THE LAUREL & HARDY MOVIE SCRIPTS,
VOLUME 2
LOST FILMS AND CLASSICS

Annotated by
Randy Skretvedt

 BONAVENTURE PRESS

For Jordan R. Young, friend and mentor

THE LAUREL & HARDY MOVIE SCRIPTS
Volume 2: Lost Films and Classics

The Laurel & Hardy Movie Scripts, Volume 2: Lost Films and Classics
Published by
Bonaventure Press
Aliso Viejo, CA
USA
bonaventure.press@gmail.com
www.bonaventurepress.com

Designed by David Koenig

Manufactured in the United States of America

Library of Congress Cataloguing-in-Publication Data
Library of Congress Control Number:
          2022939801

Skretvedt, Randy

        The Laurel & Hardy Movie Scripts, Volume 2 / by Randy Skretvedt;
        p. cm.

        1. Laurel, Stan, 1890-1965. 2. Hardy, Oliver, 1892-1957. 3. Comedy films—United States—
        History and criticism. I. Skretvedt, Randy, 1958 -

ISBN: 978-1-937878-15-3

CONTENTS

PROLOGUE

A screenwriter's initial idea rarely survives intact in the finished film. The availability of locations, sets, actors, costumes, props and just the stubbornness of the real world all affect the scenes that the writer has envisioned.

This is especially true for film comedy. Producer Hal Roach understood this thoroughly, and frequently said, "Fifty percent of what's in the script will not play," meaning that many ideas that seemed funny on the printed page did not prove to be when they were acted out in front of the cameras. For that reason, "gag men" were always on the sets at the Roach studio, ready to suggest better replacements for the comedy material that wasn't working. Mr. Roach's pronouncement is proven by many of the Laurel and Hardy scripts; about half of what we read in them is familiar to us from the films, but then they veer off into uncharted territory that sometimes sounds very funny but often seems rather odd.

During the Depression days of the '30s, the Roach studio had to be a very cost-conscious outfit. It's clear that many of the more elaborate sequences suggested by the scripts were curtailed or eliminated entirely because of budget restrictions. These were imposed by Henry Ginsberg, an executive installed at the Roach lot in 1931 specifically to cut costs in every way possible. We can't see these too-expensive sequences, but we can imagine them as we read the scripts – if they still exist.

The fact that the scripts replicated in this book survive at all, 90 or so years after they were used in filming, is a miracle considering that the folks at the Hal Roach Studios did not put a high priority on preserving their legacy. Roach's films, Laurel and Hardy films particularly, were reprinted again and again for numerous licensees until the negatives wore out; the idea of repairing and restoring the film library was all but laughed at, as every new firm wishing to use the L&H films was thought of as the absolute last entity who would ever be interested in these old things.

In 1942, the United States government took over the Hal Roach Studios – having found a convenient way to conscript its figurehead into the Signal Corps at age 50 – and remaining employees were ordered by Uncle Sam to incinerate absolutely everything that was not thought to be of further use. Scripts, stills, original music tracks all went into the fire. Roy Seawright, who had progressed from Hal Roach's office boy in 1919 to the head of the special effects department, told me in 1981, "I'm sorry, but I was probably the guy who pitched those music tracks you love so much into the fire. I hated to do it, but it was an order."

What wasn't disposed of at that time was further scattered to the winds in August 1963, when the contents of the Roach studio were auctioned in advance of the demolition of everything on the lot.

A number of scripts still survived in 1980, when I was doing research in earnest for the first version of *Laurel and Hardy: The Magic Behind the Movies*. Douglas Hart at Backlot Books in Hollywood had obtained a large collection of scripts and stills from Rosemary LaPlanche, a former Miss America and actress in Hal Roach's 1940s "streamliners," who bought them at the 1963 auction. Antiquarian bookseller John McLaughlin at The Book Sail in the city of Orange had another collection – Stan Laurel's own – which complemented Mr. Hart's. Between the two of them, and along with the scripts for the later Fox and MGM L&H films at USC, I was able to read and make notes on the majority of the team's scripts. I did not, however, retain complete copies of everything I was able to read.

Happily, in December 2021, I was alerted by Richard W. Bann – who literally rescued from destruction the 35mm master materials for the Laurel and Hardy films, and who has done so much to preserve the team's legacy – that a large collection of Roach studio scripts was available for auction. I was in the rare position of being able to afford these items, and felt obligated to obtain them for the sake of history. Many of these scripts I had seen in 1980, but quite a few were new to me, most prominently the script for Laurel and Hardy's Academy Award winning short *The Music Box*.

You will find here that most of the scripts follow Hal Roach's pronouncement, with half of the material being familiar and the other half being entirely new. Other scripts, such as the one for *Helpmates*, are virtual twins to the films. In any case, reading the descriptions of scenes that we have known and cherished for decades, written at the time of their creation, is a fascinating experience.

It seems that some of the men who thought up comedy ideas for Roach were thought of as writers, having a particular talent for constructing a story, while others were gag men, able to come up with great material on the set during the filming. Hal Roach always considered Stan Laurel a great gag man but deficient on story ideas; director George Marshall, however, felt that Stan was very talented in creating the plots. It's undeniable that the Laurel and Hardy films have stronger and better constructed stories than most of the Roach movies, which often establish a story idea without resolving it.

It's a given that Hal Roach and Stan Laurel contributed to the stories of any Laurel and Hardy picture made at the Roach lot. Most of the others, whether they were gag men or writers, never received any credit in the titles. Trade papers, however, did announce the hiring of new talent, providing some of their names. The following gentlemen added material to the Laurel and Hardy scripts, most of them without onscreen acknowledgement:

Leo McCarey – Born October 3, 1896 in Los Angeles. Died at 72 in Santa Monica, California on July 5, 1969. A failed boxer, songwriter and lawyer, McCarey became an assistant to Tod Browning at the Universal studio. Having struck up a friendship with Hal Roach, he joined that producer as a writer-director for Charley Chase, then became supervisor of the studio's entire output from 1927 through December 1928. Later director of highly regarded features such as *Duck Soup, The Awful Truth, Going My Way, Love Affair* and *An Affair to Remember*. He was of key importance to Laurel and Hardy, essentially creating the team by suggesting that Roach build a new series around them.

A working luncheon in October 1934, with gag men Frank Terry (extreme left) and Charlie Rogers (extreme right) surrounding Stan, Babe, and Ruth Laurel.

Harley Marquis Walker – Born June 27, 1878 in West Middlebury, Ohio. Died at 58 in Chicago on June 23, 1937. A sportswriter for the *Los Angeles Examiner* from 1903, he began writing scenarios and titles part-time for Hal Roach in 1917, then joined full time in 1920 as head of the editorial department. During the silent era he primarily wrote the witty titles, gave each film its name, and functioned as a severe critic before a given movie was allowed to be sent to the distributors. He's credited on more than 350 Roach comedies. Known affectionately as "Beanie," Walker was less skilled at writing dialogue, but after leaving Roach in 1932 he provided it for feature films produced by Paramount and Warner Bros.

Hal Yates – Born July 26, 1899 in Chicago. Died at 70 in Los Angeles on August 1, 1969. In vaudeville as half of the team Yates and Lawley, he broke into films in 1923 and was an editor and writer for Mack Sennett in 1924-25. At the Roach lot in 1926-29, he was continuously on the payroll as a writer with the Laurel and Hardy unit, and also directed a dozen short comedies. He was very active directing RKO comedy shorts starring Edgar Kennedy, Leon Errol and *The Newlyweds* from the late '30s through 1953, then returned to the Roach lot to make episodes of the TV series *My Little Margie* and *Blondie* before retiring in 1957.

Mauri Grashin - Born January 14, 1901 in Chicago. Died at 90 in Los Angeles on February 1, 1991. He was very active at the Roach lot in the late '20s, being one of the two writers (with Hal Yates) always on the payroll as part of the Laurel and Hardy unit in the silent era. He spent most of the '30s writing scripts for two-reel comedies at RKO and occasionally at Columbia, such as the screenplay for the Three Stooges' *Oily to Bed, Oily to Rise* in 1939. During the '40s, he wrote Westerns and comedy feature scripts for Republic, and had a late-career credit for a long dormant story which was eventually made as *The Trouble with Girls* in 1969, starring Elvis Presley.

Charles Rogers – Born January 15, 1887, Birmingham, England. Died at 69 in Los Angeles on December 20, 1956. Another graduate of the Fred Karno troupe of English comedians, Rogers played the Pantages Circuit in the USA in the early '20s with a vaudeville sketch called *The Iceman*. He was at the Roach lot as a gagman and bit player by 1928 (prominent onscreen with L&H in *Habeas Corpus* and *Double Whoopee*), and

Stan surrounded by writers James Parrott, Charlie Rogers and Felix Adler, circa 1936.

became a close associate of Stan Laurel's, directing nine Laurel and Hardy films from 1933 through 1936. He wrote for the team through the end of their term with Hal Roach in late 1939, but also contributed to the screenplay of their 1943 MGM feature *Air Raid Wardens.*

James Parrott – Born August 2, 1897, Baltimore, Maryland. Died at 42 in Los Angeles on May 10, 1939. The younger brother (by almost four years) of Roach comedian Charley Chase, James was at the studio first, supporting Harold Lloyd beginning in 1917. In 1920 he began his own series as "Paul Parrott," starring in 75 shorts through 1926. Because of his epilepsy, he moved into writing and directing in 1924, helming 89 movies through 1935. In the later '30s, he contributed to the screenplays of *The Bohemian Girl, Way Out West, Swiss Miss* and *Block-Heads.*

Frank Terry – Born May 3, 1871 in Worcester, Worcestershire, England. Died at 77 in Burbank, California on October 26, 1948. Also known as Ernest Dovay, Nat Clifford and Ernest Edwards, this man with a colorful private life involving bigamy and multiple jail escapes was a music hall comedian performing in England, South Africa, and Australia before joining the Hal Roach studio around 1919. He directed and performed with Stan that year in the Roach short *Hustling for Health*, and contributed to many of the L&H scripts in the early '30s. He's also prominent as Ollie's butler in *Me and My Pal* and as a cantankerous safecracker in *The Midnight Patrol.*

Felix Adler – Born January 22, 1884, Chicago. Died at 79 in Woodland Hills, California on March 25, 1963. A vaudeville comic in the 1910s, Adler became a title writer for Mack Sennett in 1925. He wrote scenarios for Harold Lloyd's *Welcome Danger* (1929), *Feet First* (1930), and *Movie Crazy* (1932), then wrote a few of the last Sennett shorts in 1932 and '33, and many of the first Columbia comedies in 1934. That studio would be his main employer through 1958, although he also contributed to Laurel and Hardy's *Our Relations, Way Out West, Swiss Miss, Block-Heads, A Chump at Oxford* and *Saps at Sea*. He also wrote material for Abbott and Costello (*Here Come the Coeds, The Naughty Nineties*), and is credited on more than 160 films.

Carl Harbaugh – Born November 10, 1886, Washington, D.C. Died at 73 in Hollywood on February 26, 1960. Busy as a scenario writer from 1914 through 1942, Harbaugh was Roach's chief gag writer in 1925 through 1927, and contributed to some of the earliest L&H movies. He was also a director from 1917 through 1921, making 27 films, and concentrated on acting from the early '40s through 1957. His other writing credits include Buster Keaton's *College* and *Steamboat Bill, Jr.*

Albert Austin – Born December 13, 1882, Birmingham, England. Died at 70 in North Hollywood on August 17, 1953. Remembered primarily for his work as a bit player with Charlie Chaplin, beginning with the Mutual comedies in 1916 (he's the man who watches in disbelief as Charlie dismantles his alarm clock in *The Pawnshop*) and continuing through *City Lights* in 1931. Austin directed some shorts for Educational and Fox in the early '20s and was a busy comedy writer at Universal in 1933-35, often working with frequent L&H director James Horne. Austin contributed to L&H's 1935 feature *Bonnie Scotland* and very likely made similar uncredited contributions.

John Guedel – Born October 9, 1913, Portland, Indiana. Died at 88 in Los Angeles on December 15, 2001. Beginning in 1932, Guedel wrote captions for newspaper cartoons and a humor column called *Barbs*, which brought an offer from Hal Roach. Guedel worked at the Roach studio from 1934 to 1936, writing for Laurel and Hardy and the *Our Gang* series. In later years, he said that every time Hal Roach went on a vacation, he fired the writing staff to avoid paying them; as a result, Guedel had seven layoffs in three years. Hoping to find steadier work, Guedel moved into radio and a very successful career, creating the series *People Are Funny* and *House Party*, both starring Art Linkletter, as well as *The Adventures of Ozzie* and *Harriet* and *You Bet Your Life* with Groucho Marx. All of these moved into TV for lengthy stretches.

Frank Butler – Born December 28, 1891, Oxford, England. Died at 76 in Oceanside, California on June 10, 1967. Growing up in Canada, Butler came to Hollywood in 1919 as an actor, playing very British types in feature films such as *The Sheik* with Rudolph Valentino. In 1924-25, he starred in 24 *Spat Family* shorts for Hal Roach as "Tewksberry Spat." He began writing for Roach in 1926, and in 1934 was named head of Roach's scenario department. He collaborated on the screenplays for *Babes in Toyland, Bonnie Scotland* and *The Bohemian Girl*. Later credits include *The Milky Way* with Harold Lloyd, four of the Crosby-Hope-Lamour *Road* pictures, and Leo McCarey's *Going My Way*, for which he won an Academy Award.

Frank Tashlin – Born February 19, 1913 in Weehawken, New Jersey. Died at 59 in Burbank, California on May 5, 1972. Tashlin was a brilliantly creative comedy writer

Holiday Greetings from "A Lot of Fun"

A 1934 Christmas card drawn by gag man Frank Tashlin (as "Tish Tash") shows the *Our Gang* kids, Charley Chase, Stan and Ollie, and Patsy Kelly with Thelma Todd.

in many media. He drew comic strips for his junior high school newspaper, which led to a job for the Fleischer brothers' animation studio in New York. He moved to California in 1933 and began animating *Looney Tunes* for Leon Schlesinger. Tashlin was at the Roach studio in 1935 and appears to have contributed gags for L&H's *Tit for Tat, The Fixer Uppers* and *Thicker Than Water*. Subsequent cartoon directing for Disney, Columbia and Warners led to live-action features such as *Son of Paleface* (1952) with Bob Hope, the rock 'n' roll satire *The Girl Can't Help It* (1956), and several starring Jerry Lewis. He also created a highly regarded children's book, *The Bear That Wasn't*.

Jack Jevne – Born January 25, 1892 in Provo, Utah. Died at 80 in Los Angeles on May 25, 1972. Jevne began writing comedy shorts for Al Christie in 1920, several for Educational in the late '20s, and a few for Mack Sennett in 1930-31. He was at the Roach studio by early 1935 and stayed through 1939, collaborating on many *Our Gang* shorts and Laurel and Hardy's *Our Relations* and *Way Out West*, and features including *Captain Fury*. He also contributed to the 1943 MGM Laurel and Hardy feature *Air Raid Wardens*.

Stanley Rauh – Born March 28, 1898 in Dayton, Ohio. Died at 81 in Los Angeles on September 12, 1979. Rauh wrote the scripts for Vitaphone musical shorts in New York starring Ruth Etting and Helen Morgan, and also wrote a few for MGM in Culver City before being signed by Roach in June 1933. His stay there was brief, as he was soon at RKO writing for Wheeler and Woolsey (*The Rainmakers*) and Astaire and Rogers (*The Gay Divorcée*). In the early '40s he worked at 20th Century-Fox, where he wrote the story for Laurel and Hardy's *A-Haunting We Will Go* (1942).

George Bricker – Born July 18, 1898 in St. Mary's, Ohio. Died at 56 in Los Angeles on January 22, 1955. Bricker had been a reporter for the *Ohio State Journal* and had written radio sketches for WMCA-New York when Henry Ginsberg brought him to the Roach studio late in 1933. He went to Warner Bros. in 1935 and began writing screenplays for their B-picture unit. His almost 80 screenwriting credits include cult favorites such as *Sh! The Octopus* (1937) for Warners, and the Bela Lugosi chiller *The Devil Bat* (1940) for PRC. In 1943 he wrote a screenplay for Laurel and Hardy, *A Matter of Money*, which evolved into *The Dancing Masters*.

Royal King Cole – Born June 3, 1907, New York City. Died at 86 in Mesa, Arizona on August 14, 1993. Cole was one of several new writers coming to the Roach studio in 1933, and was reported as contributing to the L&H shorts around that time. By 1934 he was writing scripts for Vitaphone shorts, but he really found his niche in 1943 when he began writing serials for Republic (*Captain America, The Purple Monster Strikes*) and Columbia (*Batman and Robin, Superman, King of the Congo*).

Walter Weems - Born June 25, 1886, Fayetteville, North Carolina. Died at 69 in Los Angeles on September 9, 1955. A comic actor in his younger days, Weems was paired with Ed Garr in the comedy team "The Two Doves" in three 1927 shorts for Vitaphone. He wrote the Fox 1929 comedy feature *Hearts in Dixie,* then moved to the Mack Sennett studio. Weems provided the stories for 36 two-reelers for Sennett and RKO through 1934, then came to the Roach lot. Trade papers noted that he was working for Laurel and Hardy; he also contributed song lyrics for four Charley Chase shorts and co-directed one of them, *Something Simple.*

It appears that supporting actor Charlie Hall – who on a given day could also be a carpenter at the lot or a dialogue coach – sometimes contributed to the gag sessions. So did musical director Marvin Hatley, when he wasn't writing scores for Laurel and Hardy or songs for Charley Chase. Hatley retained fond memories of his co-workers physically demonstrating their comedy brainstorms, even to the extent of one writer choking another to visually convey the idea.

This book is subtitled *Lost Films and Classics* because it contains the printed record of the vanished *Hats Off!* and the mostly lost *The Rogue Song*. You'll also find a detailed account of the still missing section of *The Battle of the Century*, and a 1933 script, *Tickets for Two*, which was not filmed but provided the idea for *Busy Bodies*. I am delighted to present these along with the scripts for perennial favorites such as *Helpmates, The Music Box* and *Them Thar Hills*.

The emphasis in this book is on the scripts and how they differ from the films; more information about the production of the films, and much more biographical detail, is in my book *Laurel & Hardy: The Magic Behind the Movies*, also published by Bonaventure Press.

Those of us who have cherished these films for decades owe the writers profiled above our everlasting thanks. I also owe thanks to Richard W. Bann for preserving the films and alerting me to the "new" scripts; to Claudia Bossard in Switzerland, Peter Mikkelsen in Denmark, Russ Babidge in England, and Jeff Price in Florida for further scripts; to John Carpenter and Jack Taylor for graphics; and to Craig Calman for allowing me to quote some of the studio correspondence contained in his remarkable book *100 Years of Brodies with Hal Roach*, published by BearManor Media. (A Brodie, by the way, is a high-diving comedy fall, named after Steve Brodie, who supposedly jumped off the Brooklyn Bridge and survived.)

Particular thanks to Dave Lord Heath, whose astonishing website *Another Nice Mess* (www.lordheath.com) is a monumental resource for information about all of Hal Roach's films and the people who made them. Thanks also to Bernie Hogya, whose website at www.lettersfromstan.com preserves and presents much of Mr. Laurel's very informative correspondence.

My sincere gratitude to David Koenig for his design and layout skills and for agreeing to publish this book. And thanks to you, dear reader. I hope you'll enjoy this journey through the archaeology of comedy.

WHY GIRLS LOVE SAILORS

Production history: Production S-20. Written in January 1927. Filmed Monday, January 31, 1927 through Tuesday, February 15, when production was halted due to rain. Inserts were shot on the 16th; more rain delays on the 17th. The crew shot day and night on the 18th, finishing on Saturday, February 19. Retakes were shot by Hal Yates (uncredited) on Friday, March 18 and Saturday, March 19. Copyrighted May 18, 1927 by Pathé (LU 23978). Released July 17. Two reels.

Produced by Hal Roach. Directed by Fred L. Guiol. Photographed by Floyd Jackman. Edited by Richard Currier. Gowns by [William] Lambert. Titles by H.M. Walker. Story by Hal Roach.

With Stan Laurel (Willie Brisling), Oliver Hardy (First mate), Viola Richard (Nelly, Willie's girl), Anita Garvin (The Captain's wife), Malcolm Waite (The Captain), Jerry Mandy (Sailor), Edgar Dearing (Amorous sailor), Bobby Dunn (Bemused sailor), Charles Althoff (Old fisherman fiddler).

In a seaport town, fisherman Willie Brisling (Stan) and his lovely fiancée (Viola) are at her houseboat, celebrating their engagement. Their bliss is interrupted by a ship bearing a rough captain (Malcolm Waite) and his equally tough first mate (Babe). The captain kidnaps Viola and takes her aboard his ship, where a full crew of roughnecks await. Willie comes to the rescue, climbing aboard the ship, where he conveniently finds a theatrical trunk filled with women's clothes. He dresses up as a blonde flapper and one by one conks each of the crew on the noggin. The captain's angry wife (Anita) unexpectedly comes aboard, having been left behind at the last port. Willie removes his wig and tells the wife that the ruse of flirting with the captain was "just a test to see if you really love him." As Stan and Viola depart together, a blast from the wife's blunderbuss proves the true depth of her love.

The idea of Stan and Babe appearing in a nautically themed adventure had been proposed earlier, in August 1926, when a script identified only as "S-14" was written. It co-starred Anna May Wong and Sojin Kamiyama, had many elements of action and adventure, and would have been the first teaming of Laurel and Hardy at the Hal Roach studio. (It is reprinted in full in *The Laurel & Hardy Movie Scripts*.)

Five months later, after Laurel and Hardy had appeared in *Duck Soup, Slipping Wives* and *Love 'em and Weep* – with wildly varying proportions of shared scenes – another seafaring story occurred to Hal Roach. It was very likely given fuller substance by Stan Laurel, Mauri Grashin, Hal Yates, and the other writers at the studio.

Stan and Babe were proposed for the cast at the outset of writing the script. So were burly and ominous Malcolm Waite and diminutive comic Jerry Mandy. Vaudevillian Charles Althoff, famous for donning a white wig and beard and wire-rim glasses to play "The Yankee Fiddler," a comedy violin specialty, would play the father of heroine "Little Nell," who had not yet been cast.

Althoff (1889-1959) was a buddy of Stan's. In letters written in 1962 to friends Richard Sloan and Chuck McCann, Stan noted that "Charlie appeared in one silent

Stan with Viola Richard and his vaudeville pal Charles Althoff, prominent in the script but mostly cut from the film.

film with me, he was playing at the old Pantages Theatre here (Vaudeville). He had a week's lay-off before opening in Salt Lake City, so I was able to fill in a few days for him at the Roach Studio. Charlie did a great vaudeville act, a very funny 'Rube' character, he was known as a 'Show Stopper.' The film he worked on was a fishing village story & a family of fishermen, his character was named 'Grandpa Smelt,' and I was his wayward grandson Willie – all the family Smelt & so did the film – TO HIGH HEAVENS.!!" Unfortunately, at least in the surviving print, Althoff's role has been slashed from a substantial one in the script to a "blink and you'll miss him" moment.

Richard Currier (1892-1984) is the credited editor on this picture, although he freely admitted in the 1980s that from the mid-1920s on he was more of a supervisor than an actual cutter. The actual editors around this time were Harry Lieb and assistant William Terhune.

Lieb is one of the unfairly forgotten crew members of the Roach studio; payroll ledgers show that he was the primary editor on many Laurel and Hardy silent classics, including *Big Business*. He was born in New York City as Heinrich William Lieb on July 10, 1896. He began his editing career at the Fort Lee, New Jersey Universal studio, but by 1926 he was cutting films at the Roach lot. He left Roach early in 1929 to work at Universal City, where he edited at least fifteen features, among them *See America Thirst* starring Harry Langdon. After working on the John Ford feature *Air Mail*, Lieb died in

Captain Malcolm Waite's kidnapping is interrupted by another comely lass.

his home of influenza on December 8, 1932. He was only 36 years old.

Surviving prints of *Why Girls Love Sailors* do not appear to retain the original titles written by Beanie Walker, a shame since his witty commentaries are usually a highlight of the silent Roach comedies.

Just as Pathé was releasing the picture in July 1927, Roach publicity director Ray Coffin offered his opinion to Hal Roach: "Stan does some great work, individually… Miss Richard screened well, and believe after she reduces a bit, as I understand she is now doing, and has her teeth straightened, she will be a great bet." Legions of fans today disagree with Mr. Coffin's evaluation of lovely Viola Richard, and think that her figure and teeth are just fine, thanks.

Why Girls Love Sailors was a lost film for nearly sixty years, existing only in a couple of stills and in Stan Laurel's rather hazy memory of it. French author Roland Lacourbe, in his 1975 book *Laurel et Hardy*, noted that the film had been shown on September 30, 1971 by the Cinematheque Française, but concluded that "the film is mediocre, poorly constructed, and based primarily on Stan's gift for transvestism." Even so, Laurel and Hardy devotees around the world still longed to see the film, but given the notorious disorganization of the Cinematheque's founder, Henri Langlois, the chance of it gaining wider exposure was very slim.

Peter Mikkelsen, a longtime Laurel and Hardy enthusiast based in Copenhagen who works for the Danish Filminstitut archive, was instrumental in returning this film to public view. In March 2022, he explained how this film was reclaimed with the discovery of a second print:

The first mate gives the young lovely a tour of the ship.

"It all began with [Sons of the Desert Corresponding Secretary] Dwain Smith, with whom I had been in touch for ten years. In January 1986, he wrote and told me about a young French collector, a student (who preferred to remain anonymous) and asked me if I would like to drop him a line. Of course I would, and made a point of asking him about the missing L&H films. He sent me a kind reply, telling me that the situation regarding *The Battle of the Century* and *The Rogue Song* was the same in France as everywhere else: they hadn't been found yet. But he did own a 16mm print of *Why Girls Love Sailors*, and would I like a copy? To this day, I am glad I was sitting down when I read that sentence! I spoke to him on the phone a couple of times, and he told me he had traded this print with another collector for another silent L&H film, one of the more readily available ones.

"He was fully aware of the status of *Why Girls Love Sailors* back then, and had no intention of hoarding it, but he didn't know just how to deal with the situation. Later, he called me again, telling me that he had contacted a local lab in order to have the print cleaned. They said it had various problems which meant a full and costly repair job before they could clean it for him. Being a young student, he could not afford this.

"He was somewhat alarmed over this new development. I assured him that this wasn't his problem. As important as this print was, the copyright holders should deal with the problems, and save the print for the future. He got in touch with the German copyright holders [who in 1986 were the KirchGruppe]; they sent a representative over to collect the print and a deal was made. The print was repaired, new negatives made and *Why Girls Love Sailors* was no longer a lost title.

Willie Brisling reveals all.

"It was a wonderful experience to finally watch new L&H footage, although the boys aren't together very much in this story, and of course Viola Richard is as cute as ever."

Laurel and Hardy fans throughout the world owe a debt of thanks to Peter Mikkelsen, to the late great Dwain W. Smith (1925-2017) who did so much to spread the joy of Stan and Ollie, to the anonymous French collector, and to the guy who had the very rare print before him.

The script is markedly different from the film. Stan's character had his name changed from "Willie Smelt" to "Willie Brisling," at least in the two prints which survive. The titles include cute drawings along with the text, and while the titles are in English, both prints were located in France and have a unique music-and-effects soundtrack, so they're probably from an early 1930s reissue.

The prologue with "Eight-Bell Bertha" is not in the movie, nor are the names assigned to various characters. Bertha does not leave her blonde wig behind; instead, it's found in the ship's cabin by Willie/Stan in a theatrical trunk left behind by the "Jules Ellenge" company, clearly a reference to the famous vaudeville star, female impersonator Julian Eltinge.

The piano and cats mentioned in the script's opening scene are not in the film, although the piano shows up in a couple of stills.

Neither Charlie Hall nor any other actor appears as the stowaway suggested in the script. None of the other sailors is specifically identified as a cabin boy in the film, although diminutive Jerry Mandy plays the part as prescribed in the script, shivering and shaking impressively when he sees a "headless" man.

Anita Garvin debuts with L&H as the Captain's tough wife.

Original promotional line art.

Almost all of the scenes with Willie/Stan in drag are different in the movie. The script does not propose the elaborate scene of Willie flirting with each of the crew members, knocking them out with a bludgeon and then leaving them for first mate Hardy to throw overboard. A very similar idea was employed in Laurel and Hardy's 1934 short *The Live Ghost,* and it was further reworked into the team's last film, *Atoll K* (1951), this time with heroine Suzy Delair enticing and clobbering the villains.

The captain's wife, a character vitally important to the film and its resolution, is not mentioned at all in the script. This is Anita Garvin's first appearance with Laurel and Hardy, and she dominates the last section of the film.

With Stan as the hero and Babe as the villainous first mate, *Why Girls Love Sailors* shows Laurel and Hardy working against each other as characters, but entirely in unison as performers.

WHY GIRLS LOVE SAILORS Script

Cast:

Willie Smelt	-	Stan Laurel
Little Nell	-	
Sam Salt	-	Charles Althoff
The Captain	-	Malcolm Waite
First Mate	-	Babe Hardy
Cabin Boy	-	Jerry Mandy

The story concerns a little girl who was picked up in a storm at sea by an old fisherman. Presuming that her parents were drowned, the old man adopts the child and she grows up happily in his tiny cabin on the seashore.

Into their lives comes a villainous sea Captain who plots to abduct the girl and take her out to sea. His plot, however, is foiled by a fisher boy who, motivated by his love for the girl, finally rescues her from the hands of her abductors and brings her home to her foster father.

Long shot, exterior, night. This shot will establish the atmosphere of a water front; ships, masts, wharfs, seafaring characters in evidence. In the foreground the dock, and warped to it a tramp steamer in the process of unloading.

Lap dissolve to deck of ship. We see the First Mate bawling orders to a gang of stevedores and getting over his toughness generally.

Cut to closeup of the First Mate with introductory title to the effect, "Bill Haddock, First Mate of the good ship Bread Poultice."

Cut to closeup of Captain with introductory title to the effect, "Captain Typhoon, the gentleman who preferred blondes."

Back to two-figure shot. Typhoon speaks roughly to the Mate and exits in the direction of the cabin.

Interior Captain's cabin; we see a woman of the street-walker type sitting before a mirror plastering rouge and powder on her face; she is a faded brunette with short bobbed scrawny hair. Cut to closeup of the woman with introductory title to the effect, "Eight-Bell Bertha, a friend of the Captain and sometimes the crew."

Cut to medium shot; Bertha suddenly looks towards the door, getting over that she hears someone coming. She reaches hurriedly for a blonde wig laying on the dressing table and quickly tries to get it on her head. As she does this the door flies open and the Captain enters the scene. He gets over that he has seen her put the wig on. He walks over to her slowly, snatches the wig off her head, looks at it, looks at her, hurls the wig on the floor, grabs her by the shoulder, yanks her to her feet and hustles her through the door.

Back to the deck; Captain hustles Bertha across the deck in the direction of the gang-plank; arriving there he gives her a shove which causes her to skid down the gangway onto the wharf. He stands there glaring at her. She turns and speaks title, "What about me clothes?"

The Captain takes this, steps towards her menacingly a few steps and holds it. Bertha gives him the raspberry behind her hand. Typhoon takes it big. At that moment the cabin boy passes behind him, hears the raspberry and laughs. The Captain turns on him savagely and kicks him in the fanny. The cabin boy flies out of the scene and the Captain turns and leans morosely on the rail.

Cut to medium shot of the Captain, leaning on the rail and staring angrily after Bertha. The Mate enters and indicates, "What's the matter?" The Captain speaks title to the effect, "She told me she was a blonde!" The Mate sneers and speaks title to the effect, "I knew that all the time." The Captain gets over that he resents the remark, doubles up his fist and sticks his face into the Mate's; they hold it a moment and then start to mutter at each other.

Cut to a shot of the crew, all very rough types, busy at work. One of them suddenly turns and looks towards the Captain and the Mate.

Cut back to Captain and Mate; they are still muttering savagely at each other.

Cut back to the crew; they all turn and get over that they are listening to the argument. Their jaws drop; they get over that they are shocked by the language and they stick their fingers in their ears.

Fade in, long shot of house boat, night, with a little bridge approaching from the land. We see lights in the windows, giving an atmosphere of home and comfort.

Lap dissolve to interior of house boat, with all the necessary props to make it quaint and picturesque. We discover Stan at the organ and the girl singing; the old fisherman is seated on a soap box playing a fiddle.

Cut to closeup of the old man, Sam Salt, and introduce him with title.

Closeup of Stan and introduce him as "Willie Smelt."

Closeup of the girl, and introduce her as Little Nell, a child of the storm.

Three figure shot. The old man says "Are you ready?" and they start to play. Stan starts to play fast. The old man trying to keep up time tells Stan "Not so fast!" but Stan doesn't hear him and continues his speed. The girl is also trying to keep up with Stan's fast playing. The old man's bow slips off the fiddle and gets tangled up in his shoe. Stan and the girl stop and look around. The old man manages to get the fiddle [bow] out of his shoe and it flies up and gets caught in his collar, and he gets into a general mixup. He finally rights himself, bawls Stan out and says "Don't play so fast!" Stan pantomimes O.K., and they start playing slower.

Stan gets over that one of the notes is sour. He stops them and proceeds to examine the organ. He tries one of the keys and discovers that it is the sour note. He opens the top of the organ, looks in and takes it big. He gets down on his hands and knees, opens the little slide doors at the base of the organ and a cat walks out, followed by three or four kittens. They take this with a laugh and start to play again.

Cut to close shot of the old man; he gets over he hears something and looks in the direction of the window.

Cut to close shot at the window and we see a little flexible bamboo cane nailed to the window. On the end of the cane, which is waggling violently, there is a little bell which is ringing, also a fish line running out through the window. The old man stops them and exits. He enters to the window, opens it and starts to pull in the line. He finally gives it a big heave and hauls in a large fish. He takes the fish off the hook, leaving the fish flopping on the floor, baits the hook, throws it out and exits from the scene very nonchalantly.

Back to the organ setup; the old man enters scene, picks up his fiddle, sits down and they start to play an Irish jig.

Cut to the fish flopping around as if keeping time with the music. Cut to a corner of the room and show the mother cat and kittens. They look off in the direction of the fish and all arch their backs in unison.

Back to the fish; he flops out of the setup and into the cats' setup. The cats scatter in all directions. Stay with the fish a moment, then out to a rubber boot in another part of the house. The three kittens stick their heads out of the boot, take it, hiss and duck down into the boot again.

Cut to the organ setup and get over that they have all been watching the fish and the cats. The old man says, "I'll stop this foolishness," grabs a shotgun which is up against the fireplace, aims at the fish who is flopping around, and shoots both barrels, missing the fish but blowing away half of the organ that Stan is playing. Springs, keys, etc. scatter all over the room. They all do brodies, then sit up and look at the organ. They look back at the fish. The fish finally makes a leap and goes out the window.

Cut to shot where the fish lands in the water and swims away.

Back to the three; the old man speaks title, "That's the first time I've missed a fish in twenty years." Stan and the girl get up and pick the old man up. As the old man stands up he gets over that something hurts his foot. He hops around a little bit to a chair or box and takes off his boot. In doing so the sock pulls half way off his foot. He shakes the shoe around and we see a few small rocks and sand fall out of it, and at the finish a tooth brush. Stan and the girl take this. The old man speaks title, "I've been looking for that for a week." Stan comes back with title, "Look in the other shoe, Pop, you might find the tooth paste." The old man tries to get the sock back on and it starts to whirl around like a windmill. Stan and the girl see their chance while the old man is busy and they walk over to the dining room, leaving the old man struggling trying to get his sock on.

Cut to dining room; Stan and the girl enter and their attitude is that they are very much in love with each other. Stan reaches in his pocket and pulls out a little necklace made of seashells. The girl gets over she is very happy with her present.

Cut to exterior of the cabin. Captain Typhoon enters the scene, stops as if he saw something. Cut to shot shooting through the window; we see Stan placing the necklace about the girl's neck. She is looking up at him with love in her eyes. Shoot this in such a manner that we see Stan and the girl, and the old man offside still trying to get the sock, which is whirling around. Iris down to where just the girl is visible. The Captain looks at the girl and as he does so his face, smiling crookedly, flames with lust. He exits in the direction of the door.

Cut to interior, Stan and the girl on at the table. The old man is still trying to catch his sock. The door opens and in walks the Captain. He closes the door, crosses to the old man and speaks title, "Shiver me timbers, if it ain't Sam Salt!" He slaps the old man heartily on the back and the force of the blow causes the old man to nearly lose his balance. He recovers himself and starts to cough. They shake hands.

The Captain, who is standing with his back to the fireplace, takes a bottle from his hip and hands it to the old man. The old man half empties the bottle and hands it back to the Captain, gets over it tasted great, wipes his mouth and spits into the fireplace. A big flame shoots out of the fireplace, striking the Captain on the fanny. The Captain takes it, recovers himself and looks at Stan and the girl. The girl, conscious of the man's stare, looks away uneasily.

The Captain speaks title to the old man, getting over "Who's the girl?" The old man says "That's Little Nell, the girl I saved from a wreck fourteen years ago come Christmas." The Captain looks back at the girl and gets over she is beautiful. He then looks at Stan, who is licking an all-day sucker. He crosses to Stan and the girl, places his hand on the girl's shoulder and in pantomime gets over "I knew you when you were that high."

The girl, a little embarrassed, introduces the Captain to Stan with title, "My friend, Willie Smelt." The Captain takes it and the girl looks at the Captain and says, "That's his name!" The Captain holds out his hand. Stan offers the hand in which he is holding the sucker. The Captain shakes hands vigorously and suddenly notices that the sucker is stuck to his hand. He finally pulls it off, giving Stan a dirty look, and deliberately sticks it on Stan's chin. Stan starts to struggle to remove the sucker. The Captain sits down and pulls the girl on his knee, putting his arm around her in a half parental, half familiar manner.

Cut to Stan; he manages to pull the sucker off his chin; it flies out of his hand and lands on the floor.

The Captain looks across at Stan and back to the girl, and speaks title to her, indicating Stan, "Is that your sweetie?" The girl nods her head. The Captain looks at Stan, sneers at him and then very much amused speaks title, "Do you love him?" The girl indicates "Yes," and looks proudly at Stan.

She gets an idea to show Stan off to the stranger, and speaks title, "Willie, show him your ship." Stan very much embarrassed, gets over that he would rather not. Finally the girl succeeds in coaxing him. He leans over to the Captain, baring his chest as he does so. We see on Stan's chest a tattooed picture of a four-masted schooner.

The Captain pulls out the neck of Stan's sweater to get a good look at the ship and with the other hand he grabs a pitcher of water off the table and pours it down Stan's sweater. Stan takes this and straightens up, giving the effect of a big stomach which swishes around from side to side.

The girl stands up and gives the Captain a dirty look. She gets disgusted and walks out the front door. The Captain watches her, then looks back to the old man and Stan and starts to laugh like hell.

Stan goes to the window, gets a dipper off the wall and starts dipping water from his sweater.

Back to the old man, who is roaring with laughter. He speaks title, "Your ship's leaking," and makes an exit in the direction of the bedroom.

Cut to the Captain; he gets up still looking toward the doorway, and speaks title to the old man, who stops at the arch, "Well, skipper, I got to get back to the ship; see you again." The old man pantomimes "Goodnight" and exits into his bedroom. The Captain exits, and we leave Stan dipping water out of his sweater.

Cut to exterior of the houseboat. The girl is standing by the railing. The Captain comes out, puts his arm on her shoulder, turns her around to him and speaks title, "If you take a walk with me to the ship I'll give you clothes and jewelry." The girl refuses and doesn't care to speak to him. The Captain smiles, takes her hand and pantomimes "Oh come on – let's forget that little incident inside." In doing this he comes in view of the front door.

Cut to Stan who is finishing dipping the water out of his sweater. He turns around and sees the Captain trying to pull the girl over the bridge. He takes this and exits in the direction of the Captain and the girl.

Cut to front door setup; Stan enters and tells the Captain to lay off of her. The Captain stops, giving Stan a dirty look, then shoves him in the face with his hand.

Stan goes backwards over a rocking chair, knocking a pedestal and bric-a-brac down with him. The Captain picks up the girl, putting his hand over her mouth, and carries her off.

Cut to the old man, who is by this time in a night gown and bare footed. He takes it and wonders what the crash is all about. He makes an entrance into the living room. Stan has just picked himself up, and before the old man can say anything to him Stan is gone through the front door. The old man takes a step as if to follow Stan and steps on the sucker. The sucker sticks to his foot and the old man tries to shake it off, but can't. He lifts the foot and tries to pull the sucker off with his hands. In doing so, he hops around backwards, losing his balance, trips over something and falls into the fireplace. He jumps up quickly and starts to fan his fanny, getting over that it burned him.

Cut to the Captain and the girl walking down the beach. Stan enters on the run, grabs the Captain and turns him around. Stan indicates, "That's my girl – where are you taking her?" The Captain glares at him a moment, seizes him by the front of his sweater, shakes him like a rat and throws hm out of the scene. All through this the girl is trying to take Stan's part, striking at the Captain's back, etc., to which he pays no attention.

Follow Stan out of the scene. He staggers back into a setup where there are some fish nets drying on a rack. He falls into the nets, the rack breaks away and Stan gets hopelessly tangled up in the nets. The girl enters the scene on the run, starts to help Stan out. The Captain enters, grabs the girl by the wrist, she starts to fight him but he picks her up in his arms, putting his hand over her mouth to silence her screams and exits from the scene with her, leaving Stan still struggling in the fish net.

Cut to the docks. The Captain enters with the girl in his arms, runs up the gang plank onto his ship. He hurries with her to his cabin, thrusts her inside, indicates to the cabin boy who is already on, to keep her there, and rushes back to the deck.

Cut back to Stan struggling madly to get out of the net.

Back to the ship; the Captain is on deck bellowing orders to the crew to get the ship under way, which they proceed to do.

Cut to long shot of the ship just beginning to get under way.

Back to Stan still struggling in the net. He finally gets out and exits on the run in the direction of the ship.

Back to the dock; Stan enters on the run and in some comedy manner just makes it as the ship pulls out.

Back to the ship; some of the crew are busy upon their respective duties. The First Mate is on bellowing and shouting his orders. One of the crew drags in a stowaway (type like Charley Hall). He drags him up to the Mate and speaks title, "He was trying to steal the anchor, sir."

Cut to Stan hiding somewhere on the deck behind some barrels or boxes. He sees this.

The Mate gets over, "He was, was he!" and glares at him murderously. The cabin boy assumes the attitude and actions of the Mate, and carried away by his self-importance he imitates the Mate's gestures and speech. The Mate gets over to the crew that they throw the stowaway overboard. Two of the crew grab the stowaway, pick him up over their heads and throw him overboard.

Cut to shot shooting down in the water and we show the stowaway come into the picture, land in the water and start to swim.

Cut to part of the deck where Stan is hiding. He takes this and realizes that if he is found out, the same thing will happen to him. The crew who have just thrown the stowaway overboard go by Stan, mumbling to themselves and saying "That's the only thing to do with these stowaways." Stan by this time is sweating blood.

Back to the First Mate and the crew. The crew return to their duties, the cabin boy still gesturing and getting over his importance. The First Mate stands off looking at him; the cabin boy finally turns and sees him and knowing that he is caught he tries to go through with his bluff. He finishes up with a smart salute. The Mate takes off his hat, throws it to the deck and pantomimes that the cabin boy pick it up. The boy gives him a goofy look and stoops for the hat. As he does, the Mate kicks him in the fanny and the cabin boy does a hundred and eight down through the open hatch. The Mate tightens his belt, and at that moment the cabin boy's head pops up out of the hold, gives the Mate a quick salute. The Mate makes a gesture with his foot and the cabin boy pops out of sight.

Cut to the Captain's cabin. We see the Captain showing the girl some jewels and trying to bribe her.

Cut to a porthole of the Captain's cabin; the cabin boy is on with an empty whisky bottle in his hand, getting over that he has just finished it. He pats the bottle, gives it a kiss, and puts it back through the porthole. Swaying a little on his feet he is just wiping his mouth on the back of his hand when a fist comes through the port hole and punches him in the nose. The arm is withdrawn and we see the Captain glaring at him through the porthole. The cabin boy takes it, sways, salutes and staggers out of the scene. The Captain comes out of his cabin, glares and hollers at the cabin boy as he staggers off. The Captain locks the door of his cabin and exits in the opposite direction.

Cut to Stan's setup; he looks around, sees the coast is clear, sees a cabin door and starts walking toward it. At this point the cabin boy comes staggering around the corner of the cabin. Stan sees him, takes it, sees the door of the cabin which he was going for, has a quick thought, pulls the neck of his sweater over his head, giving him the appearance of a man walking around without a head. He goes for the door, but not being able to see it he staggers around. The cabin boy sees him, takes it and staggers up against the railing shaking and trembling. Stan misses the door and bumps the cabin boy, and with his hands out starts feeling around and goes in the direction of the cabin boy. By this time the cabin boy, still giving it the "willies," is trying to keep away from Stan. Stan unconsciously keeps following the cabin boy whichever way he moves. The cabin boy finally breaks and runs.

Stan hears him running, pulls the sweater down, sees the coast is clear and ducks into the door of the cabin.

Cut to another part of the deck, the cabin boy on the run. The First Mate comes around a corner, the cabin boy bumps him in the stomach and they both do a brodie. The boy grabs the Mate around the neck, hanging on for dear life, and starts to choke him. The Mate struggles, finally knocks the boy off, grabs him and says "What the hell's the matter with you?" The cabin boy says he saw a ghost walking around without a head. The Mate takes it and goes in the direction where Stan was, and we see the Captain working in such a manner that his head and shoulders are covered from view of the Mate. The cabin boy points and says, "There he is!"

The Mate walks over and kicks the Captain in the fanny. The Captain stands up, takes it big and starts to bawl the Mate out. The cabin boy, scared, ducks out of the scene.

Close shot, Captain and Mate in a heated argument a la "What Price Glory." They both exit arguing.

Cut to interior of Mate's cabin. Stan has his ear to the door listening. He is in a panic.

Cut outside; the First Mate starts for the door of his cabin. As he gets to it he gives it a little shove with his hand as if to go in. Cut to the other side and the door bumps Stan.

Cut outside; at this point the cabin boy rushes in to one of the crew who is working backstage, all excited and pantomimes very broadly about the ghost he saw. The Mate sees them, lets go of the swinging door and starts to walk in the direction of the cabin boy.

Cut inside; by this time Stan, who has been in a panic, calms down as he hears the Mate going away. He relaxes, gets overbalanced and falls against the door, which opens onto the deck. At the exterior show Stan landing flat on the deck. The Mate stops quickly with his back to Stan. Stan is up and in the cabin. The Mate turns, just misses seeing Stan, but sees the swinging door. He takes this and gets over, "It must be something," and rushes in the door like a bull.

Cut to interior; the Mate comes in, looks around and doesn't see anybody. He gets over he feels a little creepy and would much rather be outside than inside. He exits.

At this point we see the lid of a trunk start to open and Stan comes out looking toward the door. In the trunk he discovers a woman's clothing and a blonde wig. He gets over a quick thought and starts to pull his sweater off.

Exterior of Captain's cabin; Captain enters and unlocks door.

Cut to interior, the girl on; she shows nervousness. The Captain enters, looks towards her and smiles, turns and reaches box from shelf, puts box on table, sits down, opens box and starts to take out phoney jewelry, displaying each piece to the girl, who seems to be not the least interested.

Interior of Mate's cabin. Stan with his back to the camera is looking in a small mirror, putting the finishing touches to his wig. He turns and starts to practice an effeminate walk two or three times up and down the cabin prior to making his exit.

Exterior of Mate's cabin; bring Stan out. The crew are at their respective jobs, some working on ropes, etc., at a fair distance apart. Stan walks down the deck, passes the first one of the crew, who takes it big and follows Stan. Stan doesn't notice him but keeps up this march until he has picked up every one of the crew, who go through the same routine. The cabin boy makes an appearance in the opposite direction, facing Stan and the crew, takes it big and smiles, approaching Stan.

They are by the porthole by this time. The crew are staring at Stan and the cabin boy glarey-eyed. The cabin boy winks at the crew and asks Stan for a kiss. Stan bashfully refuses. At this point they are standing on either side of the open porthole. The cabin boy insists upon kissing Stan. He turns away from the porthole and wipes his mouth on his sleeve preparing to kiss Stan.

The First Mate, hearing the conversation, puts his head through the porthole, just as the cabin boy with his eyes shut leans forward to kiss Stan, and the Mate gets the kiss. The cabin boy turns and gets over to the camera it was beautiful.

The Mate, sore as hell, exits out of the cabin, bawls out the crew and tells them to get back to work. The cabin boy helps him by bawling out to the crew, who rush to their jobs. The Mate sees the cabin boy giving orders and showing off, turns and kicks him in the fanny, then turns and smiles at Stan and inquires, "What

are you doing here?" Stan asks, "Does this boat go to Colorado?"
The Mate says, "What do you think this is, a prairie schooner?"
The Mate indicates a seat and Stan accepts.

Cut to the cabin boy who sees this and sneaks toward the
seat and hides. The Mate makes violent love to Stan. He tries
to show his love for Stan by taking off his ring and putting it on
Stan's finger. He takes hold of Stan's hand and Stan bashfully
pulls his hand free. By this time the Mate is trying to act coy.
The cabin boy sees this, extends his hand, which is taken by the
Mate, and the ring is put on the cabin boy's finger. Thinking he
has it on Stan's finger, the Mate tries to embrace Stan, but Stan
resists and pulls away.

The cabin boy is admiring the ring on his finger. The Mate
sees him, kicks him in the fanny and he rolls out of the scene. By
this time the Mate's love-making is desperate. He grabs Stan by
the arm with the idea of taking him to his cabin, and they exit.

Cut to interior of Captain's cabin. He is showing the last
piece of jewelry to the girl. He sees that this has no attraction for
her. He puts it down, stands up, throws his chair in a corner, and
without handling the girl his attitude is that she has got to do as
he tells her.

Exterior of Captain's cabin. Stan and the Mate enter. The
Mate has his arms around Stan, who is trying to pull away. They
stop opposite the porthole of the Captain's cabin and Stan is
telling him "I don't like you because you're not my type!"

Cut to reverse shot from the interior of the cabin and show
what the Captain sees through the porthole.

Exterior; Mate and Stan still struggling a little. The Captain
enters, starts to bawl out the Mate for attacking a defenseless
woman. Stan sees his opportunity and enters the Captain's
cabin, leaving the Captain and Mate arguing furiously.

Interior of Captain's cabin, girl on. Stan enters. The girl
looks a little bewildered at seeing another woman on the boat.
Stan speaks to her but she doesn't know him until he takes off
his wig to reveal his identity. Stan tells her to keep up courage,
that he will save her and everything will be O.K. We leave them
talking.

Cut outside, the Mate and Captain still arguing. The Mate
leaves after speaking title to the Captain, "You can't have every

woman in the world." The Captain shakes his fist in the Mate's direction, then turns to enter his cabin.

Interior; Stan hears the Captain approaching and hasn't time to adjust his wig. He sticks his head through the porthole just as the Captain enters. The Captain looks around and sees Stan with his head in the porthole squirming around, and asks the "girl" what is the matter. The "girl" says, "A little seasick." The Captain walks over toward Stan, puts his arm around Stan's waist and starts patting him on the back, speaking loving words to the effect that he won't be sick long.

Stan has the wig in his hand and is trying to get it on his head on the exterior of the cabin when the First Mate makes his appearance. Stan succeeds in getting the wig on his head half-way decent. The Mate sees him looking through the porthole, comes toward him with a big smile and says "Were you looking for me, dearie?" Stan tries to bluff his way through with smiles, the Captain on one side with his arm around Stan's waist and the Mate on the exterior tickling Stan under the chin. The Captain overhears the Mate speak a title to Stan, takes it big, gets sore and exits out of the cabin.

Exterior of cabin by the porthole. The Captain enters and starts to bawl out the First Mate. A fight ensues.

The Captain makes a swing at the mate, misses and strikes Stan square on the nose. Stan goes out of sight, his wig falling to the deck near the Captain and Mate.

Interior of cabin; Stan lands on his fanny, gets up, realizes that his wig is outside. He peeks through the porthole and sees the fighting. He assures the girl that she will be O.K. and hands her a blunderbuss, getting over for her to protect herself, and makes an exit out of the cabin.

Cut to the deck; Captain and Mate still fighting. Stan peeks around a corner, realizes that they might see him if he goes toward his wig, gets an idea, gets on his hands and knees and backs toward them in the direction of his wig. He starts to grab for the wig and the Mate and Captain step all over his hands. They finally get away from him and he succeeds in getting the wig. Still on his hands and knees he puts the wig on. The Captain hits the Mate and the Mate falls on Stan's fanny, which flattens him out. The Mate gets up and continues the fight, Stan getting over that it knocked the wind out of him.

At this point Stan gets up and tries to help the Captain put the Mate away. The Mate goes toward a small hatch, the Captain after him. Stan opens the hatch and tries to tell the Captain to throw the Mate into it.

Cut to the cabin boy; he sees the fight going on and starts for the Captain's cabin. He enters the door and we see a puff of smoke; he comes out on his ear with his fanny on fire. He takes it and runs down a companionway.

Cut to a part of the ship below where there are several buckets of water marked "For Fire." The cabin boy rushes in and douses his fanny in the bucket of water.

Cut to the upper deck, the fight still on. Stan sees a belaying pin which has a rope attached to it. He pulls it out as if to hit the Mate, and a block and tackle falls into the picture, crowning Stan and he disappears through the hatch.

Cut below; Stan falls in. He sees the cabin boy dousing his fanny in the bucket and dashes up a ladder.

Cut to the deck, the fight still going on. Stan comes into it. The Captain hits the Mate on the chin and knocks him out, then picks him up and throws him through the hatch.

Cut below; the First Mate falls on top of the cabin boy, which jams his fanny right into the bucket. The cabin boy tries to get up, finally gets to his feet but can't get the bucket off his fanny.

Cut to the deck, the Captain just finishing putting the cover over the hatch; he is all out of breath. He looks at Stan and Stan smiles.

Very nervously Stan looks at the Captain and says, "My hero!"

Cut to the Captain, who smiles and exits toward Stan and speaks title, "It isn't the first time I fought over a woman." The Captain puts his arm around Stan's shoulder and pulls Stan toward him in a rough hug. Stan takes it and tries to pull away. The Captain has Stan in such a position that when Stan pulls away, it opens the dress from the neck down to the waist.

The Captain draws Stan toward him with the idea of kissing him, when his eyes fall on the tattooed boat on Stan's chest. Very slowly the Captain brings his eyes up from the tattoo mark and looks at Stan. Stan looks at the Captain and then at his tattooed ship, and immediately the ship sinks (cartoon shot). The Captain realizes who Stan is, makes a grab for him and in doing so Stan's wig comes off.

We play an ad lib chase in which the girl is involved.

Cut to shot of the wheel with no one in attendance, spinning around back and forth.

Stan runs to part of the deck, followed by the Captain. This setup is with a lot of boxes, packing cases, barrels, etc. As we get to this point the ship strikes something, which causes the boxes and barrels to fall on the Captain.

The girl rushes to Stan and says "We've struck a rock!" Stan embraces her and looks around and says "To the life boat!" Business of packing life boat with barrel of water, corned beef, hard-tack, etc. Stan helps the girl up into the boat and then climbs up. He starts to lower the boat, and in doing so he releases the wrong rope and the boat disappears fast out of sight.

Cut to interior of the houseboat. The life boat comes right through the ceiling and goes through the floor into the water.

The girl says "Home at last!" then asks Stan where the old man is. Stan gets up from a sitting position while under the water and says "Here he is." The old man comes from underneath Stan and spits out a mouthful of water. FADE OUT.

DO DETECTIVES THINK?

Production history: Production S-24. Written late April 1927. Filmed Monday, April 25 through Friday, May 6, 1927. Copyrighted July 8, 1927 by Pathé (LU 24157). Released November 20. Two reels.

Produced by Hal Roach. Directed by Fred L. Guiol. Titles by H.M. Walker. Story by Hal Roach.

With Stan Laurel (Ferdinand Finkleberry), Oliver Hardy (Sherlock Pinkham), James Finlayson (Judge Foozle), Viola Richard (Mrs. Foozle), Noah Young (The Tipton Slasher), Frank Brownlee (Chief of Detectives), Wilson Benge (Butler waylaid by Slasher), Will Stanton (Slasher's friend), Charley Young (Juror), Chester A. Bachman (Officer).

In a courtroom, the Tipton Slasher has been found guilty of killing two Chinamen. Judge Foozle sentences him to death; the Slasher vows to break free from prison and exact his revenge. When newspapers report that the Slasher has indeed escaped, the judge calls a detective agency and asks for the two bravest men they've got. Alas, he instead gets Messrs. Finkleberry and Pinkham, who are spectacularly ineffective when the Slasher enters the Foozle abode, posing as the new butler. After an evening filled with hair-raising and head-losing terror, the detectives somehow manage to capture their quarry.

Do Detectives Think? is a fast-paced and consistently funny comedy, along with *Duck Soup* the best of the films before the "official" announcement of L&H as a team which heralded *The Second 100 Years*.

Laurel and Hardy are finally Stan and Ollie. They are a seamless team here, for the first time since *Duck Soup*. It's surprising that after this film, they regressed to being adversaries with virtually no footage together in *Flying Elephants*, and two very different characters in support of Finlayson in *Sugar Daddies*. The thought of Stan and Babe's teamwork in *Do Detectives Think?* might well have prompted Leo McCarey to suggest a new series built around L&H to Hal Roach.

Laurel and Hardy are almost wearing the type of clothing which they would use in most of their films. Stan wears a pinstripe suit, which after *Habeas Corpus* in 1928 would acquire a rip in its lapel. After that, Stan wore this suit, which got progressively shabbier, whenever a story cast the boys in dire economic straits. He continued to wear it (although the lapel was eventually mended) through *Hollywood Party*, filmed in the fall of 1933. Stan's bowtie here is properly tied; before long, he would make sure that it was always slightly askew.

Stan's hat is not quite yet what it would become, although it's small enough to warrant the first performance of what I call The Never-Ending Hat Routine, which would be performed in many subsequent L&H films. It starts when the boys realize

Ferdinand Finkleberry and Sherlock Pinkham introduce themselves to Mr. and Mrs. Foozle, as the Tipton Slasher awaits.

they have the wrong hats on; Ollie's is much too big for Stan, and Ollie looks ridiculous with Stan's smaller derby atop his head. Ollie gives back his hat to Stan, who manages to switch things and give Ollie back the too-small hat. This goes on and on until Ollie throws down both hats and finally picks up the right one, although this is likely to be repeated a couple of times in any given film.

Here, the brim of Stan's hat is too wide and he wears it at a rakish angle in the first scenes. He and Babe were likely given derbies to wear because this was traditional for detective characters; Frank Brownlee, as the chief of the detective agency, wears one. (For that matter, so does Wilson Benge as the real butler.) Fred Kelsey, the movies' greatest gumshoe, seems always to have worn one, as you can see in *The Laurel-Hardy Murder Case*. Starting with *The Battle of the Century*, Stan would wear an Irish children's derby, with the thinner, flat brim and a tall crown.

Everyone in this picture does wonderful "takems" and reactions. Viola Richard has such expressive eyes that one really wonders why she wasn't retained at the studio after *Should Married Men Go Home?* in March 1928. Finlayson is remembered now as much for his Scottish accent as for his physical comedy, but in this silent film he conveys fear, surprise, and irritation vividly with his face and body, especially in the scene where the Slasher tries to surprise him while he's taking a bath.

There are some wonderful directorial moments, such as the composition of the shot in which Stan forces the Slasher into a closet, not knowing that Ollie is hiding

Making friends with the new butler.

The Slasher interrupts Judge Foozle's bath, a moment not quite in the film.

A posed encounter not in the film.

inside it. The door opens and for just a second, we see Ollie's horrified reaction as Stan inadvertently puts his partner directly into harm's way, then slams the door shut. (Ollie emerges some time later with two black eyes.)

The sequence where the boys must walk by a graveyard was actually shot at night. This makes it much more effective than similar scenes in earlier films, made with less light-sensitive film stock, which were shot "day for night" and tinted dark blue on release prints. Stan and Ollie's frightened reactions throughout the film really mark them as friends and as grown-up children. When Stan is scared, he runs to hold Ollie or even jump on his back, because Ollie seems to be his human security blanket.

This is very likely the first script which repeatedly refers to "Stan and Babe," and *Do Detectives Think?* is the first film where you can truly call Laurel and Hardy "the boys."

The script's suggestions for the casting of all the key roles were followed in the film, except for the shocking surprise that Finlayson was not the original choice to play the judge. Forrest Stanley was a rather bland-looking actor, a leading man in silents of the mid-Teens, whose lack of physical magnetism didn't prevent him from having a 45-year career in movies and television. He appeared in a Roach two-reeler, *Eve's Love Letters*, around this time and that may be why he was on the writers' minds. In any event, Finlayson was much more colorful, and his energetic and expressive performance undoubtedly makes *Do Detectives Think?* a much more enjoyable film than it would have been.

The Slasher never gets this close to dispatching Ferdinand in the film.

In the early scene where the judge's wife is reading a newspaper after dinner, the sight of the headline proclaiming the Slasher's escape doesn't merely cause the judge to choke and sputter his coffee. Maybe Forrest Stanley would have done this, but Jimmy Finlayson delivers an explosive spit-take. In fact, thanks to a little error in editing, he delivers two of them with the same mouthful of coffee. We are impressed, but Viola Richard – in the line of fire – likely was not.

The dog suggested by the script was, alas, never established. Nor does the script tell us just why it should be established.

The script's suggested name for the detective agency likely would not have passed muster with the Hays Office, even in 1927 when the censors were more permissive than they would be after 1934 and the implementation of the Production Code. In the film, Ollie does not peruse the magazine suggested, nor is Stan's entrance so dramatic.

The boys' repeated confusion with their hats was evidently an inspiration that occurred during the filming. It's not in the script – nor is the cartoonish gag of Stan's arrival at the judge's house.

Surprisingly, the script's proposed gag of the boys getting tangled in each other's trousers while trying to exit the bed is not in the film; they do get into bed, but remain in their suits, so Stan is not in pajamas as suggested a few scenes later.

Diminutive Will Stanton – sort of a British alternative to Jerry Mandy – is not as prominent in the film as he is in the script. He appears in a lobby card depicting a

54   EXHIBITORS HERALD   July 16, 1927

55 SHORTS FROM SENNETT, ROACH

Four "Our Gang" Comedies Are Scheduled

Hal Roach will offer 15 two-reel comedies on the Pathe short feature program during the new season.

Three groups of comedies will figure in the 1927-28 lineup: "Our Gang" will cavort in four comedies; Charley Chase will star in three farces and a Hal Roach star series of eight two reelers enacted by such favorites as Jimmy Finlayson, Martha Sleeper, Oliver Hardy, Stan Laurel and Max Davidson will be available.

The clever Hal Roach rascals in "Our Gang" will appear in the following four releases: "The Glorious Fourth," "Chicken Feed," "Olympic Games," and "The Smile Wins." Seven youngsters have been booked on the Orpheum circuit for a summer tour. They are Joe Cobb, Farina, Jean Darling, Jackie Condon, Jary R. Smith, Aroma and Harry Spear. Anthony Mack, Charles Oelze and Robert McGowan directed the comedies. McGowan is supervisor of these pictures.

Charley Chase will star in the following three two reel comedies produced by Hal Roach: "What Women Did for Me," "Now I'll Tell One" and "Assistant Wives."

Chase is a headliner in the short feature fun field. His delineations are put over with finesse and are always human. Charley writes many of his own continuities. Lupe Valez, a Hal Roach discovery, and Edna Marion, a blonde beauty, appear opposite the comedian. James Parrott directs the Chase comedies.

Supporting casts in the two reelers include such well known comedians as Stan Laurel, Lincoln Plummer, Caryl Lincoln, Eric Mayne and members of the Roach contract players.

Unusual titles identify each of the Hal Roach star comedy releases, each of which is enacted by comedians with reputations won in the film comedy field.

Eight Roach star comedies will be presented, including: "Sailors Beware," "Should Second Husbands Come First?" "Do Detectives Think?" "Galloping Ghosts," "Flaming Fathers," "Should Tall Men Marry?" and "Flying Elephants."

Martha Sleeper, Anita Garvin, Lupe Valez, Viola Richard, Stan Laurel, Oliver Hardy, Max Davidson, David Butler, Lillian Elliott, Spec O'Donnell, Jimmy Finlayson, Noah Young, Ora Carew, John T. Murray and Fred Malatesta are in the casts of these pictures which are directed by Hal Yates, Leo McCarey, Fred Guiol and James Parrott.

Pathe Slogan Will Govern Studio Work

(Continued from page 49)

pany, and Pathe Exchange, Inc., has been taken full cognizance of by Mr. C. B. De Mille and our other producers, and we cannot conceive of any or our may pictures failing to hit at the box office.

The exhibitors must have good pictures with that "IT" called box office appeal, and if ever a great effort was put forth to establish a company to which exhibitors can turn with entire con-

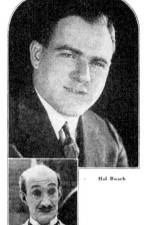

Hal Roach

Jimmy Finlayson

Martha Sleeper

Charley Chase

Max Davidson

fidence, that effort is being made today by Pathe Exchange, Inc.

We believe that the exhibitors of America believe in us. We believe they are going to accept us in the faith expressed above and every man of our excellent personnel is going to do his best to justify that confidence.

Array of Forty from Studio of Sennett

Mack Sennett will offer a tremendous array of 40 short feature comedies on the Pathe program for 1927-1928.

Three series will be offered: Mack Sennett Comedies, a series of 12 rapid-fire fun-fests enacted by such comics as Madeline Hurlock, Billy Bevan, Alma Bennett and Vernon Dent; Mack Sennett Girl Comedies, a series of 12 two-reel glorifications of the bathing girl and featuring a prominent comedienne, and "The Smith Family" comedies, a series of 12 lively domestic laugh films featuring Mary Ann Jackson, Raymond McKee and Ruth Hiatt. Also, Sennett will present two Harry Langdon and two Ben Turpin comedies.

The Mack Sennett brand for 1927-28 will offer famous beauties such as Madeline Hurlock, Alma Bennett and Mary Mabery, and clever comedians like Billy Bevan, Eddie Quillan, Andy Clyde, Vernon Dent and Barney Hellum. Included in the new lineup will be "The Gold Nut," "The Bull Fighter," "For Sale, a Bungalow," "Love in a Police Station," and "The College Kiddo."

For years the Mack Sennett girls have received tremendous publicity in every type of publication and the Mack Sennett beauty is as frequently spoken of as is the Ziegfeld charmer. In the past the Sennett girls presented as added attractions in the regular two-reel releases have been a highly valuable box office asset which exhibitors have come to realize.

According to present plans, each of the 12 releases will have some famous comedian leading the girls in the action. Daphne Pollard has been recruited from vaudeville by Sennett as one of the star comediennes in the new series.

"Why Is a Bathing Girl?" is to be the title of the first one scheduled for production.

According to Sennett's present plans, the series is to be a study in evolution—the evolution of bathing girl comedies from the days when a few sweet things in abbreviated suits capered by the sad sea waves, down to the present when a chorus of Venuses make the ensemble of the Sennett "Follies." The pictures are to burlesque the picture comedy idea, with Miss Pollard doing a travesty on bathing beauties. Special technicolor sequences of the girls will be produced.

In giving "The Smith Family" a life upon the screen in a series of Pathe domestic comedies, Mack Sennett is meeting the public demand. These comedies have been woven around the homes of the middle class.

Numbered in the 1927-28 releases of this popular series are: "Smith's Candy Shop," "Smith's Pony," "Smith's Cook," "Smith's Cousin," "Smith's Modiste Shop," "Smith's Cafeteria," "Smith's Farm Days," "Smith's Holiday" and "Smith's Army Life."

Jimmy Smith is portrayed by Raymond McKee, Mrs. Smith is enacted by Ruth Hiatt, and Bubbles Smith is played by Mary Ann Jackson.

Harry Langdon will be presented by Sennett on the Pathe program in two comedy subjects, "Soldier Man," in three reels, and "Fiddlesticks," in two reels. Both were directed by Harry Edwards and supervised by John Waldron.

Pathé distributed the short comedies of Hal Roach and Mack Sennett; the competition is one reason why Roach left for MGM.

climactic scene, but he does not make contact with the Slasher as per the script – nor do either one of them escape the clutches of the law, surprisingly. Instead, the film ends with the cops escorting the Slasher and his pal off to the pokey. Ollie, having had his eyes blackened by the Slasher, returns the favor to Stan, but the two of them manage to make a dramatic exit from the judge's home – having once again put on the wrong hats.

As *Do Detectives Think?* was being filmed, Hal Roach was seeking an exit from his distribution deal with Pathé. That company was also distributing Mack Sennett's comedies, putting the producers in direct competition. H.M. Walker, in New York, was negotiating with Felix Feist of Loew's Incorporated, MGM's parent company. On May 21st, MGM held a convention in Los Angeles, announcing the new partnership with Roach, whose films would be distributed by the most successful studio in Hollywood as of September 3rd. Roach made a wise decision in trading the Pathé rooster for Leo the Lion.

S-24

Cast:

> The Judge – Type like Forrest Stanley
> His Wife – Viola Richards
> Two Detectives – Stan Laurel & Babe Hardy
> Chief of Detectives – F. Brownlee
> The Murderer – Noah Young.

Fade in on interior of court room, the Judge, jury, prisoner, court attendants, officials, etc., in evidence. The Judge is in the act of sentencing a desperate looking murderer to hang for the brutal murder of a very prominent Chinese merchant.

The murderer gets over very dramatically to the Judge that if he ever gets out he will cut the Judge's throat from ear to ear. The Judge takes this and laughs sarcastically. Upon that the prisoner loses control, jumps to his feet and with a tremendous heave of his shoulders throws the guards from him and in the tussle his vest, coat and shirt are ripped from him, exposing his chest and muscular arms, and in the center of his chest we see a large tattooed skull and cross bones.

The Judge, jury and audience take this big and as they crowd and jam the aisles and doorways endeavoring to make an exit and the guards pile on top of the prisoner, we fade out.

Fade in on interior of the Judge's home, the judge and his wife on at dinner. The wife gets over that this is the night the servants are off and that she had to cook dinner herself, and also that she was obliged to fire the butler but she expects another one to report for duty this evening. After a little conversation the Judge gets over that this day he sentenced a desperate murderer to be hanged, who before being dragged from the court room had made a threat that if he escaped he would cut the Judge's throat. They laugh together about this.

The wife picks up a newspaper, opens it up and holds it in front of her to read. The Judge raises a cup of coffee and takes a mouthful; as he does so he sees the back of the newspaper and freezes in horror.

Insert newspaper and show enormous closeup of the
murderer with headlines to the effect that on his way to the
penitentiary he escaped after killing six of his guards, and that
to date he has not been recovered.

The Judge takes this big, choking and sputtering his coffee.
He jumps to his feet, snatches the paper, reads it closely and gets
over he is frightened to death. He strides up and down the room,
crumples the paper up and throws it in the fire. His wife follows
him after the manner of Felix the Cat, imploring him to tell
her what's happened, which he finally does, indicating that he
fears the murderer will make an attempt on his life at the first
opportunity.

(Note: Somewhere in this setup establish a dog.)

Cut to the grounds outside the Judge's house, and walking
toward the camera we see a type like Syd Crossley approaching.
He is in street clothes, carrying a grip, obviously on his way to
the Judge's house. As he approaches the house, a figure steps
across his path, whom he hails.

Cut to two figure shot and we see that this other figure is the
murderer. The butler smiles at him and gets over, "Can you tell
me if this is Judge So-and-so's residence?" The murderer, who is
by this time shaved and cleaned up, takes this and says "What do
you want to know for?" The butler says, "Well, I'm the new butler
just reporting for duty." The murderer looks him up and down
as though measuring the size of his clothes and says, "Oh, you
are, are you?" and gets over, "Step this way with me." They exit
behind a bush.

Hold it a few feet and the butler comes tearing out in his
underwear and derby hat and runs like hell away from the
camera and into small figure shot. As he does so, the murderer
appears from behind the bush wearing the butler's clothes,
carrying the suitcase and holding in his hand the letter of
recommendation. He exits in the direction of the house, getting
over he is going to take the butler's place.

Cut back to the Judge and his wife; at this moment the door
bell rings and the Judge dives under a divan. The wife reassures
him, saying that must be the new butler, and exits in the
direction of the front door.

Cut to hall; the wife admits the murderer, who is now

wearing the butler's clothes. He gets over that he is the new butler. She gives him a hurried glance, takes the letter, reads it hurriedly, and gets over she is glad he is a tall, strong man, as her husband's life is in danger and he will be a great help to them. She indicates, "Go upstairs and turn to the left and your room will be all ready."

As the wife re-enters the living room her husband peeks his head up over the back of the divan and very timidly gets over, "Who was it?" to which she replies, "The new butler."

The Judge then hurries to the telephone and picks up a telephone memorandum book. Insert page of the book; the Judge's finger runs down the page and stops opposite the name "Hitchcock & Scratchit, Private Detective Agency."

Lap dissolve to interior of the private office of the detective agency, the agency chief, type like Frank Brownlee, on. Telephone bell rings, he gets over he hears it and picks it up.

Cut to the other end and show the Judge talking.

Back to the detective agency; the chief gets over that he will send two good men up immediately. Back to the Judge; he speaks title to the effect, "It's dangerous; they may lose their lives." Back to the Chief; he smiles and says, "I have just the two men you need – I can well spare them."

Cut to the outer office and we see Babe Hardy on, his heels on the table, derby hat perched on the side of his head; he is reading the Police Gazette and getting a great kick out of a picture of a nude woman. The door opens and Stan makes a dramatic entrance and holds it in the doorway. He is very much messed up, indicating that he has had a severe tussle. Babe looks at him, smiles and says in title, "Did you get your man?" Stan very dramatically comes back with title, "I always get my man!" Babe indicates, "Tell me about it," and Stan in a short pantomime routine gets over a desperate struggle with a desperate criminal, and ends up with a title with pantomime to match, "And I drew my gun and got the drop on him."

So saying, he draws his gun from his hip pocket, points it at Babe and speaks title, "And I said, 'Stick 'em up!'" At that precise moment the gun goes off, knocks Babe's derby off his head and cuts the Chief's cigar in half as he makes an entrance. All three take it big. The chief bawls hell out of them both and gets over,

"Quit playing around; I've got a man's size job for you both; come into my office." They exit.

Follow them into the Chief's office; he explains the mission to them, emphasizes what a dangerous character this escaped murderer is, and that they must get him at all costs before he gets the Judge.

Intercut this with shots of Babe and Stan taking it. Finally Babe says, "Where's our destination?" As they wait expectantly for the information, the chief wheels on them and pointing a finger at them says dramatically, "Near the cemetery!" They take this big, looking at each other. Stan starts to ask if there isn't some other place they could go to, and the chief says, "No, be on your way!" They exit.

Cut back to the living room of the Judge's house, the Judge on extremely nervous and agitated. He rings for the butler and sits down in front of the fire with his back to the door. The butler enters and the Judge gets over, "Bring me a drink." Then without the Judge ever seeing the butler we go through a routine where the butler pours a drink for the Judge, standing a little in back of him and watching him with murder in his eye as the Judge tells him that his life is in danger. The butler reaches under his coat and starts to draw a wicked looking knife, keeping an eye on the Judge.

At this point the wife enters and breaks up the situation. As the butler exits from the scene she starts to soothe her husband.

Cut to exterior setup establishing the wall of a cemetery. Babe and Stan enter the setup and get over they are both agitated and nervous, and as they walk quickly along the wall of the cemetery Stan is edging all the time closer and closer to Babe, who finally bawls him out and tells him to pull himself together, Babe really being just as scared as Stan but not showing it so much.

They walk at a quick pace along the wall and come to the gateway of the cemetery, which is open. As they pass it a gust of wind blows through, takes Babe's hat and blows it just between the cemetery gates. They both take this a little panicky. Babe indicates to Stan, "Get my hat." Stan indicates "Get it yourself!" Babe comes back with a threatening gesture getting over "I'm running this expedition – get my hat!" Stan very timidly proceeds to do so.

In a close shot we see Stan stoop to pick up the hat, and as he does we see his shadow stoop with him. For the first time Stan sees his shadow and jumps away. As he jumps we see his shadow jump with him, which frightens him nearly to death. He looks back at Babe and Babe says, "Get it!" Stan makes a quick grab for the hat, looks over his shoulder, sees his shadow following him, hands the hat to Babe and gets over in an agitated whisper, "My God, we're followed!"

They start to walk and as they do we cut to a setup showing the two shadows on the wall walking as grotesquely as possible. In another setup we show Stan and Babe looking back at the shadows apprehensively. They break into a run. Cut to the other setup and show the shadows starting to run after them. Back to Stan and Babe; they increase their speed. Back to the shadows; they do likewise. Babe pulls his gun and fires blindly over his shoulder.

As he does so, cut to the other setup and we see Stan's shadow doing a terrific brodie.

Cut back to Babe and Stan. Stan is staggering to his feet. Babe gets over in a satisfied way, "I got one of them, anyway." They exit out of the scene. The shadows follow them. Stan looks back and says, "No you didn't, there are still two."

Play this for what it is worth until finally Babe gets wise to the fact that it is their own shadows. He bawls Stan out for getting him into this frame of mind.

They are arguing when they approach a section of the wall on which we see the shadow of a big gate similar to the one they have already passed. They get a little nervous, then get over they will run by it, holding their hats on their heads. This they do, and having crossed the supposed opening they congratulate each other.

Cut to another setup and we see a goat climbing up the side of a pile of tin cans, bottles, rubbish, etc. Half way up he slips and falls with a terrific crash.

Cut to Stan and Babe; they hear the crash, take it big and Stan jumps up and grabs Babe around the neck. Babe fights him off.

Cut back to the goat who has now regained his position and is nibbling on a can.

Back to Stan and Babe; quite near them on the wall we see the horrible profile of the goat in silhouette, resembling a devil with horns, ears, beard, etc. Stan sees this and his hat flies off his head, falls into his outstretched hands and he turns and runs like hell. Babe hears the footsteps, looks around and suddenly sees the goat shadow on the wall. His hat flies off and he turns and runs out of the scene.

Cut to a long shot; we see Stan running like hell and Babe following. Babe overtakes and passes Stan and runs out of the scene.

Carry Babe through a few setups and finally bring him on to the exterior of the Judge's house. He trips and falls and slides right up to the foot of the steps. As he gets up he sees something and gives it a triple takem.

We disclose Stan sitting in a porch chair in a very nonchalant attitude, smoking a cigar and very comfortable generally. He takes out his watch, looks at Babe, shakes his head and says, "Late, as usual." He finishes title and puts the cigar back in his mouth.

Babe gives it a double takem as he sees about three inches of ash on the end of Stan's cigar, which Stan proceeds to flip onto the floor. Babe follows the ash with his eye and gives it another takem as we disclose on the porch three or four cigar butts, getting over that Stan has been there for some time. They pull themselves together and exit to the front door.

Cut to interior, the wife and Judge on. Cut to bell ringing. At the sound of the bell the Judge makes a dive for cover. The butler goes to the door and admits to Stan and Babe, who very importantly display their badges, whereupon the butler whips back his vest and pulls out his suspender, on which we see the word "Police." Stan and Babe look at each other and nod knowingly.

The wife enters the setup and indicates that they follow her. She leads them into the living room and we see the Judge peering around from some point of concealment. He comes out and introduces himself.

Cut to hall; the butler watches the two detectives, gets over they are a couple of dumb eggs, sneaks out the front door and whistles softly.

Bill Stanton, made up as a tough little crook, runs into the setup; the butler gets over everything is OK, that he is going to wait until the family are asleep, make a smooth job of it and if Stanton will have the car ready they will make a getaway.

Cut back to the interior; the Judge gets over to the detectives that he hopes they are competent, brave and good shots. Babe gets over, "You needn't be afraid; I'll give you a demonstration of my ability with the gun." He places Stan against a wall, takes an apple from the table and puts it on Stan's head and turns away. As he does so, Stan takes a bite off the apple and puts it back on his head quickly. Play this up to the point where Babe aims and shoots, misses the apple completely and knocks a vase off the mantle about six feet to the right. Babe quickly signals to Stan to shake the apple off, which Stan does and catches it in his hand. The Judge sees this and also sees the vase; he looks inquiringly at Babe, and Babe says, "Two birds with one stone!"

Babe then takes matters in hand and assures the Judge and his wife that they are entirely in safe hands, and suggests that they retire, which they proceed to do.

Babe calls the butler to him and indicates that it would be a good idea to lock all the doors of the house. The butler agrees and Babe exits. Follow him to setup where he locks one door, removes the key, and closes one window and secures it, and we see that the windows are barred.

Cut back to Stan and the butler. Stan is filling his pockets with crackers. Babe enters the scene with a handful of keys, which he hands to Stan for safe keeping. Stan, busy with the crackers, hands the keys to the butler, who immediately puts them into his pocket and speaks title, "May I show you to your room, gentlemen?" They indicate "Yes" and he leads the way upstairs.

They enter a bedroom and the butler indicates "This is where you sleep." He produces a newspaper from his hip pocket and with an ironical smile asks Babe if he would like to read it. Babe gets over he would be delighted and takes the paper. The butler says, "May you have a long sleep," and exits. Babe and Stan start to undress.

Cut to hallway; the butler sneaking along stops and listens at the Judge's room, satisfied the Judge is asleep, then listens at the wife's bedroom door.

Cut back to Stan and Babe; they are undressed now and they hop into bed. Babe opens the newspaper. Stan is munching crackers. Play the routine of Stan munching the crackers and annoying Babe. Babe finally brushes a lot of cracker crumbs out of the bed onto the floor.

Stan then indicates that he wants to go to sleep and puts out the light. Babe indicates that he wants to read and puts it on again. Play this up until the point where they compromise and Babe continues to read, and Stan is about to go to sleep. Babe sees something in the newspaper, draws Stan's attention to it and we show insert of newspaper previously established with picture of the murderer.

They study the picture and Babe gets over to Stan, "Where have I seen that face before?" Stan starts to think.

The butler enters stealthily, goes right to a chest of drawers, brings out a long knife, tests the edge on his thumb and glances toward the bed. As he does so, Stan and Babe turn around, see him and take it big. At this point the butler, not giving them a tumble, makes an exit. They both look at each other, look at the paper and nod in unison, meaning "That's him." They get out of bed and Stan says, "What do you think?" Babe says, "I can't." They start to put their pants on.

Cut to a hand reaching to the master switch of the house lights and pulling it.

Cut back to Stan and Babe; Babe has his right foot in his pants, Stan has his left foot in his pants, and both are about to put their other foot into their pants. As the lights go out Stan puts his foot into Babe's pants and Babe puts his foot into Stan's pants, and they get into a tangle, all this action being illuminated by a shaft of light coming through a window.

They finally untangle themselves and Stan staggers back against a window. The blind flies up with a crash behind him and he leaps on Babe's neck. Babe tries to shake him off.

Cut to the wife's bedroom; she is sleeping peacefully. On the wall opposite her bed there is a patch of bright light and into this patch there suddenly appears the shadow of a man holding a long knife. The wife wakes up, sees the shadow, sits up in bed violently and lets out an awful scream and jumps out of bed. As she does so, the shadow disappears.

Cut to Stan and Babe in their bedroom; Babe has managed to quiet Stan when Stan hears the scream and leaps once more around Babe's neck, clutching him in a death-like grasp which Babe is unable to break, and they struggle out into the hallway. At this point the wife dashes out of her room; they see her and dash back into their room.

Cut to interior of bath room, the Judge in the bath covered with lather and in a listening attitude, not quite sure whether he heard the wife scream or not.

Cut to hallway; wife enters and sees Noah entering her husband's room stealthily with his knife. She takes it big and lets out another yell.

Back to the bath room; the Judge hears this, takes it big and submerges under the water. Hold this long enough to see bubbles breaking on the surface of the water.

Cut back to Stan and Babe, Stan still hanging on Babe's neck; they are in the vicinity of the door.

Cut to hall and show the wife start to enter their bedroom.

Cut to bedroom. Babe shoves Stan off, Stan makes another running jump, Babe sidesteps and Stan lands on the wife's neck and they fall to the floor. Babe helps them to their feet and gets over, "Where is he?" The wife pantomimes in the direction of her husband's bedroom. They start to exit stealthily.

Cut to the Judge's bedroom; Noah is creeping toward the bed in a menacing, stealthy way. In the dim light the bed has the appearance of holding a human form beneath the sheet. Noah sneaks up on the bed, pulls the covers back and slashes at the place where the person's neck should have been, cutting the pillow in half and spreading a shower of feathers.

Cut to the bath room; the Judge slowly coming up out of the water holding his nose and looking nervously toward the door.

Cut back to the detectives' room. Stan and Babe put on a bold front. Stan pulls out his gun and opens it again to see if the shells are there, and as he closes it the gun goes off, hitting Babe in the fanny.

Back to the bath room; the husband hearing the shot ducks down under the water again and we see more bubbles.

Back to the bedroom; Babe gives Stan a dirty look and the

wife speaks title to Stan, "Be careful – you might have blown his brains out." Babe gives her a dirty look. They exit out of the room.

Cut to the bath room; the Judge comes up out of the water again and is just about to take a breath when the door starts to open slowly and he ducks down under the water again. Noah enters, looks around in a menacing manner.

Cut to a shot of the Judge's legs trembling and shaking beneath the water, and as he draws his knees up we see that his toe is caught in the chain of the stopper, which comes out.

Cut to upper part of the bath and show the water sink quickly out of sight, revealing the Judge's body in a hunched up attitude, his eyes closed, holding his nose and still believing he is under water. He struggles to hold his breath and finally with a gesture of disgust he relaxes, flops on his back and opens his mouth as if he preferred drowning to suffocation. He fills his lungs, opens his eyes, looks around, raises up on his elbow and looks up over the edge of the bath, sees something and holds it.

Cut to Noah watching a tall clothes basket getting over he has seen a movement within. He sneaks up, draws back his knife and with a terrific lunge drives the knife right through the basket. With a savage grin he raises the lid and looks inside, sees nothing and slams down the lid. The Judge sees this and ducks out of sight into the bath tub. Noah exits.

Cut to hallway. Stan, followed by Babe and the wife, enter the scene and start to sneak along in the direction of the husband's room. Stan is holding Babe's hand. Opposite the Judge's room door, which is partially open, Stan pauses and listens. As he does so, he drops Babe's hand. At this moment the door slowly opens and we see the scowling face of Noah. He enters the scene directly behind Stan. Babe and the wife see it, try to speak but are frozen with terror.

Stan, unaware of Noah's presence, takes his hand and starts sneaking toward the other door, Babe and the wife too frightened to warn him. As Stan reaches the other door a shaft of light comes through the door; Stan turns his head to the opposite wall and to his horror sees his own shadow and the shadow of the murderer behind him with knife poised in the attitude of striking. Stan too terrified to move says a little prayer and resigns himself to his fate.

Cut to four figure shot; Babe pulls his gun out, aims at Noah and pulls the trigger. The gun refuses to go off. Babe lifts a rapier off the wall, places his hand on a table to balance himself and makes a lunge at Noah. The table breaks away, carrying Babe to the floor, the rapier at the same time striking Noah in the fanny. Noah drops the knife and falls on his back. Babe pounces on him and Stan turns and does a dive onto him and they go into a desperate struggle. In the middle of it Babe speaks title to Stan, "Quick, the handcuffs!" Stan pulls the handcuffs out of his pocket.

We go to insert of the hands all flying around wildly and we see Stan having a tough time getting on the handcuffs; he finally snaps them onto a pair of hands.

Stan gets up with a very proud attitude, getting over, "Nothing to it."

Babe in getting up pulls Noah to his feet, still thinking that Noah is handcuffed. He then turns to the camera and starts to gesture with his hands getting over "That's that." He looks down, sees that his hands are cuffed, and looks at Stan. Stan gives it a double takem. They look at Noah, who advances threateningly toward them, and they turn and run out of the scene, followed by Noah.

Follow them as they run downstairs and into the big living room. In a running shot Babe speaks title "Where are the keys to the handcuffs?" Stan gets over in a very agitated manner, "I gave them to him with the rest," indicating Noah who is pursuing them. As they duck around an archway Babe indicates a little hatchet on the wall and gets over to Stan, "Take that and cut these handcuffs off." Stan starts to do this.

Cut to Noah; he passes a huge Chinese executioner's sword hanging on the wall, sees it, stops, throws his knife away and snatches the sword off the wall and continues his pursuit. Play this chase up until a point where Stan and Babe get separated.

Noah follows Stan and just as Stan dives around a corner Noah makes a terrific swipe at his head with the sword. They both disappear around the corner.

Cut to Babe looking off wondering where Stan is. Suddenly he sees something, takes it big and freezes.

Cut to another setup; we see Stan come around the corner without a head.

Cut to Babe still paralyzed with fright. Stan enters to him, stretching his arms out toward him. Babe turns and runs from the scene, Stan after him. Play this until Stan catches up with Babe and grabs him around the neck. Babe nearly passes out with fright until he sees Stan's head pop up through the top of his pajamas.

Cut upstairs; the Judge makes an exit from the bath room and we see that he is wearing the shower bath sheet, the nickel ring to which it is attached fitting around his neck. Bring him into a setup where he trips and takes a terrific brodie, and in falling his head lands on a Chinese mask which we have previously seen fall from the wall. As he gets up we see the mask is firmly fixed on the back of his head. He is about to take a step forward when he sees something and freezes.

Cut to what he sees – Stanton working on the bars of a window attempting to force his way into the house.

As the Judge sees this he starts to back out of the set in the direction of the big living room.

Cut to living room, Noah on with the sword looking around for Babe and Stan. Suddenly he sees something and looks off, and we see the awful apparition of the Judge in the white sheet with the Chinese mask fixed on the back of his head, backing into the scene. Noah sees this, lets out an awful yell, thinks it is the ghost of the murdered Chinaman, and cowers in a corner.

Cut to Stan and Babe; they see Noah cowering and think he is afraid of them. They walk up to him, slap the handcuffs on him, drag him to his feet and are just about to congratulate each other on their work when Stan looks over his shoulder and sees the apparition approaching, draws Babe's attention to it, they let out a yell and run out of the scene.

Cut outside the house; we see Stanton climbing through a second story window directly above the front door.

Cut to inside; Noah tries to open the front door to make his escape. Above him we see Stanton climb through the window with his back to the interior; he climbs through in such a way as to get over he thinks he is climbing into an upstairs bedroom. He steps off backwards into space and falls on top of Noah, knocking him cold.

Cut outside and show posse of police led by the real butler

dashing up the drive toward the house.

Cut to interior; Babe, Stan and the Judge on. The police make an entrance. Babe and Stan point to the prisoner, taking full credit. The Sergeant of Police gets into an argument with Babe, Stan and the Judge as to who caught him, and while the argument is at its height we see the two crooks quietly exit. Finally the Sergeant says, "All right, you caught him." They turn to the prisoner and he is gone.

Cut outside and show the police on the heels of Noah.

Cut back inside for tag finish and FADE OUT.

HATS OFF!

Production history: Production S-3. Written mid-August 1927. Working title: *Rough on Hats.* Filmed Friday, August 19 through Wednesday, August 24. "Working on story" all day on the 25th. Shooting resumed Friday the 26th and finished Monday, August 29. Cutting Continuity completed September 16. Copyrighted October 17, 1927 by MGM (LP 24509). Released November 5. Two reels.

Produced by Hal Roach. Directed by Hal Yates. Supervised by Leo McCarey. Photographed by George Stevens. Edited by Richard Currier. Titles by H.M. Walker.

With Stan Laurel (Himself), Oliver Hardy (Himself), James Finlayson (Kwickway Washing Machine Co. proprietor), Anita Garvin, Dorothy Coburn (Prospective customers), Chet Brandenburg, Sam Lufkin, Ham Kinsey (Pedestrians).

The film's original press sheet provides this synopsis: "Stan and Oliver are out of work and calling on prospective bosses. At last they come in contact with a washing machine sales manager who offers them jobs soliciting. They accept and are loaded down with a sparkling, new and extremely heavy machine as a demonstrator. Many hectic adventures overtake them in their efforts to educate the ladies of the

The original title lobby card.

Mr. Finlayson displays a Kwickway washing machine to two prospective salesmen.

town to the uses of their machine, but they are apparently unable, thru no fault of their own, to make a sale. Finally a lady on top of a mountain beckons to them, and laboriously, between them, they manage to carry the machine up the nine flights of steps, only to learn that she wishes them to mail a letter for her. Heart-broken, they convey the tottering bulk of the machine again to the bottom. She calls them again. They believe she has changed her mind and will purchase one of the machines. After much travel and grief, they manage to get the machine again to the top only to learn that the lady forgot to stamp the letter. A few more experiences like this and they're ready to quit. An argument ensues over their hats. Each knocks the other's hat off. Passersby innocently become embroiled, losing their own hats. The thing becomes a riot with the whole town knocking off hats. Meanwhile a tractor runs over the sample washing machine, and it's "the end of a perfect day" for our salesmen."

This is not a script for *Hats Off!* written in advance of filming; it is a "cutting continuity" prepared by the studio, which describes the action in every shot of the film. In the case of *Hats Off!*, this is more valuable than the script, since the film has not been known to exist after 1945. Although a script has not yet surfaced, we can guess that it probably deviates from the finished movie, as does the script for *The Battle of the Century.*

This cutting continuity appears to have been written rather hastily. There are several strikeovers (which have been omitted here), and two instances of gaps in the numbering of the shots. Nevertheless, it is an important document, as it represents our only detailed account of the movie.

A lengthy sequence in the *Hats Off!* continuity has the boys encountering an apartment building with four front doors. Whenever they knock on one door, a

Ollie struggles, with the intersection of Del Monte and Vendome in the background. This site would be used later for *The Music Box* and is still recognizable.

different one opens. This gag had been used by Stan in his 1924 Roach two-reeler *Kill or Cure*, where he played a patent-medicine salesman.

It is particularly frustrating that a print of *Hats Off!* is not known to exist; it would allow us to enjoy performances by Anita Garvin and James Finlayson, both very prominent in the supporting cast. This film perpetuates The Never-Ending Hat Routine, the gag in which through some mix-up Ollie is wearing Stan's too-small derby, while Stan has on Ollie's too-big bowler; they attempt to switch hats but wind up again wearing the wrong ones. It was initiated in *Do Detectives Think?* but is given particular prominence here. It also recurs in this film's partial remake, *The Music Box*.

Speaking of *The Music Box*, you will notice later in this book that its script – a copy of which has surfaced for the first time in 90 years – contains a planned dialogue exchange, not used in the final film, which makes a direct reference to *Hats Off!* and the

The Never-Ending Hat Routine.

location both films share: the long flight of steps – 133 of them – between 923 and 935 Vendome Street, near Del Monte, in the Silver Lake district of Los Angeles.

Hats Off!, more than any other film, was given a spectacular promotional campaign, meant not only to publicize this film, but also Hal Roach's new comedy team. Babe Hardy kept many photographs and documents of this publicity onslaught in his personal collection.

One would think that the Roach studio would have taken special pains to preserve such an important and popular film. Hal Roach was not all that interested in what he had already done; he was much more interested in what was going on today and tomorrow. Unfortunately, this attitude had consequences for the preservation of the Roach film library, which was usually in general disarray and was subject to the annual endangerment of being transported in trucks across state lines into the broiling heat of Nevada, so that the film would not be taxed each year as inventory.

The Laurel and Hardy films in particular were much more popular and in demand than the studio personnel realized, and so the same negatives were printed and reprinted for new licensees until they were exhausted. The head of the editorial department, Richard Currier, said in 1980 that he knew if one series was going to be printed repeatedly over the years, it would be the Laurel and Hardy pictures. He had the foresight to tell Charlie Levin, who ran the studio laboratory, to make two fine-grain master positives (or "lavenders") of each Laurel and Hardy film instead of the usual one. This would help ensure that new negatives could be struck in the future, from which theatrical prints would be made. However, this request appears to have been made after the release of *Hats Off!*, underscoring how valuable Mr. Currier's prescience has been for the subsequent L&H films.

Anita Garvin's letter had better be important.

So, what happened to *Hats Off!*? A print, or at least a portion of one, still existed on August 2, 1932, when Stan and Babe – visiting England for what was supposed to be a vacation but turned into an unplanned publicity tour – came to the Midland Hotel in Manchester, where theater manager James Blakeley gave the boys one foot of 35mm film from *Hats Off!* Where was (or is) that print, and what happened to the other approximate 1,799 feet?

On April 20, 1945, a letter was sent from the New York offices of Loews Incorporated, the parent company of Metro-Goldwyn-Mayer, to the New York branch office of the Hal Roach Studios; it noted that the negatives for several Roach short subjects, including *Hats Off!*, were being transferred to the Mercury Laboratory at 723 Seventh Avenue in New York City, and could be used to fulfill any outstanding contracts for prints.

Sometime in the summer of 1945, Hal Yates – who had been a consistent writer for Laurel and Hardy all through the silent era and who directed *Hats Off!* – made a partial remake for RKO starring Edgar Kennedy, a two-reel comedy titled *It's Your Move*. One scene has Edgar and his brother-in-law, played by Jack Rice, hauling a washing machine up a long flight of steps. (These were not the same as those used in *Hats Off!* and *The Music Box,* although they weren't far away; these were near 327 Descanso Drive.) Could Hal Yates have borrowed a print of *Hats Off!* from the Roach studio to refresh his memory, with the print never being returned, or lost in transit, or subsequently misplaced in a Roach studio vault? We'll never know, although the decomposition that is common to nitrate film stock is the likely reason why we've never been able to see it.

Reading this cutting continuity is a fascinating and frustrating experience, as we can easily envision the action in each of the detailed shots – and wish that we had this vision available on film.

That is one sturdy washing machine.

Another young lady would love a demonstration.

Who knew that hats could cause such a melee?

At the Culver City intersection of Bagley and Venice; the buildings behind Stan and Ollie are still standing.

❧ ❧ PRESS SHEET ❧ ❧

HAL ROACH PRESENTS HIS ALL STARS in

HATS OFF

STARRING

STAN LAUREL and OLIVER HARDY

OLIVER HARDY

STAN LAUREL

New Comedy Team Sets Record for Laughs in 2 Reel Farce for M-G-M

SYNOPSIS

Stan and Oliver are out of work and calling on prospective bosses. At last they come in contact with a washing machine sales manager who offers them jobs soliciting. They accept and are loaded down with a sparkling, new and extremely heavy machine as a demonstrator. Many hectic adventures overtake them in their efforts to educate the ladies of the town to the uses of their machine, but they are apparently unable, thru no fault of their own, to make sale. Finally a lady on top of a mountain beckons to them, and laboriously, between them, they manage to carry the machine up the nine flights of steps, only to learn that she wishes them to mail a letter for her. Heartbroken, they convey the tottering bulk of the machine again to the bottom. She calls them again. They believe she has changed her mind and will purchase one of the machines. After much travel and grief, they manage to get the machine again to the top only to learn that the lady forgot to stamp the letter. A few more experiences like this and they're ready to quit. An argument ensues over their hats. Each knocks the other's hat off. Passersby innocently become embroiled, losing their own hats. The thing becomes a riot with the whole town knocking off hats. Meanwhile a tractor runs over the sample washing machine, and it's "the end of a perfect day" for our salesmen.

Released by

METRO
Goldwyn
MAYER

1540 Broadway,
New York, N. Y.

Any promotion suggestion or ideas should be sent to

HOWARD DIETZ
1540 Broadway,
New York, N. Y.

Hats Off! to Laurel and Hardy in "Hats Off" New Comedy

A new comedy starring team makes its bow on the screen of the ...... theater ...... when Hal Roach presents the M-G-M comedy, "Hat's Off," co-starring Stan Laurel and Oliver Hardy. It's built around the life of house-to-house solicitors for the sale of a particularly awkward and cantankerous washing machine.

It was because of their success with this unusual comedy offering that Roach definitely decided to co-star the pair, featuring them henceforth in his "All Star Series."

The director, Hal Yates, and the supervisor, Leo McCarey, must have lain awake nights in order to wring so much humor out of a mere washing machine (and no pun intended.) It fairly bubbles from the start, when the pair of vagrants finally connect with a job and almost ruin their new boss immediately.

Their back-breaking house-to-house canvass with their demonstrator is strictly one of the greatest comedy riots ever offered the public.

"Hats Off" is being shown in connection with the presentation of the feature production........

Just One Laugh But a Long One!

A comedy is known by the laughs it gets. That makes "Hats Off," Hal Roach's latest contribution to the M-G-M program, perfect. It just gets one laugh, which is practically continuous throughout the two reels of its length. It concerns itself with the harrowing adventures of two dumb washing machine salesmen portrayed feelingly by Stan Laurel and Oliver Hardy, two of the favorites of Hal Roach's stock company who are to be co-starred as a result of their splendid work in this picture "Hat's Off" is now showing at the .... theater.

Hats Off! was heavily promoted. Ready-to-use articles and reviews for newspapers were only part of the hoopla.

Short Paragraphs for Columnists

One must take his hat off to "Hat's Off." It's the latest half-hour of joy to emanate from the Hal Roach Studios, that hot-bed of amusement. Stan Laurel and Oliver Hardy are co-starred in this latest M-G-M comedy, which opens at the ...... theater .... Hal Yates was responsible for the direction, under the supervision of Leo McCarey.

＊ ＊ ＊

Clumsy peddlers—glistening washing machines — thousands of hats—hateful housewives — street fights—all go to make for fun in Hal Roach's newest M-G-M farce comedy, "Hat's Off," now showing at the .... theater. Stan Laurel and Oliver Hardy share the starring honors.

＊ ＊ ＊

If you're never acted as a house-to-house solicitor for the sale of washing machines, carrying a demonstrating sample by hand, you will possibly appreciate some of the annoyances which come to Stan Laurel and Oliver Hardy, the new comedy starring team, in their latest Hal Roach M-G-M comedy, "Hat's Off," which is now showing at the ...... theater.

SCENE FROM THE HAL ROACH - M - G - M. COMEDY -"HAT'S OFF"

It literally ruined hats in Culver City, near Hal Roach Studios during the making of "Hats Off," Roach's latest M-G-M comedy. A thousand hats were ruined before the very eyes of several hat dealers, but it was all for fun. Stan Laurel and Oliver Hardy star in this riot of fun, which will open at the ...... theater ....

＊ ＊ ＊

Hal Yates, latest director given a long term contract by Hal Roach, bossed the making of "Hat's Off," that producer's latest M-G-M comedy, coming to the .... theater.....

＊ ＊ ＊

One of the regular features of Hollywood life is the "preview," where new motion picture productions are "tried on the dog" without announcement of any kind, in neighborhood picture theaters. "Hat's Off," Hal Roach's latest M-G-M comedy, co-starring Stan Laurel and Oliver Hardy, was proclaimed the nearest to a perfect comic film ever witnessed by several "hard-boiled" professional preview audiences there. "Hat's Off" will serve as the risibility of the program at the ...... theater soon.

＊ ＊ ＊

Stan Laurel, co-starred with Oliver

SCENE FROM THE HAL ROACH - M - G - M COMEDY-"HATS OFF"

Hardy in the Hal Roach M-G-M comedy, "Hat's Off," now the cause of hysterical outburst of laughter at the ...... theater, originally came to America from his native England, with Charles Spencer Chaplin in the now-famous skit, "A Night in An English Music Hall."

＊ ＊ ＊

A new comedy team is introduced by Hal Roach in "Hats Off," new M-G-M funfilm now showing at the .... theater. Stan Laurel and Oliver Hardy divide the honors with such success that Roach has announced his intention of co-starring them hereafter in his "All Star Series."

＊ ＊ ＊

Stan Laurel and Oliver Hardy, Hal Roach's new starring team in M-G-M comedies, rise to undiscovered heights, in their new fun effusion, "Hat's Off", at the .... theater starting .... The boys are house-to-house solicitors for a new brand of heavy washing machine.

Try This on Your Washing Machine

Ordinarily, there's nothing so very funny about a washing machine. But it certainly has had potential comedy possibilities all these years, as witness the Hal Roach M-G-M comedy, "Hat's Off," now showing at the.... .... theater, in connection with the presentation of ......

Between the new starring team, Stan Laurel and Oliver Hardy, two favorite Hal Roach comedians, the washing machine produces more fun than any similar prop which has been hauled onto the Hal Roach Studio lot for many a moon. Then, of course, Hal Yates, the young director, and Leo McCarey, who supervised the production, are noted for their keen senses of humor. Anyway, somebody saw something very funny about a washing machine, and so will you when you visit the .... theater.

The plot of the thing is built around the efforts of these two embryo salesmen to dispose of the contraptions in a house-to-house canvass. Enough said. You'll realize what these two sterling comedians could do with an opportunity like that. It's riotous!

HAL ROACH
presents

"HATS OFF"

Starring
STAN LAUREL
and OLIVER HARDY

Directed by
HAL YATES
Supervised by
LEO McCAREY
Photographed by
GEORGE STEVENS
Edited by
RICHARD CURRIER
Titled by
H. M. WALKER

A Metro-Goldwyn-Mayer
Picture — 2 Reels.

USE THESE ADVERTISING ACCESSORIES

Stock 1 sheet
Subject 1 sheet
Subject 3 sheet
8—11x14 lobby cards
Subject slide
Music Cue
Press Sheet
2—1 col. ad mats
1—2 col. ad mat
2—1 col. scene mats
1—2 col. scene mat

Hal Roach Comedy Team Scores Big Hit in 2 Reeler

A new starring team is offered the public by Hal Roach, the king of laughter, in his latest M-G-M comedy offering, "Hat's Off," which comes to the .... theater .... Stan Laurel and Oliver Hardy will henceforth and forever, according to present plans, at least, be co-starred by the famous young producer in that series of his comedy productions called "the all-star."

It was because of their splendid work in "Hat's Off," wherein the fact of their fitness for co-starring is well demonstrated, that Roach shook each solemnly by the hand and told them they'd better get along well personally from now on — because they were to work together forever.

"Hat's Off" has to do with the hectic adventures, trials and tribulations of the pair after they secure jobs as washing machine demonstrators and house-to-house salesmen One would not imagine possible the many ludicrous situations as develop during the unfolding of this hilarious plot.

SCENE FROM THE HAL ROACH M-G-M
COMEDY "HATS OFF"

It's all right as long as prospective customers live on the level, but when they endeavor to locate their homes at the very peaks of the highest mountains, that life gets hard for our tinwear peddlers.

Laurel and Hardy have worked together frequently, but never before have been co-starred. Hal Roach himself, comedy authority as he is, flatly states that he does not believe a better starring team exists today.

ADVANCE SLIDE

This subject slide pictured at the left provides a striking full color advance announcement of the coming of The Hal Roach All Stars in "Hats Off" to your theatre. Here is the shortest way to bigger comedy profits. Flash it on your screen for bigger business!

HAL ROACH
presents
"HATS OFF"
STAN LAUREL
OLIVER HARDY
Directed by Hal Yates
Metro-Goldwyn-Mayer
PICTURE

CAMPAIGN ON LAUREL & HARDY
IN "HATS OFF" METROPOLITAN THEATER LOS ANGELES MARCH 8, 1928

ADVANCE TRAILERS: Specially prepared advertising trailers used in
                      advance.

NEWSPAPER SPACE: Additional newspaper advertising space, playing comedy
                      up equally with the feature.

BILLBOARDS: 100 special 24-sheet posters in selected locations in
                      Los Angeles, with name of comedy team, "Laurel &
                      Hardy," two sheets high, white on red. Top and
                      bottom selling copy in black on yellow.

HOUSE PROGRAMS: House organ of Metropolitan Theater gave the comedy
                      special billing, and much advance publicity,
                      capitalizing on popularity of two former Laurel &
                      Hardy comedies two weeks in advance.

"HOLLYWOOD DRY"   Fifty Owl Drug Store windows in Los Angeles, with
                      displays of Hollywood Dry Ginger Ale, tied in with
                      enlargements of the two comedians drinking the ale.

OWL DRUG TIE-UP   Five hundred soda clerks in Los Angeles, Owl and
                      affiliated drug stores, wore ribbons on their coats
                      and aprons tying in with the fact that Hollywood Dry
                      is the favorite beverage of the comedy team, and
                      carrying billing for theater.

PARADE: Put car in parade, on opening day, the auto containing
                      doubles of Laurel & Hardy, with a washing machine,
                      and appropriate billing.

ROACH ROLLING STOCK: Thirty vehicles in constant service from the Hal
                      Roach Studios, trucks, location busses and other
                      cars, carrying banners for week ahead of opening
                      advertising the return of Laurel & Hardy to the
                      Metropolitan.

MOTOR TRANSIT: Eighty Motor Transit Stages carried half-sheet cards,
                      tying in with the comedy and theater.

RALPH'S GROCERIES   The entire chain of fifty Ralph Grocery stores
                      inserted slips with copy: "Hats Off to Ralph's
                      Vacuum Coffe, Then See 'Hats Off' at the Metropolitan,
                      etc." These go in all packages during the week.

RADIO HOOK- UP   HAL ROACH STUDIOS ORCHESTRA, now a well-known musical
                      organization, on KFI, leading west coast radio station,
                      at Saturday midnight frolic, with appropriate
                      announcements all week.

RADIO WINDOW: Wurlitzer Co. gave tie-up to photo of Hardy, enlarged
                      with Wurlitzer radio, in best Broadway window.

ELEVATOR CARDS: Elevators in 100 downtown office buildings displaying
                      cards: "Hats Off! See 'Hats Off,' etc.

HAT STORES: Twelve New York Hat Stores scattered about the city
                      featuring window cards displaying a popular brand of

From Babe's private collection, a list of the amazing promotional tie-ins for the film's Los Angeles
premiere on March 8, 1928.

September 16, 1927

Cutting Continuity for S 3

"HATS OFF!"

1.   FADE IN

       Trade Mark

       Metro-Goldwyn-Mayer

       FADE OUT

2.   FADE IN

       HAL ROACH PRESENTS

       Stan Laurel

       and

       Oliver Hardy

       In

       "HATS OFF!"

       Copyright MCMXXVII in U.S.A.

       By Metro-Goldwyn-Mayer

       All Rights Reserved Under International

       Convention of Buenos Aires

       Trademark

       Passed by the National

       Board of Review

            LAP DISSOLVE TO

3.   DIRECTED by HAL YATES

       SUPERVISED by LEO McCAREY

       Photographed by George Stevens

       Edited by Richard Currier

       Titles by H.M. Walker

FADE OUT

4.   FADE IN

      [Title] The story of two boys who figure that the world owes them a living –

      But is about thirty-five years behind in the payments –

      FADE OUT

5.   FADE IN

      L.S. of the exterior of café. Babe and Stan are being thrown out by manager. He hangs up a card. He exits back into café.

6.   [Title] Pals – One pocket between them – always empty ---

7.   M.S. of Stan and Babe picking up and putting on hats. They have on wrong hats.

8.   Insert of sign. It reads: Wanted – two dishwashers.

9.   M.S. of Stan and Babe. They look at each other and see that they have on wrong hats. They change hats. They start out of scene.

10.   L.S. of Babe and Stan walking. Stan stops and looks down.

11.   Insert of brick on paper.

12.   C.U. of Stan who turns, looks at sign, then at window; gets an idea and picks up brick.

13.   L.S. of Stan picking up brick and coming to foreground. He starts to throw it but Babe rushes in and stops him.

14.   C.U. of Babe and Stan. Babe speaks title:

15.   " – Curb your terrible passion! Control your wild Corsican blood! -- "

16.   C.U. of Babe and Stan. Babe speaks title:

17.   " – Break the glass an' you'll go to jail! – Then what will become o' me? -- "

18.   L.S. of Stan and Babe. Babe throws brick.

19.   Insert of window. Brick comes in and breaks it.

20.   L.S. of Babe and Stan. They take it and exit out.

21.   L.S. of Babe and Stan go into doorway.

22.   M.S. of Stan and Babe looking back. They smile at each

other. They see a sign and start reading it.

23.   Insert – Wanted – Snappy salesmen to sell washing machines Etc.

24.   M.S. of Stan and Babe. They are reading sign. Stan speaks title:

25.   " – What does it say? -- "

26.   M.S. of Stan and Babe. Finlayson makes entrance from store and starts talking to them. He takes sign off washing machine.

27.   L.S. of the three. Stan takes cover off of machine and water comes out and squirts Finlayson and Babe. Babe bawls Stan out.

28.   C.U. of Finlayson.

29.   M.S. of Babe and Finlayson. Babe speaks title:

30.   " – We're sorry, boss – My secretary and I will accept this position -- "

31.   M.S. of Babe and Finlayson.

32.   L.S. of the three. Stan comes over and gets a hold of washing machine. He and Babe carry it out and put it on the truck which is standing at curb.

33.   C.U. of Finlayson speaking title:

34.   " – Be careful! -- That machine is worth $175! -- "

35.   C.U. of Stan and Babe. They get over okey.

36.   L.S. of Ford pulling out. The machine falls on Finlayson.

37.   M.S. of Stan and Babe drive in. They turn around and see it.

38.   C.U. of Finlayson on sidewalk with machine on top of him.

39.   M.S. of Babe and Stan backing car out of scene.

40.   L.S. of Finlayson with washing machine on top of him. Babe and Stan back Ford in. They get out and put washing machine back in Ford. They pick Finlayson up and then they get back into auto.

41.   C.U. of Finlayson who speaks title:

42.   " --- I warn you again! - Be careful! --- "

43.   L.S. of Ford pulling out. The washing machine falls out

again and lands on Finlayson. FADE OUT.

44.   FADE IN

L.S. of four-door apartment. Stan and Babe are carrying
washing machine in to one of the doors. Stan knocks.
A door on the other side opens. They see it and carry
machine over there and knock. The door that they just
left opens. They pick up machine and carry it back.
They knock and a door in the center opens. They see
the woman and they take the machine to that door. They
knock and the door next to them opens. Babe discovers it
and they carry machine to that door.

45.   C.U. of Stan and Babe at door. Stan starts to knock and
Babe starts to explain something to him. He knocks.

46.   L.S. of them carrying machine to next door. The door
opens where they just knocked. They see woman and take
it. They don't know what to do.

47.   C.U. of Stan and Babe. Babe explains to Stan what to do.
Stan does just the opposite.

48.   L.S. of Stan and Babe at doors. They both knock on the
two center doors. The two end doors open. They run
for these doors but they are closed by the time they get
there. They knock at the end doors, and the two middle
doors open. They run to get to these two middle doors. By
that time they are closed. They start sneaking to the end
doors again. They knock at all four of them. Then they
start running to all the doors. During the meantime the
women close the doors. They pick up machine and carry
it down to steps and then the two end doors open. Stan
and Babe run to opposite doors. They start talking to the
women. They both come back to machine and try to get it.
Both want it but in the meantime the women again close
the doors.

49.   M.S. of Stan and Babe. They both throw hats down. Babe
gives Stan the devil and they cross back of machine.
They pick up hats. They are the wrong ones. They
exchange hats and push machine back against wall.

50.   L.S. of Babe taking Stan over to door on one end. The
women on the other side come out and exit. Babe takes
Stan across to other side and the other two women exit

from building. They go into a routine of knocking on all the doors. A cop makes his entrance. The cop walks up the steps and stands there watching them.

51.   M.S. of Stan and Babe. Cop in foreground. They are knocking on doors. They start kicking doors and Stan kicks his open. He sticks his head in and looks around. Babe discovers cop. Stan turns around and sees cop. He does a silly grin. They go to washing machine and pick it up.

52.   L.S. of Babe and Stan as they exit past cop with the machine; they start running. Fade Out

53.   Fade In

L.S. of street as Stan and Babe drive in. There is a woman on sweeping sidewalk. They get out of Ford and walk up steps of house.

54.   C.U. of Stan and Babe knocking on door. Woman opens door. Stan starts speaking to her and Babe stands by watching him. Finally Babe stops him and he starts talking to woman.

55.   L.S. of woman slamming door. Their hats fly off out of the scene.

56.   M.S. of them entering to foreground and pick up hats. They have on the wrong hats. Babe sees this and they exchange. Babe is bawling Stan out.

57.   M.S. of woman at the head of stairway yelling.

58.   C.U. of Stan and Babe as they look around. Stan looks off and sees.

59.   Iris shot of woman at top of stairs. (Long)

60.   C.U. of Stan and Babe. Stan points off and Babe looks and sees.

61.   Iris L.S. of woman at top of stairs. The Iris opens up and shows her standing at the top of a long flight of stairs.

66.   [62 through 65 were accidentally omitted in numbering the shots.] L.S. of woman who speaks title:

67.   " --- COME ON UP HERE --- "

68.   C.U. of Stan and Babe as they make exit.

69.   M.S. of woman at top of stairs looking off.

70.   L.S. of hill and stairway. Babe and Stan carrying washing machine start up stairs.

71.   C.U. of woman watching them.

72.   M.S. of Stan and Babe making entrance with washing machine. Babe stumbles and his hat falls off. He turns around and sees:

73.   L.S. of hat falling all the way down the stairs. It lands in the street.

74.   C.U. of Stan and Babe watching hat. Babe speaks:

75.   " --- You get it --- "

76.   C.U. of Stan and Babe. Stan looks down and sees.

77.   L.S. of stairs and hat in street below.

78.   C.U. of Stan and Babe. Babe speaks title:

79.   " --- The slightest exertion – and everything goes blank with me --- "

80.   C.U. of Stan and Babe. Stan starts crying.

81.   Longer shot of Stan starting out. The machine slips and Babe gives him hell. Stan comes down steps. Babe starts struggling with machine.

82.   C.U. of Babe struggling with machine. Machine runs out of scene with him following it.

83.   L.S. of Stan on with washing machine coming in. It hits him in the back and he falls over. Babe comes rolling in to Stan. They look up and see.

84.   L.S. of Stairs with woman at top.

85.   C.U. of Stan and Babe. Babe does a silly grin.

86.   M.S. of Stan and Babe. They get up and put on wrong hats. Stan picks up machine and they exchange hats.

87.   M.S. of woman at top of stairs.

88.   L.S. shooting down stairs. Stan and Babe are carrying washing machine up.

89.   M.S. of woman as she sits down.

90.   L.S. of Stan and Babe carrying machine up steps.

91.   L.S. of top of steps. Woman is on as Stan and Babe make their entrance.

92. M.S. of the three. They tip their hats and woman speaks title:

93. " --- Will you mail this letter --- "

94. M.S. of the three. They take it and Babe takes letter and speaks title:

95. " --- Would you be interested in the world's most synchronistical washing machine? --- "

96. M.S. of the three. She speaks title:

97. " --- I would not – I have my own Chinese --- "

98. M.S. of the three. Woman makes exit. They look at each other and then turn and look down stairs.

99. L.S. of stairs.

100. L.S. of Stan and Babe looking down. They take a long breath, pick up the machine and start down.

101. End Part One

"Hats Off!"

102. Part Two

"Hats Off!"

103. L.S. shooting down stairs. Babe and Stan carrying machine down.

104. M.S. shooting upstairs. Stan and Babe are carrying machine and are coming towards camera.

105. L.S. shooting down. They are carrying machine. They both stumble and their hats fall off. They pick up hats and put them on. They discover that they have on the wrong hats and they exchange. Then they start down stairs again with the machine.

106. M.S. of woman coming running in.

107. Insert of a stamp in her hand.

108. M.S. of her yelling.

109. L.S. of Stan and Babe at the foot of the steps. They turn around and look up.

110. M.S. of woman as she yells and motions for them to come up.

111. L.S. of Stan and Babe putting down machine. They look

up and Babe speaks title:

112.   " --- Maybe the Chinaman sprained his back – you go up and see --- "

113.   L.S. of Stan and Babe on. Stan turns around and looks up.

114.   L.S. of woman. Standing at the top of stairway.

115.   L.S. of Stan and Babe. Stan starts crying. He exits out of scene.

116.   L.S. shooting down stairway. Stan is coming up slowly.

117.   M.S. of Babe at the bottom of stairway. He leans on machine and it rolls out from under him. He falls and gets up and jerks machine back again. He looks at it and leans on it again. Again it rolls out from under him and again he spills. He looks at machine and gets up. He is madder than ever. He pulls it back into set kicking it.

118.   L.S. shooting up. Stan is going up steps slowly. He is about all in.

119.   L.S. shooting down. Stan gets on his hands and knees and crawls up. Stan sits down and Babe motions for him to go on. He picks up a rock and throws at him. Stan gets up and starts up steps. As he gets near top he gets on a bum dignity and fixes his tie.

120.   M.S. of woman at the top as Stan makes entrance. He comes up to her. She speaks title:

121.   " --- I forgot to put a stamp on my letter --- "

122.   M.S. of woman and Stan. Stan looks at her. He turns around and yells to Babe at the bottom.

123.   M.S. of Babe who is still leaning on machine. He takes it.

124.   M.S. of Stan and woman. Stan motions for him to come up.

125.   M.S. of Babe who looks at machine and claps his hands and speaks title:

126.   " --- Great kid! He's made a sale! --- "

127.   M.S. of Babe picking up machine and starts out of the set.

128.   L.S. of steps shooting down. Babe is coming up the steps carrying the machine. He stumbles and drops machine.

129.   M.S. of Stan and Woman. Woman sits down. Stan speaks title:

130.   " --- He's bringing the washer – Imagine a man being that dumb --- "

131.   M.S. of Stan and woman. Stan sits down.

132.   L.S. shooting down stairway. Babe picks up the machine and falls with it again. Picks it up and starts carrying it up again.

133.   M.S. of woman and Stan. Stan looks down steps and sits down and speaks title:

134.   " --- I wouldn't be surprised if he stopped to demonstrate --- "

135.   M.S. shot of woman and Stan.

136.   L.S. of Babe carrying machine up steps. He sets the machine down and it rolls down steps. He goes after it.

137.   M.S. of Stan and woman. She speaks title:

138.   " --- He's sure getting' a lot o' mileage outta that machine --- "

139.   M.S. of Stan and woman.

140.   L.S. of Babe picking up machine and starts up again

141.   M.S. of Stan and woman.

142.   L.S. of Babe carrying machine.

143.   M.S. of Stan and woman. They get up as Babe comes in carrying machine. He sets it down.

144.   M.S. of the three. Babe starts talking as if to make a sale and Stan shakes his head no. Babe stops and looks at him. Stan speaks title:

145.   " --- She forgot the stamp – and you've got the letter --- "

146.   M.S. of the three. Woman offers him stamp. Babe looks down and sees:

147.   L.S. shooting down of the steps.

148.   M.S. of the three. Babe hits Stan in nose. It knocks his hat off. Stan starts crying. Woman hits Babe in nose. She takes letter from him and speaks:

149.   " --- You're the kind of a man that always thinks of himself first! --- "

150.   M.S. of the three. The woman exits. Babe starts crying. They pick up machine and Stan speaks title:

151.   " --- I'm growing fond of this thing --- "

152.   C.U. of Stan and Babe as they exit down stairs.

153.   L.S. shooting down. Babe and Stan are carrying machine down. Stan's legs are giving away.

154.   M.S. of Stan and Babe coming towards camera. Stan speaks title:

155.   " --- It might be worse --- "

156.   M.S. of Stan and Babe. Babe speaks title:

157.   " --- Yes – We might be selling tractors --- "

158.   C.U. of Stan and Babe as they exit past camera carrying machine.

159.   L.S. of the bottom of the steps as they come in carrying machine. They put it down. They are both all in. A woman makes her entrance. She comes up to Babe and speaks title:

160.   " --- I would love to have a demonstration --- "

161.   L.S. of the three. Babe speaks title:

162.   " --- Where do you live? --- "

163.   L.S. of the three. She points up the hill and she starts up the steps. Stan kicks her in the fanny. She takes it, turns around and comes down a step. She hits Babe in the nose. It knocks his hat off and she makes a motion at Stan and his hat goes off. She exits up stairs.

164.   C.U. of the two. Babe speaks title:

165.   " --- Thinking of myself again --- "

166.   C.U. of Stan and Babe picking up hats. They exchange before they put them on. They put on the wrong hats. Babe sees this. He takes off hat and hands it to Stan. Stan does the cross and gives Babe back the same hat. They pick up machine.

167.   L.S. of them picking up machine and carrying it to the foreground. They put it down and Babe calls Stan to the front of the machine. Babe takes off hat and hands it to Stan. Stan takes off his and does cross. Babe catching him and he says he wants that hat. Stan does another cross and hands him the wrong hat. Babe discovers it and throws it on the ground. Stan does the same with Babe's

hat. Babe pushes machine over and kicks Stan's hat out of the scene. Stan runs in and kicks Babe's out of scene. They both exit.

168.   L.S. of hats on ground. Stan and Babe come in and kick them both out of scene. They make exit.

169.   C.U. of button in middle of street. Babe's hat reels in and lands on button.

170.   L.S. of street. Stan and Babe push each other around. They are trying to keep each other from stepping on hats. Babe steps on Stan's hat. Stan starts running for the other one. Babe grabs him and they push each other around. Finally Stan pushes Babe down and Stan comes in and kicks button instead of hat. He grabs his toe and sits down on ground and is in very much pain. Babe comes in and gets his hat and looks it over.

171.   L.S. of the machine laying in the street. Finlayson makes entrance and looks it over.

172.   L.S. of Stan and Babe in street.

173.   L.S. of Finlayson coming to foreground. He is watching them as a steam roller makes entrance and goes over machine. Finlayson takes it and turns and sees what has happened. He runs over to the machine.

174.   M.S. of him looking at machine. He picks it up and drops it again. He turns around and makes exit.

175.   M.S. of Stan and Babe. Babe laughs and hits Stan on shoulder. Babe puts out his hand to shake hands and Stan gives him a razzberry and Babe knocks his hat off. Stan knocks Babe's hat off and they start pushing each other.

176.   L.S. of Stan and Babe pushing each other. Finlayson makes his entrance. He speaks to them and Stan knocks Finlayson's hat off. A man makes entrance. He talks to Stan and Babe and turns and speaks title to Finlayson:

177.   " --- I saw the whole thing – It was all your fault! --- "

178.   C.U. of Finlayson and Man. Finlayson knocks man's hat off. The man knocks Finlayson's hat off.

179.   L.S. of Finlayson picking his hat up. He goes over to man and tells him to watch him. Then he steps on man's hat. Finlayson runs out of scene. Stan points to a rock and the

man picks it up.

180.   L.S. of Finlayson running down street. The man is in the
       foreground. The man throws rock and Finlayson's hat
       drops off. Finlayson steps on it and exits.

181.   M.S. of Stan, Babe and two men on. A man with a plug hat
       makes entrance and speaks title:

182.   " --- I saw everything! --- "

183.   M.S. of Stan knocking his hat off. He knocks Babe's hat
       off. Another man makes entrance and talks to Stan and
       he knocks his hat off. The man turns and knocks another
       man's hat off. Babe knocks Stan's hat off.

184.   L.S. of other men coming in. Each gets his hat knocked
       off. It ends up in a free-for-all.

188.   [Numbers 185 through 187 accidentally omitted] M.S. of
       officer making entrance. He talks to Babe and Stan turns
       and knocks his hat off. He takes it and turns and knocks
       off plug hat. There is a big crowd on, all knocking each
       other's hat off.

189.   L.S. of crowd. Stan comes to foreground.

190.   C.U. of Stan who looks off and sees:

191.   L.S. of man standing on corner.

192.   L.S. of Stan making exit.

193.   L.S. of man on corner. Stan runs in and knocks his hat off.
       Stan runs back toward and past camera.

194.   L.S. of crowd still at it. Stan makes entrance and gets
       right into the center of it.

195.   L.S. of man on corner. He is putting hat on. A man comes
       around corner. The other man goes up and knocks his hat
       off. The other man knocks his hat off with cane.

196.   L.S. of crowd still at it. Cops come in and drive all out
       except Babe and Stan. They are laying down but come to
       a sitting position and look at each other and change hats
       as we fade out.

197.   FADE IN

       The End.

       Fade Out.

THE BATTLE OF THE CENTURY

Production history: Production S-5. Written late September 1927. Filmed Wednesday, October 5 through Thursday, October 13, at which point work was suspended due to Stan Laurel's illness. Production resumed on Thursday, October 27, but was temporarily discontinued the next day due to weather problems. Filming finished on Saturday, October 29. Retakes directed by Clyde Bruckman on Saturday, November 12. Released December 31, 1927. Copyrighted January 9, 1928 by MGM (LP 24848) Two reels.

Produced by Hal Roach. Directed by Clyde Bruckman. Supervised by Leo McCarey. Photographed by George Stevens. Edited by Richard Currier. Titles by H.M. Walker. *Uncredited assistance:* Assistant Directors, Lloyd French and Art Lloyd. Prop men, Ted Driscoll, Tom Mintz, and ? LaPlanche. Photography by R. H. Weller. Assistant Cameramen, Jack Roach, Edward L. White, and William Draper.

With Stan Laurel (Canvasback Clump), Oliver Hardy (Clump's manager), Noah Young (Thunderclap Callahan), Gene Morgan (Ring announcer), Sam Lufkin (Boxing referee), Steve Murphy (Callahan's second), Ed Brandenburg, Bob Minford (Clump's cornermen), Lou Costello, Ham Kinsey, Jack Hill (Ringside spectators), Charlie Hall (Ringside radio announcer/Delivery

The original title lobby card.

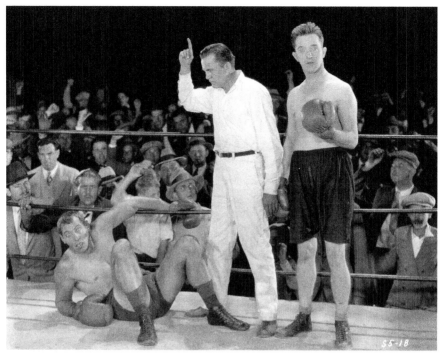

Thunderclap Callahan is down but not out, thanks to his clueless opponent.

man for Ye Olde Pie Shoppe), Eugene Pallette (Insurance salesman), Budd Fine (Cop who slips on banana peel), Dorothy Coburn (Motorist hit by pie), Hayes Robertson (Shoeshine man), Jack O'Brien (Shoeshine customer), Wilson Benge (Outraged Mayor), Jack Lloyd (Irish biddy beating rug), Dick Sutherland (Dental patient), George B. French (Dentist), Dick Gilbert (Sewer worker), Wilkie C. Mahoney (Bakery counterman), Edgar Dearing (Customer inside bakery), Al Hallett (Long-faced curious man in doorway), Pete Gordon (Barber at Max's Barber Shop with garbage can), Lyle Tayo (Woman at window with flower pot), Arthur Mund (Postman), Ellinor Vanderveer (Elegant lady in car), Jack Adams (Man posing for portrait), Bob O'Conor (Photographer), Anita Garvin (Dainty flapper at Taft Bldg.), Chester A. Bachman (Policeman who accosts L&H at end). Unknown bits: T. Marcell, Frank Butler, Harry Tenbrook, Leo Sulky, Monte Collins, Jack Herrick, Jim Farley.

Stan, incredibly, is a prizefighter; Ollie is his manager. Despite being hopelessly outmatched by his burly and terrifying opponent, Stan manages to knock the brute down, but because Stan doesn't know what a neutral corner is, he allows enough time for his combatant to revive and knock him out. The next day, an insurance man sells Ollie a policy which will pay handsomely should Stan have an accident, which Ollie immediately begins to engineer. A banana peel thrown by Ollie into Stan's path instead trips up a bakery's delivery man. The apparently inexhaustible supply of pies in his nearby wagon provides the ammunition for an argument which escalates until the occupants of an entire city block are covered with filling.

The Battle of the Century was inspired by the Jack Dempsey-Gene Tunney "Fight of the Century" boxing match, which took place on September 22, 1927 at Soldier Field in Chicago. In the seventh round, Dempsey knocked Tunney down, but stood over him. The referee, Dave Barry, could not begin the count on Tunney until Dempsey

Canvasback Clump is truly knocked out.

went to a neutral corner. Had Dempsey done this immediately, he probably would have won the fight, but his delay gave Tunney time to recuperate. In the tenth round, Tunney won the bout.

This is echoed in the film, when manager Ollie is pleading for Stan to go to a neutral corner after he knocks out Thunderclap Callahan; Stan's protracted delay gives his opponent ample time to recover and deliver a knockout punch.

Hal Roach wanted to build a comedy around this event quickly, while it was still topical. Leo McCarey's father was a boxing promoter, and Leo was still very much interested in the sport despite his own failure at it, so this was a fait accompli. The problem was, where did the story resume after Stan was knocked out?

In an interview with Peter Bogdanovich in 1969, McCarey said of the boxing sequence, "It only took up one reel to tell… We knocked off for lunch and the pie wagon pulled up. And we got the idea of starting a pie fight. Well, it was so successful that the audience forgot about the Dempsey-Tunney fight and the 'Battle of the Century' became the battle of the pies."

Stan recalled to biographer John McCabe that during a session when he and the gag men were trying to come up with a story, one of them had suggested, "We could even slip a few pies into it," but this was met with derision. The press sheet for the recent release *The Second 100 Years* had noted, "The ancient humor dependent on custard pies…now seems hopelessly stupid." But Stan thought it over and said, "Look, if we

The boys ink an insurance policy.

make a pie picture – let's make a pie picture to end all pie pictures. Let's give them so
many pies that there will never be room for any more pie pictures in the whole history
of the movies."

Hal Roach recalled to historian Richard W. Bann in 1976, "Stan came and told me
what he wanted to do. I think I liked the idea so much I was ready to purchase every
pie in Los Angeles and start baking more in the Our Gang Café if we had to!" The
studio bought a day's output of the Los Angeles Pie Company, located at 1720 Hooper
Avenue, near downtown and about nine miles east of the Roach lot.

Some recently retrieved "Daily Production Sheets," which also served as "call sheets"
notifying the actors when and where to report, provide new details about the filming.

The entire boxing sequence, most of the first reel, was all shot on Wednesday,
October 5, at the Culver City Fight Arena. The company doesn't appear to have shot
anything after that until October 11, when they worked at Exposition Park in Los
Angeles, filming the scene with Eugene Pallette selling the insurance policy. That day,
they also shot the start of the pie scene with Charlie Hall on the New York Street section
of the Roach backlot.

On October 13, they shot on the New York Street and in front of the Barber Shop.
(The cast called included Frank Butler and one T. Marcell, along with one Barber, one
"bit man for Barber Chair," and one "Man for front of bank.")

The next day, Stan's illness halted the picture; it didn't resume until two weeks later,
on October 27. We then find several actors and props called for, the most intriguing

Ollie causes an accident, but for the wrong victim.

A scene not in the film, as insurance agent Pallette inspects that "pineapple."

These extras, putting up with a hot and windy October day, the overpowering smell of pie filling, and marauding bees had reason to be genuinely angry.

being "Nita Garvin, Circular Skirt." Anita maintained for years that she was working on a Charley Chase picture and did this bit on her lunch break for free, as an impromptu favor to Stan. The call sheet indicates that her little hunk of immortality was planned before it was filmed. Anita may have been included in the cast of Chase's *All for Nothing*, which began filming on the 27th, but she's evidently not in the completed film. (She had definitely been in Chase's previous picture, *Never the Dames Shall Meet*, and perhaps some undocumented retakes were made on the 27th.) Whether it was planned or not, Anita's wonderful performance provides one of the funniest and most memorable moments of the movie.

Also filmed on the 27th were the vignettes with the dentist, the photographer, the mailman, the sewer worker, and something with Leo Sulky which doesn't seem to have made the final cut.

Bad weather caused the suspension of the picture once again on October 28th, but the company finished on the next day. Much of the pie fight was shot on the 29th, including Eugene Pallette's plea for everyone to get insurance; Dorothy Coburn's scene at the car; Wilson Benge's bit as the outraged Mayor, and Jack Lloyd's turn as the Irish biddy beating a rug. The call sheet also specifies 25 people and 200 pies, although undoubtedly many more than that were used.

Except for some retakes directed by Clyde Bruckman on November 12, principal photography was completed on the 29th. No doubt Bruckman and company shot most

S5-2

The battle escalates.

of the pie fight on this last day because it would have been very difficult to get all of those extras back into pie-splattered costuming and resume their battle on a backlot already covered in pie filling. "The *smell* of all that pie filling in the hot sun was overpowering," Anita Garvin recalled. "So sickly sweet. And every bee in Culver City came swarming to that backlot."

The script for *The Battle of the Century* is markedly different from the film, beginning with the unused mirror gag after Stan's defeat.

Portly, bald Dell Henderson graced other Laurel and Hardy films, among them *Wrong Again* and *Our Relations*, but lost out on the role of the insurance salesman. Eugene Pallette had been a svelte leading man in his early films, but as the talkies arrived and his waistline ballooned, he ultimately became a gravelly-voiced character comedian, often cast as the lone voice of sanity in screwball comedies such as *My Man Godfrey*.

The elaborate sequence with the grand piano would have been costly and difficult to film, not to mention dangerous. A banana peel was just as likely to cause an accident for Stan, and far less expensive.

The final sequence suggested by the script resembles Buster Keaton's 1922 classic *Cops*, in which the mayor and the police chief are discomfited at the start of a melee with hundreds of police involved. In that film, all of the cops are after Buster, but here "all the police" start "rushing the crowd."

As one frequently finds in scripts for Laurel and Hardy films, the finale is left to the

The New York Street of the Hal Roach Studios backlot was going to need a thorough scrubbing.

invention of the participants during the filming.

The Battle of the Century was aggressively promoted, as *Hats Off!* had been. *The Film Daily* reported in its issue of December 8, 1927, "Twenty-four sheets [billboard-sized posters] for a two-reel comedy, window cards, special trailer, radio tie-ups, all kinds of go-get-'em business – all for a two-reeler. You wonder whose brainstorm this is? Be in the dark no longer. Harold B. Franklin, whose showmanship falls into the Grade A class, proposes to do all this and more for 'The Battle of the Century,' Hal Roach release. Not only that, but a campaign of identical proportions in all West Coast theaters for this release and others in the Laurel-Hardy series."

For many years, all that seemed to survive of *The Battle of the Century* was about four minutes of the pie fight, used by Robert Youngson as the final sequence of his 1958 compilation film *The Golden Age of Comedy*. This feature-length assortment of great scenes from Hal Roach and Mack Sennett silent shorts did much to bring Laurel and Hardy back into public view. Subsequent screenings on television introduced the team to a generation or two of young viewers, including your friendly author.

While doing research for a comedy film festival to be held in conjunction with the 1976 United States Bicentennial, writer and historian Leonard Maltin discovered that most of the first reel had been held for years in the archive of the Museum of Modern Art in New York. Evidently, nobody had thought to look for it, and so it was hiding in plain sight. The 35mm amber-tinted nitrate original print of the boxing sequence was very fragile, but was successfully copied to safety film.

Early in 2015, Dr. Jon Mirsalis – a scientist and dedicated film collector as well as a talented silent film accompanist on piano – was looking through the 2,300 films which he had acquired from the estate of the late collector Gordon Berkow. Mr. Berkow had obtained much of this film in 1990 from film historian and writer William K. Everson. Mr. Everson had gotten a great deal of the collection from the estate of the aforementioned Robert Youngson. It appears that Mr. Everson and Mr. Berkow did not open the can of film marked as *Battle of the Century,* because when Dr. Mirsalis decided to run the 16mm print, he realized that he had the entire second reel, "absolutely complete from head leader to tail leader."

On June 15, 2015, he announced his discovery to the attendees of the annual "Mostly Lost" film festival held by the Library of Congress in Culpepper, Virginia. The gasps and shouts of the crowd informed him that he had a unique treasure, the only known copy in the world of this long sought-after, priceless footage. Protection prints were soon made – and in the nick of time, as this print, made by Robert Youngson as a reference copy in 1956, has since become a victim of "vinegar syndrome," which causes the film to shrink and warp and become unplayable.

After long and stressful negotiations with parties claiming the intellectual property rights to the film, producer Kit Parker and archivist Jeff Joseph made available to the public a gorgeous transfer of the film on the DVD and Blu-ray release *Laurel and Hardy: The Definitive Restorations.* Watching it today, one would think that this film had been lovingly preserved for ninety-odd years – if not for the still missing sequence with Eugene Pallette, which is bridged with a couple of photographs and titles.

As Leonard Maltin has noted, "The complete pie fight is longer and funnier. It was well worth waiting a lifetime to see."

Original line art.

Laurel – Hardy

Fade in on announcer in center of ring announcing the fighters for the main event. He introduces Noah Young and then introduces Stan as substituting for Slaughterhouse Riley, who got cold feet and ran out.

After Stan's introduction we introduce Babe Hardy as Stan's manager. Babe advises Stan on the financial necessity of winning this bout, getting over if he wins he is to receive $100, and if he loses he gets $5.

After this is established the bell rings and the fight is on. As Hoah leaves his corner he discovers that the string on one of his gloves is loose and he turns back to have one of his seconds tie it. Stan takes advantage of this, and putting everything he has into a roundhouse wallop, hits Noah on the jaw, which Noah doesn't even notice.

Stan immediately runs to a neutral corner and puts his arms on the ropes, thinking the fight is over. He suddenly discovers that Noah is still on his feet, and Babe urges him to go ahead and finish it. Stan rushes back and delivers another roundhouse wallop. This time Noah turns, brushes the side of his face as if annoyed by a mosquito, slaps at an imaginary mosquito in the air, then continues to have his glove fastened. Stan looks around to see what is holding Noah up. Babe urges Stan to go ahead and finish him, pantomiming to bring one from the ground up. Stan gets down and lays his glove on the floor, getting ready to deliver the big blow. Noah by this time has his glove fixed and as he draws back to swing, we cut to Babe fainting.

As Babe faints, the upper part of Stan's body comes into the picture in a reclining position with a silly grin on his face. They revive Babe with smelling salts, etc., and when he comes to he gives Stan a dirty look.

Go to long shot and show that the arena is empty. Stan is lying out flat in the ring.

Back to Babe; he looks at Stan, throws a pail of water on him and drags him out of the ring by one foot. They start up the aisle, their backs to the camera.

As they arrive at the rear of the arena, there is a wall

mirror, which Stan looks into, holding his jaw. Go to a shot in the mirror showing distorted reflection of Stan's face, suggesting that he got a terrible wallop. Stan starts to cry over his appearance. Fade out.

Fade in on newspaper insert to the effect that Stan is positively through as a fighter in this town because of his miserable showing last night. Lap dissolve to Babe and Stan seated on park bench. Babe has the paper; he looks up from what he is reading thoroughly disgusted with Stan.

Into this scene comes Del Henderson, an insurance agent, who recognizes Stan and speaks title that he saw Stan fight the previous night. Stan gives him a smile, and Henderson suggests that it wouldn't be a bad idea if Stan had some accident insurance, which immediately interests Babe.

Babe and Henderson go to one side and discuss the policy, pantomiming the loss of arms, etc., the idea being that if Stan is hurt Babe collects five thousand dollars or some such amount; also getting over that payment on one accident nullifies the policy. At the conclusion of this Babe signs and calls Stan over to sign. Stan puts a cross for his mark where he is to sign, and Babe takes the five dollars that Stan got for the fight from him and pays for the policy. Henderson congratulates them on their business ability and exits.

Babe sizes Stan up, then looks around as if looking for some means to cash in on the policy. He sees a grand piano being pulled up on the outside of a building, gets an idea and takes Stan by the arm, bringing him into the set where the piano is being raised.

Babe plants Stan under the piano and walks over to help the man who is pulling on the rope. As Babe takes the rope Stan, puzzled at what is going on, leaves the spot where Babe placed him and walks over behind Babe to see what he is doing. Babe deliberately lets go of the rope and the piano starts down. Babe turns and discovers Stan, and as he does so the end of the rope catches Babe's legs and takes him up out of the picture.

Cut back to long shot and show the piano on the sidewalk and Babe hanging upside down so that his head is fully ten feet above the sidewalk. Babe urges Stan to get him out of this fix, and Stan in a sort of half panic picks up the first implement handy, which is a rake, and tries to get him down with the rake, which causes Babe more damage than if he would fall.

Stan finally gives up the rake idea and takes a long handled pruning shears, and in attempting to cut the rope he cuts a wire holding up a barrel that is used as a sign in front of the hardware store. The barrel falls on Stan, breaking away and almost knocking him cold.

Stan looks off and exits, gets a picket fence from a portable house sales yard, brings it back and using it as a ladder starts climbing up toward Babe. As he reaches a point about opposite Babe he strikes the gate, which opens inward and would have plunged him to the sidewalk if he had not grabbed Babe, which leaves them both hanging on the rope, the entire fence falling out of the picture.

Stan then starts to untie the knot holding Babe. Babe realizes what Stan is doing and puts up a violent protest, telling Stan to untie the rope from the piano and let him down easy. Stan gets over he understands, and gets on the other part of the rope which holds the piano and with his pocket knife starts cutting on the rope, reassuring Babe that he will have him down in a minute.

Cut below and show a man with a five-bushel basket of eggs enter to sidewalk elevator; he puts the eggs on the elevator platform and starts down with them.

Back to Stan still sawing on the rope with his knife, until the rope finally gives way.

Go to long shot; the dummy of Babe plunges into the opening left by elevator and Stan on the other half of rope falls through the break-away piano.

Go to closeup of Stan climbing out of the piano with wires and keys draped about him. Cut and show Babe come up with elevator, wiping eggs from all parts. Stan and Babe look at each other as we fade out.

Fade in on Stan and Babe walking down the sidewalk. They pass a bunch of bananas hanging in front of fruit stand or grocery store. Babe takes a banana, and peeling the skin off throws it some distance ahead, figuring that Stan will step on it and break a leg. This leaves Babe holding the skinned banana in his hand. A cop comes around the corner, slips on the banana peel and falls. As Babe sees that he hands the banana to Stan.

The cop gets up sore as hell and sees Stan holding the banana, walks over and removes Stan's hat and socks him with his club. The cop then bawls Stan out and kicks the banana skin further down the street in front of a bakery shop. The cop then exits.

Babe looks at the bump on Stan's head, thinks of the policy, and taking it from his pocket begins to study it as Henderson walks into the scene. Babe says, "Just the man we were looking for!" Henderson asks what's the matter and Babe indicates that Stan has been injured. Henderson raises Stan's hat, looks at the bump and replaces the hat. He goes to see the amount paid on bumps. He traces down until he comes to "Bumps," looks at it and finds out that for bumps they pay five cents. He hands the nickel to Babe, and taking the policy tears it up as he exits.

Babe looks at Stan, thoroughly disgusted, and yanks the banana away from him. As he does, we go to shot of baker with tray of pies coming out of shop to load pies into a pie wagon standing in front of the shop. This pie wagon is already practically full of pies. The baker steps on the banana skin which was kicked there by the cop and goes down on the sidewalk, pies and all.

The baker looks up sore and sees Babe holding the banana. He gets up and starts over to Babe, as Babe quickly shifts the banana to Stan. The baker comes up, takes the banana away from Stan and gives it back to Babe and starts to bawl him out. Babe stands as much of this as he can, and then getting sore he drapes the banana in the baker's face. The baker takes this big and decides that two can play that game.

The baker picks up a pie and socks it at Babe, who ducks. Henderson gets it just as he has finished speaking title to a man he is trying to sell insurance to; the title reads, "Anyone is liable to have an accident."

Back to Babe; he turns from seeing this and starts laughing, as he gets a pie in the face. Stan starts laughing at Babe. Babe gets sore and picks up a pie, socking it at Stan, who ducks and it catches a man just coming out of the bakery.

From this we go to cuts of a lady looking out of second story window getting a pie; a fellow in Ford coupe; a lady with lorgnettes in a swell car; a man coming out of store and other incidental cuts, until we pull back to long shot of the street showing the street full of people involved in throwing pies.

Go to cuts of Stan and Babe in the thick of the fight.

We then establish the annual police parade and cut to an automobile decorated with bunting, in which is riding the mayor of the town and beside him the chief of police. People applaud and the mayor gets up and says, "I wish to congratulate Chief Ryan on the marvelous law and order he has prevailing in this city." The Chief gets up to take a bow and as he does a pie lands flush in his face.

The chief calls all the police and they start rushing the crowd, which starts to disperse, leaving Stan and Babe exposed to the camera. Stan and Babe run around a corner when a cop comes up behind them and suspicious of their actions accuses them of having started all the trouble. As he starts to arrest them they stop him and go into a pantomime routine of how it all happened, with the banana skin, the first officer and the baker. This winds up with Babe becoming so enthusiastic with his demonstration that he forgets and puts the pie in the cop's face when showing what the baker did to him.

The cop gets sore and picks up a pie, letting it fly at Babe. It misses Babe and hits the Chief of Police who is coming around the corner.

This again starts a pie fight which builds up to a high spot for the final fade.

One section of *The Battle of the Century* remains missing, the sequence filmed at the Los Angeles Exposition Park in which Eugene Pallette plays an insurance salesman. Fortunately, the cutting continuity survives, and precisely describes the action in each shot:

November 12, 1927

Cutting Continuity for S 5.

Fade In

M.S. of park bench with Stan and Babe sitting on it. Man comes in and looks at Stan, turns around and thinks and speaks title:

"---DIDN'T I SEE YOU FIGHT LAST NIGHT? ---"

M.S. of Babe answers yes. Man shakes hands with Babe and speaks title:

"---LISTEN! FOR FIVE DOLLARS YOU CAN INSURE THAT FELLOW – THEN IF HE GETS HURT YOU GET THE MONEY---"

M.S. of Man and Babe and Stan. Babe motions for man to back away and Babe follows. This is so Stan can't hear. Man takes out policy.

C.U. of Stan who has a dumb look.

C.U. of Babe and Man (Gene Pallette). Gene speaks:

"---THE PREMIUM WILL BE $5---"

C.U. of Babe and Gene. Babe says all right.

M.S. of three. Babe goes over to Stan and asks for five dollars. He takes off Stan's hat gets five and puts bill in pocket and walks back to man. He takes out bill and gives it to Gene.

C.U. of Stan who doesn't know what it is all about.

C.U. of Gene and Babe. Gene looks for pen and he can't find it and speaks title:

"---GOTTA PEN?---"

C.U. of Stan and Babe and Gene. Babe leaves Gene and goes over to Stan.

M.S. of Babe and Stan. Stan takes out pen and tries to take off top but can't. Babe gets disgusted and takes pen.

C.U. of Babe trying to unscrew top of pen. He succeeds and

takes top off and gets ink in face. He takes it.

C.U. of Stan who speaks title:

"---SHALL I GET YOU A BLOTTER?---"

C.U. of Babe.

M.S. of the three. Babe starts to sign policy. He tries to get ink from pen but it is dry. Stan points to Babe's nose. Babe gets ink off of face. He signs policy. Gene asks Stan to sign. Stan gets up and walks over.

C.U. shot of three. He starts to sign. The pen is still dry. He reaches back and taps Babe in the face with the pen to get ink. He signs.

C.U. of Stan and Babe. Stan asks Babe for top of pen. Babe gives it to Stan but takes other part. Again Stan asks Babe for other half and we go thru same routine. Finally Babe gets both parts and when Stan calls his attention to it Babe gets mad and throws both to background.

C.U. of the three. Gene leaves. Babe feels nose. He motions and they leave set. Fade Out.

Fade In

M.S. walking shot of Stan and Babe. Stan bumps into side of building. Babe tells Stan to look out. Stan bumps into washer. Babe tells Stan to walk on the outside. He speaks in title:

"---CLUMSY! – WALK ON THE OUTSIDE! ---"

M.S. walking. Showing Stan and Babe. Babe falls over Victrola. Stan takes center and tells Babe to walk on the outside. Babe doesn't like it and says we'll cross the street. They come to camera.

End Part One

"THE BATTLE OF THE CENTURY"

Happily, as of 2015, we have the rest of the film from this point on. Because many Laurel and Hardy rarities have been rediscovered in recent years, we can hope that the missing sequence might be located and restored, making *The Battle of the Century* truly complete.

TWO TARS

Production history: Production L-13. Written early June 1928. Filmed Friday, June 22 through the 23rd; production resumed on Tuesday, June 26 and finished on Tuesday, July 3. Copyrighted November 3, 1928 by MGM (LP 116). Released November 3. Two reels.

Produced by Hal Roach. Directed by James Parrott. Supervising director, Leo McCarey. Photographed by George Stevens. Edited by Richard Currier. Titles by H.M. Walker. *Uncredited Assistance:* Assistant Director, Lloyd French. Assistant Cameramen, Edward L. White and William A. Collins. Props by Harry Black, Charles Oelze, Thomas Benton Roberts, Roy Seawright, and Harry Hopkins. Story by Leo McCarey.

With Stan Laurel (Himself), Oliver Hardy (Himself), Thelma Hill (Thelma), Ruby Blaine (Rubie), Sam Lufkin (Pedestrian/Motorist), Charlie Hall (Shopkeeper), Edgar Kennedy (Motorist), Grace Woods (Kennedy's wife), Jack O'Brien (Diminutive motorist throttled by Kennedy), Harry Bernard (Truck driver), Thomas Benton Roberts (Motorist with tomatoes), Jack Hill (Motorist with rolled-up mattress), Charlie Rogers (Motorist who hits Ollie with car door), Edgar Dearing (Motorcycle cop), Baldwin Cooke, Helen Gilmore, Ham Kinsey, Chet Brandenburg, Frank Ellis, Fred Holmes, Dorothea Wolbert, Charles McMurphy, Lyle Tayo, Lon Poff, Retta Palmer, George Rowe, Buddy Moore, Robert "Bobby" Burns (Motorists and spectators).

Sailors Stan and Ollie, on shore leave, rent a car and set out for a day's adventure. They soon have thrills of the wrong kind, thanks to a collision with a lamppost and a near-miss of a pedestrian. Soon they find two young ladies who have encountered problems with a drugstore's gumball machine. The boys' attempts to fix the device result in its destruction, not to mention a battle with the diminutive but tough proprietor of the drugstore. All of this is merely prelude to the rest of the day's struggles, which start with a massive traffic jam on a country road. Minor arguments escalate into major ones, punctuated by the gradual and progressive destruction of one automobile after another. Finally, a patrolman and the crowd chase the two sailors' car into a tunnel – and an oncoming train. The two tars end their day sputtering along in an auto that has been squeezed by its encounter with the locomotive.

Original 1928 line art.

A scene not in the script or film.

Two Tars, like *The Battle of the Century* and several films before and after it, includes a lengthy sequence involving what biographer John McCabe called "reciprocal destruction," in which each party is allowed to inflict an increasingly humiliating embarrassment upon the other. This is done politely and methodically with no interruption from the humiliatee, who will soon get his turn.

The script for *Two Tars* proposes a lengthy opening sequence with the boys spending the first part of their precious shore leave "in a row boat in the middle of the ocean," as per Stan's suggestion. This idea doesn't have much of a finish, and it might well have played better if Stan were the one catching all of those mackerel. It doesn't appear that this sequence was ever filmed, although several stills suggest a sequence with the two sailors getting a shoeshine, and perhaps having a nautical companion in Josephine, the capuchin monkey owned by Roach studios animal trainer Tony Campanara. Josephine had just completed a co-starring role with Buster Keaton in *The Cameraman* at MGM, filmed in May and June 1928.

The film begins with section 10 of the script. Some of the most inventive comedy in the filmed drugstore scene is not in the script – for example, Stan's continual slipping and falling on the gumballs which have spilled onto the pavement. This was clearly inspired on the location, possibly as a result of someone really slipping on these confections, which are like marbles.

While many of the specific gags used in the film are detailed in the script, some exist in the script only, such as the bit involving the pigeons and the limousine. Nor is any

Two Tars stands head and shoulders above most short comedy films.

white paint spilled into another car, although a similar gag forms the finale of the team's 1929 short *The Hoose-Gow*. The idea of having eight or nine cars chasing each other around was intriguing on paper but likely impossible to perform on a narrow country road.

Likewise, many of the best gags are only in the film. One example is the scene with the tomato hitting the truck driver, who then scoops it up from the ground and lets it fly, hitting Stan on the back of the neck. (This prompts a great closeup of Stan in

Roach studios animal trainer Tony Campanaro had been an organ-grinder with Josephine as his partner; she had just finished working on Buster Keaton's *The Cameraman*, but she's not in *Two Tars*.

Drugstore proprietor Charlie Hall is not happy about the demise of his gumball machine.

Stan, Ollie and the girls are the only ones having a good time.

Jack Hill is being wrestled to the ground; other spectators are Buddy Moore (the boy wearing the cap) and Bobby Burns (between Ollie and the driver).

which he looks directly at us as the tomato slithers down his blouse.) A great unscripted running gag involves a man with bedding and other possessions rolled up on the roof of his car; he is repeatedly pushed against the auto, bringing everything collapsing to the ground. He gets it all rolled back up, just in time for someone to send it crashing down again. This unfortunate fellow is played by Laurence Young "Jack" Hill (1887-1963), whose unmistakable face and large ears are plainly seen in 36 Laurel and Hardy films.

 Two Tars was received rapturously by audiences, exhibitors and reviewers. One writer for the *Shamokin* [Pennsylvania] *News Dispatch* wrote that Laurel and Hardy were "the greatest of all comedians of the time," and noted, "These masters of fun are to be offered in *Two Tars* and funny as have been some of their success of the past, this is the zenith of their combined efforts to date."

L-13   Laurel-Hardy

Open on title, "The Navy!"

1   Cut to stock shot of the fleet arriving.

       Cut to title to the effect, "After nine months at sea the boys arrived in port, ocean-weary and glad to get ashore."

2   Fade in on Stan and Babe in a row boat in the middle of the ocean. Babe looks at Stan disgustedly and speaks title, "So this is your idea of a good time!" Stan just looks dumb, kind of half surprised at Babe's attitude.

3   Stan already has his fishing line in the water. Babe picks up his pole, puts some bait on the hook and throws it out. His line no sooner hits the water when he gets a bite and pulls in a big mackerel. Babe doesn't show any enthusiasm at all. He takes the fish off, throws out his line again, and it no sooner hits the water when he gets another fish. Repeat the same business, Stan still with his line in the water and not a sign of a bite.

4   Babe throws his line out again. Stan pulls his line out and throws it over near Babe's. Babe moves his pole away, and Stan gets over he wants to sit where Babe was sitting. Babe says, "All right, then – anything to satisfy you." They exchange places, the boat wobbling about. Babe puts his line where Stan's was, gets another bite and pulls in another big fish. Stan is still waiting, full of expectancy. Babe catches another one. Stan then gets over he wants to change poles. Babe does so, and no sooner takes Stan's pole than he gets a bit on that one and pulls in another fish.

5   Stan by this time is getting mad. He takes his pole from Babe again, throws the line into the water, and still no bite. Babe pulls up another mackerel with that pole and takes it off. All the while Babe is doing his business in a half-peeved attitude, not a bit thrilled at catching fish. Stan would give his left eye if he only had a nibble.

6   Finally Stan asks Babe to give him his bait. Babe does so and as Stan is putting it on the hook, Babe's line accidentally

falls into the water without any bait. He gets a bite and pulls in another big fish.

7   Stan throws his line into the water and gets a big bite at the same time Babe's pole bends. They both pull up and the lines are tangled. Stan is all excited – there is a big mackerel on the line. He tries to get the fish off and Babe says, "Wait a minute – I'll do it." He gets hold of the two lines to unravel them, the fish spins around and when the lines are separated we see that the fish is on Babe's hook.

9   Stan's hat falls off and as he walks to back of the boat to get it, the boat sinks.   FADE OUT.

10   Fade in on Stan and Babe coming along the road in a Ford roadster. Hanging on the door is a sign, "For Rent." Stan is driving. Babe with a very pleased expression is talking to Stan and gets over title, "This is what you should have done in the first place." Stan turns to nod to him and they run into a lamp post. Babe looks disgusted, tells Stan to move over and he will take the wheel. Babe backs the car away (no damage has been done to it) and they start off again.

11   Babe turns to Stan and speaks title, "You never did do anything right." He no sooner gets the words out of his mouth than he runs smack into a telegraph pole and a globe falls on Babe's head.

12   Cut to setup outside a drug store with a penny-in-the-slot gum machine (the kind with a glass globe holding balls of gum). Two rather tough flappers put a penny in the machine and no gum comes out. They start to shake it and get over they are having a little trouble with it.

13   Stan and Babe drive into the scene and notice the girls in trouble. Babe stops the car and gets over title, "In trouble, girls?" The girls get over they can't get any gum out. Stan jumps out of the car and starts to play around with the gum machine to help them, but with no success. Finally Babe gets that "leave-it-to-me" attitude, steps out of the car very graciously and starts to monkey with the machine.

14   Babe gives the machine a hard shake and the globe drops off, spreading gum all over the sidewalk. Stan takes it, runs and jumps in the car and calls to the two girls to join him and pretend they don't know anything about it.

15   Babe gets on his hands and knees and starts putting handfuls of gum down his blouse. He quickly gathers them all, and as he gets the last handful the druggist (type like Charley Hall) comes out and just stands looking at Babe.

16   Babe gets over his embarrassment and acts like a little school boy caught in the act. The druggist looks down and sees the broken machine, looks back at Babe and smacks Babe's hand, knocking out the balls of gum. Babe looks terribly hurt. The druggist then smacks Babe's other hand, knocking more gum out, and gets over, "What do you mean, busting our machine?" He gives Babe a little push and all the gum drops out of his blouse.

17   The druggist starts getting rough with Babe, flicking him under the nose, pulling his ear, etc. Stan gets a little sore at this, pushes his cap on one side, gets out of the car, comes over to the druggist and gets over, "What are you trying to do to my pal?" The druggist turns and looks at Stan and gives him a poke on the chin.

18   The two girls take this, get out of the car and deliberately kick the druggist in the shins and push him into the doorway. The girls get into the car with Stan and Babe and drive off, leaving the druggist bewildered. Fade Out.

Title, "Only one hour before the end of a perfect day."

19   Cut to running insert, Stan and Babe and the two girls in the roadster moving very slowly along a line of cars two abreast. They are making no headway, probably moving a couple of feet at a time.

20   Babe gets an idea and decides to pull out of the line and make some headway by going down the wrong side of the road, which he does, much to the resentment of the other drivers.

21   Running insert of the roadster moving along very swiftly, showing the other line of cars in the background standing still with the tourists waving and yelling at him to get back in line.

22   Cut to the girls gesticulating as if giving the tourists the razz. The girls have on the sailor hats and ties, and Stan and Babe have the girls' hats on.

23   They enter setup where there is a large concrete mixer at work. This is the cause of the line moving so slowly. They

come to an abrupt stop, realizing they have made a mistake and should have remained in line. Two other drivers who have seen Babe pull out of the line have followed suit and are coming along behind the roadster. The car that is following directly behind accidentally give the roadster a slight bump.

24   Go to closeup of the four taking the jar and looking back.

25   Cut to closeup of the man in the car that has bumped them. He makes an apologetic gesture.

26   One of the girls looks at Babe and speaks title, "You're not going to stand for that, are you?" Immediately after this title Babe puts his car in reverse and gives the car in back a slight bump as if to say, "Take that." The man in the second car becomes angered, pulls back and gives the roadster a harder bump, jarring the two girls and Stan and Babe. Babe becomes angry, pulls forward about ten feet, comes back very swiftly and gives the second car a terrific smash.

27   The driver of the second car becomes more angered; he puts the car in reverse and starts back to take a run at the roadster, but in doing so hits a third car behind him, breaking a headlight glass. The man in the third car becomes angered, gets out and starts to argue with the man in the second car. He gets out pencil and pad and starts to take numbers and names.

28   The man in the second car has become very angry. Realizing that Stan and Babe were the cause of his misfortune, he puts his car in gear and starts forward at a terrific rate. He takes a good run and hits the roadster with a terrific crash, almost throwing Stan and Babe and the girls from the seat. This greatly angers Stan. He steps from the roadster, walks back to the second car and without any conversation jerks a headlight from the man's car and throws it down. Immediately on top of this he gives the headlight a kick which sends it flying from him.

29   Follow the headlight into another setup where there is a limousine, and it goes crashing through the glass window.

30   Stan looks around at the two girls and Babe and they are cheering him, speaking title, "Atta sailor boy!" Stan gets over nobody can put anything over on him, and starts toward the roadster. The man in the second car jumps out very angry and

walks toward the roadster. He becomes so angry he does not know what to do. He reaches over to the radiator cap where there is a balloon tied to a string, and clapping his hands together he squashes the balloon. He looks at Stan and says, "Take that!"

31   One of the girls sees the balloon busted and says, "Aw, he busted my balloon!" She gets all broken up about it and almost breaks into a cry. Stan takes this and becomes angry. He reaches in a wheelbarrow nearby, grabs a large handful of new cement, takes off the man's hat, slaps the gob of cement on the man's head, replaces the hat and takes a big swing at it, knocking it down on the man's head.

32   The man in the third car steps forward and tells the second man to get back in his car and they'll get out of here – that he is partly the cause of the trouble. Turning to Babe and Stan he makes a motion for them to pull out also.

33   Babe tells Stan to crank up the roadster. Stan exits to front of the car and starts to crank it. The man in the second car, who is very angry over the cement on his head, steps on the gas and bumps the roadster, knocking Stan to the ground and the roadster passes over him. When Stan sits up he is at the bottom of the radiator of the second car. He gets to his feet burning with anger and without any further argument gives the radiator a terrific jerk, pulling it down to about a forty-five degree angle.

34   The man with the broken radiator is now in a burning rage. He pulls back and takes another run at the roadster, crashing into it with terrific force. This time one of the girls is thrown half out of the roadster and is grabbed by the other girl to keep her from falling to the ground. The girls turn to Babe and get over, "Are you going to stand for that?"

35   Babe says "No" and pulls forward about ten feet, then puts the car in reverse with the intention of crashing the second car, but coming back with terrific speed he loses control of the steering wheel, causing him to swerve, and he entirely misses the second car and crashes into a truck in the other line loaded with crates of pigeons. The bump causes the lids to fly off the crates and the pigeons all fly out into the air, followed by a big cloud of feathers.

36   Cut to a large limousine. Eight or nine of these pigeons fly

in through the windows, fluttering around in the faces of the occupants.

37   Closeup of the owner of the pigeon truck. He sticks his head out from a window of the truck, looks up at the birds flying away and receives an egg which spatters all over his face.

38   Cut to Stan and Babe; they figure it is about time to get out, and start back toward the roadster.

39   Cut to the third car. The driver decides to get out of the line. In trying to wig-wag back and forth he bumps a truck which has a large pole extending from it, causing the truck to back up and the end of the pole hits a limousine, going through the windshield and directly through the car, bumping the back end and causing the whole rear of the car to fall completely out. The occupants of the rear seat go tumbling to the street.

40   This causes all the tourists to become greatly angered. The man in the third car, realizing that he is the cause but also realizing that Stan and Babe are at fault for all the commotion, steps from his car, goes to the roadster, takes a pen-knife and cuts a large gash in the rear tire, causing the tube to protrude through the hole in a large blister. The blister starts to swell and finally explodes, causing the man to take a brodie. This greatly angers Stan and Babe. They walk to the third car, Stan on one side and Babe on the other, give each front wheel a terrific kick, causing the wheels to cave in and the whole front end of the car collapses down to the ground. Stan and Babe say "Take that," and exit.

41   Another car decides to get out of the line, starts to zig-zag back and forth, but in doing so rips the rear tire, trunk rack and bumper from another car. He doesn't stop. The other car gives chase. Follow them into a large field with one car chasing the other, trying to bump it.

42   Back to the man whose car has collapsed. He walks over to Stan so angry he doesn't know what to do, and in waving his arms he gives Stan a slight push. Stan and Babe look at each other, give each other a nod and both rush the man, giving him a terrific push and almost lifting him off his feet. The man goes flying from the scene.

43   Follow the man into another set; he comes in with such

terrific force that he crashes into a Ford Sedan, causing it to
fall over on its side, and the man lands on top.

44   Stan and Babe see this and get over an attitude to the
man, "By god, you can't push us!" The girls cheer the boys for
not taking any back talk.

45   Further up the line there is a painter's truck loaded
with barrels of white paint. In front of the truck is a small car
tightly pinned in. The man in the small car turns to the truck
driver and motions for him to back up so that he can get out.
The truck starts back, but in doing so gives a small car in back
of him a terrific bump, causing the barrels to upset and spill
white paint all over the rear car.

46   Cut to a field and show eight or nine cars bumping each
other and chasing each other around like a free for all fight.

47   Cut down the line to a setup under a tree where there is a
motorcycle cop. He looks off with a dumbfounded expression.

48   Cut to what he sees: Long shot of the traffic jam, people
arguing with each other, running around kicking cars, smoke
coming up, etc.; in other words it looks like the Battle of the
Marne.

49   The cop jumps on his motorcycle and tears out of scene.

50   The motor cop enters to roadster where the girls are
standing up waving their arms and getting over they are
delighted. The cop jacks up his motorcycle and as he is looking
off toward Stan and Babe, the two girls turn, see him, get over
there is going to be hell popping, and decide the best thing for
them to do is to beat it. They jump from the car very nervous
and exit on the run.

51   The cop enters where Stan and Babe are on arguing with
the other tourists. By this time the thing is at such a height
that at any minute it may come to blows. The cop walks in
with his hands on his hips and watches them, then reaches
in his pocket, gets a whistle and gives it a toot. The tourists
all see the cop and scramble like mice, trying to get into their
cars, people getting into the wrong cars, being pulled out,
dashing hither and thither, etc.

52   Stan and Babe turn and stand looking at the cop. The cop
turns and yells title, "Who started this?" The tourists all point
to Stan and Babe. The cop walks to Stan and Babe and gets

over title, "You two guys wait here," and motions for the rest of the cars to move from the scene. They start moving slowly forward.

53   Move back to long shot, and between the camera and the cop we see the different wrecks move slowly through the scene. The truck with the long pole on it has hooked up the limousine and it is hanging from the pole. When that leaves, the small car covered with white paint comes through. This is followed by a car turned completely upside down, being towed by another car. This is followed by people walking, carrying different parts of their cars. The large truck enters scene and exits. Follow it into setup where the cop has left his motorcycle. The truck hits the motorcycle, tipping it over and passing over it.

54   Cut to the rear four wheels of the truck and show them pass over the motorcycle, crushing it flat.

55   Back to Babe and Stan and the cop. The cop orders them to the car and they exit. Arriving at the set where the roadster is, he orders Stan and Babe into it and speaks title, "You're under arrest – follow me." He reaches down for his motorcycle and discovers that it has been smashed flat. This greatly angers him and he throws the motorcycle to the ground. He exits to a car directly in back, telling the man to follow Stan and Babe to the police station. He starts forward with great force as Stan and Babe move out of his line, causing him to go head-on into the concrete mixer, completely collapsing the car and leaving the cop and the man sitting amongst a bunch of tin.

56   Stan and Babe see this, get their car out of the line and tear out with great speed. The cop jumps out with rage, runs to another car, jumps on the running board and says, "Follow those guys!" The running board collapses and he does a brodie. He rushes for another car, jumps on the tire and tells the driver to follow Stan and Babe. The tire falls off and he goes to the ground again. He rushes out of this set, jumps on another car and orders the driver to follow. The car starts out and we discover that it has egg-shaped wheels, bobbing up and down. Other cars follow the cop in the chase.

57   Cut to Stan and Babe coming along in the roadster, with fifteen or twenty cars chasing them at some distance behind.

58   Cut to follow shot shooting directly at Stan and Babe in the roadster. They come to a turn in the road and several cars are coming toward them. The drivers look forward, see what is coming and all scatter for safety, running off into fields, ditches or anything to get out of the way.

59   Follow Stan and Babe into an open field, followed by the other cars. They chase across the field and down over a hill, disappearing from sight.

60   Pick them up at the entrance of a tunnel. The roadster dashes in. Cut to other end of tunnel and show a locomotive approaching. Cut back to the other end and show the fifteen or twenty cars trying to crowd into the tunnel. Stay with this setup and we see all the cars quickly skirmish out of the tunnel backwards as if they had seen the approaching train. They just clear the tracks as the train passes through.

61   Cut to the other end of the tunnel and we see Stan and Babe come through in their roadster but it has been squashed almost flat, giving the impression that it has gotten by between the wall of the tunnel and the train. They approach the camera and we see the condition of the car. FADE OUT.

Gobs of fun, indeed.

THE ROGUE SONG

Production history: Production 450. Filming began Thursday, August 22, 1929. Laurel and Hardy signed to appear on Monday, September 16 and started filming on Tuesday, the 24th. Principal photography was completed Thursday, October 17. World premiere was held at Grauman's Chinese Theatre in Hollywood, Friday, January 17, 1930. New York premiere, Tuesday, January 28, 1930. Copyrighted March 26, 1930 (LP 1176). Two-color Technicolor; 9,723 feet, 108 minutes.

Produced (without credit) by Irving G. Thalberg and Paul Bern. Directed by Lionel Barrymore and (uncredited) James Parrott and Arthur Rose. Photographed by Percy Hilburn and Charles Edgar Schoenbaum. Edited by Margaret Booth. Story by Frances Marion and John Colton, suggested by Wells Root. Based on the 1910 operetta *Zigeunerliebe* (*Gypsy Love*) by Franz Lehar, story by Alfred Maria Willner and Robert Bodanzky. Original Music by William Axt. Art Direction by Cedric Gibbons. Costume Design by Adrian. Assistant Director, Charles Dorian. Sound recording by Paul Neal and Douglas Shearer. Music conducted by Roy Isnor. Dance direction by Albertina Rasch.

With Lawrence Tibbett (Yegor), Catherine Dale Owen (Princess Vera), Nance O'Neil (Princess Alexandra), Judith Vosselli (Countess Tatiana), Ullric Haupt (Prince Serge), Elsa Alsen (Yegor's Mother), Florence Lake (Nadja), Lionel Belmore (Ossman), Wallace MacDonald (Hassan), Kate Price (Petrovna), H. A. Morgan (Frolov), Burr MacIntosh (Count Peter), James Bradbury, Jr. (Azamat), Stan Laurel (Ali-Bek), Oliver Hardy (Murza-Bek), Harry Bernard (Guard), John Carroll (Bandit), The Albertina Rasch Ballet.

Yegor (Tibbett) is "the singing bandit of Agrakhan." His retinue includes Ali-Bek (Laurel) and Murza-Bek (Hardy), who are usually taking care of the bandit gang's horses. Yegor hates the Cossacks but still falls in love with Princess Vera, whose brother, Prince Serge, commands a Cossack region. Yegor

Caricatures from the *Los Angeles Record* by future Disney artist Joe Grant.

and Vera have a love-hate relationship and alternately romance and berate each other. Yegor is captured
and receives a lashing, but manages to ride off into the sunset with a song on his lips, as Ali-Bek and
Murza-Bek clean up after the horses.

Lawrence Tibbett (1896-1960) was born in Bakersfield, California and grew up in
Los Angeles. He served in the Merchant Marine during the World War, and after he was
discharged he began singing in the prologues to movies at Sid Grauman's Million Dollar
Theater in Los Angeles. He acquired vocal training in New York and signed a contract
with the Metropolitan Opera in 1923, at 26. Three years later, gaining an ever-greater
reputation, he began preserving his magnificent baritone voice on records for the Victor
Taking Machine Company.

MGM tailored *The Rogue Song* for Tibbett; filmed entirely in two-color Technicolor,
this was a lavish and expensive production. After the movie was thought to be
completed, producer Irving Thalberg felt that it needed some comedy relief. He called
his friend Hal Roach, who agreed to loan the team for the relatively brief time that their
approximately eleven minutes' worth of footage would take to complete.

Stan Laurel in later years recalled that Lionel Barrymore attempted to direct him
and Babe, but on his first try he fell asleep. Stills indicate that James Parrott oversaw the
Laurel and Hardy scenes, a logical choice since he was the team's most frequent director
at this point. The November 2, 1929 issue of *Exhibitors Herald World* confirms this:
"James Parrott directed Laurel and Hardy in the comedy sequences of 'Rogues Song'
[sic] for MGM. Lawrence Tibbett has the featured role. The film is completed and the
comedians have returned to the Roach studios to prepare for their next picture."

The following descriptions of the action and dialogue are taken from a "Dialogue
Cutting Continuity" of the domestic, English-language version of *The Rogue Song*,
prepared by film editor Margaret Booth and dated February 5, 1930. A vault fire in
1967 reportedly destroyed all existing film sources on this title. Because most of the
picture element of the film is not known to survive, a cutting continuity in this instance
is more valuable to us, since it details the action of the final cut. (Laurel and Hardy's
characters are nowhere to be found in the shooting script.) The complete soundtrack,
which was issued to theaters on discs as well as on optical-sound prints, does survive, as
does about 15 minutes of footage from varied sources. Only about three minutes of this
material includes Laurel and Hardy.

Lawrence Tibbett's character in the script is named "Nadir," but was changed in
the movie to "Yegor," probably since somebody at MGM realized that "nadir" means
the lowest level, usually of quality. Stan Laurel plays "Ali-Bek" and Oliver Hardy
portrays "Murza-Bek," but you'd never know it from this continuity, which refers to
them, mostly, as Laurel and Hardy. In a surprising number of cases, they're referred
to as "Oliver and Hardy" (something which never would have happened at the Roach
studio!), but I have corrected this lapse for our mutual benefit.

The cutting continuity describes every shot of the film and gives its length in feet and
frames. In 35mm film running at 24 frames per second, one minute equaled 90 feet.
Here we must do some subtracting to determine the actual length of each shot, since,
for example, shot number 14 is listed at 180 feet and eight frames, with number 15
listed as 184 feet and 12 frames. Therefore, shot 14 runs for four feet and four frames.

The three columns of numbers are the shot number in that reel (it starts over again with each new reel), the length in feet, and the amount of frames thereafter.

Dialogue which likely was integrated into the action is often stated separately after a description of the entire visual element of a given shot.

Laurel and Hardy are introduced very quickly, in shot 14 of Reel One. LS means Long Shot; MS is Medium Shot; CU is Closeup; MCU is Medium Closeup; MLS is Medium Long Shot. Off-screen or Out of Shot is "o.s."

The film opens with a title, "A sudden unseasonable snowstorm disordered the high passes in the Kaisher Mountains in South Russia. One mid-summer day in 1910…." (It's rather surprising to think that this takes place only 19 years and a few months before the film was made, as it seems to belong to a much earlier time.) We hear Yegor and his men singing "The Rogue Song" as they ride into the courtyard of an inn and dismount, bringing servants Ali-Bek and Murza-Bek with them.

In countries where English was not the primary spoken language, MGM released a "Foreign Scored Version," which was essentially a silent film with a synchronized musical score, and titles for spoken dialogue. Tibbett's voice was only heard when he sang. Judging from its cutting continuity, this edition had some notable differences from the domestic sound version. Thus, there were two distinct versions of *The Rogue Song*. Each one may have had unique footage; there were definitely two different edits.

The Foreign Scored Version describes a bit of visual slapstick in Laurel and Hardy's first scene:

REEL ONE

13   136   3   LS Yegor's men dismount… finish song & start into the inn.

14   146   1   MS Int. Yegor's men enter, dragging servant with them.

15   150   4   MS Ext. door. Yegor enters followed by Laurel & Hardy. Yegor turns to Laurel & Hardy and says title.

16   155   2   "Stay here with the horses."

17   159   2   CS Laurel & Hardy hear title.

18   161   13   CU Yegor turns and enters inn.

19   164   3   MS Int. Yegor enters to men and starts giving orders.

20   170   11   MS Laurel & Hardy. Hardy says title.

21   174   0   "Shut that door!"

22   177   7   MS Hardy finishes title; Laurel goes inside & closes door; Hardy opens door suddenly, hitting Laurel in nose. Laurel comes outside. Hardy says:

23   206   9   "You can't even shut a door right … watch me."

Lawrence Tibbett enjoyed working with the boys.

24 213 12 MS Hardy finishes title, steps to door & closes it.

25 218   3 CU Snow as it slides off roof.

26 219   9 CU Hardy as snow falls on him.

27 222   3 CU Laurel sees snow fall on Hardy.

28 224 12 MS Laurel & Hardy looking at each other.

A scene like this occurs in the second reel of the domestic sound version, which instead gives Stan and Ollie a dialogue exchange for their introduction, or more accurately a monologue from Ollie:

12 160   0 MLS Courtyard. Tribesmen getting off horses; they start to exit into inn.

(Ad lib talking and laughter from men)

13 169 14 LS Int. Turk's Inn. Men come up toward fire. (Ad lib talking and laughter from men)

MAN   I smell a goat.

ANOTHER MAN Look, it's cooking there.

14 180 8 MS Yegor entering door. Laurel and Hardy follow. Yegor pushes them away.

YEGOR Outside there.

15 184 12 MCU Laurel and Hardy looking o.s. at Yegor.

YEGOR'S VOICE Take care of the horses

16 189 2 MS Yegor looks at Laurel and Hardy. Yegor enters inn.

17 194 2 LS Int. inn. Yegor enters in b.g. (ad lib talking and laughing)

18 197 15 MS Yegor coming thro' crowd of men. He starts to unfasten cape. (ad lib talking)

YEGOR Quiet, here – quiet – quiet – a man can't hear himself think in here. Where is that Turkish pig?

SERVANT He's upstairs.

YEGOR Well, go upstairs and get him and tell him to hurry. I want to see him.

SERVANT Yes, sir.

19 214 1 MCS Laurel and Hardy. Oliver looking thro' entrance. He looks over to Stan.

HARDY He always talks to me like that. That's for the benefit of the other men. I was with his father before him. In fact, -- I –

20 238 9 MCU Stan reacts to Oliver.

HARDY – saved his father's life once.

21 243 4 MCU Oliver looking o.s.

OLIVER There were lions – mountain lions –

22 246 12 CU Stan reacting.

HARDY'S VOICE -- four of them.

23 250 14 MCU Oliver looking o.s.

HARDY Was I afraid?

24 253 15 CU Stan looking o.s. at Oliver. He reacts.

HARDY (laughs) No!

Roach studios perennial Harry Bernard appeared as a soldier.

25 258 6 CU Oliver looking o.s. raises his hand. Pulls out
            dagger.

            HARDY I just finished polishing my sabre, not
            wishing to dirty it –

26 264 11 MS Laurel and Hardy. Stan joins in end of story.

            LAUREL & HARDY (speaking together) – I slapped

them to death.

27　270　11 CU Oliver looks o.s. at Stan.

18　272　12 CU Stan looks o.s. at Oliver, smiles.

Yegor and his bandits try to sell their most recently acquired loot to Osman the Turk (Lionel Belmore), who is the innkeeper. The Turk tells Yegor to be careful, as he has nobility in the house this night. That would be the matronly Countess Alexandra (Nance O'Neill), the young and pretty Princess Vera (Catherine Dale Owen), and their servant, Petrovna (Kate Price). As Yegor launches into another chorus of "The Rogue Song," the Countess instructs Petrovna to "go down immediately and fetch this tall strong singer." Petrovna hurries downstairs to summon Yegor, who responds with, "Go tell your mistress if she wants to see me she can come down here." Hearing this, the Countess and young Vera walk out to a balcony and listen to Yegor's singing; he climbs up onto the balcony and into their room with them, singing all the while.

When he concludes, the Countess indicates that she knows that he's Yegor, "that disreputable robber," but he tries to put one over on them with "I'm Yegor, chief of the Kaisher tribesmen. I'm known for my singing from Baku to Samarkand." Yegor then starts singing "And Then Forget," and he and Vera begin making eyes at each other. When Yegor finishes his song, the Countess tells Petrovna to bring her purse, but Yegor wants no payment except for Vera's hat, "with its funny little feather." But Vera tells him, "You should learn that there are some things you cannot take," then hastily exits. The Countess says, "I'd give you anything you ask. I've always wanted to meet a real thief." Yegor laughs, "Why? Do you want something stolen?" The Countess enthuses, "How delicious! You're looking at my pearls. Take them if you like. I have boxes of them. What are pearls compared to a moment in life when one isn't bored?"

There is one brief moment (Reel 2, shots 14 through 16) with Laurel and Hardy standing outside the door of the inn; it opens and Yegor's men come out and past them.

Meanwhile, the Countess double-crosses Yegor by sending for Osman the Turk and telling him that she plans to hang Yegor because "he stole my pearls." Osman protests, "But, Excellency, he says you gave them to him." She replies, "It's a lie. He stole my pearls."

At this point, the domestic sound continuity has a scene similar to the "snow" gag that introduced Laurel and Hardy in the Foreign Scored Version:

REEL TWO

19　390　9　MS Laurel and Hardy – Oliver puts dagger away in holder. Stan goes in and closes door. Oliver opens door. Stan comes out of Inn holding his nose. Oliver closes door from outside.

HARDY Close that door. (door slams) (door slams again)

LAUREL You hit me on the nose.

Ali-Bek and Murza-Bek have trouble mounting their horses.

HARDY Well it serves you right. Close it from the outside. Watch me. (door slams)

20 434 1 CU snow sliding off shelter of doorway.

21 435 10 MCU Oliver looking off scene at Stan, holding his arms out as snow falls on him.

22 438 3 CU Stan looking off scene at Oliver.

23 440 13 MS Laurel and Hardy looking at each other. Stan points his finger at Oliver, smiling.

Yegor sneaks into Vera's bedroom through the window, causing Vera's maid to scream. Yegor tells Vera, "I… I came for the hat." She tells him to take it, and that seems to be all he wants for now, as he bids the "little white dove" adieu and climbs back out through the window. Laurel and Hardy, at the porch of the inn, see Yegor start to ride away on his horse.

44 616 15 MS Laurel and Hardy standing by horses; a barrel in f.g. Yegor enters, pushes them away. Mounts horse and exits. Laurel and Hardy watch

Yegor exit.

45   626   2   MCU Vera and Petrovna looking out of window. Vera turns and looks at Petrovna.

VERA Petrovna, why did you scream?

46   633   15 MS Oliver trying to get on horse; starts to put foot into stirrup.

47   637   12 CU Oliver's foot in stirrup. Stirrup breaks.

48   640   9   MS Laurel sitting on horse; Oliver leans down. Picks up stirrup, tries to fix it onto saddle.

Stan looks at him. Oliver tries to jump on horse. Stan leans over and looks. Oliver looks down and up at Stan. Stan speaks. Oliver looks o.s. back at Stanley. Oliver exits scene, leading horse.

LAUREL May I suggest something?

HARDY What?

LAUREL Why don't you get on the barrel, then get on to the horse?

HARDY Thank you.

LAUREL You're welcome.

49   690   5   MS Laurel and Hardy. Oliver gets on top of barrel. He looks o.s. at Stan. Oliver raises his foot, about to get onto horse.

HARDY At last you have shown some intelligence.

(Sound of crashing as he lifts his foot)

50   710   4   CU Oliver's feet on top of barrel. Ice breaks. He falls into barrel of water into CU. He comes up and looks o.s. (Sound of water splashing)

51   723   8   MCU Stan looking o.s. at Oliver. He waves for him to follow. Stan starts to ride out as we

FADE OUT.

Now follows a scene where Yegor and his friend Hassan (Wallace MacDonald) ride up to Yegor's family home. He meets his mother (Elsa Alsen), who asks, "So they didn't kill you this time, my son?" Yegor alludes to being smitten with Princess Vera by replying, "No, but I was almost caught – caught by a little white dove, when I got this present for Nadja." Nadja is Yegor's younger sister (Florence Lake). Yegor's mother frets,

"I'm worried about Nadja – she hasn't been herself since the Saint Lankas Day dance in the Thieves' Market."

Yegor goes to visit Nadja and brings her the hat he appropriated from Princess Vera. Nadja spurns it with, "I don't want anything that belongs to a Russian Princess – they're rotten, all of them." Yegor notes, "I know what's the matter with you – you're in love." She replies, "No, I'm in hate." We don't yet know whom the object of her anger might be. Yegor gives his younger sister a hug and a kiss, and we fade out.

Now we fade in to "The Thieves' Market – rich in looted treasure – its stir of hidden danger hinting at reckless adventure." The Turk who is the innkeeper and the fence for Yegor's stolen goods drives up in a carriage, accompanied by a Cossack Captain. The Captain asks, "Any sign of Yegor yet?" and the Turk replies, "Not yet, but patience – he is sure to come." As the carriage drives out of the scene, Yegor and his gang ride up on horses.

REEL THREE

26 490 5 MLS Yegor, Hassan, Azmat, Laurel and Hardy ride into s. Yegor gets off horse. Azmat and Hassan get off their horses. Yegor walks around in front of Laurel and Hardy.

27 506 5 MS Laurel and Hardy on horses; Yegor looking up at them. Laurel and Hardy looking at Yegor.

28 509 0 CU Oliver looking down at Yegor and smiling.

29 511 9 CU Yegor looking up at Oliver, then turns and looks at Stan.

30 513 10 MCU Stan looking down at Yegor. Gives a silly grin.

31 516 10 MCU Yegor. Turns, faces camera, starts to put up sleeve.

YEGOR You stay here and take care of these horses.

32 520 4 CU Oliver reacting.

YEGOR'S VOICE Come on.

33 522 3 MS Yegor, Laurel and Hardy. Yegor exits s. followed by Azamat.

34 527 2 MCU Capt. of Cossacks and soldier. Soldiers salute and start to exit.

CAPTAIN Isn't there anybody else that knows Yegor beside this Turk?

SOLDIER None that we know of.

CAPTAIN Be ready.

35 537 3   MS Laurel and Hardy. Laurel starts to get off horse.
             He gets foot caught in Oliver's pocket. Oliver takes
             hold of his foot, swings it around, rips his pocket.
             Stan tries to fix it for him; Oliver slaps his hands.
             Stan pokes Oliver in the eye with his finger. Stanley
             gets back on horse. (Sound of coat ripping).

             HARDY Get your hands off of it.

             LAUREL You're always picking on me for
             everything.

             HARDY Well, it serves you right. Oh – oh- oh-
             (Hardy groans)

At this point, Princess Vera is shown asking a woman with a baby if she has seen "the
singing tribesman, Yegor, today?" The woman shakes her head no, but soon Vera hears
Yegor singing – he is standing on a table in a nearby inn, and when he finishes his song,
he jumps off the table and walks to Vera in the doorway. "By the liver of Lucifer!," he
exclaims. "My little white dove!" Vera warns Yegor, "You're to be hanged for stealing the
Countess' pearls. The Turk is waiting to signal the Cossacks when he sees you." Yegor
protests that the Countess gave him her pearls, and Vera says, "I know, but they'll hang
you just the same." She adds that she came to tell Yegor this because "it is unjust to hang
a man for something he did not do." Yegor sees some stairs and tells Vera, "These stairs
lead to the roof… wait for me there." Meanwhile, Yegor has some business to attend to,
and he dashes out of the scene.

[This next L&H scene was placed before the preceding "plot" sequence in the foreign
edition.]

REEL FOUR

7   199 6   MS Oliver fixing saddle on horse. Soldier enters
             with cane. Soldier gooses Oliver; Oliver jumps up,
             looks at soldier; then at horse. Soldier points cane
             toward horse, turns and looks o.s.

             (ad lib street noises)

             CAPTAIN Say, whose horses are these?

             HARDY I don't know.

             CAPTAIN You don't, eh?

             HARDY No, sir.

8   232 12 MCU Stan by horse, turns and looks o.s. at officers.
             He lowers his eyes and looks back at officer.

9   239 3   MS Oliver and soldier. Soldier turns back to Oliver.

Oliver puts his arms out.

CAPTAIN Who is that fellow.

HARDY Never saw him before –

10 254 1 MCU Stan looking o.s. at soldier and Oliver. Gives silly grin and looks back at horse.

HARDY'S VOICE – in my life.

11 257 5 MS Oliver, Captain. Captain looks at Oliver. Turns, looks o.s. at Stan. He starts to exit.

CAPTAIN You didn't, eh?

12 270 15 MS Captain enters to Stan; Stan is petting horse's neck; starts to polish saddle; is about to mount horse; Captain stops him.

(Laurel blows dust off horse – slaps horse)

CAPTAIN Wait a minute. Whose horse is that?

LAUREL What horse?

CAPTAIN That horse. Say, who are you with?

LAUREL Who – me?

13 314 4 CU Oliver looking o.s. at Captain and Stan. Waves hand at them.

CAPTAIN Yes, you.

14 316 15 MS Stan looks o.s. at Oliver. Laughs. Captain looks o.s. and laughs.

LAUREL I'm with him.

CAPTAIN Thank you. (laughs)

15 324 3 CU Oliver looking o.s. at Captain and Stan. Waves hands. He finally stops, starts to pick his finger nails.

16 330 8 MS Stan and Captain. Stan smiles, turns and starts to get on horse. Captain stops him.

CAPTAIN You stay right here.

17 338 11 LS Stan and Oliver standing by horses. Soldier enters scene, looks o.s., gives orders to soldiers o.s. Stan runs over to Oliver.

CAPTAIN You, too, Men!

18 346 3 MCS Stan with Oliver; Oliver waving hands, Stan crying.

(bugle sounds)

CAPTAIN'S VOICE Arrest those men.

(ad lib)

19 349 11 LS Soldier, Laurel and Hardy. Soldier has stick up in air. Squad comes in; soldier gives orders to squad; they turn. Laurel and Hardy run out of s. followed by soldiers.

Yegor and Vera meet in a wine cellar. He tells her, "I've been to Samarkand – and as far as Moscow, even, but I've never seen anything as lovely as you." She admits to him, "Yes, there is something about you." Vera says that Yegor must have many sweethearts among the "Robbing Lark ladies," but Yegor says, "Until today, I only allowed two women in my house – my mother and my sister. My sister is about as old as you and as like you as a pair of beads in a string – except you're fair and she's dark." He then sings "The White Dove." Vera concedes, "That was beautiful."

[The following bit of business was originally planned for L&H's 1929 two-reeler *The Hoose-Gow*.]

REEL FIVE

4 459 11 MS Laurel and Hardy – they sit down – Stan starts to eat cheese. Oliver takes it away from him, breaks cheese in two – gives smallest piece to Stanley. They start eating it. (Laughter ad lib.)

HARDY Just a moment.

(Bee buzzing)

5 498 6 CU Stan eating cheese – he looks at it as flies are on it.

6 502 4 INSERT flies on cheese.

7 506 1 CU Stan looks at flies, then off scene, back at flies.

8 509 3 INSERT cheese, flies on cheese. Stan's hand shooing flies off cheese.

9 514 10 MCU Stanley trying to shoo flies off cheese –

10 518 2 MCS Laurel and Hardy. Oliver eating cheese, Stan shooing flies away. Oliver looks at him.

11 528 2 INSERT cheese, flies on it.

A frame enlargement from the trailer, which includes part of the "bee" sequence.

12 531 13 MCU Laurel and Hardy. Oliver looing at Stan, Stan looks at Oliver, then back to cheese – starts to flick flies off cheese.

13 534 8 INSERT cheese. Stan's hand comes in, chases last fly off cheese.

14 536 15 MCS Laurel and Hardy – Stanley waving hands around shooing flies away as they continue to hang around. He finally hides cheese under his coat. Oliver pulls Stan's coat back, brings out cheese, takes out a corner of it and places it on ground.

15 562 7 CU piece of cheese on ground, fly on it.

16 564 14 MCS Laurel and Hardy looking down at piece of cheese on ground – Oliver looks at Stanley.

17 569 8 CU Stanley puts out his hand, agreeing, cleans off cheese and is about to eat it.

18 578 1 CU piece of cheese – sees flies on it – calls over to corner.

19 587 15 CU Stanley looking at Oliver off scene, turns and takes big bite of cheese, eats it, turns and looks at

Oliver o.s., smiles, looks down at piece of cheese, gets ready to take a bit of cheese. Bee buzzes.

BEE Buzz

20 606 10 CU Oliver looks off scene at Stanley

21 610 5 MCU Laurel and Hardy – Stanley looks at Oliver. Stanley and Oliver prepare to have another bite of cheese.

22 616 5 CU Stanley about to take bite of cheese, bee buzzes, he looks at cheese, about to take another bite, bee buzzes, he looks off scene at Oliver – is about to take another bite, bee buzzes, Stanley brings his hands up into scene, bee buzzes, Stanley starts to cry, bee buzzes, starts to frown.

BEE Buzz -

Buzz –

Buzz – buzz –

Buzz – buzz –

Buzz

23 646 14 MCU Laurel and Hardy. Oliver looking at Stanley. Stan tries to take another bite of cheese, bee buzzes. Oliver looks at his piece of cheese, Stanley turns and looks at him. Stanley about to take another bite of cheese, bee buzzes, he waves his hands around, bee buzzes, he looks down at stomach, bee buzzes, he looks down and pokes himself on other side, bee buzzes. He looks at Oliver – presses him in stomach. Oliver brings his hand out and presses Stanley in stomach and Stanley leaps.

BEE Buzz – buzz –

Buzz –

Buzz –

HARDY What is that?

BEE Buzz – Buzz

LAUREL Oh, what's the matter with me?

BEE Buzz – buzz

LAUREL Oh, what's –

BEE Buzz –

LAUREL Oh, something's happened –

BEE Buzz – buzz – buzz

LAUREL Oooh! Ooooh!

24 687 14 MS Stanley jumps up holding his stomach, grabs a knot in his hand, Oliver gets a long stick, tries to hit bee, misses and hits Stan on hand with stick, Oliver swings back again, hits mule.

BEE Buzz – buzz

HARDY What is it? What is it?

LAUREL I think I swallowed a bee – or something

BEE Buzz – buzz

HARDY A bee!

BEE Buzz

HARDY Wait – wait there it is – there it is – I'm holding it

LAUREL Ohh – there – there

HARDY There – right there – hold it right there – and I'll get it.

BEE Buzz – buzz –

LAUREL Oh – oh – oh –

HARDY Hold it there. (Ad lib from Hardy, Laurel & Bee)

25 718 6 MCS mule being hit with stick, breaks loose from wagon and runs out of scene.

26 720 15 MCS Laurel & Hardy seeing mule coming after them, they exit scene followed by mule.

Laurel and Hardy now disappear from the film for five and one-half reels (roughly 50 minutes); the preceding sequence was in the middle of Reel Four, and the boys don't show up again until the start of Reel Ten.

In between is a great deal of plot footage, in which Yegor and Vera flirt in a tavern. Yegor stabs the Turk in his carriage for being a traitor.

Back at his family home, Yegor learns that his sister, Nadja, has been assaulted by Vera's brother, Prince Serge (Ullrich Haupt). Finding that the Prince will be at a ball being given by Countess Alexandra, Yegor strangles Prince Serge and then kidnaps

Princess Vera. Yegor tells Vera, "You're going to know what it means to be a bandit's drab… a robber's trull." Vera is not exactly smitten with Yegor at this point.

As the bandit gang ekes out a nomadic existence, she learns about "weary journeying through sun and sand – the drudgery of animals to feed – coarse food to prepare – tents to fold." Yegor tries to win back her favor, but Vera responds, "I can bear anything – even the braying of your animals – but your singing drives me mad! If you have finished with your caterwauling perhaps you will tell me where we are going." Yegor responds, "I tell no one where I'm going. It is very far… but have no fear, you will last." After a fade out and back in, we at long last again see Ali-Bek and Murza-Bek.

REEL TEN

2   0   0   MS Laurel and hardy; Stan putting lather on Oliver's face. He starts to put brush down in lather.

HARDY Whew! Wasn't that a long ride today?

LAUREL It sure was.

HARDY And wasn't that desert hot?

LAUREL And sandy, too.

HARDY Say, you know Yegor was so tired he wouldn't even talk to me.

LAUREL I noticed that.

(Hardy snaps fingers)

3   57   2   CU Boiler of water. Hand with shaving brush comes into scene.

4   59   5   MS Laurel and Hardy. Laurel looks at Hardy. Oliver gives Stan instructions; Stan starts to put lather on Oliver's face.

HARDY And don't dip your brush in the soup.

LAUREL I thought it was water.

HARDY Come on and let's get this over with. Now be careful.

5   87   9   CU Oliver getting lather in his face.

6   91   7   MS Laurel and Hardy. Stan putting lather on Oliver's face; a few women walk by, Stan starts to look at them.

7   95   10   CU Stan looking o.s. at girls. Smiles at them.

8   98   12   CU Oliver. Stan putting lather on his face. Brush goes into his mouth.

(Oliver blub-blubs)

9   103   8   MS Laurel and Hardy struggling.

(Oliver blub-blubs)

10   108   8   CU Oliver, shaving brush in mouth. He pushes Stan's hand away; Oliver starts taking hair of brush out of his mouth.

11   118   2   MCS Laurel and Hardy. Oliver taking hairs out of his mouth; Stan looking at empty brush holder.

12   126   1   CU Oliver finishes taking hair out of his mouth. Looks o.s. at Stan.

13   130   7   MCS Laurel and Hardy. Stan holding razor; leans out o.s., picks up rock, is about to sharpen razor on rock.

14   137   13   CU Stan sharpening razor on rock. He looks at razor.
(Sound of sharpening razor)

15   147   7   MCS Laurel and Hardy; Stan looks at razor. Stan continues sharpening. Drops rock on Oliver's toe. Oliver yells. Stan goes out of s., picks up rock. Oliver pushes it out of his hands; it falls on his toe again. Oliver yells. Stan starts to look at razor.

(Sound of sharpening razor on stone.)

HARDY Oh! Oh! Oh! Oh! Why don't you shave me?

LAUREL Wait a minute – wait a minute

(Sound of rock dropping)

16   177   11   CU Stan tests razor, making sound.

(Tests razor. Boom sound.)

17   180   12   CU Oliver reacting to sound.

18   183   14   CU Stan looks at razor, then at Oliver. Looks out o.s.; gets rock; starts to sharpen, gets razor and tests it again making sound.

(Sound of sharpening razor.)

19   200   13   CU Oliver reacting to sound of razor.

(Sound of razor being tested)

20   202   7   CU Stanley; looks o.s. at Oliver and smiles.

(Sound of chickens clucking. Clucking heard thru following scene)

21 203 12 MCS Laurel and Hardy. Stan starts to shave him. Stan puts lather on Oliver's shirt; Oliver takes hand away and takes lather off shirt. Stan takes Oliver by nose, starts to shave front of neck [throat]; Oliver reacts. Stan takes lather off with razor; puts it on back of Oliver's neck. Stan starts to shave back of neck.

HARDY Oh! I think you'd better shave the back of my neck.

(Sound of shaving back of neck.)

22 259 3 CU Stan shaving back of Oliver's neck.

(Noise of scraping neck with razor.)

23 267 0 CU Stan sitting on crate. Chicken's head comes out of crate; pecks him on seat of pants.

24 268 9 DOUBLE CS Laurel and Hardy. Stan gets up, drops razor down back of Oliver's neck. Oliver starts trembling, starts to squirm.

25 278 8 MCS Laurel and Hardy. Stan rubs seat of pants. He leans down to Oliver. He gets up and looks around. Oliver points down his back. Stan starts to lean over. He puts hand down his back, pulls razor up. Oliver puts hand back to see if he has been cut; stands and puts shoulder forward, turns and faces Stan.

HARDY Oh – oh!

LAUREL What's the matter?

HARDY The razor – the razor – Oh!

LAUREL Where is it?

HARDY Down my back. Get it out – get – get – oh! Oh!

LAUREL Relax – relax –

HARDY All right –

LAUREL Now be careful –

HARDY Oh!

LAUREL Don't move now.

HARDY I won't

LAUREL Don't get excited –

HARDY I'm not excited –

LAUREL I've found it –

HARDY Take it easy – take it easy –

(Sound of tear. Sound of chickens clucking around them all thru this episode.)

The next bit of plot has Yegor and Vera's love-hate relationship in full force. Despite the fact that Princess Vera is now chopping wood and doing other menial work for Yegor and his bandit gang, she maintains her pride. Yegor hasn't decided whether to continue the gang's journey through the sand dunes or by the mountains. When Vera says, "The road through the mountains is much nearer. I used to go there as a child in the summer. There's a lake there set deep in the rocks – like tourmaline, and the roses grow all around it as large as cabbages." Because of this, Yegor spitefully decides that "you're not going near the mountains – you'll see nothing but sand and sand, and still more sand." A windstorm begins. Hassan, one of Yegor's henchmen, and Vera speak with Yegor in front of a tent.

[This is the portion of the film which was discovered in 1982.]

39 635 1 MCS Vera and Hassan. Yegor enters to them, Hassan exits. Vera tries to follow; Yegor pulls her back.

YEGOR Hassan, get to the tents. Can't you see there's a storm –

(Thunder starts)

-- coming? There's work to be done. The women say you've cast a spell on Hassan. He is not the same. I warn you he's like a brother to me, and he has a heart, even if you haven't, and I'll not have it broken.

VERA (laughs)

(ad lib camp noise – thunder.)

40 657 3 LS Clouds; lightning flashes.

(Wind increases)

41 660 1 MCU Yegor looking at clouds; points c.s., brings hands up to mouth and yells.

YEGOR Hey, there, take care of those tents.

42 667 2 LS Camp; people rushing around.

(Storm sound effects)

YEGOR'S VOICE Look after the animals. Hurry up.
Go over there --

43 671 13 MCU Yegor and Vera. Yegor yelling.

YEGOR – and get those carts and wagons up on the
high ground.

44 674 7 MS People running around.

YEGOR'S VOICE Hurry up,

45 677 5 MCS Yegor and Vera. Yegor finishes yelling, starts
to pull down tent.

(ad lib camp noise.)

46 683 15 LS Camp. People rushing around.

(ad lib – wind)

47 688 14 MLS Laurel and Hardy. Tent blows away. Oliver sits
up.

(ad lib – wind, rain)

48 695 10 MCU Laurel and Hardy. They get up, look around,
look at each other. They pull blankets over them.

(Storm noise)

49 714 14 MLS Yegor and Vera in front of tent. Lightning
flashes. She tries to help Yegor.

(Storm noise)

50 724 9 MCS Vera pulling rope of tent. Lightning flashes.
She leans back; looks o.s.

(Storm noise)

51 737 2 MLS Camp. Lady runs in and picks up little lamb
out of mud puddle.

(Storm noise)

52 740 4 LS Camp. People running around

(Storm noise)

53 743 12 MLS Front of cave. Bear enters.

(Storm noise)

Rain causes the boys to find a cave – with a bear inside.

54 748 3 MS in front of tent. Lady comes out and picks up little lamb, takes it to tent.

(Storm noise)

55 753 1 MLS Front of cave. Laurel and Hardy enter.

HARDY Whew! Isn't it dark in here?

LAUREL It sure is.

HARDY I can't see a thing.

LAUREL So can I.

HARDY What do you mean – so can I? Lie down. Hi-ho! Say, where did you get that fur coat?

LAUREL What fur coat?

HARDY Haven't you got a fur coat on?

LAUREL Why, I've got no fur coat.

HARDY Well, it feels like a fur coat.

(The bear growls.)

HARDY & LAUREL Oh – oh – oh --

(ad lib – storm noise.)

Laurel and Hardy come running out and exit to right.

After the storm subsides, Yegor tries to quell the storm that Vera has churning inside her against him. He tries to curry her favor by saying, "Would it make you very happy if I changed the route and we went thru the mountains toward Kars, and you saw your little lake?" Vera dismisses this with, "Do as you like."

After Yegor exits, Vera looks around then runs toward his henchman, Hassan. He kisses her hand. She says, "We're going to Kars by the mountain road. You know what I asked of you. Will you help me?" Hassan replies, "I'll do anything you ask. I love you." Vera whispers, "When we get to camp tomorrow night you can slip away." Hassan is a bit nervous about this; he wants reassurance that "no harm shall come to my brothers," nor to Yegor. Vera responds cryptically, "I promise no harm shall come to the Kaisher men. As for Yegor, he shall learn how a Borisoff forgives."

The next day, Vera and Yegor are enjoying an idyll at the edge of the lake where Vera "used to come in the summer as a child." Soldiers sneak up behind Yegor and grab him. Vera says, "You have brought me home. Take him, men, take him!" Hassan, realizing that he has unwittingly betrayed Yegor, stabs himself. "I didn't mean this; she promised -- " he cries. "A knife is too much honor for me, but I have no rope like Judas had."

Yegor is taken to a fortress to be lashed, and manages to sing "The Lash" by Stothart & Grey all the while. Vera, demonstrating her amazing ability for vacillation, now wails to her maid, "What's to be done, Petrovna? They'll kill him! Oh, I wish he'd stop singing – he's driving me mad." Yegor faints from the lashing; Vera faints from stress.

The next day, in a dungeon, Yegor is lying on a straw bed, with Vera's uncle Peter watching over him. Vera enters and asks her uncle for some privacy. She tells Yegor, "I know now that hate and death are littler things than love. Forgive me." Yegor responds, "Forgive you? There's nothing to forgive. I tried to hate you and you tried to hate me. We couldn't…. You're here and I'm happy." Vera notes, "And I'm happy too, now, but I'm afraid – afraid for the future."

REEL 12

11 134 2 MS Laurel and Hardy in tree, looking o.s.

LAUREL Look –

HARDY Where?

Waiting for news about Yegor.

12 140 12 MS people gathered around gate – soldier enters from gate –

MAN What do you people want?

13 143 8 MS Laurel and Hardy in tree looking o.s.

VOICE What happened to Yegor?

14 146 6 MS people and soldier at gate

MAN Oh, that bandit will bother you no more. Go on, clear out –

15 154 3 MCS Laurel and Hardy in tree, looking o.s.

VOICE He's dead?

MAN Yes, he's dead.

VOICE He's gone.

16 157 9 MCS group of people around gate –

(ad lib conversation)

MAN Yes, Yegor is dead –

17 160 1   MCU Laurel and Hardy in tree – it starts to go
            down. They both look down toward the bottom of
            the tree.

            HARDY Oh, get off my foot.

            (Sound of tree breaking)

            HARDY What's that?

18 169 1   CU trunk of tree breaking.

            (Sound of tree cracking)

19 171 8   MCS Laurel and Hardy react to what they see – tree
            starts to fall.

            LAUREL It's the tree.

            LAUREL AND HARDY Oh – oh – oh

20 177 9   LS Lake – tree falls into lake with Laurel and Hardy

            (Sound of tree falling in lake)

            FADE OUT

    In the film's finale, Yegor and Vera seem to have finally decided they are sweethearts
– just in time for Yegor to leave for further adventures, or maybe plunder. He says,
"Perhaps one day all these foolish barriers between us will be torn down, and then –
then I'll come back for you." He begins singing "Looking at You." Meanwhile, news of
Yegor's survival of the lashing has not yet come to the rest of his crew.

26 367 1   MLS camp – tribesmen swarmed around – Laurel
            and Hardy enter

            (ad lib camp noise)

27 379 3   MS Laurel and Hardy enter to Azamat and
            tribesmen

28 381 4   MCU Azamat and tribesmen looking o.s. at Yegor

            MAN Any news of Yegor?

29 383 3   MCU Laurel and Hardy looking o.s. at Azamat and
            tribesmen.

            HARDY Yegor is dead

30 388 8   MCS Azamat and tribesmen looking o.s. at Yegor

            VOICES Dead –

31 401 6   MCS Laurel and Hardy looking o.s. at Azamat and
            tribesmen

The boys take care of the horses and bring up the rear.

MAN Did he have anything to say before he died?

HARDY His last words were: 'Oliver, I want you to carry on.'

LAUREL He never –

HARDY Shh – and if you boys don't mind, I'm your chief.

32 437 8 MCS Azamat and tribesmen start laughing

(laughing)

33 440 7 MCS Laurel and Hardy –

(sound of laughter)

34 447 8 MS Laurel and Hardy in group – they react to o.s. voice – Laurel and Hardy look around and exit to camera-right. Tribesmen start to exit to camera-left.

(Music: ROGUE SONG by Stothart and Grey)

YEGOR (singing) Beyond the dawn, we belong.

Fun on the MGM backlot with actor Lew Cody.

35 [accidentally omitted in numbering]

36 463 3 MLS lineup of horses – Laurel and Hardy – they
           walk down line of horses with shovels over their
           shoulders.

           (Music)

Having established what Ali-Bek and Murza-Bek's continuing status with the bandit gang will be, Yegor and his tribesmen continue singing "The Rogue Song," on their horses. Yegor rides up to a medium close-up and raises his hand as he finishes his song with "Beyond the dawn, we belong where the frowning hills guard us forever!" Fade out. (This was followed by exit music, an "Exit March" by Herbert Stothart.)

NIGHT OWLS

Production history: Production L-30. Written mid-October 1929. Filmed Wednesday, October 30, 1929 through Tuesday, November 12. Released January 4, 1930. Copyrighted January 6, 1930 by MGM (LP 977). Two reels.

Produced by Hal Roach. Directed by James Parrott. Photographed by George Stevens. Edited by Richard Currier. Dialogue by H.M. Walker. Sound by Elmer Raguse.

With Stan Laurel (Himself), Oliver Hardy (Himself), Edgar Kennedy (Officer Kennedy), Anders Randolf (The Chief of Police), James Finlayson (Meadows, the butler), Harry Bernard (Police Station desk clerk), Baldwin Cooke, Charles McMurphy (Officers scoffing at Kennedy). *Part cut from final release print:* Charles McAvoy (Policeman apprehending Laurel and Hardy in the chief's home).

The police chief is sore at officer Kennedy, who hasn't been able to capture the crook who has been committing burglaries all over the neighborhood. When a desk sergeant jokes that the only way Kennedy will make an arrest is to frame it himself, he decides to do just that. Stan and Ollie, sleeping on a park bench, seem to be prime candidates to do the job, especially after Kennedy threatens them with 90 days on the rockpile for vagrancy. After getting inside the chief's house and locking themselves out again numerous times, they finally accomplish the burglary. However, they cause a great deal of racket, topped by their accidentally starting a player piano. Too scared to wait for Kennedy to show up, the boys escape through a window. Just then, Kennedy bursts through the door and picks up their bag of loot. The chief naturally accuses Kennedy for this robbery – and all of the others.

Night Owls may be a talkie, but it offers very little dialogue from its participants. It's really more of a "crashie," thanks to the astonishing number of booms, bangs and crashes that Stan and Ollie induce while trying to quietly burgle the chief's house. (Something else crashed very loudly the day before filming began – the New York stock market.)

As usual, the script and the film have some interesting differences. For example, the number of robberies has been increased in the film to 42 burglaries in one week.

The script notes that the desk sergeant "speaks title." This script was written in October 1929, and although the Roach studio had been making talkies exclusively since March, clearly it took a while for the writers to lose old habits.

Stan's "not shaking" remark is not in the film.

The "cucumber frames" as described in the script are a small greenhouse covering some shrubs on the ground.

The script proposes, "They go through the door and window routine and Babe finally gets inside." Obviously, the writers knew that once Laurel and Hardy were on the soundstage, presented with locked doors and windows, they would be able to

Officer Kennedy finds two potential accomplices.

create seemingly endless variations on getting in and locking themselves out again. The premise of burglars trying to get into a house formed the basis of Stan's vaudeville routines *The Nutty Burglars* and *The Keystone Trio*. Similar scenes show up in *Duck Soup, Bacon Grabbers, Another Fine Mess, Laughing Gravy, The Music Box, The Chimp, Scram!, The Midnight Patrol, Sons of the Desert, Way Out West, The Flying Deuces, The Dancing Masters*, and the team's 1952 stage routine *A Spot of Trouble*.

The scripted ending has the dramatic flourish of Laurel and Hardy exposing Kennedy's plot, but it isn't funny. The film has a much better ending, with Kennedy bursting into the house just as Stan and Ollie are escaping through a window, so that when the chief switches on the lights, he sees Kennedy literally holding the bag. The chief naturally figures that he's the burglar who has been terrorizing the neighborhood. We then see Laurel and Hardy again struggling to get over the wall surrounding the chief's house, with Stan tearing what's left of Babe's trousers. They fall into the garbage cans below; Stan falls deeply into one and it gets stuck on his posterior. He hobbles off on all fours as Ollie hurls rocks at him.

Since Hal Roach did not want to lose the huge international audience that his silent films had enjoyed, he began producing his talking comedies in Spanish (almost always) and French, German or Italian (alternately), continuing through 1931. The first Roach short released in another language was *Ladrones*, the Spanish equivalent of *Night Owls*. It was expanded from 21 minutes to 36 and included some new gags. Enrique Acosta now played the role of the chief. Edgar Kennedy remained and spoke Spanish, as did

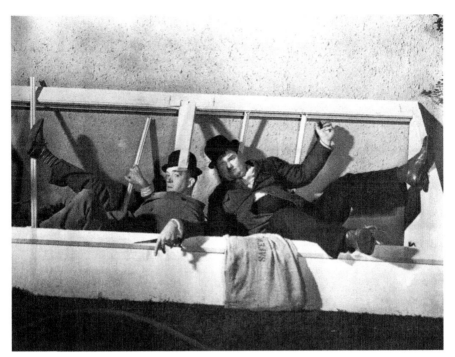

Scaling a wall brings an unexpected landing.

James Finlayson as the butler – named Meadows in the English-language edition, but Juan in the Spanish-language film.

As filmed, *Ladrones* retains the finish that was proposed by the *Night Owls* script, up to the point where the other cops start to take Laurel, Hardy and Kennedy to jail. Stan and Ollie sit in the back seat of an open police car; the chief and his butler follow behind in a second open car. As the first car approaches a tree with a low overhanging branch, Stan and Ollie get the idea to jump up and hang from it, thus evading their captors. They then fall into the back seat of the second car, not realizing that the chief is driving. This startles the chief, who runs off the road and sends the car and its inhabitants hurtling into a nearby pond.

Stan may have been happier with *Ladrones* than he was with *Night Owls*, since the English-language version was cut to conform with the expected length of two reels. He explained to *Los Angeles Times* film critic Philip K. Scheuer, "Nineteen hundred feet is the usual length for a two-reeler, and it necessitates some regrettable cuts. We were compelled to eliminate much of the business leading up to the big laughs in *Night Owls*, and the laughs themselves suffered by it. Comedy, especially our type of comedy, must be cumulative in effect, not abrupt. So it may be that we shall make arrangements to release our comedies in whatever footage they show to best advantage, from 1900 up to 2500 feet."

Stan got his wish, as the team's very next film, *Blotto*, was released in three reels. So were some of the other films whose scripts are contained in this book – *The Music Box*, *The Chimp*, and *Oliver the Eighth*. Hal Roach agreed with this idea to the extent of releasing *Beau Hunks*, also in this book, in the highly unusual length of four reels.

Stan finds many ways to enter the house – and lock himself out again.

A gag cut from *Night Owls* but retained in *Ladrones* – Ollie has a vase stuck on his head, helpfully removed by Stan.

Ladrones had an elaborate ending not in the English-language film or script.

Stan's mentor, producer Fred Karno, was briefly employed at the Roach studio. Stan, Babe and director James Parrott look on as Mr. Karno refuses to clean up the refuse.

In 1952, Laurel and Hardy toured England in a stage sketch, *A Spot of Trouble*, reworked from *Night Owls*. Police chief Kenneth Henry aims the gun, while officer Leslie Spurling climbs through the window.

L-29

Fade in on interior of police station, shooting toward the street through swinging doors upstage. At the desk on the left of the set we see the desk sergeant, Kennedy and two other cops. Out in the street pedestrians and automobiles are passing. From the same setup we see a car drive up in front of the station. The Chief of Police (Anders Randolph) gets out of car and enters the station. He is upset over something and has a newspaper in his hand. He walks right in to the desk sergeant and speaks title in a gruff way, "Sergeant, who was on duty in my district last night?"

Kennedy, thinking he is to be congratulated for something, jumps to his feet and says, "I was, sir." The Chief whirls around and glares at Kennedy and very angrily says, "You were, huh? Did you see the morning paper? You didn't huh? Well, there were five robberies in two blocks last night. It's a good thing it wasn't my house!" The Chief glares angrily at Kennedy for a moment and then continues, "Kennedy, you must do something to clean up this situation. If there are any more robberies and you don't make an arrest, you're through! This is your last chance!" He exits into his office and slams the door.

The desk sergeant and cops all laugh at Kennedy and start to kid him. The sergeant speaks title, "Poor Kennedy, you're always in wrong." He laughs again and continues, "I guess the only way you'll ever make an arrest is to frame it yourself."

Cut to Kennedy pouting. He thinks over the last remark about framing it himself and thinks this is not a bad idea. He gets over a little smile, and as he exits from scene we fade out.

Fade in on a park: night. Two characters are lying on a bench, head to head, with newspapers over their faces, snoring. It is a moonlight night and we see the shadows of the trees hitting the walk. Kennedy enters to the bench, notices the two characters and gets over a thought. He starts tapping one of them on the foot with his club. The man wakes up and we see it is Laurel. He shakes the other character, who sits up and we see it is Hardy. They look at Kennedy frightened. Kennedy speaks title, "Come on, come on! What do you think this is? The Biltmore Hotel? Do you know you can get ninety days for sleeping in the park?"

Babe: "Yes."

Kennedy: "Well, what are you doing here?"

Stan: "We're looking for odd jobs."

Kennedy: "How would you like to do an odd job for me?"

Babe: "We'd love to."

Kennedy: "Well, here's the proposition --- "

All three sit down on the bench and become kind of chummy.

Kennedy: "The Chief and I are on the outs, and I want to get on the good side of him"

Stan: "We'll do all we can to help you."

Kennedy: "That's great! I want you two boys to rob the Chief's house."

Stan and Babe take it big.

Stan: Why, we'll be arrested!"

Kennedy: "That's the idea! I'll arrest you and that will put me in good with the chief."

Stan: And they'll put us in for the winter. We won't do it!"

Kennedy: "All right, then. It's the rock pile for you."

Babe: "Just a minute, officer. Are you sure that no harm will come to us?"

Kennedy: "Why, no. You leave it to me and I'll get you out of it. Come on, now, and I'll show you the house."

Stan: "No good will come of this!"

Babe: "Be quiet! Do you want to go to jail? Haven't you any confidence in the officer?"

Stan: "Yes, but I don't trust him."

Fade out as they exit.

Fade in on alley. Kennedy enters and beckons off. Stan and Babe enter and all three quietly come down to the foreground. Kennedy points to the house and says, "There's the house. Go to it, and be as quiet as you can. I'll see you later."

Kennedy starts to tiptoe away, looking back toward the two boys, and collides with four big garbage cans stacked against the wall. They crash to the ground and Kennedy falls with them. He jumps to his feet and dashes down the alley, followed by Stan and Babe. They run around the corner out of sight.

Cut to bedroom; the Chief is just getting into bed and Finlayson, the butler, is straightening up the Chief's clothes. They take the crash and the Chief says, "Meadows, see what that is." Finlayson opens the window and looks out, turns back and says, "It must be the garbage man, sir." The Chief says, "All right, Meadows, you may retire."

Cut back to the alley. Kennedy sends Stan and Babe back to the wall and tells them to go ahead.

Stan and Babe come down to the foreground again. Stan's legs are shaking violently. Babe asks him what he is trembling for, and Stan says "I'm not trembling." Babe says, "If you're not trembling, what are you shaking for?" and Stan answers, "I'm not shaking – it's the wind blowing up me trousers."

Babe tells Stan to climb the wall and open the gate. Stan gets on a garbage can and starts to climb up. A couple of cats run along the wall, scaring Stan. He falls off the garbage cans and the two of them scramble out of the alley again.

Cut to Finlayson reacting at the window. He looks out and the window falls, clunking him on the head.

Stan and Babe finally come back to the wall. Babe helps Stan up on the wall and Stan tries to assist Babe. Babe gets one arm and one leg over the wall and is hanging there. Stan reaches down to pull him over by the seat of his pants. We hear a big tear and Stan comes up with the seat of Babe's pants in his hand. He tries again and gives a big heave, and both fall over the other side of the wall. There is a big crash of glass.

Cut to inside of yard and show Stan and Babe have crashed through the cucumber frames.

Cut to bedroom. The Chief sits up and takes it, and says "Meadows, see what that noise is!" Finlayson goes to the window, and shooting from his angle he sees a couple of cats dash back along the wall and start "meowing." He turns to the Chief and says, "It's the cats, sir."

Back to Stan and Babe. Babe says, "Pretend we're cats!" and they both start meowing.

Back to the bedroom. The Chief tells Finlayson to do

something. Finlayson picks up a shoe and throws it out the window.

The shoe hits Babe in the face. He takes it and Stan continues the meowing. Finlayson throws another shoe. This time it hits Stan. Stan gets sore, picks up the shoe and throws it back at Finlayson. The shoe hits Finlayson in the face. He takes it and as he throws it back, the window drops and the shoe crashes through the glass. Finlayson looks silly and the Chief says, "Meadows, stop that playing!"

The shoe just misses Stan. He gets sore, picks up a big rock and is just about to heave it back at Finlayson when Babe stops him, takes the rock from him and throws it out of the scene.

Follow the rock into the alley. It crashes into the globe on a light post where Kennedy is standing looking at his watch. There is a terrific crash and the rock comes down on Kennedy's head, knocking him cold.

Back to Stan and Babe. They suddenly see the Chief lift the shade and look out. They sneak to cover and kneel down beside the garden hose. The Chief pulls down the shade, and Babe motions for Stan to come on. Stan steps on the hose and the water from the nozzle squirts into Babe's face. Babe gives Stan a dirty look and again motions for him to come on.

They start toward the door and Stan steps on a rake, the handle of which flies up and hits Babe. Babe bawls Stan out, picks up the rake and throws it out of scene toward the house.

They go to the door, which is a double door with two handles. Shooting from the outside, the left side of the door is latched. Babe tries the handle of the left side. They go through the door and window routine and Babe finally gets inside. Stan climbs out the window, closes it and finds the door locked. He knocks on the door and rings the bell. We hear an awful commotion inside and Babe comes tearing out. He dashes past Stan and Stan follows. They hide around the corner of the house.

The door opens and Finlayson in his night gown and cap looks out, sees no one, goes back in and closes the door, and we hear a heavy key turn in the lock.

Babe gives Stan a dirty look and starts working on the window. Stan goes back to the window near the door, finds he can open it and climbs in.

Back to Babe working on the window. Stan opens it from the inside and gives Babe such a scare that he topples over. He gets to his feet and climbs in through the window.

Cut to dining room; Stan and Babe enter. Stan holds the sack while Babe starts putting the silverware in. He puts in a few pieces and Stan shakes them down. Babe finally gets the sack full and tells Stan to find something to tie it with.

Stan looks around, sees the bell cord and gives it a yank to pull it off the wall. We hear the bell jangle upstairs. Babe drops the silverware, Stan takes it big and they both quickly hide.

Cut to Finlayson at the top of the stairs, very nervous. He exits.

Cut to the Chief's bedroom. Finlayson enters and says, "Did you ring, sir?" The Chief bawls him out for waking him up and tells him he is getting old and going nutty.

Cut to Stan and Babe in the living room. They start to go back to get the silver and Babe trips over a bear rug. As he falls, his head hits the drawer of the player piano and it starts playing.

The Chief upstairs hears the piano, gets out of bed and calls downstairs, "Meadows, will you stop playing this time of night!" He discovers Finlayson standing right behind him and both take it big. Cuts of Stan and Babe frantically trying to stop the piano. The Chief orders Finlayson to phone the police station, then puts on his robe, grabs a revolver and starts downstairs.

The Chief enters the living room and switches on the lights, taking Stan and Babe by surprise, and says, "Hands up! So you're the fellows who have been robbing this neighborhood!" Stan starts to cry and Babe says, "Don't worry – Kennedy will fix it."

Cut to flash of Kennedy, still out.

Back to Stan and Babe, confident that Kennedy will get them out O.K. We hear the police car siren coming, and the Chief, still keeping Stan and Babe covered, opens the door and admits about four cops. The Chief orders them to arrest Stan and Babe.

Cut to Kennedy; he comes to, suddenly realizes that he may be late and rushes out of the scene.

Back to interior. The Chief is giving the cops orders to take Stan and Babe away. At this point we hear a police whistle blowing violently, and a couple of shots are fired. Everybody takes it. Stan and Babe smile at each other knowingly.

Cut outside and show Kennedy running and bumping against the front door.

Cut to interior; the Chief opens the door and Kennedy falls in. He gets up and takes it big when he sees all the cops. The chief says, "Late as usual, Kennedy!" He tells the cops to take Stan and Babe away, then turns to Kennedy and says "You stay here – I want to talk to you."

Stan gets a little worried as the cops start to take them out. He turns to Kennedy and says, "Aren't you going to help us?" Kennedy and the policemen take it. The Chief says, "What's this?" He looks at Kennedy and says, "Kennedy, do you know these two men?" Kennedy says "I never saw them before in my life!"

Stan: "Why, he did too! He hired us to rob your house and promised to get us out of it!"

Babe: "Yes, and he said he would be made Chief if we did it."

The Chief gets sore, tears Kennedy's badge off and orders the cops to take him to jail.

Finish with Stan, Babe, the Chief and Finlayson in living room.

COME CLEAN

Production history: Written late April-early May 1931. Filmed Thursday, May 7 through Thursday, May 14. Copyrighted September 1, 1931 by MGM (LP 2431). Released September 19, 1931. Two reels.

Produced by Hal Roach. Directed by James W. Horne. Photographed by Art Lloyd. Edited by Richard Currier. Sound by Elmer Raguse. Dialogue by H.M. Walker.

With Stan Laurel (Himself), Oliver Hardy (Himself), Mae Busch (Kate), Gertrude Astor (Mrs. Hardy), Linda Loredo (Mrs. Laurel), Charlie Hall (Soda jerk at Nason's Drugs), Eddie Baker (Detective), Tiny Sandford (Apartment doorman), Gordon Douglas (Desk clerk). *Part cut from final release print:* Harry Bernard (Policeman).

Ollie and his wife are enjoying a private, romantic dinner until it's interrupted by the unexpected and unwanted intrusion of "those Laurels." Mrs. Hardy puts on a brave (if unconvincing) face as they enter, and the boys soon leave to indulge Stan's hankering for ice cream. Returning home, they find a woman about to commit suicide by jumping off a bridge into a river. They save her from a watery demise – Ollie almost meeting one himself – and are paid for their chivalry by her threat that if they don't take care of her from now on, she'll tell the whole world that they tried to murder her. The boys try to escape her, but she follows them to Ollie's apartment, where a frenzied evening results as they try to conceal their unruly visitor.

Come Clean is one of the funniest Laurel and Hardy shorts, and certainly one of the noisiest, thanks in large part to the lungpower of Mae Busch, whose screaming is a piercing accompaniment to most of the second reel. She would display her formidable presence in 13 films with the boys, sometimes as Ollie's wife, occasionally as a friendly acquaintance, periodically as a lady of dubious virtue and once (in *Oliver the Eighth*) as a genuinely lethal adversary.

This film is identified on its script only as "L-1," but it's clear that the phrase "come clean" was being thought of as a running gag. It was originally intended for the final sequence when Stan is in the bathtub, fully clothed. In the script, Stan says, "I wanted to come clean," but it appears that in the film Ollie said it after "He's gone to the beach." He takes a breath to say something else, but a splice in the negative omits that next line. Presumably, preview audiences laughed so much at what was supposed to be a set-up line that it instead became the payoff.

The script's opening scene is entirely different, with the Laurels already in the Hardys' apartment and sharing dinner. This was replaced by a reworking of a scene from the 1928 silent *Should Married Men Go Home?* It establishes Mrs. Hardy as a tough dame who goes in a flash from a loving companion to a hissing harridan, calling Ollie a "sap," "chump," and a "big lunk."

An early scene has the boys repeatedly just missing each other in side-by-side elevators. In the movie, one of those conveyances clearly has a broken chair inside,

Gertrude Astor (Mrs. Hardy) and Linda Loredo (Mrs. Laurel) pretend to enjoy this unexpected visit, while Ollie is more candid with Stan.

indicating that some Laurel and Hardy knockabout caused the breakage. This was omitted in the film and is not mentioned in the script.

The soda fountain scene has a neat ending in the script, which Ollie accidentally breaking just enough eggs to cover the change for 75 cents from his five-dollar bill. The film retains the breaking of eggs, but doesn't include Charlie Hall determining that they cost this precise amount. One wonders if this was filmed, and if so why it was cut.

The "two detectives" mentioned here are reduced in the film to just one, played by Eddie Baker, later to become a patrolman for the Los Angeles Police Department. The actors in the supporting cast are not specified in the script, except for "Mae Busch, a desperate character." She gives a superb performance in the film, and one wonders how any other actress could have equaled it.

The scripted gag of Babe taking off his coat while preparing to save Mae from a watery grave, Stan mimicking him and then going one further by starting to remove his pants, was likely ignored to keep the tempo of the scene from lagging.

The film doesn't include the script's gag of Stan grabbing Babe by the seat of his pants and ripping them, nor does it have the crab that bites Babe in his nether regions,

Charlie Hall expects that those straws will soon be strewn.

a reworking of a memorable gag in the L&H silent *Liberty*.

The gag detailed in paragraph 27 is more pointedly made in the film, with Stan saying, "I got her in this apartment," and Ollie replying, "Ohhhh, that's my bedroom, you bonehead!" The fact that this is the entrance to the Hardys' bedroom is not mentioned earlier in the film as it is in the script. Neither entity explains why the entrance to someone's bedroom would be located in the main hallway of an apartment building.

In the film, the explanation for the boys returning without ice cream is not that the drug store didn't have any, it's that Stan ate it. "He couldn't wait," Ollie adds helpfully. And the music suddenly emanating from the Hardy bedroom is not Mae Busch singing, but instead a rousing rendition of Sousa's "Stars and Stripes Forever" – Mae seems to have turned on the radio out of sheer deviltry. The boys try to cover the din by singing along and using tea cups and saucers for percussion.

The script's suggested gag with Mae Busch hiding in the Hardys' bed while Stan mistakenly pushes Mrs. Hardy into a closet is not in the film, where the final attempt to keep Mae hidden from the wives is less complicated.

The ending of the film is much improved from the script, which fails to bring the detectives into the action after their introduction. Also, Stan doesn't just pretend to take a bath until after he's discovered – he begins to really take one, fully clothed, as soon as he hears Ollie say, "He's in the bathroom – taking a bath!" There are no shower curtains nor a gag with a brush handle in the film; this probably proved too cumbersome to film.

Stan, Ollie and "Kate" all try to keep mum. Officer Harry Bernard does not appear in the film.

The final paragraph of the script is one of the strangest and unfunniest endings ever proposed for a Laurel and Hardy film. It would have required the building of a new set, and would have removed the action from its point of origin. The suggestion of a men's restroom would have been considered tasteless by many and probably would have been removed from prints by several regional censor boards.

The film's ending brings back the detective, as well as the idea of Stan wanting ice cream. Stan literally going down the drain is a much more outlandish and impossible gag than one usually finds in L&H comedies, but it gets a laugh, as does Ollie's explanation of Stan's whereabouts – "He's gone to the beach" – which, again, as a following splice suggests, was probably a set-up for Ollie to then say, "He wanted to come clean." If the "beach" line got as big a laugh in 1931 as it does today, there was no need for the "come clean" addition, as it would have been drowned out by laughter anyway.

FORM 21 11-30 5M HOME PTG. CO

Hal Roach Studios, Inc.

DATE **5/8/31**

PICTURE No. **L-1**

DAILY PRODUCTION SHEET

Hopkins   Lloyd

DIRECTOR **Horne**   ASST. DIRECTOR **Lightfoot**   PROP **King**   CAMERA **White**

TIME OF CALL   **9 a.m.**   WHERE TO REPORT   **Studio**

WHERE COMPANY WILL WORK

A	B
1. Int. Babes Apt.	1.
2. Int. Drug Store	2.
3.	3.

PEOPLE CALLED

NAME	WARDROBE	HAND PROPS.
Stan		
Babe		
Chas. Hall		
Gertie Astor		
Linda Loreda	ok	ok

TRANSPORTATION	EXTRA EQUIPMENT	SPECIAL EQUIPMENT

REMARKS:

NEGATIVE EXPOSED YESTERDAY_____ NO. OF DAYS ON PICTURE **2**

This production sheet, the only one that calls for "Chas. Hall," tells us that his scene was filmed on May 8, 1931.

Detective Eddie Baker leads his quarry off to the pokey in this scene that's not quite in the movie.

Stan wants to come clean in every possible way.

PRESS SHEET

HAL ROACH - Metro-Goldwyn-Mayer

STAN LAUREL
AND
OLIVER HARDY
COMEDIES

Comedies That Pull Like Feature Pictures! The Greatest
of All Comedy Teams Will Mean Plenty at the
B.O. if You Get Behind—

COME CLEAN

SYNOPSIS

The Hardys' anticipation of a nice quiet evening at home was shattered with the appearance of the Laurels, Mr. and Mrs. At the suggestion of Mr. Laurel the men go out for some ice cream, and on the way back encounter a woman with suicide in her mind. This desperate woman jumped over the parapet and into the swirling waters below. Mr. Hardy followed with the intentions of saving her. It was up to Mr. Laurel to save them both. The woman, who has a reward on her head, calls them both meddlesome fools because she didn't want to live, and therefore Messrs. Laurel and Hardy must take care of her. With no small amount of screaming they are finally compelled to take her up to Mr. Hardy's apartment, and hide her in the bedroom beyond the suspicious eyes of their wives. In the meanwhile detectives, having seen her enter, surround the apartment house. The wives discover the woman and Babe shoves her and Stan into the bathroom, absolving himself of all blame and committing Stan. The detectives, hearing the commotion, enter and break down the bathroom door. Stan is in the tub, a la ostrich style and the woman behind the door. The detectives capture the woman and tell Stan to appear at the station to collect the reward. Mr. Hardy is so mad that he pulls the stopper out of the bathtub and sends Mr. Laurel to the beach via the pipe line.

SHORT PARAGRAPHS

With the capable assistance of Gertrude Astor, Linda Loredo and Mae Busch, Stan Laurel and Oliver Hardy have produced two of the funniest and fastest reels in comedy history. "COME CLEAN", their latest Hal Roach comedy, which is now on the program at the ...... Theatre is another notch in the careers of these irresistible comedians.

⁕ ⁕ ⁕

For an inexhaustible amount of fun and laughter Laurel and Hardy, famed Hal Roach comedians, can always be depended upon. Their latest fun fest, "COME CLEAN", which is now on the program at the ...... Theatre is the best bit of nonsense yet enacted by these popular comedians.

LAUREL-HARDY ABSURD? PERHAPS, BUT CERTAINLY FUNNY

"Come Clean", latest comedy, ranks high among their screen successes

Laurel and Hardy welcome absurd situations if only for the fact that they have to get out of them. After the usual exclamation of Mr. Hardy, "Here's another nice mess you've got me into", the boys proceed in their own bunglesome manner to absolve themselves.

In "COME CLEAN", which is now on the program at the ...... Theatre, Laurel and Hardy aimlessly wander from one ticklish "mess" to another. One often wonders how two men could

be so dumb, so utterly brainless, and live, although both Mr. Laurel and Mr. Hardy claim that it took long years of study and practicing to appear as fatuous as they do on the screen.

"COME CLEAN" is the story of two men, their wives, and a desperate woman. Laurel and Hardy have the hard luck of rescuing a woman from the river and this woman rewards them by forcing herself on them regardless of their lives. The boys have a hard time keeping their little secret when the woman hides herself in the Hardy bedroom and the two wives converse in the room beyond.

Gertrude Astor and Linda Loredo play the boys' wives, and Mae Busch is the other woman. They are all good and there is no gainsaying the fact that for real laughs on comedians on the screen today can approach Stan Laurel and Oliver Hardy.

IT COULD HAVE HAPPENED TO ANYONE!

That's why Laurel & Hardy's "Come Clean" Is Rare Comedy Treat

All Laurel and Hardy comedies are laugh successes because these boys seem to have the capacity to extract fun from the most everyday things in life. Laughter is spontaneous throughout any one of their comedies because of their famed Laurel and Hardy manner. To bump one's nose is maddening, but to bump one's nose in the Laurel and Hardy way is quite laughable.

The comedians' latest Hal Roach comedy, "COME CLEAN", which is now showing at the ...... Theatre, is a series of laugh enticing escapades. Mr. Laurel is funny, screamingly funny, when he writes a note to Mr. Hardy, telling him be called. Mr. Hardy is doubly funny in the receiving of the note. They are both a howling success in the purchase of a quart of ice cream, and when they try to hide a woman from their wives —well, if you don't enjoy Laurel and Hardy you have no sense of humor.

"COME CLEAN" is the pitiful story of two unexperienced men trying to hide a woman, a desperate woman, from their wives. The woman, a character of rather uncertain virtues, is portrayed by Mae Busch, and she certainly puts the comedians through their paces. As well as Miss Busch, Linda Loredo and Gertrude Astor, have important parts as the respective wives of Laurel and Hardy.

James W. Horne directed this fun fest, with dialogue by H. M. Walker.

A Hal Roach — M-G-M
Laurel and Hardy Comedy
"COME CLEAN"
starring
Laurel and Hardy

Director
James W. Horne
Cameraman
Art Lloyd
Sound Engineer
Elmer Raguse
Story Editor
H. M. Walker
Film Editor
Richard Currier
A Victor Recording
Western Electric System
Running Time — 21 Minutes
Footage — 1890 Feet

MGM COMEDY SPECIALS

While the mention of "B.O." might be appropriate for a film titled *Come Clean*, in this case it means Box Office.

L-1   Laurel-Hardy

1.   Fade in on dining room of Mr. and Mrs. Hardy's
        apartment, where we see Babe, Stan and their wives seated
        around a table just finishing dinner. Mrs. Hardy asks her
        guests if they would like any kore, and Babe replies, "No,
        thank you, I've had two helpings already." She then asks Stan
        if he would like some more, and Stan says that he would. She
        proceeds to fill Stan's plate up with meat, vegetables, etc. Babe
        turns to Mrs. Laurel with some slight remark about Stan's
        appetite, and when he turns to look at Stan we see that Stan's
        plate is absolutely empty and he is wiping up the plate with a
        piece of bread.

2.   Babe turns to Stan and says, "I suppose there's nothing
        else you can't think of that you wouldn't like?" Stan says he
        would like some ice cream. Mrs. Hardy says, "If Stanley wants
        some ice cream, he can have it. Now Oliver, you just get your
        hat and go down to the store." Stan butts in and says, "Is he
        going to get it in his hat?" Babe says, "No, we're going to get
        it in a pitcher. Go in the kitchen and get one." Stan exists into
        the kitchen and comes back carrying a calendar on which is a
        large picture. Babe grabs it, throws it down and says, "Never
        mind! Meet me in the hall." Stan exits to the hall and Babe
        goes to the bedroom to get his hat.

3.   Cut to the hall. Stan walks along toward the elevators and
        as he is passing the bedroom door it opens suddenly and Babe
        comes out, frightening Stan.

4.   They go down the hall where we see two elevators side by
        side. Babe pushes the bell between the elevators and the two
        come up simultaneously and the doors open. Babe beckons
        Stan to follow him and Stan gets into one elevator and Babe
        into the other, and they go down simultaneously. After a
        moment's pause the elevator containing Babe comes up and
        Babe opens the door and looks out to see where Stan is. He
        quickly closes the door again and goes down. Immediately
        afterwards the elevator containing Stan comes up. Stan pokes
        his head out looking for Babe. Not seeing him, he goes down
        in the elevator again. After another pause the two elevators
        come up again together, both doors open and Babe and Stan
        look out and bump heads. Babe grabs Stan and pulls him into

his elevator, and the elevator starts to descend.

5.   Lap dissolve to interior of drug store at soda fountain. Babe and Stan enter and the clerk says, "What are you going to have, gents?"

   Babe: We want a quart of ice cream.

   Clerk: What flavor would you like?

   Stan: What flavors have you got?

   Clerk: Strawberry, pineapple and vanilla.

   Stan: I'll have some chocolate.

   Clerk: I'm sorry, but we're out of chocolate.

   Babe: Well, how about some pineapple?

   Stan: I don't like pineapple.

   Babe: Come on, make up your mind. What kind do you want?

   Stan: What other kinds are you out of?

6.   The clerk starts to repeat, "Strawberry, pineapple and vanilla," then gives Stan a dirty look and says, "We're out of orange, walnut and chocolate!" Stan says, "All right, give it to me without chocolate." Babe says, "Didn't the gentleman just tell you he had no chocolate?" Babe turns to the clerk and says, "Just give us a quart of ice cream."

7.   The clerk takes a quart container of ice cream, puts it in a bag and gives it to them. Stan asks, "What flavor is that?" and the clerk replies, "Chocolate!" They both take it and Babe says, "How much do we owe you?" The clerk tells them it is seventy five cents. Babe pulls out a lone five dollar bill and hands it to the clerk, saying, "Can you change a five dollar bill? It's the smallest I have." The clerk takes the bill, turns and rings up 75 cents.

8.   Stan meanwhile starts to pull out the straws from the holder. Babe seeing him, smacks him on the hands. While trying to slap Stan's hands away from the straws, Babe accidentally brings his hand down in a bowl full of eggs, smashing nearly all of them. The clerk turns and just goes to hand Babe his change when he sees the bowl of broken eggs, and after counting the eggs he gives Babe a dirty look, goes back to the cash register and rings up the $4.25. Babe looks

at the eggs, and seeing one egg left uncracked in the bowl, he takes that and throws it on the floor with a crash.

9.   Here plant two detectives talking about Mae Busch, a desperate character, and showing her picture.

10.   Cut to a wall overlooking the river on the opposite side of the street from the apartment house. We see a girl (Mae Busch) nervously pacing up and down and stopping to look in each direction as if anticipating suicide. She then starts to mount the wall in preparation for the jump.

11.   Cut to exterior of the apartment house. Stan and Babe enter and are just about to go into the apartment when Stan notices the girl on the wall and calls Babe's attention to her.

12.   Cut to the girl standing on the wall with her head raised to the heavens saying, "Farewell to all – goodbye – goodbye!"

13.   Back to Stan and Babe. Stan raises his hat and says "Goodbye." Babe, however, realizes the situation. He tears out toward the girl, with Stan following him.

14.   Back to the girl on the wall. She turns and makes her fatal leap, going out of sight. The two boys enter the scene and look over the wall just as a big splash of water comes up and covers them. Babe and Stan both take this and realize what has happened. Babe starts to remove his coat and Stan starts to do likewise. Stan is just in the act of taking off his pants when Babe stops him and says, "That won't be necessary. Quick, get me a rope!"

15.   Stan hands Babe the ice cream. Babe takes it, then realizes what he is doing and throws it to the ground, saying "Didn't I tell you to get me a rope?" Stan exits to get a rope.

16.   Babe then gets ready to make a running dive into the water. He goes to the center of the road and just as he starts to make the run, Stan crosses in front of him with the rope, which is taut. Babe trips over it and goes sprawling with his face right in the ice cream. They both take this big, and feeling there is no time to lose Babe takes another running leap and dives head first over the wall. We hear a loud crumpling of splinters, and as Stan looks over the wall he sees that Babe has dived into a boat, which is now folded up, and as Babe unfolds it he reveals himself tangled in a fishing net. The boat starts to sink.

17.   Stan runs to the foot of the steps carrying a life buoy. He sees Babe struggling in the water and throws the life buoy towards him. Just as Babe starts to reach for the buoy it sinks.

18.   Stan rescues the girl, unseen by Babe, who is doing porpoise dives into the water with his fanny in the air. Stan then tries to signal Babe, finally giving him the Laurel whistle. Babe looks up and sees that Stan has rescued the girl. All exhausted, he tries to climb up on the landing, aided by Stan, who grabs him by the seat of the pants, causing them to rip open. Babe takes this big and looking in back of him to see what happened he discovers a big crab attached to his rear end. He takes this big and knocks the crab off, then gets onto the landing.

19.   Babe then tells Stan to grab hold of the girl, who is unconscious, and they start carrying her up the steps. Stan in the lead starts backing up the steps and backs right off into the water again. He quickly gets out of the water and comes back to assist Babe.

20.   They place the girl under a lamp and start working out on her, giving her first aid treatment by working her arms up and down. Babe is bending over her and Stan's knee comes in contact with her stomach, causing her to spout a stream of water out of her mouth right into Babe's face.

21.   The girl starts to regain consciousness and goes into a beautiful talk about seeing a lovely face, at the same time looking at Babe. She gradually turns toward Stan, and one look at his pan brings her to consciousness and she realizes that she is not in heaven. She immediately starts to upbraid them for rescuing her, and tells them that now they have saved her they will have to look after her, and if they try to leave her she will scream and accuse them of pushing her into the water.

22.   Cut to a policeman on the other side of the street, taking in the whole situation. He becomes somewhat suspicious and exits toward them.

23.   The policeman comes into the setup where they are and starts questioning them. They try to explain that they all fell out of a boat. The policeman accepts their explanation and leaves.

24.   Thinking that they are in the clear, they hurriedly start

in the direction of the apartment, but the girl follows closely at their heels. When they get outside the apartment the girl starts to scream and threatens to call for help if they leave her. They try to explain to her that they are respectable married men. She gets over that that will help her cause all the more, and says, "That's fine. Now you'll either listen to me or else!" She once more starts to scream, but they duck into the elevator.

25.   Cut to the upper hallway. Stan and Babe step out of the elevator and just as they do so the door of the adjoining elevator opens and the girl steps out. Stan and Babe both take it big. Babe turns to Stan and gets over that the only thing they can do is to go and explain the whole situation to their wives, lay the cards on the table and come clean. He makes a flowery speech about what they should tell the wives, then tells Stan to go in and do it. Stan takes this very surprised and wants to know why he should have to go in. The girl interrupts and says, "Well, make up your minds!" Babe says to Stan, "All right. If that's the way you feel about it, I'll do it myself." He exits into his apartment, leaving Stan and the girl in the hallway.

26.   When Babe enters the dining room he hears his wife talking to Mrs. Laurel. He starts to interrupt, but his wife stops him and goes on relating to Mrs. Laurel a circumstance very similar to the one they have just encountered, and finishes saying "—and he expected his wife to believe that!" She then turns to Babe and says, "Now, dear, what was it you wanted to tell me?" Babe by this time has wilted, and says "Nothing, dear." She asks where Stan is, and Babe says he will go out and look for him.

27.   Cut to Stan in the hall. He hears someone coming out of the dining room, thinks it is the wife, and pushes the girl into the bedroom just as Babe comes out. Babe says, "Well, did you get rid of her?" Stan says "Yes," and Babe asks, "Where is she?" Stan points to the bedroom and says, "In there." Babe, furious, rushes to the bedroom door and tries to get the girl to come out, but she insists upon staying in the bedroom.

28.   At that moment we hear Babe's wife calling him. They hurriedly close the bedroom door, leaving the girl in there, and come back into the dining room.

29.   The wife asks, "Where's the ice cream?" and Babe tells her they didn't have any. The wife then suggests that they sit down and drink their coffee. Just as Stan starts to pour Babe a cup of coffee they hear loud singing from the bedroom. Stan looks at Babe and they all turn in the direction of the singing. In doing this Stan pours the coffee into Babe's lap. Babe takes this, but realizing there is no time to lose he quickly gets up and says to his wife, "It must be the radio." He goes in the direction of the bedroom.

30.   Babe enters the bedroom where he sees that the girl has taken off some of her wet clothes, but hearing his wife and Mrs. Laurel following him, he quickly pushes the girl into a closet, throwing her clothes in after her, closes the door, then rushes to the radio just as his wife and Mrs. Laurel enter with Stan. Babe starts manipulating the dial of the radio, and turning to his wife says, "Can you imagine anybody leaving this radio on all this time?"

31.   The wives accept this explanation and start to exit toward the dining room. Stan starts looking around wondering what Babe has done with the girl. He then whispers to Babe, "Where is she?" Babe tries to pantomime that she is in the closet, and Stan starts to look in. Babe quickly stops him just as the wives turn and look at them suspiciously, then exit back to the dining room, followed by Stan.

32.   When the wives reach the dining room, cut back to the girl pounding on the door. The wives hear this and take it. Stan, who is still in the passage, tries to cover up the noise by knocking on the door. The wife looks at him and says, "What are you doing?" Stan alibis it by saying, "May I come in?"

33.   Cut back to Babe. The girl comes out of the closet and bawls him out, asking him what he thinks he is trying to do. Babe, all confused, takes a roll of bills out of his pocket and gives them to the girl on the condition that she will go. She accepts the money and tells Babe that she will see him later. She exits, taking Mrs. Hardy's fur coat from the hall tree.

34.   Cut to the hotel clerk and a detective. The detective is asking the clerk if he has seen "Suicide Annie," showing him a picture of Mae Busch. At this point Mae steps out of the elevator, catches sight of the detective, hurriedly steps back, closes the door and starts up. The detective catches a glimpse

of her and starts to follow.

35.   Back to the bedroom of Babe's apartment. Mae enters hurriedly and slams the door after her.

36.   Cut to Stan and Babe and the wives in the dining room. They all take it big and Babe nearly chokes on his coffee. Both he and Stan become very nervous and give each other a look getting over that the girl must have returned. The wives are more suspicious than ever now. Mrs. Hardy looks at Babe and says, "Oliver Hardy, you're protecting someone here, and I believe it's a woman!" They jump up from the table and exit toward the bedroom.

37.   They enter the bedroom and start searching in closets, under the bed, etc. While the wives are looking under the bed, Stan opens the bath room door and we see that the girl is in there. Stan draws Babe's attention to this and they just slam the bath room door as the wives look up and just miss seeing the girl.

38.   Becoming very suspicious, the wives go to the bath room door and look in. They go into the bathroom just as the girl comes out of the bath room door in the passage and comes into the bedroom. She hides herself in the bed, pulling the covers over her. Stan, who has his back turned, doesn't see all this, but Babe's wife comes right through the bath room, through the passage and into the bedroom again. Stan turns, sees it is a woman, and thinking it is the girl he pushes her into the closet and beckons to Babe that at last he has got her hidden.

39.   Babe's wife in the closet starts pounding on the door and trying to pull it open, but Babe holds it closed. Babe pantomimes to Stan to get a sheet from the bed, which Stan does, exposing the girl on the bed. Then Babe opens the door and as his wife starts out he throws the sheet over her and starts struggling on the floor with her. Stan looks around and sees the girl exposed on the bed, realizes their mistake and frantically tries to warn Babe. Babe finally looks over, sees the girl and stops struggling. Mrs. Hardy takes the sheet off and gives Babe a poke on the nose.

40.   Wondering what has happened to the girl, Stan and Babe look around and see the folding bed gradually start to rise and we see the girl underneath hiding. Babe rushes to the bed and lies on it in order to keep it down.

41. The wives then start toward the living room. As soon as they get into the passage, Babe closes the door, lifts up the bed, grabs the girl and tells her that she has got to get out of here. He rushes her toward the hall door, but finds it locked.

42. We hear Mrs. Hardy call out, "Are you coming, Oliver?" Babe quickly pushes the girl into the bath room and pushes Stan in after her, saying, "Lock the door, quick!" At that moment the wives return and looking around the room Mrs. Laurel says, "Where's Stanley?" Babe, all flustered, says, "He's taking a bath." Stan takes his cue and says, "Yeah, I'm taking a bath."

43. The wives give each other the nod and exit to the passage, going to the side door of the bath room. They look in and see Stan in the bath room talking through the locked door – "You can't come in. I'm all undressed." He gets a little cocky and adds, "Believe it or not!" On this he turns and sees the wives in the other doorway. He takes this, and keeping his eyes on them he slowly gets into the bath tub, picks up the long handled brush and starts scrubbing like hell, catching the hook of the brush in the shower curtains ands pulling them down, revealing Mae all exposed.

44. Stan sees what has happened and tries to hide by ducking his head down under the water. Mrs. Laurel becomes exasperated and say, "Stanley, what do you think you're doing?" Stan comes up and says, "I'm looking for the soap. I want to come clean." Mrs. Laurel says, "Who is this woman?"

45. At that moment Babe enters and takes in the whole situation. He starts to upbraid Stan for daring to bring this woman into his house. Mae hearing this turns on Babe and says, "Why, you big bozo, you brought me in here yourself!" Babe at first tries to deny this, but Mrs. Hardy says, "What's she doing with my clothes on?" Stan and Babe both take this big and rush out of the bath room, followed by the wives.

46. Cut to exterior setup of board fence with a sign reading "Gents" and a hand pointing. Seeing the door open, Babe and Stan duck in. The wives come up to the entrance just as a man comes walking out, and seeing the sign, they pass on. Stan and Babe poke their heads out, see that the coast is clear, and come out. As they close the door after them, we see that the sign says "Gents Furnishings." FADE OUT.

Beau Hunks

Production history: Production L-3. Written early July 1931. Filmed Wednesday, July 15, 1931 through Saturday, July 18. On Sunday, July 19, the studio closed for one week. Shooting resumed on Monday, July 27, finishing on Tuesday, August 11. Added scenes were filmed on Monday, August 24. Copyrighted by MGM on November 3, 1931 (LP 2607). Released December 12, 1931. Reissued September 18, 1937. Four reels.

Produced by Hal Roach. Directed by James W. Horne. Photographed by Art Lloyd and Jack Stevens. Edited by Richard Currier. Sound by Elmer R. Raguse. *Uncredited Assistance:* Assistant Director, Morrie Lightfoot. Assistant Cameraman, Edward L. White. Props, Harry Hopkins, and Paul King.

With Stan Laurel (Himself), Oliver Hardy (Himself), Charles Middleton (Commandant), Broderick O'Farrell (Fort Arid Commander), Harry Schultz (Captain Schultz), Tiny Sandford (Legion officer), Jean Harlow ("Jeanie Weenie," in photographs), "Abul Kasim K'Horne (In person)"/James W. Horne (Chief of the Riff-Raff), Billy Bletcher (New recruit 11), Charlie Hall (New recruit 13), Albert Austin (New recruit 19), Baldwin Cooke, Leo Willis (New recruits in

The original 1931 title lobby card.

barracks), Dick Gilbert (Weeping new recruit), Leo Sulky (Fort Arid Legionnaire/Arab), Gordon Douglas (Fort Arid Legionnaire), Hollywood American Legion members (Legionnaires), "3897 Arabs, 1921 Riffians, and four native Swede guides" (Gag title).

Ollie divulges the news that he's going to be married – to his beloved "Jeanie-Weenie." A letter then arrives from his sweetheart, with the sad news that she loves another. Ollie joins the Foreign Legion to forget – with Stan naturally coming along. Forgetting proves to be difficult when most of their fellow inductees have the same photo of Jeanie-Weenie. The boys decide to "leave before it's too late," which only prompts a tirade from their commandant – whose office is adorned with a framed photo of Jeanie-Weenie. The Legionnaires hear of an attack on another outpost, Fort Arid, and are sent to defend it; entirely by accident, Stan and Ollie arrive there long before the rest of the men. They vanquish the barefooted Riff assailants by using barrels filled with tacks. The boys are ordered to search "the chief of the Riff-Raff" before taking him away, and discover his most prized possession – a photo of Jeanie-Weenie.

This film's title is a pun combining the vintage slang word "bohunk," meaning an uncouth person, and the titles of three then-popular novels about the French Foreign Legion written by P.C. Wren – *Beau Geste, Beau Sabreur,* and *Beau Ideal.* The last had been made into an RKO feature starring Ralph Forbes and Loretta Young, released on January 25, 1931. It must have still been on the mind of somebody at the Roach writing staff in July, as many elements of the Laurel and Hardy picture are direct references to the RKO feature. For example, one character in that film is "Major LeBaudy," pronounced as "Lebbidy." Surely this must be the inspiration for the references in the Laurel and Hardy film to "Mr. Levity." In Britain, "bohunk" was evidently not a well-known term, and the title was changed to *Beau Chumps.*

Beau Hunks is the team's only four-reeler, running 37 minutes. MGM, as the film's distributor, capitalized on this by giving the film extra promotion to exhibitors. Hal Roach did not profit from the film's extra length, because it only counted as one of the two-reel comedies paid for by exhibitors at the start of the 1931-32 season. He explained in January 1981, "It was already sold as a two-reeler; we couldn't get any more dough out of all the circuits because they'd already bought it. It was intended to be a two-reel comedy, but it kept getting funnier, and it ended up as a four-reeler. And it was so good that we didn't want to cut it, you know what I mean?" This is one of many examples where Hal Roach proved that, as he said, "Never in my life was it 'Oh, my God, the money I'm going to lose on this,' or 'The money I'm going to make on that.' The whole basis was either how good or how bad the picture was. That applies to everything I made. I never in my whole career paid any particular attention to the finances."

One area where Mr. Roach did save money was in the choice of this film's leading lady – in fact, the only female in the entire cast. It's Jean Harlow, who in July 1931 was becoming an audience favorite thanks to her performances in the World War epic *Hell's Angels* and the gritty gangster drama *The Public Enemy.* The photograph is a portrait of her in the revealing black dress she wore in *Double Whoopee,* filmed in early February 1929. Hal Roach recalled, "Jean Harlow, who started with me and then went to Metro, gave me the permission to use her [photo] for free… I got a very nice leading lady for nothing!"

Deeply in love with Jeanie Weenie, Ollie plays and sings a blissful serenade –

Before *Beau Hunks* was reissued in September 1937, someone at the Roach studio, quite possibly Stan Laurel or Hal Roach himself, decided to tighten the film and eliminate some footage. The prints we have today all derive from this reissue, which omits the first moments of the original cut, in which Ollie sang "Pagan Love Song." The film now starts at the end of what the script calls section 4. We have the gag of Stan cutting the fertilizer ad out of the newspaper and inadvertently cutting away a section of the chair's leather seat, but we don't get the dialogue exchange about strawberries.

One surprise yielded by the script is that Stan, too, is one of Jeanie-Weenie's paramours, thus has a more pressing need to join the Foreign Legion than just being Ollie's faithful companion.

In the film, it's Ollie who bounces so high on a spring, and he doesn't just cause all of

-- which has a discordant finale.

"You vampire. You wrecker of men's happiness!" Miss Harlow is in the dress she wore (sort of) in *Double Whoopee* (1929).

Commandant Charles Middleton and Captain Harry Schultz inspect two new recruits.

the pictures to fall off the wall; he lands on, and destroys, the piano that only moments before was providing such lovely accompaniment to his singing.

The film's budget evidently allowed for more extras playing recruits than anticipated, because Ollie is not recruit twelve, but twenty-one. Stan also has a different number – his phone number in the film is Hollywood 4368.

One wonders if Hal Roach Studios casting director Joe Collum had a ready supply of "awful looking gorilla types."

Charles Middleton delivers the Commander's monologue virtually as written here, with a few embellishments. Laurel and Hardy also speak their dialogue mostly as written, although Stan usually adds a bit of comedy business. For example, when Ollie tells the commandant, "Well, most luckily, sir, we found out just in time that this woman wasn't worth it," Stan adds, "No sir. You know what she did? She –" and Ollie has to shush him before saying, "and we've decided to leave before it's too late."

The routine of Ollie taking off Stan's boot and massaging his foot, mistakenly thinking it's his own, was first used in the boys' final silent film, *Angora Love* (1929). In *Beau Hunks*, this takes place inside their barracks, after they return from a long, exhausting march. The script places it during a march outside. No doubt Stan and company figured that this routine had to be performed indoors, since it depends on subtlety, much of which would have been lost with shadows, wind noise and the other unavoidable elements of outdoor location filming.

"You forgot what you came here to forget?" Someone forgot to remove the clapper board from the commandant's desk.

The hats that Laurel and Hardy and the other Foreign Legion members wear is more precisely a "Kepi Blanc," with the distinctive white flap of fabric in back to protect the neck from sunburn. Stan wears his backwards in an attempt to protect his face, not realizing that he won't be able to see anything in front of him.

The script's proposed gag of a Riff sticking Babe with a knife as he patrols the high fortress wall is not in the film; the script doesn't explain how the Riff could get up there without being seen, nor where he goes after the gag. Often, when gag writers come up with one good idea, physical reality proves that it can't be put on film.

The script does not include the film's great scene where the commander of Fort Arid awaits help from more Legionnaires, then hears a voice behind the gates saying, "Left – Left – Left foot left –" As the commander and his weary men shout for joy, the gates open to reveal only Stan and Ollie. This would take the place of scenes 72 and 73, which in the script are played seriously and have little entertainment value.

Likewise, the script does not include the scene played with gusto by James Horne where the Riff rides in under a flag of truce and threatens the men of Fort Arid. This would probably go after scene 71 in the script.

Scenes 83 and 84 are replaced in the film by a moment where the Fort Arid Commander asks, "Who will volunteer?" Stan accidentally sticks Ollie with his bayonet and Ollie lifts his arm in surprise and pain, which is mistaken for his volunteering.

Proud Legionnaires.

In the script's section 86, the penknife that is described in the early scenes comes back into play. This cute moment in the script might have been in the original cut of the film, but it is not included in the 1937 reissue that we have today.

Scene 100 in the script shows that the writers hadn't yet thought of the funny and characteristic way in which Laurel and Hardy vanquish the Riffs – by taking barrels of tacks and spreading them on the ground, thus rendering the barefooted attackers

Capturing "the chief of the Riff-Raff," played by director James Horne. Commander Broderick O'Farrell and Captain Schultz look on.

unable to advance. Whoever was writing this script was focusing a bit too much on the dramatic aspects of the story – not necessarily a bad thing, but there's precious little comedy in the Fort Arid scenes as written.

The script really loses its way during and after the Fort Arid battle. The mutiny among the Legionnaires – and the dispute that separates Stan and Ollie – is nowhere to be found in the film, happily.

Poor Jeanie-Weenie, who provides the film's final gag, absolutely disappears from the script after the scenes in the barracks, and it's surprising that the writers didn't have this wrap-up planned from the beginning. Jeanie's final appearance provides a much funnier finish than the script's business with the penknife.

The script's finale would have provided a nice scene of affection and bonding between Stan and Ollie, but would have been difficult to film – these are night scenes, and how would Ollie take Stan's knapsack and put it over his own shoulder, or give Stan a big hug, while still marching at night? Likewise, the business of Stan cleaning his nails is a bit too intricate to perform as the boys continue marching. The ending as filmed is more direct and germane to the story. It was clearly cheaper and easier to film, is much funnier, and provides a satisfying conclusion in every regard.

L-3 – LAUREL-HARDY

1.   Fade in on interior of bachelor apartment. Stan is seated
        on a chair near the fireplace reading newspaper and smoking
        a pipe. Babe is seated at the piano playing and singing "The
        Pagan Love Song."

2.   Closeup of Stan looking worried.

3.   Cut to insert of newspaper showing a fertilizer
        advertisement.

4.   Stan calls over to Babe, and Babe stops playing. Stan
        says, "Say, what do they use fertilizer for?" and Babe replies,
        "Oh, they use it for lots of things. Some people put it on their
        strawberries."

        Stan: "On their strawberries?"

        Babe: "Certainly!"

        Stan: "I must try it – I've always put sugar and cream on
        mine."

        Babe gives him a dirty look and resumes playing the
        piano and singing "I Love You" etc.

5.   Stan gets up and lays the paper on the leather chair,
        then taking a pen-knife out of his pocket he cuts out the ad,
        incidentally cutting a big piece of the leather out of the seat
        of the chair. When he lifts the paper off the chair we see the
        leather is cut through, which reveals the top of a big spring.
        Stan takes it and sits down quickly to cover it up. He starts to
        close up the knife. Babe sees it, crosses to him, takes the knife
        from him and says "What are you doing with my knife?" He
        puts the knife in his pocket and goes back to the piano.

6.   Cut to Babe singing "I Love You, I Love You."

7.   Cut back to Stan looking over at Babe and listening. Then
        he says, "What are you looking so mushy about?"

8.   Back to Babe; he gets over gushingly, "I'm glad you asked
        me. I can't keep it from you any longer."

        Stan: "What?"

        Babe: "I'm going to be married."

        Stan: "You don't believe me! Who to?"

Babe: "Why, a woman, of course. Did you ever hear of anybody marrying a man?"

Stan: "Yes."

Babe: "Who?"

Stan: "My sister."

9.   Babe gives Stan a dirty look and says, "This is no time for levity." The word "levity" worries Stan. Babe continues, "She's the sweetest girl you ever saw. To know her is to love her. Well read, travelled all over the world; everybody loves her – and she's mine, all mine!" Babe looks to Stan for a reaction and Stan says, "What does 'levity' mean?"

10.   Babe is about to try and explain when we hear a knock at the door. Stan picks up the phone and says "Hello."

Babe: "What are you doing?"

Stan: "Someone was knocking on the phone."

Babe: (Disgusted) "That's levity!"

Stan: (Into phone) "Hello, Mr. Levity."

11.   There is another knock on the door and Babe annoyed says, "Answer that door." Stan crosses to the door, disclosing the spring attached to his pants. Babe resumes playing and singing.

12.   Stan opens the door and a bellboy hands him a letter. He takes it and says "Thank you, Mr. Levity." Stan hands the letter to Babe, who takes it, gets up from the piano and smells the envelope, getting over he recognizes the perfume. He starts to look around the room, looking in drawers, etc., and finally says, "I can't find my glasses – you read it."

13.   Stan takes the letter, smells it and his hat blows off. He opens the letter and starts to read: "Dearest, darling Oliver -- " Babe smiles.

Stan: (reading) "As I sit writing this note to you, with your picture in front of me –"

Babe smiles gushingly.

Stan: (reading) "—I have decided that all is over between us, for I love another. Your one time sweetheart."

Babe: "Oh!"

Stan: "What's the matter?"

Babe: "Didn't you read it?"

Stan: "Yes, but I wasn't listening. It's addressed to you. Wait a minute – there's some more. (Reading:) B.S. – It's best we never see each other again."

Babe: "What does she mean, B. S.?"

Stan: (Thinking) "Big sucker, I guess."

14.   Babe takes it again and reaches in his pocket, taking out a picture, and we insert photograph of Jean Harlow signed "Occasionally yours, Jean."

15.   Closeup of Babe as he says, "You vampire! You temptress! You wrecker of men! A rag, a bone and a hank of hair! I've learned about women from you!" He tears the picture to pieces and gives a big sigh.

16.   Stan having seen the picture also gives a big sigh. He then pulls a picture out of his pocket and we insert it. It is the same picture of Jean Harlow, only signed "Sometimes yours, Jeanie Weenie." Stan looking at the picture starts to upbraid it, saying, "You vampire – you temptress – you wrecker of men – you levity!"

17.   Babe pushes Stan and Stan falls to the floor. The spring makes him bounce way up in the air, falling down on Babe and they both go to the floor, causing all the pictures to fall off the wall.

18.   Go to closeup. They get up and Babe says, "I see it all. So you're the 'another.' That B. S. meant that we're both suckers." Then pointing towards the open door Babe says "Come!" Stan asks, "Where are we going?" and Babe replies, "We're going to forget!" FADE OUT

19.   Fade in on long shot of court yard of the Foreign Legion headquarters. A band is heard playing and a command is given for the soldiers to stand at attention.

20.   The gates are opened and the band enters, followed by new recruits, including Stan and Babe, with officers in charge, etc. They halt and the officer hands some papers to the Commander.

21.   The Commander looks over the papers and another officer goes to the end of the line and yells "Count off!" The

recruits start counting off, "One, two, three," etc., and we pan down the line until we come to Babe and Stan. Babe calls out "Twelve." Stan is looing around and hasn't been listening. The Commander calls to him to attract his attention and says, "Hey! What's your number?" Stan looks dumb and replies, "Morningside 4876." All the recruits laugh and the Commander looks very stern and yells out, "Silence! This is no place for levity!"

22.   Stan does a big takem and the Commander looks sternly at him and says, "What's your name?" Babe figuring that Stan is in a jam, tries to help him out by stepping out and introducing him to the Commander, saying "This is my friend Mr. Laurel." Stan extends his hand to shake hands and Babe smacks it away, then introduces himself, saying, "My name is Mr. Hardy – Oliver Hardy." He fiddles with his tie as the Commander looks at them and says, "Joined up together, huh?" They both nod and Stan says, "Yes, Ma'am." Babe smacks Stan's hand again. The Commander says, "You're a sorry looking pair," and Stan says, "We're not sorry."

23.   The Commander asks them what prompted them to join the Legion. Babe gets all fussed and doesn't want to say, but Stan pipes in and says, "We came to forget." The Commander says, "Forget what?" Stan looks blank and then says, "I forgot."

24.   The Commander turns to his aide and says, "He forgot what he came to forget!" He turns back to the boys and says, "Well, we won't let you forget what you're here for."

25.   The Commander turns to his Captain and says "Put them through the routine and tomorrow we'll start to whip them into shape." He exits. The Captain commences giving orders. "Right about face – forward march!" and they all exit.

26.   Lap dissolve to the dormitory; the men are on with uniforms on their bunks. They are opening bundles, suitcases, etc.

27.   Cut to Stan and Babe beside their bunks. They have their uniforms and are starting to change.

28.   Cut to a bunk alongside of Stan. A man is taking things out of his suitcase. He throws out a picture of Jean Harlow onto the bed. Stan does a double takem when he sees it. He

nudges Babe and Babe looks over and sees the picture. He does a takem, and Stan does another takem as he looks in another direction. Babe takes it and we cut and show another guy with Jean's picture, crying over it.

29.   Stan and Babe look at each other and Stan does another double takem; Babe also, and we show a guy across the way nailing a picture of Jean on the wall with his boot. Stan and Babe look at each other again and do another takem. Each one of these characters is an awful looking gorilla type.

30.   Stan repeats some of the lines that Babe spoke in the first part of the picture: "To know her is to love her; travelled all over the world; everybody loves her, and she's mine, all mine!" Babe reacts to each line, then suddenly swells his chest and gets over he has made a decision. He says to Stan, "Come on." Stan says, "Where are you going?" Babe says, "Never mind; come on!" They exit.

31.   Lap dissolve to the Commander's quarters, two Senegalese soldiers guarding the door and the Commander seated at his desk. There is a knock on the door and the Commander says, "Come in."

32.   An officer enters to the Commander, salutes and says, "Two of the recruits wish to see you, sir." The Commander says, "Oh, I can't be bothered!"

Officer: "I beg to remind you, sir, it is their prerogative."

Commander: "All right – show them in."

33.   The officer signals to the guards, the doors are opened and Stan and Babe walk in and stand by the desk. The Commander without looking up says, "Well?"

Babe: We would like to rectify a small mistake.

Com: Mistake?

Babe: Yes, sir. Since joining your army we find we've been disillusioned.

Com: Disillusioned?

Babe: Yes, sir – you see, sir, it's like this: We came here because of a woman.

Com: Yes, ninety percent of us do. What of it?

Babe: Luckily we found out just in time that this one

wasn't worth it, so we've decided to leave before it was too late.

    Com: You've decided to leave?

    Stan: Yes, and you don't have to fire us, because we quit.

34.   The Commander looks at them and says, "You quit, eh?" Babe and Stan both nod their heads, and the Commander suddenly bursts forth like a firecracker and says, "What do you think this is? A picnic? You're here to stay! This is the army of forgotten souls. Men come here to forget – to accept the hardships of the desert and the wastes – to be without food and water, and to laugh at it all. Comrades will fall by your side, and you will take their place!" He continues giving a heavy description of what it means to be in the Foreign Legion, and as he finishes he sits back in his chair and says, "Go back to your quarters." Babe very meekly says, "Yes, sir," and they start for the door.

35.   Stan gives a double takem, nudges Babe and they both look out of scene. We show a big picture of Jean hanging on the wall. The boys look helplessly at each other and exit.

36.   Hold the scene and there is a knock on the door. The Commander says, "Come in." Stan and Babe come back in and they do the hat routine.

37.   At the finish of the hat routine the Commander calls his officer and tells him to get the recruits ready and take them for a good stiff march, saying "That ought to bring them to realize what they're here for." The officer salutes, and as he exits the Commander says to himself, "I'll show them!" We hear a bugle call as we fade out.

38.   Fade in on the court yard. The regulars are all lined up with a couple of officers giving commands. Over this scene the title is running: "Eight Hours Later." As the title dissolves, we hear the sound of drums, the gates open and in come the recruits in uniform, headed by an officer on horseback and two drummers. The outfit is all bedraggled, worn out, tired and dirty. The command is given to halt and right-face.

39.   The commander looks them over and says, "You're looking better already." He turns to his captain and says, "Well, fix them up, and after a good night's rest we'll take them on a real march." Stan and Babe take this as the Commander exits. The captain calls out some orders and the soldiers turn

and march out.

40. Cut to the gates and we hear a bugle call. The gates are opened by a couple of guards and an Arab rides in, dismounts and exits out of the scene.

41. Cut to the officers' quarters. The Arab enters and bows to the Commander, who says, "What news?" The Arab gets over that "the Riffs are preparing to make an attack on Fort Arid and we must have reinforcements or the Fort is doomed."

42. The Commander calls to his captain and says, "We're leaving at once for Fort Arid." The captain has a big takem, salutes and says, "But not the new recruits, sir?" The Commander says, "Take them! I need every man!" The captain says, "Yes, my Colonel," and starts to exit.

43. Cut to the barracks; some of the men are in bed, some half undressed, some lying on the beds in their uniforms, too tired to take them off, and Stan and Babe are in their night shirts. Stan sits on his bed and looks all in. Babe is fixing his bed, patting the pillow, etc., and making it very comfortable. As he walks around to the other side of the bed, Stan crawls into Babe's bed and immediately falls asleep. Babe walks around, gets in and immediately he falls asleep. Stan in his sleep starts murmuring, "We came here to forget." Babe takes it, realizes that Stan is in bed with him and hustles him out.

44. Stan starts to get into his own bed, and as Babe makes himself comfortable we hear the bugle call. All the men take it and start dressing quickly, grabbing their guns, etc. Stan and Babe also start getting dressed, Stan getting into Babe's coat and getting all mixed up.

45. Cut to the court yard, troops already lined up, some rushing into line buttoning their coats. The last out are Stan and Babe and they fall into line.

46. The officer walks up and down inspecting them. He comes to Stan and Babe, who are half asleep, then walks in back of them to inspect the second line and does a big takem. We show Stan has on his long underwear and no pants, with the flap showing in back. The officer says, "What's the meaning of this?" Stan starts crying and tries to explain. The officer interrupts him and says, "I'll see you at Fort Arid – if you get there!"

47.   The officer shouts some orders and the company starts to march out of the Fort, the band playing the Legion number as they exit. FADE OUT

48.   Fade in on stock shot of soldiers marching over the desert.

49.   Close shot of Stan and Babe, both perspiring, Stan wiping his face with his handkerchief. He gets the idea to turn his hat around so that the neckpiece covers his face. They march along a little further and he lifts up the cover and says to Babe, "Why don't you try this? It's great. It keeps the sun off your face." Babe says, "That's a good idea – I think I'll try it." Babe turns his hat around.

50.   They are on the end of the line and as they continue to march they suddenly come to the edge of a bank. The company makes a sharp turn but Stan and Babe keep on going and fall over the cliff. A couple of the men from the rear rush to save them. We see the officer in the background and he yells for them to come on. They rejoin the ranks and make a sharp turn to the right, going down the hill over which Stan and Babe have fallen.

51.   Cut and show Stan and Babe rolling over and over.

52.   Cut to the roadway at the bottom. As Stan and Babe land at the bottom, the officer walks in with his back to them, telling the men to come on. He falls over Stan and Babe and they all fall in a heap.

53.   They finally pick themselves up and the officer says, "I guess we better call a rest period." The troops sit down exhausted, and Stan and Babe sit on a big rock.

54.   Babe pulls his foot up on his knee and rubs it like it is sore. He puts his foot on the ground again, turns to Stan and says, "My feet are just killing me." Stan says, "Mine too." Babe goes to lift his leg up and by mistake picks up Stan's right foot and puts it across his knee. He starts to take Stan's shoe off.

55.   Cut to Stan watching and wondering what Babe is doing.

56.   Babe takes Stan's shoe off, drops it, pats his foot and massages it and says, "What a relief!" Stan looks at him and says, "Scratch my back." Babe takes it and says, "Scratch your own back – I've got troubles of my own." He turns back to pat the foot and discovers it isn't his. He throws it down in disgust and starts to take his own shoe off.

57.   Stan takes his shoe and starts to pour sand out of it, making an enormous pile. When the sand finally stops running, he looks into the shoe, puts his hand in and brings out a big rock, throwing it away. Babe gives a takem.

58.   The order comes to fall in. They quickly put their shoes back on and start to march out.

59.   Lap dissolve to stock shot of the soldiers marching with a sand storm approaching.

60.   Cut to the captain and he gives the order, "Indian file!" The soldiers form a single file and each man takes hold of the scabbard of the man in front of him. They start marching in this formation. The storm is getting worse.

61.   Stan kind of stumbles to his knees, holding onto the scabbard in front of him. The scabbard leaves the bayonet and the man ahead continues on. Stan gets back to his feet holding the scabbard in front of him, and with the terrific storm we get over that he can't see where he is going. Stan and Babe start marching around in a circle, and in the background we see the troops going away from them.

62.   Cut to the captain. He turns and sees what happened, calls a halt and stands watching.

63.   Cut back to Stan and Babe from the captain's angle and they are still going around and around in circles.

64.   The captain finally calls to them. Stan and Babe look up, see what has happened and run to join the ranks.

65.   As they join the ranks, the Captain issues an order to lie down flat, as the storm will only last about ten minutes. Men start kneeling down, covering their heads, and the storm gets terrific.

66.   Lap dissolve. The storm has settled down and we see mounds of sand covering the soldiers. The captain gets up, says "Attention!" and the soldiers all start getting out of the sand.

67.   Cut to Stan and Babe, their fannies sticking up out of the sand. They both get up shaking the sand off, and Stan starts hitting his head and the sand pours out of his ear. Babe says, "Wait a minute, I'll help you." Babe starts to blow in Stan's ear and the sand comes out of the other ear, going out of the scene.

68.   Cut to the captain and as he turns, the stream of sand goes into his eye. He goes nuts.

69.   Back to Stan and Babe, Babe still blowing the sand. Stan sees what has happened and puts his finger to his ear to stop the sand, causing it to backfire at Babe. Babe takes it big and gets over he has swallowed a lot of sand.

70.   The captain gives the orders to fall in and they continue to march. They march along a few feet, and Babe suddenly looks at Stan and says, "Where's your knapsack? Did you leave it behind?" Stan says, "No, I wrapped it up with yours." Babe takes it big, pushes Stan out of the line and steps out with him, and starts to take off the knapsack, which we see is larger than the others.

71.   Cut to the captain; he hollers to Babe, "Get back in line and stay there!" Stan and Babe take it and get back into the line, Babe giving Stan dirty looks and bawling him out.

72.   Lap dissolve to the interior of Fort Arid. The men are all excited. The gates are opening and troops marching in. They halt, the captain dismisses them and they exit.

73.   Cut to the commander of the Fort talking to the commander of the re-enforcements. They are congratulating each other on being on time, etc.

74.   Cut to the barracks; the soldiers on, some lying on the beds again – a replica of the first barracks scene, with Stan and Babe back in their night shirts just getting into bed. An orderly comes in and says, "Sentry duty" to Stan and Babe. They take it big.

75.   Lap dissolve to long shot of the court yard, two sentries marching up and down on the wall.

76.   Go to close shot of Stan and Babe half asleep patrolling the wall. As they meet in the center of the wall there isn't room enough for them to pass, so they have to climb around each other. They salute each other with "All's well," and continue on their way. A Riff climbs over the wall with a knife in his mouth and carrying a box of dynamite. Stan and Babe with their backs to each other do not see him. Just as he drops into the yard, the Riff takes the knife out of his mouth and sticks Babe in the fanny. Babe takes it, runs back along the wall and sticks Stan in the fanny with his bayonet, waking him

up, and says, "Never do that again!"

77.   They continue the march, coming together again and going through the routine of passing. They salute and say "All's well," and continue on. Another Riff comes over the wall carrying a large coil of wire. He sticks Stan in the fanny as he drops over the wall. Stan takes it and sticks Babe with his bayonet. As Babe takes it we hear a voice in the distance say "All's well." This stops Stan and Babe from any further encounter.

78.   They try to pass each other again, but this time it gets a little precarious and they make a complete circle, going back in the direction they came. As they do so, another Riff is climbing over the wall with a "plunger." Stan makes a quick turn to go back, but falls over the Riff. His gun goes off, shooting Babe in the fanny and he does a brodie.

79.   Intercut above with shot of the first two Riffs hooking up the wire and the dynamite.

80.   A bugle is heard and we cut to the yard, where soldiers run out and capture the three Riffs. They are taken prisoners and the Commanders and officers surround them. The officers see the dynamite all rigged up, and one Commander tells the other, "Find out the enemy's position. Make them talk!" He exits.

81.   Cut to Stan and Babe in line with the troops. Their commander walks over to Stan, kisses him on both cheeks and Stan takes it. The Commander stands back admiringly and says, "Stout fellow!" Stan looks at Babe and says, "He means you."

82.   The other commander comes in with a map and the first one says, "What news?" The second commander says, "We made them talk – we were lucky enough to get the plans of the enemy position. Their strongest point is there." (Pointing to the map.)

83.   The first Commander turns to the troops and says, "Legionnaires, we are outnumbered six to one. Our only chance is to silence the enemy's machine gun nest, and that means certain death. Who will volunteer?"

84.   We hear a voice of an officer giving an unintelligible order. The two lines of soldiers take a pace to the rear, leaving

Stan and Babe alone in front. The commander turns and sees them, a big smile comes over his face and he goes to Stan, salutes him and says, "Mon brave!" He shakes Stan by the hand and says, "But we only need one." The Commander takes Babe by the arm and says, "Come," leading him out of the scene. An order is given again and the troops dismiss.

85.   Cut to the gate. Babe is on and the commander is giving him the box of dynamite, attached to which is the coil of wire. He asks one of the soldiers if everything is connected up.

86.   Stan enters with a few soldiers as the Commander says to Babe, "Now go ahead." He opens the gate and Babe looks out worried. He turns to Stan and says, "Good bye." He and Stan shake hands and Stan says, "Good bye, Ollie. Be careful of the riff-raffs." Babe looks kindly at Stan, feels in his pocket, pulls out the little pen-knife and says, "You always did like this, didn't you?" Stan nods and Babe hands it to him.

87.   The officer interrupts and says, "Come on, there's no time to be lost." Stan and Babe shake hands again. The officer hands Babe a gun and says, "When you've got it planted, signal with this." Babe takes the gun and exits. The soldiers all crowd around watching.

88.   Cut to shot of some Riffs behind rocks, with a machine gun pointed over the top.

89.   Cut to Babe crawling along inch by inch.

90.   Back to the gate. Stan is trying to look over the heads of the soldiers to see how Babe is getting along.

91.   Cut to the spinner uncoiling the wire.

92.   Stan, unable to see good, steps up onto the box of the plunger.

93.   Back to Babe crawling along.

94.   Back to the Riffs; they see something and fire a few shots.

95.   Cut to Babe; the bullets just miss him. He leaves the box and crawls back out of the scene.

96.   Back to Stan and the rest, all excited. Stan can't see, so he steps higher onto the plunger and we hear a big explosion.

97.   The Riffs start firing. They leave their position and start charging toward the Fort.

98.   Babe comes running back all in rags. The troops are taking positions on the walls and an officer yells, "Hold those gates!"

99.   Stan and Babe run to hold the gates, and stand with their shoulder against the left side of the gate. The right side opens unnoticed by them and millions of Riffs run through. Stan and Babe turn and see them all coming in and run out of the scene, followed by a lot of Riffs.

100.   A battle ensues, winding up with the Legion victorious.

101.   Lap dissolve to the officers getting the troops back into line. The Commander addresses them, saying "Men, France is proud of you." He salutes them. An order is given, "Right about face – forward march," and the soldiers do not move. There is mumbling heard in the ranks.

102.   Cut to a few soldiers and one says, "We can't march back now; we're all in." Another says, "I can't face that desert – it's murder." The officers all start shouting commands and a small mutiny starts, some of the soldiers running in different directions. Stan and Babe run into a little room.

103.   An officer shouts, "Don't forget, men, we are Legionnaires, soldiers of France – pull yourselves together!" There is a mumbling amongst the crowd which breaks into a cheer.

104.   As the commands are being given again, we cut to Stan and Babe. Babe says, "Come on, let's go." Stan starts to cry and says, "I can't make it," then gets mad and says, "I won't do it!" Babe says, "Do you know what this means?" Stan says he doesn't care what it means – he can't go another step. Babe says, "All right, take the consequences – I'm going."

105.   Babe exits and takes his place in line. The drums start and the soldiers start to march out singing a Legion number.

106.   As they march out the gate, we cut back to Stan and we hear the singing over his scene. He is fighting with himself whether to stay or go. He finally makes his decision and rushes out of the room.

107.   Cut to a shot of the soldiers marching along the desert.

108.   Close shot of Babe marching, looking straight ahead. The others are still singing.

109. Cut to a shot of Stan running across the desert. He finally catches up with the troops, runs alongside of them and takes his place beside Babe. Babe doesn't notice him. Stan keeps looking at Babe, then quietly slips his arm through Babe's. Babe turns and takes it when he sees Stan. Stan gives him the grin and Babe gives a nod of approval.

110. They continue marching, and Stan keeps lifting up his knapsack, getting over it is heavy. Babe watches him, then quietly takes the knapsack and puts it over his own shoulder. He gives Stan a big hug and they continue marching, with the soldiers still humming the song.

111. Stan pulls out the pen-knife and starts to clean his nails. Babe takes it, goes right back into his character again, roughly takes the knife from Stan and gives him a push. Stan is a little bit bewildered, thinking he was all set with Babe, and gives one of those helpless looks as they continue marching. FADE OUT.

ANY OLD PORT

Production history: Production L-4. Action script and H.M. Walker's dialogue script written circa September 9 through 14, 1931. Filmed Monday, September 14 through Wednesday, September 23. Added scenes shot Monday, November 9 through Wednesday, November 11. Copyrighted February 4, 1932 by MGM (LP 2818). Released March 5, 1932. Two reels.

Produced by Hal Roach. Directed by James W. Horne. Photographed by Art Lloyd. Edited by Richard Currier. Sound by Elmer Raguse. Dialogue by H.M. Walker. *Uncredited Assistance:* Director, James Parrott. Assistant Cameraman, Edward L. White.

With Stan Laurel (Himself), Oliver Hardy (Himself), Walter Long (Mugsie Long), Jacqueline Wells (The reluctant bride), Harry Bernard (Harry Bernard, boxing stadium manager), Robert "Bobby" Burns (Justice of the Peace), Eddie Baker (Policeman), Frank Terry (Lunch wagon proprietor), Dick Gilbert, Pete Gordon (Mugsie's seconds), Charlie Hall (Stan's second), Sam Lufkin (Referee), Will Stanton (Drunken spectator), Baldwin Cooke, Charles Lloyd, Sammy Brooks, Helen Gilmore, Ed Brandenburg, Jack Hill (Spectators).

Stan and Ollie, sailors returning from a whaling voyage, check into a run-down hotel and discover that the manager, Mugsie Long, is trying to trap his servant girl into an unwanted marriage. The boys do their best to prevent it – the fracas results in the girl making her escape and Mugsie falling off a pier into the sea. Long vows to get even with Stan and Ollie if he ever sees them again. The boys discover that they've left all of their pay in their hotel room and clearly don't want to return to it. Help arrives in the form of Ollie's old pal Harry, a boxing promoter, who offers the boys $50 to fight a preliminary match. At the stadium, they discover that Stan's opponent will be Mugsie Long.

Any Old Port is a showcase for Walter Huntley Long, making his second of five appearances with Laurel and Hardy. Like Charles Middleton and Arthur Housman, although his films with the team were few, his performances were so vivid that he remains one of the favorite L&H supporting players.

The fair maiden rescued by Stan and Ollie from an unwanted marriage is played by Jacqueline Wells, who had just turned 18 at the time of filming. Among her almost 100 films are six at the Hal Roach Studios; two with Charley Chase (*Skip the Maloo!* and *In Walked Charley*), two *Boy Friends* comedies (*The Knockout* and *You're Telling Me*) and a return appearance with Laurel and Hardy as Arline, the title character of their 1936 feature *The Bohemian Girl*.

Stan utters one of his malaprops in *Any Old Port* when he hears about the imminent nuptials, and Miss Wells recalled it fondly. In the 1990s, she told interviewer Mike Fitzgerald, "The skinny one, Stan Laurel, was supposed to say, 'Oh, what a terrible catastrophe,' but it came out, 'Oh, what a terrible catsafterme.' That struck me as so funny. I've never forgotten it!" Indeed, her daughter, actress Pamela Susan Shoop,

In a deleted scene, Tiny Sandford and James Finlayson are glad to be rid of Stan's "African canary."

recalled, "Mom used the line 'terrible catsafterme' all of her life after she cracked up when Stan ad-libbed it in *Any Old Port*."

As you can discern from the above production history, *Any Old Port* was shot over nine days in mid-September 1931 (the crew usually took Sundays off). Then, 46 days elapsed before the Laurel and Hardy unit, with James Parrott replacing James Horne as director, shot three days' worth of retakes. During the interlude, Stan and Babe filmed their cameo for the ZaSu Pitts-Thelma Todd short *On the Loose*, and the entirety of *Helpmates*. It appears that after the L&H crew thought they'd finished *Any Old Port*, preview audiences, or their own intuition, told them that the entire first reel wasn't working.

As a result, this is one of the most informative and valuable scripts, as it fully details ten minutes' worth of comedy material which was cut before the film's release. What was intended to be the second reel of the film became its first, and a new second section was added which is nowhere to be found in this script.

Tantalizing stills showing Stan and his pet "African canary" (an ostrich) survive, and they reveal that the elimination of this footage deprived us of another performance from Jimmy Finlayson – and from Tiny Sandford. Other stills illustrate Ollie teaching Stan how he can "share" his pay, and a few depict the boys tying the ostrich to a hitching post outside Mugsie Long's hotel. Had this footage been retained, *Any Old Port* might well have been a funnier and more cohesive film than the final cut, which is often rather abrupt, forced and unnecessarily violent.

Another cut scene: Ollie knows how to divide Stan's pay.

A few frames of a cartoon showing the ostrich flying away survived long enough to be incorporated into *That's That*, a bizarre reel of out-takes that was compiled by editor Bert Jordan for Stan's 48th birthday on June 16, 1938, during the filming of *Block-Heads*. Presumably, this was drawn and animated by Roy Seawright. W.C. Fields also thought that having a pet ostrich was funny, as he struggled with one on a leash in his Paramount feature *You're Telling Me!*, released in April 1934.

The routine of counting the money with, "That's two for you and one, two for me," probably originated on the stage in British Christmas pantomimes, and Stan may well have seen it as a youngster. It shows up in the Harold Lloyd film *The Kid Brother* (1927) when Flash and Sandoni are counting some stolen money, and in the 1931 *Our Gang* film *Helping Grandma* as Wheezer counts out pieces of candy. Chico Marx used it in *Animal Crackers* (1930), and Abbott and Costello performed it in *One Night in the Tropics* (1940). It returned in the Bugs Bunny cartoon *Racketeer Rabbit* (1946) and in a scene with Peter Sellers and Terry-Thomas in George Pal's film *Tom Thumb* (1958).

Paragraph 7 in the script contains Stan's twist on a then-current and unfortunate expression. Lest anyone think that the "n-word" was something that either Stan or Babe used in off-camera conversation, Babe's widow Lucille told me that neither Stan nor Babe could understand racial prejudice. Babe had essentially been raised by an African-American maid, whom he called "Mama," because his real mother, whom he called "Miss Emmie," was very busy running the Milledgeville Hotel. Matthew "Stymie"

Stan ties his canary to an impromptu hitching post as hotelier Walter Long gapes.

Stan's canary has broken loose from his leash, in an animated bit that survived in *That's That,* a gag reel assembled for Stan's 48th birthday in 1938 by editor Bert Jordan.

Beard of the *Our Gang* series often referred to Stan Laurel as his second father, and his trademark derby was a gift from Stan. In later years, Mr. Beard recounted, "The last two years of his life I used to go visit him there in Santa Monica. It made me feel good to tell him what his friendship meant to me."

On August 26, 1956, 12 African-Americans became the first students to integrate

The boys prevent Jacqueline Wells' unwanted marriage to Mugsie Long.

previously all-white Clinton High School in Tennessee. They faced threats of violence, and whites rioted during the Labor Day weekend of September 1st and 2nd. Stan commented on this in a letter to his friend, Earl Shank, Jr., on September 14th: "I think the negro question down South is terrible & for no reason, its about time the die hard whites paid attention to the L&M cigarette ads – "Live Modern", they do'nt object to the color line when the guys go to war & give their lives to protect them & their beloved South, I certainly do think it very un-American & a disgrace to this great Country."

If scenes 12, 14 and 37 were filmed, another actor besides Finlayson and Sandford would have been eliminated from the film. One wonders who would have played "the juvenile." A possible candidate might be David Sharpe from Roach's concurrent series *The Boy Friends*. Apparently, no stills survive to solve this riddle. It would have been nice to see a happy ending for the servant girl. As the film now exists, she escapes from the closet in which Mugsie has trapped her, and that's her final scene.

Somewhere a supplemental script may exist which describes the action that we now know as the second reel of this film. Having temporarily thwarted Walter Long, the boys make a hasty escape, and soon encounter Ollie's old pal Harry Bernard at a lunch wagon. (Typical of Hal Roach comedies, his real name – or at least his adopted stage name – is his character's name here.) Mr. Bernard is a fight promoter. Since the boys have left their money in Long's hotel and surely can't retrieve it, Harry offers them fifty bucks to participate in a preliminary bout. Ollie jumps at the chance – and takes the entire fifty in advance.

Mugsie has a terrible temper –

-- as the boys discover when he's Stan's prizefight opponent.

Only after ordering himself a sumptuous meal, and telling Stan that he can't have the same, does Ollie reveal to Stan that he is to be the pugilist in that evening's bout. When the time comes for the boxing match, the boys discover that Stan's opponent is none other than Mugsie Long, who now has an extra incentive to provide a knockout wallop.

Behind the scenes at the pier, with Walter Long, Babe, Stan, director James Horne kneeling, Art Lloyd behind the camera, and Edward L. White in front helping with focus. We don't know who the script girl keeping continuity might be.

Through a series of comic events, Stan winds up wearing the loaded glove intended for Long, and emerges victorious when Mugsie pulls the glove off Stan's hand and knocks himself out. Unfortunately, Ollie has snatched defeat from the jaws of victory, having bet on Long to win. Stan is not happy at this betrayal, and starts swinging his overloaded glove. He accidentally clobbers the policeman who has been inspecting the glove; Stan and Ollie make a hasty getaway.

L-4

LAUREL-HARDY

1   Fade in on long shot of the docks. Lap dissolve to medium shot of the good ship Bread Poultice. There is activity going on, the boat having just docked.

2   The captain and first mate are standing by a gang plank. A couple of sailors come up out of the hatchway. One has a monkey and the other has a parrot in a cage. One of them speaks to the captain and says "Where do we get paid off?" The captain replies "Right here," and hands them their pay envelopes. Looking at the pets they are carrying he says, "And let me tell you something – on the next trip we don't want any of these animals aboard. Turning my ship into a floating zoo!"

3   At that moment a few more of the crew pass by the captain with various pets, and as he hands them their pay envelopes he takes it big as he sees the mascots they are carrying and says, "Say, what do you think this is? A Noah's Ark?" He then looks over toward the hatchway and sees Babe, who is holding a small bird cage, and Stan who is pulling on the end of a rope. The captain and mate look at each other, wondering what all the pulling is about, then looking back at Stan we see an ostrich come out of the hatchway on the other end of the rope that Stan is pulling. The captain turns to them and says, "How did you get that thing aboard?" Babe replies, "Well, you see, Captain, it's like this. A man in Port Said sold it to us in this cage." The captain looks at the cage bewildered and says, "In that cage?" Stan replies, "Yes, sir. He told us it was an African canary." The Captain hands Stan his pay envelope and says, "Well, get it off this ship, and don't bring it back!" Stan exits.

4   Babe holds out his hand for his envelope. The captain gives him a dirty look and says, "What do you want?" Babe replies, "Some money, sir." The captain says, "You've got no money coming to you. You blew it all in Shanghai." Babe trying to get on the better side of the captain becomes a little subservient and says, "Well, captain, could you advance me a little on account of our next trip?" The captain just gives him an abrupt "No!" and Babe exits.

5   Cut to Stan seated on a packing case counting his money.
Babe enters, looks at Stan and gives him one of those friendly
smiles. Stan smiles back at him, puts the money into his
pocket and says, "Well, let's go find a room." Babe says, "I can't
go," and Stan asks why. Babe tells him, "I've got no money."
Stan, being big-hearted, takes the money out of his pocket and
starts counting out some bills. Babe gets all enthused. After a
lot of counting Stan hands him one dollar. Babe takes this big.

Babe: What can anybody do with a dollar?

Stan: What did you expect?

Babe: You could at least share it with me.

Stan: What? The dollar?

Babe: No, not the dollar. Share what you've got.

Stan: Well, I've only got fifteen dollars.

Babe: Well, what about it?

Stan: I can't share that.

Babe: Why?

Stan: I haven't any change.

Babe: You don't need any change. I'll show you how it's
done.

6   Babe takes the money from Stan and proceeds to count it
out on top of the packing case. He lays a bill down alongside of
Stan and says, "That's one for you." He then lays one alongside
of himself and says, "That's one for me." He lays another
bill on Stan's pile and says, "That's two for you." He counts
two bills for himself and says, "That's two for me." He places
another bill on Stan's pile and says, "That's three for you." He
counts off three bills for himself and says, "That's three for
me." He continues this with "four," and has one dollar left. He
places that dollar on Stan's pile and says, "That's five for you."
He then picks up Stan's pile and counts the five onto his own
pile and says "That's five for me."

7   Babe puts the money into his pocket and says, "See
how simple it is?" Stan looks a little worried and Babe says,
"What's the matter?" Stan says, "There's a woodpile in the
nigger somewhere." Babe says, "All right, you count it." He
hands the money to Stan. Stan counts it in the same manner
that Babe did, which ends up with the money being all on one

pile on Stan's side. Stan is still in a quandary. He picks up all the money and hands it to Babe and says, "You're right." Babe says, "Certainly I'm right. You don't think I would cheat you, do you?" Stan says, "No, but I didn't want to be taken for a sucker." They start to exit.

8   Lap dissolve to exterior of "Ye Mariners Rest," which is a sailors' rooming and boarding house. Over this we hear a cheap player piano.

9   Lap dissolve to interior. There are three or four sailors sitting around drinking. Introduce the heavy, Walter Long, reading a newspaper.

10   The girl enters and's crosses over to a table where there is a drunken sailor. As she starts to clear off the table he asks, "How much do I owe you?" She replies, "Thirty cents." He says, "How about a little kiss for dessert?" He grabs her and struggles with her and she finally gets away from him. The guy laughs, gets up and exits.

11   Long comes from behind the counter, shakes the girl and says, "What are you trying to do? Drive away my customers? Why don't you treat 'em nice?" The girl shrinks from him and he says, "Now get back to your work!" She gets down and starts to scrub the floor as he exits upstairs.

12   The juvenile enters, stands in back of the girl and looks down at her admiringly. He then picks her up, embraces her and lifts her up onto the counter. He takes a ring box from his pocket, opens it and we insert a cheap little engagement ring with very small diamond. The girl is all thrilled. He puts the ring on her finger and she admires it.

13   At this point cut and show Long at the top of the stairs looking down at the scene.

14   Back to the boy and girl. The boy says, "Get your clothes and I'll be back for you. We sail at noon and the captain is going to marry us aboard ship." The girl says, "Sh-h-h—Not so loud. If my guardian finds out he'll kill us both!" The boy laughs and says, "Don't worry about that big mug. By this time tomorrow we'll be on the high seas, and we'll let him do the worrying." He kisses here and exits.

15   The girl sits admiring the ring, and kisses it. In back of her we see Long coming down the stairs. The girl sees him, conceals the ring and hurries back to her scrubbing.

16   Long comes over, sits in the chair, looks at the girl with a sneer and says, "So, you're going to get married, huh? You ungrateful little hound! After all I've done for you. Didn't I take you out of the orphanage? And give you a nice home? Didn't I bring you up to be a fine lady? And now you want to run away and leave me flat! If you want to get married, what's the matter with me? I'll marry you. Why not? I don't mind. Come to think of it, it's a pretty good idea."

17   He gets up, picks up the girl and starts to maul her, and says, "How about a little kiss?" The girl is horrified and says, "Please don't." Long says, "Come on, be nice to me." The girl says, "But I don't love you." He says, "What's that got to do with it? We're going to be married, ain't we? Gimmie a kiss!" She slaps his face and he grabs her, when the front door bell rings, which stops the proceedings. Long pushes the girl and tells her to get back to work, and shouts, "Come in."

18   Stan and Babe enter and Long asks them what they want. Babe says, "We'd like to have a room and bath." Long says "O.K." and goes behind the counter.

19   Stan and Babe come up to the counter and Babe says, "Could I see a plan of the rooms?" Long looks puzzled and Stan says, "We'd like to have a room with a southern explosion." Babe quickly says to Stan, "Not explosion! Exposure!" Long hands Stan the pen.

20   Stan takes the pen and goes to write with the wrong end of it, and discovers there is no point on it. Thinking it is a pencil, he picks up a knife and starts to sharpen it. Babe smacks Stan's hands and takes the pen from him, and signs his name with a big flourish. We see that the register is about three-quarters filled with names. Babe hands the pen to Stan and motions for him to sign. Stan is just going to sign when Babe reminds him to remove his hat, so Stan hands Babe the pen, takes off his hat and places it on the desk. Babe hands him back the pen and Stan picks up his hat again and goes into a routine of trying to sign his name. The ink splatters all over the page, and Stan tears the page out and starts all over again. He finally gets down to it and we go to insert showing his pen making a cross.

21   Long then turns and gets a key and hands it to them, and starts to leave. Stan stops Babe and whispers in his ear. Babe says, "Oh, yes," then turns to Long and says, "Have you any

objection to us keeping our pet in our room?"

  Long: What kind of a pet?

  Babe: An African canary.

  Long: All right, as long as he don't sing at night.

  Stan: He don't even sing in the day time.

22 Stan goes out to get the ostrich and discovers it is not on the end of the rope tied to the rail. He looks around, then calls Babe and they both look. They hear a honking sound and wings flapping and both look up and have a double takem. Cut to a cartoon shot of the ostrich flying away in the sky. Fade out.

23 Fade in on interior, downstairs. Long is on at the telephone talking to the Justice of the Peace. He says, "Come on over right away. I've got a little ceremony for you to perform."

24 Cut to dining room where the girl is setting the table. She listens.

25 Back to Long. He continues, "Yes, we want to get married. – O.K., I'll pick up the license."

26 Back to the girl; she drops some plates with a nervous exclamation, runs out of the dining room and passes Stan and Babe on the stairs as they are coming down dressed in their regular clothes with derbies. The girl exits to her room.

27 Long hangs up the phone with a laugh as Stan and Babe enter to him. He puts on his cap and starts for the door. Babe says, "Pardon me, what time do we partake of the cuisine?" Long just looks at him dumbly and says "What?" Babe says, "The dejuener." Long says, "Come again!" Babe becomes all bashful and says, "When do we eat?" and Long says, "Chow will be ready in half an hour." He exits out the front door.

28 Babe says to Stan, "How about a little pool while we're waiting?" They go over and take down the cues and start to chalk them.

  Babe: Let's make this interesting. How about ten cents a ball?

  Stan: I haven't any money.

  Babe: Well, if you lose, I'll accept your I.O.U.

  Stan: I.O.U.?

  Babe: Certainly.

Stan: What do you mean? You owe me!

Babe: What do you mean, you owe me?

Stan: I never got my share.

Babe: Oh, you're going to bring that up again. Let's settle this once and for all. I'll give you a chance to win it all back. (He takes out the money.) I'm going to think of a number from one to five. If you tell me the number I think of, you can have the money. Are you ready?

Stan: Yes.

Babe: I've thought of a number. What is it?

Stan: Four.

Babe: Wrong. It was five.

Babe picks up the money and puts it back in his pocket. Stan looks a little amazed and says, "Just a minute. Let me think of a number."

Babe: All right, you think of a number from one to five. Have you got it?

Stan: Yes.

Babe: What is it.

Stan: Fourteen.

Babe: Right. (He takes the money.) Now never bring up the matter again. Let me see, where are we?

Stan: We're here.

Babe gives him a disgusted look and says, "Oh, yes – a game of pool!"

29   The girl enters down the stairs dressed ready to leave, with a little package under her arm. She is very nervous and looking around cautiously. As she gets to the bottom of the stairs she runs quickly to the front door, and as she opens it, Long is standing there. She gives a startled little cry and runs to Babe as Long steps in. Stan seeing the girl run, covers up in fright. The girl says, "Help me, help me." Babe asks her what's the matter and she says, "He's forcing me to marry him!"

30   As Long comes up, Babe steps up to him and says, "Pardon me, don't you think you're overstepping your bounds?" Long just hits Babe right on the nose. The girl screams and rushes toward the door. Long grabs her and says,

"No you don't! I'll put you where you'll stay put!" He pushes her into a closet and as he is locking the door Stan picks up a pool ball and throws it. It hits Long on the head but doesn't take any effect. Stan picks up another ball and goes to throw it harder, as Long turns and sees him. Being caught, Stan throws the ball at Babe. Babe takes it, gets sore, picks up a ball and throws it at Stan.

31   The Justice of the Peace comes in and says, "Well, where's the blushing bride?" Long says, "She's all ready – willing and waiting" (or waiting and willing). The Justice asks, "Have you got your witnesses?" and Long says "Sure." He looks around at Stan and Babe and says, "Hey, you mugs, come here!"

32   Long turns and puts the key in the door. Babe says, "We won't do it!" Long turns from the door, leaving the key, walks over to Babe menacingly and says, "You won't what?"

33   Stan grabs the key out of the door. Long turns and sees him. Stan passes the key to Babe. Long rushes at Babe and Babe passes the key back to Stan. Stan misses it and it drops to the floor. The Justice grabs the key. Stan pushes him against the electric fan and his hair gets shaved off the back of his head, and he drops the key. Stan picks it up and throws it to Babe and the chase is on. The Justice takes it big and beats it.

34   Routine a chase, going into the kitchen where various gags happen, the Heavy being pushed against the hot stove, hit with frying pans, etc.

35   Stan is bumped against another door. The key drops out of this door. Stan picks it up and throws it to Babe. The chase is now on with the wrong key, Long trying to get it.

36   Finally they run out on the dock, followed by Long. Stan throws the key into the water and Long dives in after it.

37   Stan and Babe run back to the hotel. The juvenile enters and they deliver the girl to him. The two lovers embrace and leave.

38   Stan and Babe come onto the front porch waving them goodbye. They look off and see Long coming up over the dock with murder in his eyes. Stan and Babe run over and push him back into the water. At this point a big truck passes behind them and honks its horn, scaring them and they go into the water with Long. Fade out as Stan and Babe are swimming away from Long.

HELPMATES

Production history: Production L-5. Action script written early October, 1931. Dialogue script by H.M. Walker completed October 6. Filmed Monday, October 19 through Monday, October 26. Copyrighted December 21, 1931 by MGM (LP 2714). Released January 23, 1932. Two reels.

Produced by Hal Roach. Directed by James Parrott. Photographed by Art Lloyd. Edited by Richard Currier. Sound by Elmer Raguse. Dialogue by H.M. Walker. *Uncredited Assistance:* Assistant Director, Morrie Lightfoot. Assistant Cameraman, Edward L. White. Props, Harry Black, Chet Brandenburg.

With Stan Laurel (Himself), Oliver Hardy (Himself), Blanche Payson (Mrs. Hardy), Robert Callahan (Telegram messenger), Robert "Bobby" Burns (Neighbor watering lawn).

Ollie, hungover and remorseful, is berating himself in the mirror for having "pulled a wild party" the night before, since his wife is away in Chicago. A telegram arrives, stating that she's going to be home earlier than expected – at noon. The house is a shambles, filled with liquor bottles and other evidence of Ollie's revelry, so he calls Stan for help. The boys create more messes than they clean, and nothing is put in order until Ollie leaves to meet the missus at the depot. With the house now spotless and tidy, Stan decides to light a nice cheery fire in the fireplace to welcome the happy couple. Matches don't light the logs, so Stan douses them with kerosene. Ollie returns home, minus his wife but with a black eye, to find Stan hosing down the smoldering remains of his house.

Helpmates may be the perfect Laurel and Hardy comedy. As with many of the shorts, it revolves around a particular task, in this case cleaning Ollie's home. It also brings back the idea of the boys having naughty fun away from their wives. Ultimately, however, it's a prime illustration of the resilience of Stan and Ollie's friendship. Stan is eager to help clean up the aftermath of the party, even though he wasn't present at the evening's merrymaking. The boys squabble at times, but Stan never seriously thinks about following through on his threat to walk out. When Stan accidentally burns down Ollie's house and sobs out an apology, Ollie lets it go with a wave of his fingers, as if this is just something to be expected.

Production reports indicate that the first day's filming was Monday, October 19, 1931, starting at 8:30 in the morning. The location given is "1645 La Bonia," evidently a gag as no such street existed in Culver City then or now. The prop house, probably just a façade for the opening scene and later a burned back wall, was built on a little finger of property owned by the Roach studio on Carson Street. An actual home was beside it, and others were across the street. The home next to Ollie's burned-out wall is 8885 Carson Street; a parking lot now sits where Ollie's home stood. The house we see behind Stan as Ollie asks him to close the door is 8880 Carson Street, still standing but with a

Stan immediately arrives to help.

The happy bride.

The end of one of Ollie's suits, blackened with soot and whitened with flour.

large addition behind the main house. One wonders what the neighbors thought about the Roach crew's shenanigans happening in such close proximity.

Since the October 19th report calls for Laurel, Hardy and "1 Messenger Boy," we can deduce that Robert Callahan's scene was filmed this day, and possibly the ending sequences, although Stan always preferred to shoot everything in sequence – a very unusual way of making movies, but one which accommodated Laurel and Hardy's penchant for improvising.

The reports for October 20 through 24 call for Stan, Babe (so designated) and "1 double," presumably for Ollie's 108 off the carpet sweeper and his later dive into the stack of dishes. Sunday, October 25 was an off day, but the company came back at 9:00 on Monday, the 26th, the final day of filming. They photographed the scenes with Blanche Payson at the railroad station telephone booth, and the single shot of Bobby Burns, doing another 108 as he waters a lawn. The location specified is still "Int. House" (on a studio sound stage) as on the previous five days, but the interior of Blanche's phone booth was also likely on a sound stage. Bobby Burns' pratfall was probably shot near the façade of the Hardy home.

Studio publicity must always be taken with several grains of salt, but for whatever it's worth, here's what the Hal Roach Studio publicists wrote about Ollie's house and its demise: "A regular five bedroom bungalow was built on the edge of the studio property within a few yards of an adjoining home. Every precaution was taken to prevent the film fire from spreading to the neighboring property but for realism it was necessary to

A attempt to light the stove causes the demise of Ollie's other suit.

be as close as possible to the other house… In order to get the desired results from the ruins of the burned building the studio fire department stood by and took charge of the blaze when the director considered enough of the house had gone up in smoke. Many of the inside timbers of the building were "doped" to keep them from burning through completely and with the help of water some of the house was saved."

Let's remember that the interior scenes for the film were shot on a Roach studio sound stage, and it's quite possible that the crew assembled a "pre-burned" wall and didn't really have to set anything ablaze near the actual residents of Carson Street.

When *Helpmates* went into production in mid-October 1931, changes were about to arrive at the Lot of Fun, the most drastic in the person of Henry Ginsberg, hired at the behest of Hal Roach to cut costs and increase efficiency. The Depression was having a huge effect on box office returns, and Roach had to do everything he could to keep his studio profitable. Within a year, cameraman George Stevens, sound engineer Elmer Raguse, and film editor Richard Currier, all longtime Roach employees, would be terminated.

That lay in the future, but an immediate problem for Stan was *Any Old Port*, which had been shelved and seemed to need some massive reworking. Fortunately, the script for *Helpmates* was a gem. Hal Roach was fond of saying that "Fifty percent of what's in the script will not play," but *Helpmates* was a rare exception. The differences between script and film are slight and few.

The film opens with a dolly shot of Mr. Hardy's living room and dining area, strewn

Ollie learns that his fire insurance has just run out, a scripted bit not in the film's final cut.

with liquor bottles and other litter implicating him as the host of a very wild party indeed. Where did he get all of those liquor bottles in 1931, more than three years before Prohibition would be repealed? (Possibly from film editor Richard Currier, who was the studio contact for "the good stuff.")

Ollie's soliloquy of remorse – "Now, aren't you ashamed of yourself…" – does not appear in the "action" script, nor in Harley M. Walker's dialogue script of October 6, 1931, so it must have been the product of some on-the-set inspiration.

In the movie, the telegram does not indicate that Mr. Hardy's wife is named Mary, nor that her mother has been ill. And it certainly doesn't contain the word "love," since even the wedding picture that Ollie shows Stan indicates that she has been grouchy from the first day of their marriage.

The gag of Stan wearing his bedspread "like a kimono" or more accurately a poncho, is not in the movie – however, the "China vessel," implying a chamber pot, is.

The telephone conversation is so beautifully timed and played, it's surprising to remember that they were shot separately, on different sets, and then intercut. I would presume that Babe was off camera and feeding his lines to Stan, and vice versa, to preserve the correct timing.

Ollie does not say "What took you so long?" when Stan arrives almost immediately after hanging up. It's better that Stan's amazing speed in getting dressed and traveling to Ollie's house isn't examined. In the movie, this scene ends with a closeup of Ollie rubbing his head after doing that "high gruesome" off the carpet sweeper; the huge pile of dirty dishes isn't revealed until the next scene, when Stan has washed them all – again showing some amazing speed.

The boys don't attempt to clean up the dishes in the film; Stan somehow takes care of it. Likewise, Stan doesn't try to put the flour back into the canister.

After Stan drenches Ollie with the water from the sink, in the film Stan has a different line as Mr. Hardy stands there dripping: "How 'bout some breakfast?"

One of the longest differences in the script is a dialogue exchange after Stan has agreed that it's certainly a good thing that he hasn't any sense. It appears that this was filmed; a lap dissolve (something very rare in Laurel and Hardy comedies) takes us from Stan's confused closeup to Ollie at the stove saying, "Take these pants and wring 'em out, while I dry the coat," essentially the last line of the scripted routine.

Ollie's chapeau and sword in the final scenes resemble the regalia worn by the Knights of Columbus, although their uniforms don't have the frilly epaulets. Similar costuming is worn by a group of dignitaries waiting at a train station in the W.C. Fields film *The Old Fashioned Way* (1934).

The last sequences are quite different in the script. In the film, the results of Stan's attempt to build a warm, cozy fire aren't revealed to him, or to us, until a fade out and a fade in to Ollie's arrival back home. The film doesn't mention fire insurance, and when Ollie asks Stan to close the door, he adds, "I'd like to be alone," which is why he sits in that chair in the pouring rain by himself, picking away a piece of lint from his uniform and looking at us as the image fades out.

The original 1931 one-sheet poster.

L-5

LAUREL & HARDY.

1   Fade in on Babe; business getting over he has had a bad night.

2   Cut to the front door; a telegraph boy rings the bell.

3   Babe gets up and goes to the door. As he enters the living room we see evidence of a wild party the night before. Babe gets a telegram opens it and we insert message to the effect: "Mother is better and I'm returning today at noon – Meet me, Love, Mary." Babe takes it and looks over the room, and seeing the state it is in, shakes his head, then goes to the phone and calls a number.

4   Cut to Stan in bed at his home. The bell is ringing. Stan wakes up and turns off the alarm clock. The bell continues to ring at telephone. Stan gets mad and throws the alarm clock under the bed, and we hear a noise like it hit a China vessel. Stan takes it, looks under the bed and brings up a water pitcher and places it on the night table, then lies down in bed again. The phone rings again. Stan now realizes what it is. He sits up in bed and starts to get out. He shows one bare leg, then pulls it back, thinks a minute, then pulling up the bed spread which has a hole in the center of it, he places this over his head and gets out of bed. The spread is hanging on him like a kimono as he goes to the phone.

5   Cut to Babe at the telephone and he says, "Where have you been?"

       STAN: I was here with me.

       BABE: Why didn't you come over to the party last night?

       STAN: I couldn't make it. I was bitten by a dog.

       BABE: Where?

Stan puts down the phone and shows his wrist bandaged up to the phone and says, "There." He reaches to pick up the phone again but by mistake picks up a small nude statue which is on the table by the phone, and continues, speaking to the fanny of the statue:

STAN: And they took me to the hospital.

BABE: Get closer to the phone. I can't hear you.

Stan goes to speak closer into the phone and discovers it is the statue. He takes it, then picks up the phone again and says, "I said they took me to the hospital."

BABE: Was it serious?

STAN: Yes, the doctor said I might get hydrophosphates.

BABE: Hydro phosphates! You mean hydrophobia. Did they cauterize it?

STAN: No, I think they shot it.

BABE: Listen, I want to see you. What are you doing?

STAN: Eh?

BABE: What are you doing?

STAN: I'm talking to you.

BABE: I know you're talking to me! Come on over, I want to see you, and make it snappy.

6   Babe hangs up the phone disgustedly and says, "Talking to me!" The door bell rings. Babe goes to the door and opens it and Stan walks in. Babe does a big takem and when he recovers he says, "What took you so long!" Stan does a big takem and says, "What do you want?"

BABE: I'm in a slight predicament. My wife's coming home unexpectedly, and look at this house!

Stan looks around the room and says, "What's the matter with it?"

BABE: What's the matter with it! You never met my wife, did you?

STAN: Yes, I never did.

BABE: What do you mean, 'yes I never did'? Listen, she's arriving at noon, and if she sees the place like this, she'll know I've had a party.

STAN: What's that got to do with me?

BABE: I haven't time to clean it all up myself, so I want you to help me. You know I'd do the same for you.

STAN: No, you wouldn't.

BABE: Yes I would.

STAN: No you wouldn't.

BABE: How do you know I wouldn't?

STAN: Because I'm not going to get married.

BABE: Will you help me or will you not?

STAN: Sure I'll help you. What do you want me to do first?

BABE: That's the spirit! You clean up the dirty dishes while I go and get dressed, then we'll have a nice breakfast and after that we'll start right in and put this house in perfect order, so that the wife will suspect nothing. We'll put our shoulder to the wheel, take the bull by the horns and put our best foot forward.

Babe goes to exit to the bedroom, steps on a carpet sweeper and does a high gruesome. Stan picks up some dirty dishes, etc., off the table and starts to the kitchen.

7   Cut to the kitchen; Stan enters and takes it big as he sees dirty dishes piled up everywhere. FADE OUT.

8   Fade in on Babe in the bedroom all dressed; he is singing and making up the bed.

9   Cut to kitchen; Stan has finished all the dishes and they are piled up on the table in the center of the set. He then ties a line to the door leading into the porch and hangs the dish cloth over it to dry. Stan then gets a butter dish, places it on the sink near a piece of soap, gets butter out of the ice box and takes off paper wrapper.

10   Babe enters the living room singing and crosses toward the kitchen. He steps on the carpet sweeper again and does a flying leap through the kitchen door, hitting the table and smashing all the dishes.

11   Babe sits up, looks at Stan and says, "Why don't you be careful?" Stan does a takem and lays the butter down near the soap. Babe says, "Help me get rid of this mess." Stan gets the clothes basket and they shovel the broken dishes into it. When it is piled full, Stan tries to lift it but can't. Babe, disgusted, pushes him aside and lifts it up, and as he starts to walk away

with it the bottom falls out of the basket. Babe says, "Why don't you do things right?"

12   Babe starts out to the back porch to get something, and as he pushes open the door we cut to the other end of the cord and show it is tied around the stove pipe. Back to the porch door; the pipe falls into the scene, causing a cloud of black soot all over Babe. Babe turns around with an exasperated look. Stan crosses over to him and starts to brush him off with his hand. Babe smacks at him, then crosses to the sink to wash his hand.

13   Babe turns on the water and reaches for the soap, but gets the butter by mistake, and giving Stan a dirty look he squashes the butter all in his hands as he says, "Why do you always do everything wrong?" He then sees the butter all over his hands and takes it big, grabs the soap and cleans it off.

     BABE: Get me a towel.

     STAN: Where do you keep them?

     BABE: In the cupboard.

14   Stan goes to the cupboard, has trouble in opening it, and as Babe comes in behind him the cupboard door flies open. Insert a big can of flour tipping over. The flour pours all over Babe. He goes nuts and exits.

15   Stan surveys the mess, gets the broom and dust pan, sweeps the flour off the floor and puts it back into the can, then places the can back on the shelf. Fade out.

16   Fade in on Babe in the bedroom, trying to put a collar button in his shirt. It drops to the floor and rolls under the dressing table. Babe gets down on his hands and knees to look for it. Stan enters looking for a handkerchief. He crosses over to the dressing table, pulls out one of the drawers, takes out a handkerchief and starts out of the room blowing his nose, leaving the drawer open. Babe finds the button, backs from under the dresser and as he comes up his head comes right through the drawer with a crash.

17   Stan enters the kitchen just finishing blowing his nose. He goes to the sink, which is full of dirty water, pulls up his sleeve and tries to make the water run out, but discovers that the sink is stopped up. He looks around and finds a sink vacuum with a long stick on it, puts it over the hole and tries to work

it. He finally gives one big tug. The stick comes detached from the vacuum cup just as babe enters the kitchen, and the stick goes into Babe's eye. He lets out a double "Oh."

BABE: What are you trying to do?

STAN: The sink's stopped up. What will I do with the water?

BABE: (Disgustedly) Use your own judgment.

18   Stan opens the kitchen window and as he throws the water out, the window closes and the water all splashes back in the room. Babe steps back out of the way and says, "Do you want to ruin the only suit I have left?" He pushes Stan aside and Stran steps his foot into a bucket.

19   Babe tries to open the window, but it is stuck. He pushes Stan aside again and exits, and enters to the exterior of the window. Stan recovers himself and as he turns to the window he sees Babe, and it scares him for a minute. Babe violently opens the window and the glass falls out. He sticks a piece of wood under the window to keep it up and pantomimes to Stan that that's the way to do it.

20   Cut to exterior and the plant pot falls off the window sill. Babe stoops to pick it up and as he comes up with it, a load of water comes through the window and almost drowns him. He takes it to the camera with disgust. Stan's head pops out of the window into the scene and he says, "What happened?" Babe goes nuts, pushes Stan back into the kitchen and we hear a terrific crash. (See Mr. Raguse) Babe takes it and looks in the window. Show Stan lying under the sink, which has collapsed. The piece of wood falls from under the window and the window comes down on Babe's neck. (See Finlayson re this gag.)

21   Babe enters the kitchen. Stan is picking himself up out of the debris. Babe says, "Now look what you've done! This is my last suit. It's enough to make a man burst out crying." Stan starts to cry and says, "I couldn't help it" etc. Babe says, "Shut up and get this mess cleaned up. Do you realize my wife will be home at noon?" Stan says, "What do you think I am – Cinderella?" Babe takes it and Stan continues, "If I had any sense, I'd walk out on you." Babe says, "It's a good thing you haven't any sense," and exits. Stan shouts after him, "It

certainly is!" He takes it and wonders whether he was right or wrong.   Fade out.

22   Fade in on Stan mopping the floor. He dips the mop in the bucket as Babe enters in his bathrobe, carrying his coat and pants, which are wringing wet.

STAN: What did I say to you before you went out of here?

BABE: Why, you said If you had any sense you'd walk out of here.

STAN: Then what did you say?

BABE: I said it was a good thing you hadn't any sense.

STAN: And what did I say?

BABE: You said it certainly was.

STAN: Now, here's what I want to find out. Did you agree with you or me?

BABE: Why, I agreed with you.

STAN: Well, that's different.

BABE: Suppose I hadn't agreed with you, what then?

STAN: I'd have walked out on you.

BABE: Here, take these pants and wring them out.

23   Stan takes the pants and exits to the back porch. Babe hangs his coat over a chair, places it near the stove and starts to light the oven.

24   Cut to Stan at the wash tub. He puts the pants in the wringer and as he starts winding the pants through we show that they are dropping through the other side of the wringer into the tub half full of water. When he discovers it he picks them out soaking wet.

25   Cut to Babe in the kitchen, just about to light the oven. He sees Stan and exits, leaving the gas going.

26   Babe enters to Stan and sees what's happened. He gets mad again and shows Stan how it should be done. He finally gets the pants wrung out, gives Stan a dirty look and exits.

27   Cut to the kitchen; Babe enters, goes to the stove and places the pants delicately over the chair. He then reaches for a match and as he strikes it, we cut to the living room and

hear a terrific explosion. The kitchen door flies open and Babe
comes flying through, followed by flame, smoke, tin pans, etc.
He lands on the table and a big collapse follows. As everything
quiets down, Stan enters in ribbons and face blacked. Babe
gives on of his helpless looks.

28   The telephone rings. Babe answers it gruffly, "Hello!" He
does a takem and softens, saying, "Hello, Honey Baby. Where
are you? At the depot? You've been waiting half an hour?
Don't be mad, darling, I'll be right down." We hear the phone
hung up on the other end and Babe says to Stan, "Quick!
Get me my suit. My wife's here at the depot and she ain't
laughing."

29   Babe starts to straighten things up as Stan exits to the
kitchen and re-enters with the remains of Babe's suit. Babe
sees it, takes it big and thinks a minute.

BABE: I have it!

STAN: What?

STAN: Never mind what. You go ahead and straighten
things up, and do something to help me.

Stan starts running around fixing things, then gets a
feather duster and starts to dust things off ad lib.

30   Babe finally enters from the bedroom all dressed up in
his lodge uniform – sword, plumed hat, white gloves, etc. Stan
sees him and salutes him, then does a double takem.

BABE: What's the matter?

STAN: Are you going like that?

BABE: Certainly.

STAN: Where's your horse?

The telephone rings again and Stan goes to answer it, but
Babe stops him.

BABE: Don't answer it! It's the wife. Quick, get the place
cleaned up.

STAN: I won't have time.

BABE: Well, do the best you can. I'll stall her.

Babe exits and Stan starts to clean up.

31   Lap dissolve to the set now all in order. Stan enters from

the kitchen and places some flowers on the table. He stands back and admires his work, then notices the empty fireplace and decides to build a fire. He gets paper and wood from a small wood box near the fireplace, sets it, strikes a match, lights the paper and throws the match in back of him. It sets the curtains on fire. Stan is blowing on the fire, trying to make it burn, while the room behind him is starting into flames.

32 Lap dissolve to front of house. Taxi drives up and Babe gets out alone, and we see he has a big black eye. He goes to the front door, opens it and falls right in on his fanny.

33 Cut and show reverse angle, and the placed is all burned down to the ground. Stan is on with a garden hose putting out the embers. Babe takes it big and says, "What happened?" Stan says, "I had a slight accident." Babe sits down on the half burned chair near the telephone and Stan says, "Where's your wife?" Babe feels his black eye and says, "She went home to her mother."

34 The phone rings and Babe answers it, receives the message and says, "Never mind, let it go." He gives a sigh. Stan says, "Anything wrong?" Babe nods and says, "Oh, not much. My fire insurance ran out yesterday."

> STAN: Well, I guess there's nothing more I can do.
>
> BABE: (looking around the place) No, I guess not.
>
> STAN: Well, I'll be going now. Good bye.

He starts to exit, and Babe says, "So long." Stan exits through the front door and Babe calls him back. Stan re-enters and Babe says, "Would you mind closing the door?" Stan closes the door.

35 We hear heavy thunder, and as Stan looks up it starts to rain. Stan puts up his coat collar and starts to go, but the rain gets heavier. Another big crack of thunder. It scares Stan and he runs back into the house and quickly closes the door. Babe is on still seated, holding an umbrella over him. Stan stands alongside of him in the pouring rain. Babe sees him and motions to him to come over and as Babe moves over Stan sits down with him under the umbrella. Stan slips his arm into Babe's and gives a big grin. Babe replies with a smirk. There is another peal of thunder and the rain pours down heavier. Fade out.

THE MUSIC BOX

Production history: Production L-6. Action script and H.M. Walker's dialogue script written circa early December 1931. Filmed Monday, December 7 through Thursday, December 17. Copyrighted March 14, 1932 by MGM (LP 2914). Released April 16. Three reels.

Produced by Hal Roach. Directed by James Parrott. Photographed by Len Powers. Edited by Richard Currier. Sound by James Greene. Dialogue by H.M. Walker. *Uncredited assistance:* Assistant Director, Morey Lightfoot. Assistant Cameraman, Harold Graham. Film editing by Bert Jordan. Sound crew, John C. Whitaker, E. Rowland, Adelbert H. Nece, Sig Baden, Ralph Butler, Harvey Wasden, R.H. Raguse, Al Blodgett. Laborers, John Hill, Fred Opitz, Wayne Murray. Carpenter, Bones Vreeland. Grips, A.J. Wark, C. Goettman. Painter, Luis Betancourt. Electrician, Felix Grisilhardon. Props, Bob Sanders, Ted Driscoll, and Roy Seawright. Piano effects by Marvin Hatley.

With Stan Laurel (Himself), Oliver Hardy (Himself), William Gillespie (Piano salesman), Hazel Howell (Mrs. Schwarzenhoffer), Charlie Hall (Postman), Lilyan Irene (Nursemaid), Sam Lufkin (Policeman), Billy Gilbert (Professor Theodore von Schwarzenhoffer, M.D., A.D., D.D.S., F.L.D., F.F.F. and F.), Billy Algren (Extra).

The founders of the Laurel & Hardy Transfer Co. ("Foundered 1931") are sent to deliver a player piano to a home at 1127 Walnut Avenue, which – as a friendly postman shows them – is situated high atop a long, long flight of steps. Stan, Ollie and the piano make several trips up them and down again; along the way, they encounter a condescending nursemaid, a grouchy policeman, and the contentious and egotistical Professor Theodore von Schwarzenhoffer. Nobody is home at the delivery address, but Stan and Ollie manage to get the piano inside the living room. Soon they are met with a tirade from the professor, whose home this is. He insists that the delivery is a mistake; he hates pianos and proves it by hacking the new arrival to pieces with an axe. Just then, his wife arrives and explains that she'd bought the piano as a surprise birthday present (evidently not knowing about her husband's extreme dislike of the instrument!). Apologetically, the professor agrees to sign for the delivery – but a faceful of ink from the boys' fountain pen sends him into another tirade, and Stan and Ollie fleeing from the house.

Probably owing to its prestige as an Academy Award winning film, *The Music Box* has often been compared to the myth of Sisyphus (say that six times real fast), the poor guy in ancient Greek stories who is condemned to forever roll a giant boulder to a mountaintop, only to have it roll back down. Others might think of it as a metaphor about the frustration of living in the material world, or as a sterling example of "Man plans, God laughs." Stan Laurel, Babe Hardy, and Hal Roach's only concern would have been if the movie makes you laugh, and that it does in abundance.

The ever-deepening Depression prompted the increasing popularity of the double-feature movie bill – which gave you a big-budget "A" feature and a lower-budget "B"

Postman Charlie Hall points to 1127 Walnut Avenue, "right on top of the stoop."

feature instead of the supporting program of a newsreel, cartoon and comedy short. This was supposed to be a better value to the movie patron. That was debatable, but it was definitely affecting the Roach studio, which needed to cut costs and increase efficiency. One of the belt-tightening measures was to re-use story lines from the silent pictures; those old films were thought of as obsolete, but they still retained some value in providing plots. (We're very lucky that Hal Roach didn't destroy his backlog of silent films, as the Universal studio did.)

Using an old story was faster and cheaper than creating a new one from scratch. *Below Zero* was a partial remake of a 1925 Clyde Cook short *Starvation Blues*. *Another Fine Mess* was a remake of *Duck Soup* (1927), both based on a sketch called *Home from the Honeymoon*, written by Stan Laurel's father. *Chickens Come Home* revisited the story of *Love 'em and Weep* (1927). *Laughing Gravy* clearly had similarities to *Angora Love* (1929), which also provided a scene remade in *Beau Hunks*. *The Music Box* was at least partially inspired by the 1927 success *Hats Off!*

Such an economy measure would have pleased Henry Ginsberg, who arrived at the Roach studio in mid-November 1931. He was immediately made vice president and general manager. He would remain at the Roach lot through January 1936, and during his reign – especially the first year – he terminated a lot of the studio's longtime employees. Anita Garvin recalled, "Stan called him 'The Expeditor.' He was always

The day begins promisingly – or ominously.

trying to get everyone to work as quickly as possible." To give him his due, Ginsberg did in fact cut costs at the Roach lot at a time when this was necessary – and in May 1933 he prevented the Loew's executives from pulling the plug on the *Our Gang* series, which would continue for another five years at Roach's.

Speaking of *Our Gang*, the usual L&H cameraman, Art Lloyd, appears to have been working on the concurrently filmed *Spanky*, so Len Powers and assistant Harold Graham substituted on *The Music Box*.

Shooting the long sequence outdoors on the steps was difficult, primarily because the crew was filming in mid-December, the days with the fewest hours of daylight. Even when the sun was shining, the sky was often overcast, so time to shoot in acceptable light was at a premium. (The crew started work at 8:30 each morning, but had to quit between 3:45 and 4:30.)

The crew anticipated these problems and when clouds prevented filming at the Vendome Street location, sets remained standing on a Roach soundstage so that interior scenes could be completed. As a result, *The Music Box* was not shot in sequence, "right through from beginning to end," as Laurel and Hardy preferred.

Daily production reports reveal that the crew shot at the steps on December 7th (filming the opening scenes, including Charlie Hall's helpful directions), 10th (the scenes with the nurse, and Billy Gilbert and Sam Lufkin's first scenes), 16th (more Gilbert scenes) and 17th (the final Gilbert and Lufkin material). The scene where

Nursemaid Lilyan Irene howls at "all the dumb things" she meets right in the middle of her daily duties.

Charlie Hall explains that there's an access road was filmed on December 8th, and the material in the living room was shot on the 12th and 14th, with Marvin Hatley required just off camera on the 14th to play "Arkansas Traveler," "Dixie" and "The Star-Spangled Banner." President Herbert Hoover had signed a congressional act making this the official national anthem of the United States on March 3, 1931, so the boys' dropping everything to salute was a topical reference.

The crew shot a total of 164 scenes, exposing 10,264 feet of film, with the "estimated good footage" at 3,425. This was 38 minutes' worth, which was whittled down to a final cut of 2,680 feet, just a whisker shy of 30 minutes. The shooting ratio of total film shot to footage used was 3.8 to 1, remarkably efficient since most movies at the major studios had shooting ratios between 6 to 1 and 10 to 1.

Despite the Depression, one could still be paid very handsomely in the movie industry. Stan Laurel earned $2,333.33 during the week ending December 26, 1931. Babe Hardy received $2,000. Billy Gilbert was working for $150 per week, as was cameraman Len Powers. Assistant Cameraman Harold Graham got $50, while cartoonist and prop man Roy Seawright earned $45 per week.

On November 18, 1932, in the Fiesta Room of the Ambassador Hotel, *The Music Box* won a certificate as the "Best Short Subject (Comedy)" of 1931-32, the first time short subjects were considered for awards. This was competing with Mack Sennett's

Professor Theodore von Schwarzenhoffer (Billy Gilbert) wants these "two numbskulls" to "get this thing out of the way."

short *The Loud Mouth*, and the RKO Clark and McCullough comedy *Scratch-As-Catch-Can*, which also featured Charlie Hall in its cast. *The Music Box* was not precisely an Oscar-winner, but was honored instead with "a parchment scroll affair," as Stan wrote in 1962. Hal Roach accepted the prize with Stan and Babe and later generously gave it to Stan.

Acknowledging short subjects was the idea of none other than Henry Ginsberg, who on July 5, 1932, had written to the Academy thusly: "Would it not be in keeping with the Academy's purpose to include in your yearly awards some token of recognition for the accomplishments of the comedy and short subject producer, player, writer and director?" The Academy didn't go quite that far, but did create three new short subject categories. Along with the Best Short Comedy, awards were given to the Best Animated Short (Walt Disney's *Flowers and Trees*) and the Best Novelty Short (Mack Sennett's *Wrestling Swordfish*).

There are notable differences between the film and its script. The film's opening dialogue between customer Hazel Howell and salesman William Gillespie was largely improvised on the set. 418 Walnut Avenue was changed to "1127 Walnut Avenue." What significance 1127 may have had to Stan or to any of the other writers, we don't know, although 1127 has a better rhythm and weight to it than 418.

The most surprising revelation of the script is the dialogue exchange between Stan

The combination of Stan, Ollie and the piano is unsafe even at the front door.

and Ollie which directly refers to their having been at the same location for *Hats Off!*, made in 1927. That film was heavily promoted, more than any of the other early L&H shorts, and it's possible that audiences in 1932 might have remembered it. However, since this is also the one Laurel and Hardy film which appears to have vanished entirely, the reference would be lost on most audiences today.

The gag with Ollie creating an indentation in the street after having the piano fall on him is not in the film. It would have been costly and time consuming to dig a hole in the actual city street, and likely would have been frowned upon by nearby residents and by the local government. Also, it's basically a cheap joke about Babe's weight and not terribly funny.

The scene where the cop yells for the boys' attention was given an added laugh in the film, when Stan walks all the way down the steps only to be told, "I don't want you; I want that other monkey." Stan then accurately conveys the message by hollering to Ollie, "He don't want me, he wants the other monkey!" Ollie is perplexed by this strange statement until Stan clarifies it by pointing and yelling, "You!" Ollie says, "Oh," then reacts with disgust when he realizes what he's just been called.

The script indicates that Billy Gilbert was definitely the preferred actor for the role of the professor, and also spells his last name as "Swassenhoffer," although as Billy pronounces it in the film it sounds more like "Schwarzenhoffer." Billy also extends the professor's credentials a bit, with "M.D., A.D., D.D.S., F.L.D., F.F.F.and F."

They could have just let themselves in through the top floor, opened the front door and moved the piano in. Oh, well. There's more than one way to get a piano indoors --

-- and out again.

The complicated sequence proposed by the script wherein Ollie lands on the piano dolly and nearly rolls down the steps was discarded, replaced in the film by an elegantly performed but painful gag in which Stan is carrying a ladder; the edge of it disappears behind the piano crate and after a thud, we hear a howl from Mr. Hardy, who emerges from behind the crate, rubbing his newly-injured eye.

The many repetitions here of The Never-Ending Hat Routine, in which the boys repeatedly and accidentally don each other's derbies, are not mentioned in the script.

Had Billy Gilbert's character told the cop that "They were here fifteen minutes ago" in the film, it would have introduced a continuity error, since this scene is supposed to take place at least two hours after his initial encounter with Stan and Ollie. The film retains only the cop's "If I see them, I'll run them in," and Gilbert's "Thank you, officer."

The grumblings of the piano when Laurel and Hardy are grappling with it at the base of the steps and further upward were added in post-production. The film has no underscoring for a specific reason. Hal Roach explained this in 1986 after a video release added color and a musical score to the film, much to Roach's disapproval. He told historian Richard W. Bann, "Stan Laurel's whole idea there was to clear the track of everything—dialogue, music, everything except the discordant sounds the damn piano made as they crash-banged it around and wrecked it. How could anyone miss that? It's the point of the film: how they're wrecking this piano and just listen to the thing as it complains and tries to tell you so! That's what he wanted people to focus on and hear."

The professor makes a gift return.

While the idea of the player piano rendering a "Medley of Patriotic Songs" is in the script, Stan and Ollie's charming dance while cleaning up the living room is not. Nor is the idea of Gilbert's character seeing the boys' horse, Susie, contentedly drinking out of the decorative pond. Gilbert's line about pianos being "mechanical blunderbusses" was evidently an ad-lib, while his fanatical hatred of the instruments is in both script and film.

Marvin Hatley recalled providing the voice of the piano in the final scenes. "I played with a lot of tremeloes, like a player piano, as fast as I could play it. And finally, when old Billy came in with an axe and chopped it all to pieces, I played that right on the set.... I remember one gag where some of the keys were on the floor, and Billy was running around trying to hit them with the axe, and I'd play a note for each key. But they cut it out of the picture."

What was left in the picture is easily one of the finest Laurel and Hardy films, fully deserving of its status; in November 1997 it was added by the Library of Congress to the National Film Registry as one of 25 motion pictures that year deemed to be "culturally, historically or aesthetically significant." Indeed it is, and it's a lot more fun than the myth of Sisyphus.

L-6 – LAUREL-HARDY.

Fade in on music store. A salesman is demonstrating a small upright player piano. A lady buys it and wants it delivered right away, saying "It's a birthday present for my husband and I want to surprise him." The salesman takes down the address and says, "We'll send it over right away, madame."

Lap dissolve to Stan and Babe coming along the street with a horse and wagon and a piano case on the back. They are driving along slowly, getting over they are looking for a number. They finally pull up to the curb.

A postman comes into the scene and Babe asks him very politely if he will be kind enough to tell them where 418 Walnut Avenue is. The postman thinks a minute, then points out of scene and says, "That's the house up there – right at the top of the stoop." Stan and Babe look off and we show the long flight of stairs.

STAN: Do we have to go up there again?

BABE: What do you mean, again?

STAN: Don't you remember when we went up there with a washing machine?

BABE: Oh, yes. Well, we can profit by that experience. Now we know how to go about it.

They both get out of the wagon and start to work. Stan lets down the tail gate and as he starts to pull the piano case out of the truck Babe stops him and says, "Just a minute – this has got to be done with great care and caution. Let me handle it." Babe gets on his hands and knees and says, "Now ease it down onto my back."

Stan slides the piano case part way out the back of the truck and stops to spit on his hands. He grabs the case again and the horse steps forward, pulling the wagon from under the piano and the piano drops with a dull thud onto Babe's back, knocking the wind out of him.

Babe gets up from under the piano and we see that the force of the piano hitting him has made an indentation in the street. Stan goes to walk around the other side of the piano, steps into the hole and takes it. They pick up the piano case and start up the steps with it.

They struggle about half way up when they meet a nursemaid on the way down with a perambulator and a baby. Babe very graciously decides to put the piano on the side of the steps to let the maid pass. As they get it off the steps, she passes and thanks them. Stan and Babe let go of the piano to tip their hats and the piano rolls down the hill to the bottom. They start after it on the run.

Cut to the bottom of the steps; the piano falls in and we hear the sound effect like chimes from it. They enter and pick it up, and as they get it righted the nurse comes into the scene and starts laughing at their predicament. Stan gets sore at this and kicks her in the fanny. She takes it, turns and pokes Stan in the nose. Babe laughs and she reaches in the carriage, brings out a milk bottle with nipple on it, lifts Babe's hat up, socks him with the bottle, puts the hat back on him and exits.

Babe wipes the milk off his face and motions to Stan to help him with the piano again, and they start up the steps.

Cut to the corner of the street. The nursemaid and a cop are on and she is pointing in the direction of Stan and Babe. The cop says, "Oh, they did, huh?" and exits.

Cut to Stan and Babe half way up the steps struggling with the piano. The cop walks in to bottom of the steps and hollers, "Hey!"

BABE: What?

COP: I want to talk to you.

BABE: (to Stan) Go down and see what he wants.

Stan exits and comes in to the bottom of the steps and says, "What do you want?" The cop says, "I don't want you – I want the other guy." Stan turns and whistles to Babe.

Cut to Babe; he takes it.

Back to Stan, who waves for Babe to come down and says, "He wants you."

Back to Babe a little bit flustered. Forgetting the piano he lets go of it and starts to walk down. The piano starts to roll after him. He turns and sees it and starts to run to get out of its way. Show cut of Babe running, and a cut of the piano gaining on him. Babe trips and sprawls on the steps and the piano enters scene, skids right over him and continues on its way. Babe gets up and we see his face is all dirty.

Cut to Stan and the cop. The piano enters the scene and as it hits the sidewalk it falls over on its side and we hear the noise of the chimes again. Babe enters the scene and the cop says, "What's the idea of molesting that girl?" Babe says, "Who, me?" and the cop says "Yes, you," and kicks Babe in the fanny. Babe takes it and the cop says, "No let that be a lesson to you!" The cop exits.

Stan and Babe pick up the piano again and struggle about three-quarters of the way to the top, where they sit down on the steps to rest. A character like Billy Gilbert, with high hat and cutaway (the owner of the house where the piano is being delivered) starts down the steps. He gets as far as the piano and can't go any further. He stands there a while waiting to see just what Stan and Babe are going to do, and starts getting very impatient. He finally pokes Babe with his stick. Babe and Stan turn and see him.

GILBERT: Just how long are you numskulls going to sit here with this thing?

BABE: What's it to you?

GILBERT: What's it to me! I want to get down those stairs!

BABE: Well, walk around.

Gilbert becomes furious. He has never been talked to like that in his life.

GILBERT: I, the great Professor Theodore Swassenhoffer, M.D., A.D., P.P.S. – I should walk around in the dirt and get my shoes all filthy? Get this thing out of the way immediately!

Babe and Stan get up a little scared at the man's bellowing. They start to move the piano and are doing it so awkwardly that it is getting on Gilbert's nerves. He again becomes infuriated and starts showing them. Stan resents this and knocks Gilbert's silk hat off. The hat bounces down the stairs and the three of them stand and watch it. Gilbert takes it big and in an effort to save his hat he runs around the piano, off the stairway, and steps in a small mud hole up to his knees. He goes nuts and dashes out of scene after his hat.

Cut to the street at the bottom of the steps. The hat rolls into the street. Gilbert enters to pick it up and we hear a loud automobile horn; Gilbert jumps back and the car runs over his hat. He picks up the hat, puts it on, shakes his fist at Stan and

Babe and says, "I'll have you arrested for this!" He turns to exit and we see he has only half a hat.

Cut back to Stan and Babe. They struggle to the top of the steps, where there is a sidewalk and continuing from that are three more steps up to a lily pond which is alongside of the house that the piano is to be delivered to. They reach the top and instead of turning and going along the sidewalk to the house, they continue backing up the steps to the lily pond, and finally fall in the pond, piano and all.

They get themselves out, take the piano back onto the sidewalk and roll it up to the front of the house. This sidewalk is on a gradual slope. They stop at the front of the house and as they go to ring the door bell the piano starts rolling back down the sidewalk. They turn and see it and start to run after it. Follow the piano and it rolls right down the steps again to the bottom. Stan and Babe start down after it.

Fade out.

Title: "Two hours later."

Lap to the top of the stars showing about ten or twelve steps. Stan and Babe enter with the piano and just do make it to the top, all in. They sit down on the top step as the same postman walks in. Babe takes it when he sees him.

POSTMAN: Did you fellows carry that piano all the way up those steps?

Stan looks at him with a sad expression and says, "I don't know and I wouldn't say positively, but I'm afraid we did."

POSTMAN: Why, you didn't have to do that. If you had asked me, I could have told you which way to go. All you had to do is drive around that corner and come up here. The road runs right around.

He exits and Stan and Babe look at each other.

BABE: Why didn't we think of that before?

STAN: Well, we can profit by the experience. Now we know how to go about it.

BABE: You're getting dumber and dumber every day. Come on.

They pick up the piano and start down the steps with it.

Fade out.

Fade in on the top of the steps. Stan and Babe drive in. The piano case is now on the wagon again. They both get off and Stan lets down the tail gate. Babe starts to kneel down the same as he did at first. Stan takes a hold of the piano case. Babe stops him and says, "Wait a minute." He gets up, takes the horse out of the shafts, comes back and kneels down again.

Lap dissolve to them pushing the piano to the front door. The piano case is now on a little piano dolly. They ring the bell but nobody answers. Stan says, "There's nobody home. Now what are we going to do?" Babe looks up and sees the French windows of the little balcony over the front door; one half of the window is open.

BABE: Get the block and tackle.

STAN: What for?

BABE: We'll take the piano through that window, carry it downstairs and put it in the living room. Now don't ask any more questions.

STAN: But after we're in there, how are we going to get out?

BABE: I never thought of that.

STAN: I have it. When we get in the living room we can come out the front door.

BABE: At last you're getting some intelligence. Now make it snappy.

Stan exits and Babe starts twisting the piano around into position, lifting it off the dolly, which is pushed toward the door. Stan enters with the block and tackle and a straight ladder. He drops the block and tackle alongside of Babe, walks over to the door, and looking up at the window he sets the ladder on the dolly, not seeing it. He exits to Babe, picks up the block while Babe is tying the other end of the rope around the case, and starts up the ladder with the block under his arm.

As Stan gets to the top rung he gives himself a little boost to jump over onto the balcony, and the force of this jars the dolly from under the ladder and it runs into Babe's scene, knocking his feet from under him. Babe lands on the dolly and it scoots down the sidewalk and starts down a couple of steps, where Babe rolls off, doing a lot of "Oh's." He gives one of his looks to Stan.

Cut to Stan; he takes Babe's look and hooks the block onto an awning.

Cut to Babe; he shoves the piano toward the front door, gets the other end of the rope, climbs up the ladder and starts to pull the piano up. The piano is balanced straight until it reaches the rail of the balcony, and as Stan starts to pull it in, it tips and the water starts pouring out of the case onto Babe. Babe is in such a position that he has to take it all.

Stan finally gets the piano onto the rail of the balcony. Babe reaches to give it a push when the front door flies open, the ladder fall in with Babe and there is a big glass crash. Stan is pulling the piano into the room from the window.

Cut to interior of bedroom as Stan pulls the piano case into the room.

Cut to Babe on interior starting up the stairs.

Back to Stan in the bedroom. He gets over he hears the footsteps, goes to the window and whistles.

Cut to Babe half way up the stairs. He hears the whistle.

Back to Stan; he says, "Hey, Ollie!"

Back to Babe on the stairs; he exits down again out of a closeup.

Babe goes to the front door and looks up to the French windows.

STAN: There's somebody home.

BABE: Are they up there?

STAN: No, but I heard them coming up the stairs.

BABE: You heard them coming up the – THAT WAS ME, STUPID!

Stan takes it with a dumb expression and Babe exits back into the house.

Cut to bedroom, Stan pulling the piano toward the door. Babe enters and starts to help him through the door with it.

They start down the steps, Babe on the end backing down. They reach the first landing and Babe, instead of making the turn, continues backing and falls through the French windows. Stay with the landing shot; we hear Babe's "Oh-h-h!" and a big splash, and the water comes in through the window, drenching

Stan. Stan looks out the window and we cut and show Babe in the pond again.

Cut to the bottom of the steps. Gilbert comes in with the cop. They look around and Gilbert says, "They were here fifteen minutes ago." The cop says, "Well, their wagon's gone; they must have beat it. But I'll keep my eye open and if I see them around here I'll run them in." Gilbert says, "Thank you, officer," and starts up the steps.

Cut to Stan and Babe just carrying the piano in through the front door.

They get it into the living room and Stan gets a hammer and opens the side of the crate. As he does so the water pour out of it all over the floor. Babe pushes Stan and says, "Why don't you be careful?" Stan takes out his handkerchief and tries to mop it up. Babe smacks him again, then goes to pull the piano out and steps on a board that has a couple of nails in it. The board sticks to the sole of his shoe. He tries to kick it off and gives a helpless look. Stan starts to take the piano out of the case.

Cut to individual shot of Babe. He stands on the board with one foot and tries to pull the other one off the nails. He makes a couple of motions, finally gives a big yank and his foot comes off the board, but the sole of his shoe remains there. Babe's foot is now sticking out the bottom of his shoe.

The piano is now out of the case. Stan has the cord with plug on the end of it and is looking for a place to plug the piano in. He looks up, sees the chandelier, climbs up on the piano and takes one of the bulbs out. It slips and falls on Babe's head with an explosion. It scares Babe and he jumps out of the way, accidentally knocking against the piano, which throws Stan off balance and he grabs the chandelier to save himself. The chandelier comes out of the ceiling with a lot of plaster.

Babe takes it big and Stan picks himself up.

BABE: What were you doing up there?

STAN: I was trying to plug it in.

BABE: That's not the place to plug it in!

He takes the plug, looks around the room and sees a place in the baseboard and plugs it in.

Insert the roll of music in the piano: "Medley of Patriotic

Songs." It starts to play "Dixie."

Cut outside to the sidewalk. Gilbert comes along and hears the music playing. He takes it big and starts into the house.

Gilbert enters, looks around the house, takes it big and goes nuts. He rushes over to the piano and turns off the switch.

GILBERT: What's the meaning of this?

BABE: Do you live here?

GILBERT: Do I live here? This is my home! What are you doing here?

BABE: We just delivered your piano.

GILBERT: I ordered no piano! I hate pianos! Get that thing out of here before I commit murder!

Stan and Babe a little nervous start to pick up the piano to exit, and they bump into a statue or something and break it. Gilbert goes off his nut again and says, "Stop!" Stan and Babe put the piano down, not knowing what is going to happen next. Gilbert rushes to the wall where there is a shield and a couple of battle axes. He grabs one of the axes and starts smashing the piano. As he smacks it a couple of times it starts playing "The Star Spangled Banner," and all three unconsciously stop and salute. Gilbert catches himself, turns the piano off and starts beating on it again.

Cut to exterior and we see the wife arrive. Over her scene we hear Gilbert smashing the piano and bellowing like a bull.

Cut to living room; she enters, looks around and says, "Theodore, what has happened?" He stops swinging his weapon and says, "These two imbeciles delivered a piano here by mistake and wrecked our home!" The wife says, "There was no mistake, darling. I bought that as a surprise for your birthday." She starts to cry.

Gilbert becomes remorseful, crosses over to Stan and Babe, puts his hand on Babe's shoulder and says, "What can I do to show you how sorry I am?" Stan pulls out a delivery book and says, "Sign here." He hands Gilbert the book and a fountain pen. Gilbert places the book on top of the piano, pulls the top off the pen and ink squirts in his face. He goes nuts again and chases Stan and Babe out. FADE OUT.

THE CHIMP

Production history: Production L-7. Script written early January 1932. Dialogue script completed by H.M. Walker January 13. Filmed Monday, January 18 through Tuesday, January 26. Released May 21. Copyrighted May 26, 1932, by MGM (LP 3055). Three reels.

Produced by Hal Roach. Directed by James Parrott. Photographed by Len Powers. Edited by Richard Currier. Sound by James Greene. Dialogue by H.M. Walker. *Uncredited assistance:* Assistant Director, Morey Lightfoot. Props, Harry Hopkins and Bob Sanders. Assistant Cameraman, Harold Graham.

With Stan Laurel (Himself), Oliver Hardy (Himself), James Finlayson (Colonel Finn, the ringmaster), Charles Gemora (Ethel, the gorilla), Tiny Sandford (Destructo, the Cannonball King), William J. O'Brien (Circus manager), Baldwin Cooke, Dorothy Layton, Estelle Etterre (Circus performers), Jack Hill, Lois Laurel (Audience members) Billy Gilbert (Joe, the landlord), Dorothy Granger (Ethel, Joe's wife), Bobby Burns (Tenant reading paper).

Stan and Ollie are roustabouts for a ramshackle circus which soon goes bankrupt. In lieu of payment, the manager gives each of the employees a part of the show. Stan gets a flea circus, while Ollie wins "Ethel, the human chimpanzee," who is really a gorilla. The boys have to find lodging for the night, and do their best to sneak Ethel past the bombastic and hot-tempered landlord, who is particularly overwrought because his wife – conveniently and coincidentally named Ethel – is out on the town late at night. When the landlord overhears Ollie reproaching the roisterous ape with "Ethel! Will you stop that and come to bed?," he understandably gets the wrong idea.

All of the cast members for this movie will probably never be known, as the "Daily Production Sheet" for January 18th calls for "Stan, Babe, 2 doubles, 7 girls, 6 attendants, 4 clowns, 1 bareback rider, 20 people, 2 butcher boys" – and "J. Finlayson." Well, we know who *he* is, and the other actors named above, but the most memorable performance is given by someone who receives no billing in the film's credits, and is listed on the production sheets only as "Monkey Man."

He's credited on the Internet Movie Database for varied work on nearly 150 films, but there must be dozens more, because Charlie Gemora was a true Renaissance Man, talented as a painter, sculptor, makeup artist, prop and costume designer, and entrepreneur in addition to his best remembered talent as the finest of Hollywood's "gorilla men."

Gemora only made two films with Laurel and Hardy – *The Chimp* and *Swiss Miss* (1938), but he was no stranger to the Hal Roach lot, having earlier appeared in *Do Gentlemen Snore?* (1928) with Max Davidson, *The Holy Terror* (1929) and *Bear Shooters* (1930) with *Our Gang*, and *Sealskins* (1932) with ZaSu Pitts and Thelma Todd. He would return for *Nature in the Wrong* (1933) with Charley Chase, *Bum Voyage* (1934)

Circus manager William J. O'Brien directs the boys to their next job in a gag not in script or film.

Ringmaster Finlayson presents his proud troupe.

Roustabouts Stan and Ollie light Destructo's cannon a little too soon.

with Thelma Todd and Patsy Kelly, and *Who Killed Doc Robbin?* (1948), an attempt to create a new version of *Our Gang*.

Gemora as Ethel is not only entirely convincing with the gorilla pantomime, he manages to imbue her with an impish and beguiling personality, especially when she overhears another boarder playing his phonograph. (The tune is Marvin Hatley's gorgeous "Monkey Waltz." We sure wish we had a record of that.) Ethel dons her ballet tutu and begins dancing around Stan and Ollie's room, pulling Stan in as a partner when the music suddenly breaks into hot jazz.

Charlie Gemora is so fascinating that space doesn't permit detailing all of his adventures here, but you can read much more about him in essays written by his daughter Diana Isabel Gemora Fox Jones, on her website westgate-works.com; he's also the subject of a feature-length documentary written and directed by Jason Barnett, *Charlie Gemora: Uncredited* (2016).

The script for *The Chimp* includes quite a few differences from the movie. The working title was *Monkeydoodle*, which fortunately was rejected because it had been the title of a cartoon by animator Les Elton released the year before. You'd think that *The Chimp* would have been inspired by MGM's recent hit *The Champ*, especially since Laurel and Hardy were reported to have attended the premiere at Grauman's Chinese Theatre on November 13, 1931.

The gag with the drunk not realizing that rain is pouring on him is not in the film. The Lady Godiva routine is filmed very much as scripted, however.

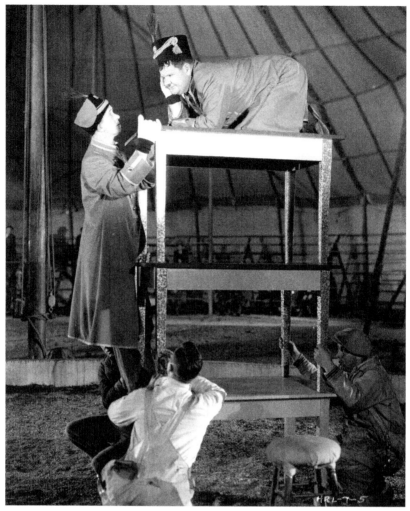

The prop man on the right is Byron "Bones" Vreeland, who worked his way up to being CEO of the Hal Roach Studios.

"The Cannonball King," referred to in the script as "the great So-and-so," was given a more fitting sobriquet in the film – "Destructo." Stan and Ollie, as the circus roustabouts, destroy much more than Destructo does.

The script proposes that when the proprietor announces that he's going to split up the show, two or three of the now ex-employees say, "I'll take the trained seal," and so on. Giving each element of the circus to someone who actually wants it seems like a good idea in the real world, but for purposes of this story Stan and Ollie have to get something they don't want. In the film, the manager says that he's going to write down each item, put them in a hat, and give them to the employees to draw before anyone can say what they want.

The script's scene with Ethel, the crate and the banana is not as elaborate in the film, but one gag survived in Laurel and Hardy's 1936 feature film *The Bohemian Girl:* As

Stan and Ethel are getting along famously, to Ollie's consternation.

Stan munches away, Ollie says, "Give me part of the banana." Stan obliges by handing him the peel.

The porcupine gag is not in the film, but may well have been filmed, as the daily production sheet for January 21 calls for a total cast of Stan, Babe, William J. O'Brien, one lion, and one porcupine.

Beanie Walker came up with a good title to mark the transition to the late-night sequence: "The night was dark – they usually are."

"Monkeys" is misspelled here as "monkies," but I retained it in the interest of not rewriting history. Also, it's cute.

Although the gorilla is referred to as Ethel and "she" all through the movie, the writers seem to have forgotten her gender and routinely refer to Ethel as "him" in the script.

Harley M. Walker wrote a dialogue-only script, dated January 13, 1932, which has some rather ornate dialogue not in the movie. When Billy Gilbert is telling the boys that they can't bring Ethel into the boarding house, he's supposed to say, "Get that quadruped out of here!" And when Stan has accidentally opened the box for the flea circus in the boys' bed, Ollie is supposed to yell, "Put that menageria away!"

One surprise is that a storage bin or waste bin next to the garage in the nighttime sequences is referred to as "the piano box." One wonders if this was a prop left over from *The Music Box*.

Ollie's bedtime lament to Stan of "How many times have I told you to trim your

Landlord Billy Gilbert wants "no monkeys in my hotel!"

toenails?" remains in the film, but his scripted request that Stan shave his legs was probably thought as going a bit too far.

The idea of Stan knowing each of the fleas in the circus by name is a funny one, but it's not in the film. Stan evidently thought that Oscar was a funny name for a pet, because in the team's last film, *Atoll K* (1951), he has a pet lobster who goes by that moniker.

The scripted dialogue which ensues when landlord Billy Gilbert thinks that his wife is the "Ethel" in bed with Stan and Ollie is just about the most "Pre-Code" passage in any of the Laurel and Hardy scripts, especially with the added suggestion of the squeaky bedsprings. Even though the Production Code had not yet gone into effect, it's doubtful that this would have passed muster with the Hays Office, or with regional censor boards which often ordered theater managers to delete certain sections of films before patrons were allowed to see them.

The final scene takes place in the boys' room, not in Gilbert's adjoining room as scripted. This would have necessitated the assembly of another set for a very brief scene, so this idea may have been vetoed by cost-conscious executive Henry Ginsberg.

Happily, the witty repartee suggested for Ethel (the gorilla) in the last shot was not used in the film. (If Ethel is such a sparkling conversationalist, why didn't she use such a unique skill in the circus, which surely would have helped it avert bankruptcy?) Walker had added a line for Ollie to say to Stan, "Now, see, even a monkey knows you're dumb!" Ethel was to respond to Ollie, "That goes for you too, Windy!" In the film, Ethel simply grabs Billy Gilbert's pistol and begins shooting wildly, sending everyone running into the end title.

Stan, Ollie, Billy Gilbert, and two Ethels; Dorothy Granger is the one standing.

Charles Gemora and his alter ego.

L-7 – LAUREL & HARDY

Fade in on long shot of a small one-ring circus. The spieler is outside announcing "This way for the big show" etc. It is night and pouring with rain, and no customers are in evidence.

Lap dissolve to the interior; the Ring Master, Finlayson, dressed in typical outfit with silk hat, riding breeches, etc., is announcing the stupendous show about to commence, finishing with "All right, let 'er go!"

We hear a lousy brass band strike up a march, "The Stars and Stripes Forever." The two curtains open at the side of the ring and the parade starts in, led by two horses, a couple of girls with white plumes, etc., followed by the animal wagons, ponies, goats and what have you. One of the wagons contains "Ethel, the Human Chimp." As each wagon or performer passes in review, Finlayson stands on the sideline raving over their qualities. Might get a gag from each act that Finlayson talks about, for instance a monkey knocks his hat off, the goat butts him, etc. We see that the audience is composed of about a dozen disinterested spectators.

Cut to a drunk sitting all by himself. Rain is pouring in on his head. Show a hole in the canvas where the rain is pouring in. The drunk hasn't sense enough to move out of the way.

At the tail end of the parade is a prop horse, a couple of clowns following it, and riding on it is another clown made up as Lady Godiva. One of the clowns in back is carrying a large prop key-hole and peeking through it. Finlayson announces them as Lady Godiva and Pepping Tom. The band is playing over all this and Finlayson is shouting at the top of his voice.

Another clown walks in dressed up like a foney cop, takes it big on seeing Peeping Tom looking through the key-hole. He snatches the key-hole away from Peeping Tom, picks up a big prop mallet, which explodes when he socks the clown on the head with it.

This scares the horse, which throws Lady Godiva on her fanny, and the horse tears out of the scene. The back end trips over something and sprawls out, and the front end continues running, dragging the rear end after it. They exit from the ring.

Cut to a section of the tent like a prop room, with wardrobe, trunks, etc. The horse comes running in dragging the hind end and stops. The hind end picks himself up and gets out of the skin and we introduce Babe. He gives Stan a push, takes down a flunkey's coat and hat and puts them on, then starts to put his white gloves on.

Cut to Stan; he has the skin off but the horse's head is still on his head. Stan puts his coat on, puts the hat on top of the horse's head and starts to exit. Babe stops him, roughly takes the head off, tells him to come on and they both exit.

Cut to the ring; Finlayson is announcing "LaBelle Henderson, the world's greatest bareback rider." The band strikes a chord and the little equestrienne enters doing "cuts." Finlayson helps her onto the horse, cracks his whip and she starts riding around the ring, the band playing a suitable number.

Stan and Babe enter to the entrance of the ring and discover that they haven't taken off the horse's legs. Babe very annoyed sits down on a trunk and tells Stan to pull them off. He holds up his legs and Stan takes his feet by the heels and gives a pull. Babe loses his balance and falls off the trunk as the pants come off. Babe stands up very annoyed and doesn't realize that Stan pulled off his regular pants with the others. Stan sits on the trunk and Babe pulls off Stan's "horse" pants.

Cut to the girl on the horse. She does some finishing trick, such as jumping through a paper hoop. The band gives her a chord and the drunk applauds. The Ring Master helps the girl off the horse.

Stan and Babe run in and Babe starts to escort the girl out. He discovers he hasn't any pants and makes a bashful exit. Stan leads the horse out.

Finlayson announces "The Cannonball King" in true circus fashion. Stan and Babe re-enter, open up a big trunk and start setting up the paraphernalia – a small teeter-totter, cannon balls, etc. Babe gets two kitchen tables, puts one on top of the other and starts to climb up to see if he has them the right distance from the teeter-tot. Stan rolls one of the cannon balls onto the low end of the teeter-tot, then comes around, doesn't see Babe on top of the tables, and tries to straighten them up. Babe nearly falls off. He gets mad and makes a pass at Stan, which causes Stan to stumble backwards onto the high end of the teeter. The cannon ball goes into the air and lands on Babe's head, sending him with a crash through the two tables.

Stan picks up the cannon ball. Babe is so mad he kicks Stan in the fanny. Stan drops the cannon ball on Babe's foot. Babe takes it, picks up the cannon ball and starts to throw it at Stan. He changes his mind and puts it into Stan's hands. While Stan is holding it, Babe again kicks him in the fanny. Stan then hands Babe the cannon ball. Babe takes it a little bewildered and Stan kicks him in the fanny.

At this point the strong man enters, glares at Babe, takes the cannon ball from him and offers it to Stan, saying, "Hold that." Stan waves him away, rubs his fanny and exits. The strong man turns to Babe and says, "You've spoiled my first trick. Get the cannon ready!" Babe exits.

Cut to Finlayson; he starts to announce that the great So-and-so at the risk of his life will catch a cannon ball shot from a real cannon eighty five feet in the air onto the nape of his neck – "And that is not all, ladies and gentlemen, he will be blindfolded! This trick has never been done before, so watch closely." He starts to put the blindfold on the guy.

Cut to Stan and Babe loading up the cannon with gun powder, etc. The guy with his back to the cannon is waiting. Babe starts to put the ball into the mouth of the cannon. Stan in back of him lights the fuse and it starts spluttering. Stan then comes around to help Babe put the cannon ball in. They finally get it in and put some more powder on top of it and ram it down.

BABE: Give me a match.

STAN: What for?

BABE: To light the cannon; what do you think?

STAN: I did.

Stan points to the fuse and we see it just spluttering into the little hole. Babe gives a big "Oh" and drags Stan out of the scene.

Cut to the exterior; we hear a terrific explosion and the tent all collapses. FADE OUT.

Fade in next morning on the circus proprietor's wagon. Around the wagon are the vacant looking sideshows. Several characters are on with the proprietor, including the strong man, the ring master, etc. The proprietor is pacing up and down worried. He finally stops and says to the gang, "Well, fellows, after seven weeks of continuous rain and no business, I'm flat broke. I'm afraid it's the end. We'll have to fold up." There is a chorus of "What about our money?" "How about my salary," etc. The proprietor says, "Just a minute – you can't get blood from a stone. I've got a plan. I'm going to split the show up amongst you." The strong man asks, "What do you mean?" The proprietor says, "I mean you will each get some part of the show in place of your salary."

Two or three speak up, "I'll take the trained seal," "I'll take the lions," etc. The proprietor stops them and says, "No, you're not going to take anything. I'm going to write each item on a piece of paper and place them in a hat, and what you draw, you get." He takes off his big hat, places it on a table and starts tearing pieces of paper as all the performers mumble to themselves.

Lap dissolve to Babe building a wooden crate. Stan enters with a little box under his arm, looks at Babe and says, "What are you doing?"

BABE: I'm building a crate.

STAN: What for?

BABE: Look what I drew.

He points out of scene and we cut and show Ethel, the monk, sitting on a barrel or something, eating a banana.

STAN: What are you going to do with her?

BABE: I'm going to sell her to the zoo. What did you draw?

Stan shows him the little box and says, "I got the flea circus." Babe takes it.

The monk makes a hissing noise and Stan and Babe look toward her. The monk motions Stan over to her and offers him a piece of the banana. Stan breaks off a piece. Babe steps over and holds out his hand for some. The monk peels the skin off the rest of the banana and hands Babe the skin. Babe throws it back at the monk, who takes it. Babe turns to work on the crate and the monk picks up a dish pan and throws it at him, hitting him on the back of the head with a big "bong." Babe takes it a little bit scared and says to the monk, "Come on, get in this crate." The monk doesn't budge. Babe takes her by the hand and tries to pull her over. The monk lets out a squawk and Babe starts to run, but slips on the banana peel.

Insert Babe's foot on the banana peel, then pick him up in the air turning. Cut to a small box-cage which is standing nearby with a porcupine in it. Insert the porcupine's quills straightening up, then show Babe drop into the box, landing on his fanny.

Closeup of Babe taking it big. He gets out of it with a lot of quills sticking to his fanny. He starts running around pulling the quills out, Stan helping him.

They finally get the quills out and Babe becomes resigned again. He says, "See if you can get her into the crate – she seems to like you better than me." Stan entices the monk into the crate and locks the door. Babe says, "At last you're of some use to me. Now give me a hand." They lift up the cage to move it, the monk remaining on the ground.

They discover what happened and Babe says, "Get a rope while I put her in here." Babe is mad now. He starts to take off his coat as Stan exits.

Stan enters to another setup, finds a piece of rope and picks it up. He starts to exit and hears a great commotion, Babe's "Oh's" and a lot of hammering. He exits quickly.

Cut to Babe's scene. The monk has got Babe in the crate and is nailing it up. Stan enters, takes the hammer away from the monk and lets Babe out of the crate.

Babe picks up the rope and says, "You put her in the crate and I'll tie it up." Stan turns the crate over and Babe starts pulling the rope.

Cut and show the setup that Stan just left, and a lion comes out with the other end of the rope tied around his neck.

Back to Babe still pulling and bawling Stan out. He suddenly turns.

Cut and show the lion coming.

Back to Babe; he lets out a yell. Stan and the monk look off and take it big. The monk starts hollering and the three of them beat it hell bent for election out of the set.

Run the lion through a longer set in the direction of Stan and Babe and the monk. Fade out.

Fade in on title, "That Night," or "Twenty-five Miles Later." Fade out.

Fade in on a quiet street. The Monk's head peeps around a corner. Seeing that the coast is clear, he turns and beckons in back of him.

Cut to another street corner; Stan peeks around and getting the signal from the monk he turns and motions in back of him.

Cut and show Babe at the next street corner peeking around.

Back to Stan. He whistles and Babe steps from behind the corner. Stan says, "Ethel says it's all right." All three get together and Babe says, "Well, I guess we better get a room."

STAN: How are we going to pay for it?

BABE: Simple – tomorrow we'll sell Ethel and we'll be on Easy Street.

STAN: O.K. Let's get a room with twin beds.

BABE: What for?

STAN: One for me.

BABE: Why, I can't sleep with Ethel!

STAN: She won't mind – go on, ask her.

Babe takes it big and says "Come on," and they exit.

Lap dissolve to the exterior of rooming house with sign over the door, "Rooms and Board."

Lap dissolve to interior hallway. Gilbert, the proprietor, is on pacing up and down. An old character is seated in a chair reading a newspaper. He looks up from his paper and says, "What seems to be the trouble?" Gilbert says, "Oh, it's that frivolous wife of mine. She's at it again." The old man asks, "What's she up to now?" Gilbert says, "She went out this afternoon and here it is eleven o'clock and she's not home yet. If I thought she was chasing around – I wouldn't be responsible for my actions!"

Cut outside. Stan and Babe and the monk enter. Babe says, "You stay here while I go see if we can get a room."

Cut to the inside; Gilbert is still pacing up and down, looking at his watch. The door bell rings. The old man says, "There she is now. I think I'll be going." He starts up the stairs.

Gilbert looks ferociously at the door and works himself up to a pitch where he is going to give her a good bawling out. He rushes to the door opens it quickly and Babe is standing there. He grabs Babe and pulls him in, saying, "What do you mean by staying out at this hour?" Then he notices that it is not his wife, takes it and says, "I beg your pardon. I thought you were my wife." Babe says, "No apologies necessary. I would like to get a room." Gilbert says "With pleasure. Just register here." Babe registers and Gilbert gives him a key, points upstairs and says, "That's your room."

Cut to Stan and the monk on the exterior. Stan looks down the street, does a double takem and we cut and show the lion looking around a corner. Stan and the monk take it big and the monk yells. They both rush into the house and close the door.

This scares Babe, who starts up the stairs, and Gilbert does one leap into his living room. Gilbert says, "What the devil is that?" Babe gets very coy and says, "I forgot to mention it, but we would like to keep our monkey here for the night too."

GILBERT: No monkey is going to stay in my hotel!

BABE: You don't understand. This is a human monk – has more brains than most people.

GILBERT: After looking at you guys, I thoroughly agree with you. Get it out of here!

BABE: We can't leave it outside.

STAN: No, it might get cold and die of ammonia.

BABE: Not ammonia – PEW-monia!

GILBERT: I don't care if you all die of pew-monia. Get it out of here!

BABE: If we leave it outside, can we have our room?

GILBERT: O.K., but understand, no monkies!

Stan and Babe go outside. Babe pushes Stan and says, "What did you want to run in with that thing for?" Stan says, "I just saw M-G-M." Babe: "What do you mean, M-G-M?" Stan says, "The lion!" Babe takes it big and they look around. Stan says,

"What'll we do now?" Babe thinks, then says, "I have it!' He looks down the alley and says, "Come on." They exit hurriedly into the garage adjoining the house and close the sliding door.

Lap dissolve; garage door opens, Stan looks out to see if the coast is clear, then brings out the monk dressed in Babe's clothes. Babe follows the monk out, looking around. He has on the ballet skirt and Eugenie hat with feather. He says, "You take him upstairs quietly, then throw the clothes down to me and I'll come up after." Stan exits.

Cut to interior; Stan enters with the monk and they start for the stairs.

Cut to Babe at the garage looking out of the scene. We hear the lion's roar; Babe takes it and looks the other way. Show the lion running toward Babe. Babe does a big takem, rushes into the garage and closes the door. The lion stops and starts pawing at the door.

Cut to Stan half way up the stairs. Gilbert comes out and looks kind of suspiciously at them. As Stan is exiting he raises his hat and gives Gilbert a grin.

Cut to the bedroom. Stan enters with the monk and starts to undress him.

Cut back to the lion pawing the garage door, and he accidentally opens it a little. He runs into the garage and we hear a lot of "Oh's" from Babe. He slides open the other side of the door, slams it shut, rushes and slams the first side of the door and locks it. He gives a sigh of relief.

Cut to Stan at the window with the clothes. He throws Babe the coat and hat, but the pants stick on a nail in the wall out of Babe's reach, about half way up. Babe tries to jump up to reach them but can't make it. Stan leans out and tries to reach them but can't. Babe says, "Have Ethel get them – she can reach farther than you." Stan pantomimes to the monk to get the pants. The monk leans out of the window trying to reach them and Stan holds onto his legs. The monk loses his balance and both drop into the alley onto Babe. They pick themselves up. Babe tells Stan to put the monkey in the piano box and lock it in. He starts to get dressed.

Stan lifts the lid of the box, gets the monk into it and locks it. The piano box has evidently been used for a dust bin.

Back to Babe just putting his coat and hat on. Picking up the monk's dress and hat, he tells Stan to come on. They exit.

Cut to the interior. Stan and Babe enter and start up the stairs. Gilbert enters from the top of the stairs and takes it big as he passes them. They both raise their hats and exit.

Cut to the room; they enter and start to undress.

Cut to the alley and show the monk inside the box. He discovers that the side of the box is out. He climbs out and starts looking around the alley.

Back to Stan and Babe, now in their night shirts. Stan walks over to the window to pull the shade down.

Cut to the alley; the monk looks up and sees the lighted room and sees Stan pulling the shade down. He walks over to the wall and starts examining the drain pipe.

Cut to the hall; Gilbert is on still pacing. The old character enters in bath robe with a towel around his neck, and says, "Any news of the wife?" Gilbert looks wild-eyed and says, "No, no news, but there will be news if I find out where she is. I'm cursed with a jealous nature, and not to be trifled with!" The man says, "Don't get excited. She'll be back."

Cut to Stan and Babe. Babe is asleep snoring, and keeps edging Stan out of the bed. Stan falls to the floor but Babe doesn't wake up. Stan tries to get back into bed again, then looks over and sees a single bed and decides to sleep in it. He gets into bed and lies down to sleep.

The window shade goes up quietly and the monk gets into the room, looks around and climbs into bed with Babe. Babe feels him getting in and half wakes up, but not looking says, "Why don't you be quiet and go to sleep? Can't you lie still? I never saw such a fidgety person as you." He lets out an "Ouch" and says, "Why don't you cut your toe nails? And how many times have I told you to shave your legs?"

Cut to Stan waking up, sitting up in bed and looking.

Back to Babe; the monk gives him a big kiss. Babe takes it big, sits up in bed and sees Stan over in the other bed. He does a double takem and sees the monk, and jumps out of bed. He looks over at Stan and Stan does a big grin.

Babe tries to get the monk out of bed, but the monk

makes a pass at him, which scares Babe. Babe tells Stan to help him. Stan gets the monk out of the bed and Babe says, "Make a bed on the floor for her." Stan throws down a couple of cushions or whatever is around there. Babe goes to arrange them, bending over. The monk, behind him, starts to lift up Babe's night shirt. Babe takes it, runs and gets into bed, then tells Stan, "Go to bed and let's get some sleep." Stan gets into his bed while Babe settles down, pulling the covers over him.

Cut to the monk; he starts to lie down on the cushions, then looks around. He looks over toward Babe's bed, gets up, goes to Babe's bed, takes all the covers off and again lies down on the cushions, covering himself up. Babe takes it, gets up, crosses to Stan's bed and says "Move over." They both settle down to sleep.

Stan starts scratching and Babe picks it up and starts. They build this scratching business up until Babe suddenly stops and says, "What did you do with the flea circus?" Stan reaches under the pillow, pulls the little box out and says, "I've got it here." Babe takes it again. Stan looks at the box and says, "Where's Oscar?" Babe says, "How should I know where he is? Put that thing away and let's go to sleep." Stan starts to put it under the pillow. Babe grabs it and says, "Not there!" The lid falls off, spilling the fleas in the bed. There is a general scramble. They pull the covers back and start brushing the sheet, throwing the fleas in the direction of the monk. They then get back into bed.

Cut to Ethel; she starts into a scratching routine.

Cut to the landlord coming into his bedroom, adjoining Babe and Stan's. He is still in a jealous state of mind. He walks over to the dressing table where there is a framed picture of his wife. Insert the writing on the picture: "Your loving wife, Ethel." Gilbert sneers at the picture.

Cut to Stan and Babe. The monk is still scratching. Babe sits up and says, "Ethel, will you lie still?"

Cut to Gilbert; he takes it big and listens.

Back to Stan and Babe; Babe gets out of bed. The monk is walking around the room, scratching. Babe says, "Ethel, will you please go to bed?"

Back to Gilbert; he is now convinced that it is his wife in the room. He opens the drawer, takes out a gun and exits to the hall, where he stops to listen again.

Back to the bedroom; the monk is still carrying on. Babe turns and says, "See what you can do with her. She likes you better than me." (Another takem from Gilbert.) Stan gets out of bed a little bit mad, picks up the monk's dress and says, "Here, you put these clothes on and stop dancing around."

Cut to Gilbert for another takem.

Back to the bedroom. Stan says "Maybe she would rather sleep in your bed." Babe says "I don't care where she sleeps if she will only keep still." Stan takes the monk by the hand and tugs her onto the bed. The monk starts struggling and Stan and Babe tussle trying to get her to lie down. (Have a squeaky spring in the bed.) Cut to Gilbert for takems. Babe says, "Don't make so much noise. If that fat-headed landlord knows she's here we'll all be thrown out."

Gilbert starts hammering on the door and says, "I know she's here. Open that door!" He keeps banging on the door.

Stan and Babe get all excited and try to hide the monk under the bed and in the cupboard. They suddenly get the idea to put her in the next room, which they enter through the adjoining door.

They quickly put the monk into Gilbert's bed and cover it up, then run back to their room, jump into bed and start to snore. Gilbert shoots the lock off the door and bursts in, saying "Where is she?" Stan starts to point toward the door, but Babe knocks his hand down. Babe says "Who?" Gilbert says, "You know who! Ethel, that's who!" He starts looking under the bed and in the cupboard. Babe says "What are you going to do?" Gilbert tells him, "I'm going to shoot her, and I'll deal with you after."

Gilbert suddenly sees the half open adjoining door to his room, gives a maniacal "Ah-ha!" and rushes into his room, followed by Stan and Babe.

Cut to the bedroom; Gilbert is holding the gun over the monk, who is covered up, and says, "You deceitful wretch! How could you after all these years? The mother of my children!" He continues upbraiding the monk, thinking it is his wife, while Stan and Babe do big takems. Gilbert finally breaks down sobbing, and kneeling on the bed puts his arm around the monkey.

Gilbert's wife streps in the door and takes it big. Gilbert is saying to the monk, "Honey, why did you do this thing to me? You know I love you better than anyone in the world," etc., etc. He finally looks around to upbraid Stan and Babe and sees his wife standing in the doorway. He does a big takem and says, "Where have you been?" The wife says, "You should question me, when I find you in the arms of another. Who is this woman?"

Gilbert throws the bed covers back and the monk sits up. They all take it. The monk says, "If this is civilization, back to the jungles for me!" He goes to the window, then turns to Stan and says, "You're the dumbest thing I ever saw." With that he jumps out the window. Babe says to Stan, "See, even the monkey thinks you're dumb." The monk pokes his head back in the window, points at Babe and says, "That goes for you, too." Babe takes it big. FADE OUT.

County Hospital

Production history: Production L-8. Script and H.M. Walker dialogue script written early February 1932. Filmed from Monday, February 15 through Thursday, February 25. Copyrighted May 31, 1932 by MGM (LP 3060). Released June 25. Foreign dialogue soundtrack completed October 21, 1932. Reissued January 22, 1938. Two reels.

Produced by Hal Roach. Directed by James Parrott. Photographed by Art Lloyd. Edited by Bert Jordan. Sound by James Greene. Dialogue by H.M. Walker. Assistant Director, Morrie Lightfoot. Props, Chet Brandenburg and Bob Sanders. Assistant Cameraman, Edward L. White. Supervising Editor, Richard Currier. Visual Effects, Roy Seawright.

With Stan Laurel (Himself), Oliver Hardy (Himself), Billy Gilbert (Doctor), William Austin (Ollie's English roommate), May Wallace (Nurse Wallace), Estelle Etterre (Nurse Smith), Sam Lufkin (Policeman), Dorothy Layton (Nurse at reception desk), Lilyan Irene (Nurse carrying baby), Betty Danko (Desk nurse), Baldwin Cooke (Orderly), Ham Kinsey (Orderly/Stunt double for Stan), Frank Holliday (Visitor), Bob Minford (Hospital orderly), Carl M. Leviness (Doctor extra).

The original 1932 title lobby card.

Stan arrives to visit his friend; the crane lifting the car can be seen at top right.

Ollie is enjoying a wonderful rest, even if it is in a hospital, where he's recovering from a broken leg. One wonders if that injury was somehow caused by his friend Mr. Laurel, who unexpectedly shows up and makes Mr. Hardy's recuperation much less restful. Ollie doesn't care for Stan's gift of hard-boiled eggs and nuts, nor does he appreciate it when Stan curiously inspects a weight, which sends Ollie flying up to the ceiling dangling by his leg – and his doctor hanging for his life from a top-story window. The angry physician orders them both to leave. Unfortunately, Stan has accidentally sat upon a hypodermic needle filled with enough sedative to make him "sleep for a month!" as a head nurse quips with an alarming lack of concern. Stan's attempt to drive Ollie home is a wild ride through traffic, ending only when his Model T is smashed into a semi-circle by two streetcars.

The opening titles for Hal Roach comedies usually give credit to very few of the actual cast and crew members, but those for *County Hospital* are particularly sparse, consisting only of "Hal Roach Presents Stan Laurel and Oliver Hardy" and a second title giving the name of the film. For this film, all of the crew members are "uncredited assistants," with the names listed above provided by the daily film reports. The performers are identified thanks to the eagle eyes of several L&H devotées, particularly Dave Lord Heath, who maintains the magnificent *Another Nice Mess* website (www.lordheath.com).

The only prints known to exist of *County Hospital* are from the reissue version, which was created in September 1937 and released on January 22, 1938. This enhanced the 1932 original with a musical score, taken primarily from cues that Leroy Shield had written for the 1936 feature *Our Relations*. It also removed Beanie Walker's introductory titles: "Mr. Hardy fell on his leg, and was laid up for two months. Mr. Laurel fell on his head – and hadn't felt better in years."

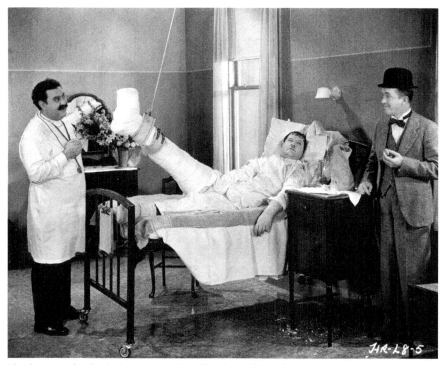

The doctor wishes his little patient and his friend a triple good morning.

After the titles, there's a fade out and fade in to the opening scene – which boasts some impressive special effects work from Roy Seawright. As Stan drives his Model T to the front of the hospital (which was really the Culver City City Hall building at 9770 Culver Boulevard, near Duquesne Avenue), it backfires and the rear of the car lifts up. This was accomplished with a crane, which was still visible in the shot. In a 1980 interview, editor Richard Currier remembered asking Seawright if he could somehow remove the crane and the section that was connected to the back of the car. Roy accomplished it so well that it's a surprise to see the crane in stills.

Daily production reports tell us that the film was not quite shot in sequence. Estelle Ettere's scenes were filmed on the production's second day, February 16. William Austin's contribution was shot on February 17, which also called for "Stan, Babe, Billy Gilbert, 6 nurses, 3 internes, 2 orderlies, 2 doubles, 1 telephone operator, 6 visitors working in Int. Hospital."

The last two filming dates, February 24 and 25, are puzzling because each session started at 6:30 in the evening and continued to 9 p.m. (on the 24th) or 11 p.m. (on the 25th). There are no night sequences in the film, so maybe the schedule had to do with the availability of the crew or equipment, as the only cast members called for are Stan, Babe and two doubles.

All told, the crew shot 114 scenes and exposed 9,395 feet of 35mm film, 3,143 of which were considered to be "good footage." This was almost 35 minutes' worth, which

Now it's not so good, as orderlies Baldwin Cooke and Ham Kinsey, and nurse Estelle Etterre, bear witness.

was edited to a final cut of 1,743 feet or just over 19 minutes.

As always, there are many differences between the film and the script. The film expands the opening scenes with Stan looking for the room in which his friend is staying. Stan is confused when a desk clerk tells him that Room 14 is "next to the solarium." Also, the rather involved gag with the half doors is not in the film, nor is the Japanese baby; the idea of Ollie being in the maternity ward was confusing enough for Stan.

Anyone who has seen this film will notice that the best-known phrase from it is not found in the script, which suggests that Stan's gift to Ollie should be "fruit and nuts." This is not nearly as endearing as what we hear in the film: not only does "hard-boiled eggs and nuts" have a much better rhythm, it also makes sense comedically. What could be more difficult or messier to eat in a hospital bed than hard-boiled eggs, which need their shells removed, or nuts, which would require a nutcracker?

In the script, Stan eats an apple; in the film, it's a hard-boiled egg. Stan would get his chance for a lengthy sequence eating an apple, a wax one, in *Sons of the Desert.*

The gag with the apple dropping into an unseen vessel at the side of Ollie's bed and eliciting a splash is clearly meant to imply a bedpan or a chamber pot, before it's revealed to be a water pitcher. There's a similar gag in *Helpmates.* This one survived the censorship of the Production Code when *County Hospital* was reissued in 1938. Ollie here does hit Stan with a real bedpan after Stan upsets the water pitcher into Ollie's bed.

Jolly roommate William Austin has put on Ollie's trousers by mistake, but the boys have made a bigger mistake with his.

Stan's attempt to crack a walnut with the weight keeping Ollie's broken leg extended upward is amplified and improved in the film; instead of the doctor merely jumping on Ollie's bed in an attempt to pull him down from the ceiling, he grabs the weight and flies out of the window, which a nurse in earlier scene has informed us is in Room 14 "on the top floor." Roy Seawright's split-screen optical effects work in this sequence is exemplary.

The film adds another moment of confusion for Stan when he's having difficulty getting Ollie's trousers over the cast. Ollie says, "Get the scissors and cut the leg off." Stan begins to feel Ollie's cast, wondering where, or if, he should start the incision – until Ollie exasperatedly explains, "The leg of the pants!"

The script refers to "Bertie Johns." Bertram Johns was an actor, born in Plymouth, England in 1874; he came to Hollywood in 1915 and appeared in comedies for Al Christie and Paramount; he was also the manager of film comedienne Billie Rhodes. He was well-known for his "silly ass" characterizations and was consulted by studios as a "technical director on things British," according to the *Illustrated Daily News* of February 28, 1934; he died that year in Los Angeles.

The English roommate's scripted line of "I have on your pants by mistake" was changed in the film to "I have on your trousers by mistake," as "pants" to the British specifically refers to underwear. The script does provide the roommate with a last name,

"He'll sleep for a month" – or at least while trying to drive Ollie home.

Twittingham, as well as his reason for being in the hospital – and for his immediate return.

The proposed finale, which takes almost two full pages of a six-page script, would have been very expensive to film. It would have involved outdoor filming at several locations, and required several other cars (and another actor as the man whose car is unwittingly towed by Stan and Ollie). The fire hydrant and sewer gags would have needed some special effects work.

It's likely that Henry Ginsberg vetoed the sequence. Instead, the final two minutes have Stan and Ollie in the Model T on a studio stage, Ollie gesticulating frantically to highly unconvincing rear-projection footage of a wild ride through traffic. As Roy Seawright noted, "We had to have the ingenuity to solve each problem as economically as possible – if you needed a lot of money, they'd say, 'Forget it! We'll write something else!'"

Hal Roach told historian Richard W. Bann in 1986, "We had to accommodate Ginsberg. There was no money. We tried to make a gag out of the rear projection by showing the audience we knew the thing looked phony." (W.C. Fields would use intentionally fake-looking rear projection footage for his 1933 short *The Fatal Glass of Beer.*)

Mr. Roach concluded, "That year was one time when Metro wouldn't give me the financing I wanted. You do the best you can."

The boys' car is caught between streetcars, a scripted idea not in the film.

Policeman Sam Lufkin wants Stan and Ollie's car to "pull over there," but it only goes around and around.

L-8 – LAUREL & HARDY.

Fade in on long shot of hospital. Cut to Auto Club sign: "Hospital – Quiet."

Closer shot in front of hospital. Stan drives in in the Ford, which is backfiring and making a lot of noise. He finally gets it stopped. The rear end of the Ford lifts up and it gives one final explosion. Stan gets out of the car, lifts out a big bag of fruit and starts toward the hospital.

Lap dissolve to interior of the hospital reception room; various characters are on, mostly men. A nurse seated at a desk asks Stan who he wishes to see and he says he would like to see Mr. Hardy. The nurse says "Room 14."

Lap dissolve to the corridor. Stan is walking along looking at the numbers on the doors; internes and nurses crossing through scene.

Cut to a room with half doors. At the lower part is a man's feet and legs, and leaning on the upper part of the doors is a baby. As Stan passes, the baby says "Hello." Stan replies "Hello," and does a double takem as he notices the man's feet at the bottom of the doors. A little bewildered, he opens the door to look in and we see a man standing holding a baby in his arms. Stan exits a little bit fussed.

Stan finally gets to room 14 and is just about to knock when a nurse comes out of the room with a baby in her arms. Stan looks at the number on the door and takes it big, watches her go down the hall, then looks back at the number again. The door opens again and another nurse comes out with a baby. Closeup of a Japanese baby. Stan does another takem.

Nurse: "Did you want to see somebody?"

Stan: "Yes, I want to see Mr. Hardy."

Nurse: "Top floor, in the convalescent ward."

Stan starts to exit.

Lap dissolve to interior of Babe's room, shooting at the door from Babe's angle. We hear the whistle and a knock comes at the door. Babe's voice comes over scene, "Come in." Stan enters and looks.

Cut to Babe in bed with his leg in a cast and strung up on a pulley. Stan comes into the scene.

Stan: "How do you feel?"

Babe: "Fine. I didn't expect to see you here."

Stan: "Well, I didn't have anything else to do, so I thought I'd drop in to see you."

Babe: "What have you got there?"

Stan: "I brought you some fruit and nuts."

Babe: "Now you know I don't like fruit and nuts! Why didn't you bring me a box of candy?"

Stan: "Well, you never paid me for the last box I brought you."

Stan starts to take the fruit out of the bag and sets it on a plate. He takes one of the apples, polishes it on his chest, sits down and starts to eat it.

Cuts to Babe for looks.

Stan finishes the apple, gets up and takes another one. He starts to polish it but it slips out of his hand and drops at the side of the bed and we hear a splash. Babe takes it and looks over. Stan stoops down and picks up a pitcher three-quarters full of water, with the apple in it. He goes to get the apple out of the water, but Babe says, "Don't get your hand in there – I have to drink that."

Stan thinks of an idea and starts pouring the water out into glasses, the apple remaining in the pitcher. He finally gets rid of the water and rolls the apple out of the pitcher into his hand, then puts the pitcher back on the table and replaces the water from the glasses, etc., into the pitcher.

There is a little towel on the table, and as Stan starts to wipe off the apple he pulls on the towel, upsetting the pitcher of water and it falls into Babe's bed. Babe takes it big, reaches under the bed out of scene, brings up a bed pan, hits Stan on the head with it and puts it right back. As it hits Stan we hear a loud "bong." Stan takes it, picks the apple up and starts to eat it. Repeat the same scene as before, with cuts of Babe looking.

Stan finishes the second apple, gets up and picks out a walnut. He tries to crack it with his heel. Babe is watching him all the time. Stan decides to crack it in the hinge of the swinging door. He places it there and gives the door a terrific push.

Cut to the hall; the doctor is standing outside the door just about to enter. The door swings out and hits him, knocking him on his fanny. He picks himself up and enters the room.

As he gets inside, he steps on the uncracked nut and does another high brodie, landing with his fanny on the nut. He gets up and we insert the nut broken.

Babe says, "Good morning, doctor." The doctor says "Good morning," giving Stan a dirty look. Babe introduces Stan, saying "This is my friend Mr. Laurel." Stan says "How do you do?" Stan picks up the broken nut and starts to eat it. The doctor takes the chart at the foot of the bed and reads it.

Stan gets another nut and tries to crack it with his heel.

Cut to the corridor, two nurses on. One hands the other a hypodermic needle and says, "Give this sleeping potion to the patient in room 22." The other nurse takes the needle and exits.

Back to Stan trying to crack the nut. Seeing the weights connected to the pulley holding Babe's leg up, he gets an idea. He places the nut on the sill of the open window.

Cut to the doctor. He places the chart on the bed and starts to write something on it. His head is directly underneath Babe's leg.

Stan lifts the weights to crack the nut, which causes Babe's leg to drop and hit the doctor on the head. Babe lets out a holler. Stan takes it and drops the weight and it slides out of the window, taking Babe up to the ceiling and leaving him hanging there. The doctor jumps up on the bed frantically trying to get Babe down. Stan realizing what happened tries to pull the weights up into the window, each time taking Babe up and down. Insert the cord being cut in half on the window ledge. It finally breaks, Babe drops onto the doctor and the bed collapses.

Show the weights dropping down the outside of the building, and they land on the top of the main door in a balancing position.

Cut to the hall. The nurse with the hypodermic needle is passing the door and hearing the crash she runs in.

Seeing what has happened, the nurse lays the needle

on a chair and helps Babe and the doctor pick themselves up. The doctor thanks her and says "You may go." The nurse exits nervously. The doctor bawls Babe out, telling him to get his clothes and get out of the hospital at once. He exits.

Babe looks over at Stan and says, "Well, you had nothing else to do, so you thought you'd drop in and see me. Here was I for the first time in my life having a nice, peaceful time, and you had to come along and spoil it. Get my clothes!"

Stan goes to a closet and brings out Babe's clothes. He tries to help Babe on with his pants but can't get the pants leg over Babe's cast. Babe says, "Get the scissors and cut them off."

Stan takes the pants off again as Babe starts to put on his shirt.

Stan crosses to a dresser, gets the scissors and cuts off the pants leg. He takes them back to Babe, who now has his shirt, collar and tie on. Stan helps Babe on with the pants and they slip on easy. As Babe stands up he realizes that they are on back to front and Stan has cut off the wrong leg. Babe sits down again in utter disgust. He makes Stan pull the pants off again and says, "Give me those scissors!" Stan hands him the scissors and Babe starts cutting the other leg.

The door opens and in comes another patient in his bath robe, who is sharing the room with Babe. He is a type like Bertie Johns, wearing a monocle. He says, "Congratulate me, Hardy old thing – the doctor says I may go home." Babe says, "That's great. I'm going, too." The fellow reaching into the cupboard for his clothes says, "How perfectly ripping!" He throws the clothes onto the bed and starts to dress.

Cut to Babe. Stan is helping him on with the short pants. Babe gets them on and looks at himself with disgust.

Cut to the other character putting on the pants. He gets over they don't fit him too good, then looks inside and sees a tag with Hardy's name on it. He does a silly-ass laugh and says, "Hardy, old bean, what do you think?" Hardy says "What?" The man laughs again and says, "You dear old thing, I have on your pants by mistake." Babe takes it and says, "Well, these must be yours." The guy starts to laugh, then seeing the pants all cut he stops the laugh and gives Hardy a dirty look. Babe takes it, turns and gives Stan a dirty look. Stan all embarrassed again sits down, picks up another apple and starts to eat it.

Insert the hypodermic needle on the chair as Stan sits down and show it go into his fanny.

Stan jumps up, turns to look at the chair, and the needle is hanging onto the back of his pants. At this point the nurse comes in looking for the needle. She looks at the chair, then discovers the needle hanging on the back of Stan. She pulls it off, examines it, and seeing that the fluid has been shot out of it she starts laughing, getting more hysterical as she exits. Stan looks at Babe bewildered.

Lap dissolve to the hall. Stan and Babe enter from the room, Stan helping Babe who is limping. As they are passing one of the rooms we hear a loud groan. Stan stops and looks under the swinging half-doors. He motions to Babe to look. Babe gets down on his knees to look. The door opens and the doctor comes walking out and falls over Babe, slides across the hall into a tray with mashed potatoes, etc., that is on the floor outside a room. Stan and Babe exit as the doctor is picking himself up. The English character enters from room 14, wearing felt hat with small feather, dark coat with light vest, monocle, spats and the short pants that Babe cut off. He starts to exit down the hall.

Lap dissolve to the reception room. The Johnny enters and the nurse behind the desk says, "So you're leaving us, Mr. Twittingham?" He says, "Yes, old raspberry pot, after eight months I'm sorry I have to leave you." The nurse tells him, "Well, when you have hay fever again, come in and see us." He says "I will. Cheerio," and starts to exit.

Cut to the front of the hospital. Twittingham comes out and as he pushes the door a little further open the weights fall off the top and hit him on the head, knocking him cold. Two attendants walk out with a stretcher, place him on it and carry him back in.

Cut to the Ford. Stan is fixing Babe in the back seat, ad lib.

Cut to the two nurses in the hallway. One of them hands the other the hypodermic needle and says, "Can I have this re-filled? A visitor in 14 sat on it." Both girls laugh heartily.

Cut back to Stan getting into the Ford. He is starting to get drowsy. He slowly releases the brake, turns on the gas and steps on the starter. Each thing he does is more of an effort. As he pulls out of the scene he is fast asleep, with Babe unconscious of what has happened.

Go into a routine of driving in traffic, missing cars, etc., cutting to Babe taking it big as they just miss things, giving Stan dirty looks and telling him to go easy, etc. Babe's leg is sticking out the side of the car as they pass close to a truck, which knocks the leg completely around in back and Babe goes down in the bottom of the car.

Babe finally discovers that Stan is asleep. He frantically grabs the steering wheel and pulls in to the curb. He shakes Stan and Stan wakes up. Babe makes him get out.

Babe gets into the driver's seat with his leg up on the windshield and starts to drive. They turn a corner and start up a hill. Stan by this time has again fallen asleep.

They reach the top of the hill and are just about to go over when the stop signal goes against them. Babe stops the car but has no foot to put on the brake, and the car backs all the way down the hill, bumping into another car which is parked diagonally at the bottom.

A party in the car leans out the window and bawls Babe out. Babe says he is sorry, but he has a bum leg and couldn't keep his foot on the brake. Stan is half awake by this time. The man in the car tells Babe he has no business driving in that condition, and to let the little fellow take it.

Babe motions for Stan to take the wheel. Stan tries to get over and under Babe's leg, and Babe finally gets moved to the back seat, as there is no room in the front for him.

They start out and Stan again falls asleep. Insert shows that the bumper of Stan's car is caught in the bumper of the other car, and Stan is dragging the other car backwards up the hill. The man starts honking his horn. Babe says, "Pull over and let the gentleman pass." Stan keeps going and the man is still honking his horn. Stan hasn't paid any attention to Babe, being asleep. Babe reaches over and shakes him. Stan wakes up for a minute and Babe says, "Pull over and let the gentleman pass!" Stan pulls over to the side but the guy still keeps honking his horn. Babe gets a little mad and waves to the car in back of him and says, "Come on! Do you want the whole street?" The guy keeps honking his born. Babe manages to turn around and takes it big when he sees what has happened. He waves Stan up and tells him to stop and keep his foot on the brake while he helps the gentleman out of his trouble.

Stan stops the car and Babe gets out. The other man gets out of his car. Babe apologizes for the accident and they both unlock the bumpers. The guy gets into his car and pulls out. Babe is standing in back of the Ford doing one of his characteristic waves.

Cut to Stan fallen asleep again. Insert his foot slipping off the brake. The car moves back out of the picture.

Cut to Babe at the front end of the Ford, getting over that the car just backed over him. Stan is asleep and the car is going down the hill, Babe hobbling after it. He finally makes it, hanging onto the bumper. He yells, which wakes Stan up. Stan not knowing what has happened, steers the car backwards onto the sidewalk, knocking off the top of a fire hydrant and the water squirts out.

Babe picks himself up and tries to stop the water. Stan gets out and also tries. Stan tells Babe to sit on it. Babe does so and the water carries him high into the air. He falls down into the gutter, which is flowing pretty heavy with water, and it carries him all the way down the gutter with his leg in the air, and we see him disappear down a sewer.

Stan gets into the car and starts down the hill. He gets to the bottom and swings the car around just as Babe is getting out of the sewer. Babe makes a pass at Stan and says, "Get out of there! I'll drive this car if it's the last thing I do!" Stan gets into the back seat and falls asleep as Babe starts the car.

Babe backs the car up to take a run at the hill. As he backs, a car just misses him in front, and as he starts forward another car just misses in back of him.

He takes a run at the hill, makes the top and swings to the right onto a street car track where there is a steam roller standing and a man waving a red flag. Babe stops the car in back of the steam roller and we hear the street car bell clanging. Stan wakes up and looks; Babe looks and they both cover their faces. The street car comes into the scene, smacking the back of the Ford.

Cut to a cop standing on the corner and over his scene as

he does a big takem we hear a terrific crash.

Back to Stan and Babe and show the bent Ford. The street car and steam roller back out of the scene. The cop enters, bawls Babe out and says, "Get that thing out of here!" Babe starts the car and it goes around and around in a circle. The cop starts writing tickets and handing them to Stan and Babe as they pass him. FADE OUT.

THEIR FIRST MISTAKE

Production history: Production L-10. Script written mid-September 1932. Filmed from Wednesday, September 21 to Wednesday, September 28. Released November 5. Copyrighted November 22, 1932 by MGM (LP 3426). Two reels.

Produced by Hal Roach. Directed by George Marshall. Photographed by Art Lloyd. Recording Engineer, James Greene. Edited by Richard Currier.

With Stan Laurel (Himself), Oliver Hardy (Himself), Mae Busch (Mrs. Arabella Hardy), Marjorie Campbell (The baby), George Marshall (Friendly neighbor), Billy Gilbert (Process server).

Ollie's wife is sick and tired of her husband spending so much time with his friend, Stan, who lives just across the hall from their apartment. Stan suggests that Ollie adopt a baby to keep the wife occupied while they go out at night. This is quickly accomplished, but when they try to surprise Mrs. Hardy with the blessed event, they are surprised instead by a process server who informs them that Ollie is being sued for divorce, and Stan for alienation of affections. The two "parents" endure a hectic night trying to take care of the new arrival.

The team's latest opus showed the drive toward economy that Henry Ginsberg was imposing on the studio's output. Costs had been cut considerably over the past year. A month before *Their First Mistake* began production, Ginsberg had written to executive David Loew in New York: "… our negative costs for the season so far show a difference in costs of between 35 and 40% and from our observations here the quality is being maintained." The new film took place on only four inexpensive sets – the Hardy living room, their bedroom, the apartment house hallway, and Stan's room. Further, there was no outdoor or location filming.

Using director George Marshall in a brief appearance as a neighbor may well have been another way to tighten the budget. Marshall was an old friend of Hal Roach; they had broken into the picture business together around 1913.

Little Marjorie Campbell was six months and one week old when she began filming with Laurel and Hardy on September 21, 1932, having been born on March 14th. This wasn't her first film, however; she'd already appeared in *Life Begins*, a Warner Bros. drama starring Loretta Young and Eric Linden, which was released on September 10th. She was in one more film, Fox's *Tess of the Storm Country* with Janet Gaynor and Charles Farrell, released November 20, 1932. Miss Campbell was cast for the Mary Pickford feature *Secrets* (1933), but was replaced because she couldn't stop crying. After this, Marjorie left the movie business, but returned as a celebrity guest at the 2014 convention of the Sons of the Desert.

Mister Jones arrives.

Mae Busch returns as Mrs. Hardy. Although she's not nearly as dangerous here as she is in *Come Clean* and *Oliver the Eighth*, she's awfully high-strung. One can see how that angry, piercing voice would drive Ollie to spend as much time as possible away from her.

Billy Gilbert has a brief scene as an ominous process server, one not nearly as amiable and naïve as the one he'd portray in *His Girl Friday* (1940). His character here is gruff and humorless, except perhaps for the grim delight he takes in telling Ollie that his wife will "take you hook, line and sinker!"

The script suggests several changes, a few of them very significant.

The gag with Babe standing on a table and looking over the transom was reworked so that it's Stan looking over the transom of the Hardys' apartment as they have a fight.

The opening scenes sound as though Stan is following the Hardys around because they provide food. Ollie tells Stan not to come over for breakfast because the missus is angry but promises to give him some leftovers. This recalls the "victims of the Depression" speech in *One Good Turn* where the boys ask for a meal.

This script takes an awfully long time to start having a point. All of the material with the lodger was scrapped, which seems to be for the best. In the film, the only interaction with another dweller in the apartment is the very brief encounter with George Marshall, who is much more congenial than the lodger in the script. The boys give him a cigar to celebrate the adoption, and he congratulates them.

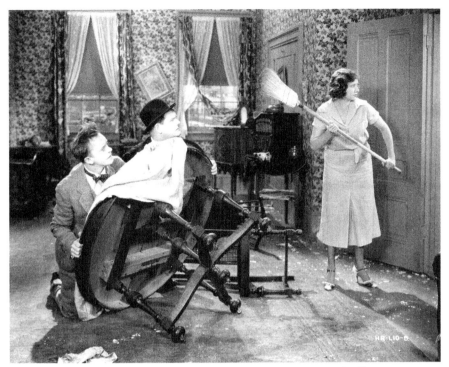

Stan and Ollie shield themselves from the wrath of Arabella, a gag not in the film.

The "Glassblowers' Blowout" is changed in the film to the Cement Workers' Bazaar. We can't decide which sounds like the wilder party.

The story as we know it from the film doesn't start until the fourth page of this script; some L&H scripts only run four pages in total. In the film, Ollie incurs his wife's wrath even further by attempting the subterfuge of talking to "Mr. Jones," his new boss, on the phone when he's really talking to Stan. This is a reworking of an earlier routine used in the 1928 silent *We Faw Down*. The script doesn't include this bit, instead merely suggesting that the wife becomes angry when Ollie asks to go out with Stan yet again.

The best-remembered dialogue exchange from this film is when Ollie says of his wife, "She says that I think more of you than I do of her." When Stan counters with, "Well, you do, don't you?," Ollie responds with "Well, we won't go into that," which is a better line than "Well, yes and no," as offered by the script.

The movie adds a nice punchline to the discussion about adoption; when Ollie says, "We're going to adopt a baby," Stan asks, "What for?," having just forgotten the entire preceding sequence when he was making a case for doing so.

The scripted idea of the wife misinterpreting Ollie's remark of "I know where there's a lot of swell babies" is a clever one, and one wonders why it wasn't used in the movie.

In the script, when Stan strikes a match to see if the light switch was off, Ollie merely asks Stan to bring the lamp near the bed as a night light. The film, however, gives Mr. Hardy an ingenious added line: "Get that floor lamp. I don't want you striking matches

Stan's trip through the transom is a gag not in the film.

all night long!"

The film never really provides an end to the story, it just stops. The script, however, introduces a clever finale (with several new characters), made even more clever by the exact repetition of some of Stan's dialogue earlier in the proceedings.

A still showing Ollie bouncing twin infants on his knees indicates that the script's finale was indeed filmed but deleted. One wonders what that "short finish to be added" would be.

One marvels at how quickly the legal system works in this film, with Ollie and his wife separately able to adopt and bring home infants within an hour or so of hatching the idea, and a process server arriving with two writs just as quickly.

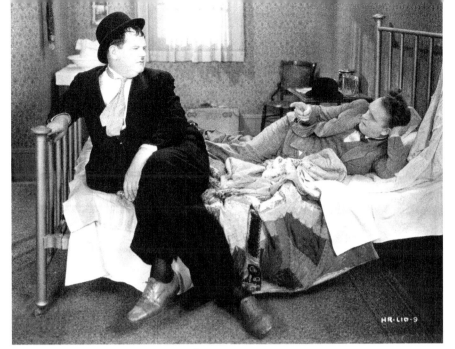

"What you need is a baby in your house."

Director George Marshall is a neighbor much friendlier than the one described in the script.

Little Marjorie Campbell is the new addition to the household.

Process server Billy Gilbert has a little present for each of the boys.

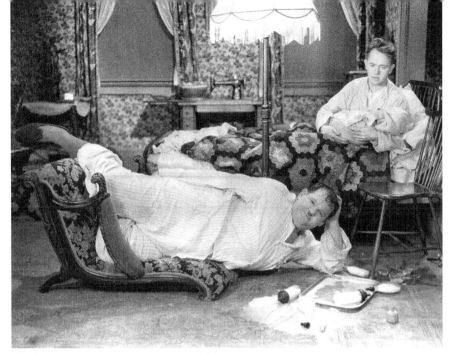

It's a long night trying to take care of the baby.

In a scripted scene filmed but deleted, Ollie's wife has had an even better idea than Stan's, shown by the arrival of twins.

L-10 – LAUREL & HARDY.

Fade in on combination living and dining room of Babe's apartment. Babe's wife is on fixing the breakfast, just putting the coffee on, etc. She goes to the bedroom door and calls, "Oliver." Babe's voice comes over, "What?" The wife says, "Breakfast is on the table." She returns to the table and starts pouring the coffee.

Babe comes out of the room a little bit sleepy-eyed and says, "Why so early?" The wife says, "This is one morning we're going to get breakfast over with before your friend Mr. Laurel oozes himself in. I'm sick and tired of his sponging." Babe acts a little embarrassed at this and sits down, and the wife continues, "You know he's getting on my nerves. Everywhere we go he trails along. We've moved four times in the last six months trying to get away from him, and for some reason or other he always manages to get a room next door."

Babe: "Oh, he's all right - - you just don't understand him."

Wife: "No, and I don't want to!"

Babe: "Well, we've been together for so many years he just can't get along without me."

Wife: "Then why didn't you marry him instead of me?"

Babe gets a little fussed and she says, "Go get the milk." Babe goes to the hall door as the wife exits to the kitchen.

Cut to hallway; Babe enters, picks up a bottle of milk and a bottle of cream, and tiptoes over to Stan's door. Stan is occupying a hall room. Babe tries the door but it is locked. He goes to knock, then realizes he mustn't make any noise in case his wife hears him. He gets an idea, pulls a little hall table over in front of the door, carefully climbs up and looks through the transom which is partly open.

We shoot from his angle and show Stan in funny position in bed.

Cut back to Stan's angle, with Babe's head at the transom. Babe says "Hey!"

Back to Stan; he wakes up and sees Babe.

Cut back to Babe. The transom slips into place so Stan can't hear Babe speak. Stan walks over to the door and in the business of opening the transom it swings up and catches Babe under the chin. Babe gives him a dirty look and says, "Don't come over for breakfast this morning. The wife is sore. I'll hold out something for you and you can have it later." Stan whispers "O.K." and goes to close the transom. It swings over and hits Babe another bump on the head, and from Stan's angle Babe disappears from the transom and we hear a big crash.

Cut to the outside and Babe is sitting in a funny position with the milk pouring all over him and the table collapsed.

Cut to the room next door. One of the lodgers comes out and looks. At this point Babe's wife rushes out and says, "Whatever are you doing?" Babe picks himself up, gives the lodger a dirty look and says, "Never push me again like that!" He takes his wife quickly and exits into the apartment, leaving the lodger dumbfounded.

Cut to the living room. Babe enters with the wife and closes the door. The wife asks, "What did he push you for?" At this point the door opens slowly in back of them and the lodger is standing in the doorway. Babe says, "Why, the dirty thief, I caught him in the act of stealing our milk!" The wife says, "That's terrible - - we ought to report him," and exits to the kitchen. Babe says, "I'll do that the first thing." He turns and takes it big as he sees the lodger. The lodger hits Babe a terrific punch on the nose and Babe does a high-gruesome, causing a China cabinet or something to fall over. The man exits quietly and quickly.

The wife enters, just misses seeing the lodger, and takes it big when she sees Babe in the middle of the wreckage holding his nose. Babe thinks quickly, jumps to his feet, runs to the door and shouts into the hallway, "Now let that be a lesson to you!" and slams the door. The wife asks what happened now, and Babe says, "Oh, it's only that lodger. He came back for more." As the wife turns away, Babe holds his nose again and they both proceed to sit down to breakfast.

Cut back to Stan finishing dressing, standing in front of a mirror. He picks up a perfume atomizer, closes his eyes and it sprays the wall, which he gradually takes and tries to rub it off with his hand. He picks up a towel, starts to rub it off with that and rubs off the wall paper. He becomes all confused and finally pushes the dresser in front of it.

On the dresser he sees two tickets for the Glassblowers' Blowout. Insert the tickets: "Admit One to the Glassblowers' Blowout. Lots of fun – lots to eat. For Men only. (Hold a lighted match in back of this.)" On the reverse side are pictures of dancing women.

Stan strikes a match and holds the card in front of it, and we see a shadow of a hula dancer. As Stan moves the card back and forth the figure goes into motion. Stan gets interested in this and the match burns his fingers, which brings him out of it. He crosses over to the phone and asks for apartment 18.

Cut to Babe's apartment. He and the wife are on having breakfast. The phone rings. The wife gets up and answers it.

Cut to Stan and he says "Hello."

Back to the wife. She looks disgusted and walks away leaving the receiver off the hook.

Back to Stan and he says "Hello" again and wiggles the hook.

Cut downstairs to the apartment house manager sitting at a small switchboard; he says "Hello?"

Back to Stan; he tells the manager he can't get apartment 18.

Back to the manager. He plugs in and waits a second, then speaking to Stan says, "They were in there a minute ago – maybe they left the receiver off the hook." Stan says, "What for?" and the manager says, "Well, maybe they didn't have ---" He gets all burned up and says, "How do I know what for?" Stan takes it, hangs the receiver up and exits.

Back to Babe's apartment and they are both eating hotcakes. Babe has one on his plate and is pouring syrup over it. He finishes this, picks up the newspaper and starts to read. A knock comes on the door, they both take it and the wife says, "See who that is." Babe not thinking lays his newspaper down on top of the hotcake, then crosses over to the door.

Cut to hallway; Stan is outside Babe's door. He hears Babe coming and thinking it might be the wife, exits quickly back to his room and closes the door. Babe comes out and looks around. Stan opens his door a little, peeks out and whispers to Babe, "You left your telephone receiver off the hook," and closes the door again. Babe exits back into his room.

Cut to Babe's living room. He sheepishly picks up the receiver and hangs it up on the hook. The wife is still looking disgusted. Babe sits down at the table, picks up his newspaper to continue reading, and the hotcake is stuck to the paper, Babe not noticing it. The telephone rings. Babe looks a little annoyed, folds his paper, folding the hot cake inside it, lays it down on the table goes to the phone and says "Hello."

Stan: "Is that you, Ollie?"

Babe: "Yes."

Stan: "Are you there?"

Babe: "Certainly I'm here."

Stan: "I want to talk to you."

Babe: "All right."

Stan hangs up the phone. Babe stands waiting a second, looks very annoyed and hangs up. He goes and sits at the table, picks up the newspaper, this time keeping it folded. Not looking at his plate, he picks up his fork and starts feeling for the hotcake. He finally looks, discovers the hotcake is gone and starts looking around for it. As he does so, a knock comes on the door. Babe and the wife both start for the door and they collide. The wife picks up some plates and exits to the kitchen. Babe throws the newspaper down on the chair and exits to the hall.

Cut to hall. Stan is on again and repeats the last business of running back to his room. Babe comes out, Stan peeks back through his door and Babe says, "What do you want?"

Stan: "Are you alone?"

Babe: "No, my wife's here."

Stan: "Oh, I wanted to talk to you privately."

Stan goes back into his room, leaving Babe bewildered again.

Babe goes back to the table, lifts the paper off the chair and the hotcake slides out onto the chair. He sits down on it and the phone bell rings again. Babe now disgusted lays the paper open with the sticky side up on the chair. He goes to the phone and says, "What do you want?"

Stan: "On my way home last night I found a couple of

tickets for the glassblowers' blowout. They're having a big affair tonight. Lots of fun – lots to eat. It's for men only. Can you go?"

Babe: "Wait a minute - - I'll ask the wife."

Babe walks away leaving the receiver hanging again.

Cut to the kitchen; the wife is on washing dishes as Babe enters. She takes a plate out of the water and starts to dry it. Babe gallantly takes it away from her and says, "Let me do it, honey." The wife gives him a dirty look and says, "Now what are you after?" Babe gets a little fussed and says, "Stan's been invited to a quiet little affair tonight and he wanted me to go along." She still keeps looking at him, and Babe getting a little more fussed continues, "All the big business men in town are going to be there and I might do some good for myself." The wife just continues to look at him. Babe adds, "And he said it would rest my nerves to get a little relaxation." Babe at this point has dried the dish. He puts it back in the water, takes out another wet one and starts to dry it. The wife says, "Nothing doing! You're not going out of this house tonight!" Babe says, "Now wait a minute, honey. You don't understand. This might be my big opportunity."

Cut to Stan who is listening over the phone, and a big row starts, Babe and his wife arguing back and forth, and we hear China breaking, tin pans, etc., and the war is on. Stan gets a little nervous and hangs up. The crashing and argument continue and over this scene we hear the voice of the wife, crying, "I'm going home to mother!"

Cut to hallway. Stan comes out, listens at Babe's door, the crashes still going on. He gets a high-backed chair and pulls it in front of Babe's door and steps up on the back of the chair. The transom is open a little and Stan sees Babe come running out of the kitchen followed by the wife. Babe rushes to the door and opens it to make a hurried exit. As the door opens, Stan's chair overbalances and collapses, and Babe falls over Stan and the chair. The wife rushes in to the doorway and stands watching them pick themselves up. On the way to the door, Babe has grabbed his hat and coat, and they exit into Stan's room.

Cut to interior of Stan's room. Babe sits on the bed, all in. Stan looks a little dumb and says, "What did she say?" Babe says, "Well, I went in the kitchen, and she said that --- What do you mean, what did she say? You heard what she said!"

Stan: "Well, what seems to be the matter?"

Babe: "Oh, I don't know. It just seems we can't get along. She thinks that I think more of you than I do of her."

Stan: "Well, you do, don't you?"

Babe takes it and says, "Well, yes and no."

Stan: "You know what the trouble is?"

Babe: "No."

Stan: "What you need is a baby in the family."

Babe: "Now what difference would that make?"

Stan: "Well, it's a well known fact, there can be no domestic happiness without a child."

Babe: "I don't see how that would help any."

Stan: "It would keep her mind occupied – you could go out nights and she wouldn't think a thing about it. All your troubles would be over."

Babe: "That's a good idea. At last you're getting some intelligence."

Stan: "Certainly. I'm not so dumb as you look."

Babe: "You bet your life you're not so dumb as I look."

Babe suddenly takes it and corrects himself, then says, "Come on, let's go."

Stan: "What are you going to do?"

Babe: "I'm going to adopt a baby."

They put on their hats and coats and start down the hall. The wife opens the door quietly and looks after them, watching them go. Stan says, "Where do we go to get one?" Babe says, "Leave it to me. I know where there's a lot of swell babies." They exit down the hall.

The wife takes it big, rushes to her bedroom, brings out a suitcase and starts packing hurriedly. In the midst of this she quickly starts to write a letter. Fade out.

Title: "Without even fainting, Mr. Hardy became the proud father of a bouncing baby boy - - - Mr. Laurel remained throughout the crisis, and is pleased to state that father and child are doing nicely."

Fade in on the upper hall. Stan and Babe enter, Babe carrying the baby and looking all pleased. Stan is all smiles and carrying several small packages and a box of cigars. The lodger enters from his room. Stan offers him a cigar. Babe attracts Stan's attention and motions not to give the lodger any cigars. Stan obeys and Babe gives the lodger a dirty look and flounces to the door of his own apartment. He then hands the baby to Stan and says, "You wait here until I call you. I want to give Arabella a big surprise."

Cut to interior of the apartment. Babe enters, teeming with excitement, looks around, and not seeing his wife, tiptoes and looks into the kitchen. He starts to look a little worried, comes back to the center of the room and "yoo-hoos." He listens for an answer and does it again.

Cut outside to Stan. He hears Babe and replies "Yoo-hoo."

Back to Babe; he takes it and smiles, then says, "Where are you, honey?"

Cut back to Stan and he says "I'm out here."

Babe takes it big, exits to the hall and says, "I don't mean you! Come on in." Stan enters with Babe and says, "What's the matter?"

Babe: "Aarabella isn't home."

Stan: "Where is she?"

Babe: "Maybe she went out to do some – How do I know where she is? You mind your own business!

At this point a knock comes on the door. Babe says, "Come in." A character, who looks like a typical process server, enters and speaks to Babe, asking him if he is Mr. Hardy. Babe replies "Yes, sir," and the man reaches into his pocket and hands Babe a summons.

Babe: "What's this?"

Man: "Your wife's suing you for divorce, and that's a restraining order forbidding you to dispose of anything till she gets it."

Babe takes it big. The man then looks over at Stan and asks if he is Mr. Laurel. Stan says, "Yes ma'am – Yes, sir." The man hands Stan a writ and Stan says, 'What's this for?" The man says, "You're being sued for alienation of Mr. Hardy's affections."

The man exits and slams the door.

Stan hands Babe the baby, puts the packages, milk bottle, etc., on the table, then pulls out an envelope, lays that on the table and says, "There's the adoption papers." He starts for the door. Babe takes the attitude of a brokenhearted wife.

Babe: "Listen! You can't leave me here alone with this child!"

Stan: "Why?"

Babe: "You know you're just as much responsible for it as I am."

Stan: "What have I got to do with it?"

Babe: (Very indignant) "What have you got to do with it? You're the one that wanted me to have a baby, and now that I've got one you won't stay and help me take care of it!"

Stan: "I don't know anything about babies."

Babe: "You should have thought of that before we got it."

Stan has a takem and again starts to exit.

Babe: "So you're going to desert me just at the time when I need you most?"

Stan: "Well, I can't afford to get mixed up in this. I have my life, my career to think of."

He again starts for the door. Babe grabs him and slams the door.

Babe: "You're not going out of this room!"

The baby starts to cry and Babe orders Stan to give it some milk. Fade Out.

Fade in at the home of the wife's father and mother. The wife is crying and the father is consoling her.

Father: "Come, come, my dear, you mustn't jump at conclusions this way. Divorce is a serious thing."

Wife: "I'm through. He thinks more of that friend of his than he does of me. I might as well be divorced, for all I see of him.

Mother: "You know what the trouble is, don't you? What you need is a baby in the family."

The wife starts to give this some thought and says, "Do you really think that would make any difference?" The

father says, "All the difference in the world. It would give him
something to occupy his mind and keep him at home nights. It
wouldn't be any time at all before he forgot that friend of his."
The other says, "Come along, darling. You've got to go home – I'll
go with you." Fade Out.

Fade in back at the apartment, night, with lights of the
city in background through window. Stan and Babe are now
in night shirts, etc. The baby is crying and Babe is walking the
floor with it. Stan is walking along with him up and down. Babe
finally gets annoyed and says, "Don't keep following me around!
Do something to help me!" He hands the baby to Stan and says,
"Here, give it something to eat. Maybe it's hungry again."

Stan sits on a chair, places the baby on his lap and
bounces it up and down. The baby continues to cry. Stan starts
to undo his night shirt at the neck. He gets the front of his night
shirt open and looks down, then reaches in and brings out a milk
bottle with a nipple on it.

Babe gives a takem at this and says, "What are you
keeping the milk there for?" Stan says, "I put it there to keep
it warm." He feeds the baby the milk and the baby finally stops
crying.

They now decide to put the baby to bed. They do so and
Babe says, "Now don't make any noise. Come on." Babe quietly
gets into bed. Stan turns the lights off at a switch, and through
the shaft of moonlight he quietly gets into bed. The baby is now
in the middle of them.

Stan suddenly starts to get up again. Babe watches him.
Stan strikes a match, goes over and looks at the switch.

Babe: "What are you doing?"

Stan: "I wanted to be sure I turned the lights off."

Babe: "Come on back to bed!"

Stan starts back to bed and Babe says, "Wait a minute –
bring that lamp over here. We might need a night light. I'll fix a
bottle of milk in case the baby wakes up."

Stan goes over, gets the lamp, takes the plug out and
carries it over alongside the bed, as Babe gets up and tiptoes
toward the kitchen. As Stan is bringing the lamp over, Babe trips
over the cord with a loud crash. The baby starts crying again.

Babe switches on the lights, rushes into the kitchen, grabs a bottle of milk from among several in a basin of water, rushes back to the bed and gives it to the baby, who stops crying. Babe says to Stan, "Why don't you be careful?" He crosses over to the switch, puts the lights out and tiptoes back to the kitchen. He quietly puts the switch on in the kitchen and closes the door.

Stan now can't find a place to plug in the lamp. He happens to glance out of the window and we see the electric sign reading "Rooms." The electric light keeps going on and off every minute. Stan opens the window takes a bulb out of the sign and puts the lamp plug in. The lamp in the room immediately lights up, and Stan is perfectly satisfied that he had a good idea.

During this business, cut to Babe in the kitchen fiddling with the milk bottles, trying to put the nipples on etc.

Stan gets into bed and is just about to lie down when the light goes off. He sits up and goes to turn it on when it comes on by itself. He has a takem, then lies down again and again the light goes out.

Cut to Babe. He has all the milk bottles, etc., placed on a tray. He opens the kitchen door and starts to exit. As Babe starts across the room the lamp goes out again and we hear a terrific crash. The light comes up again and Babe says, "Stop fiddling with that light!" Babe smacks at Stan, then goes over and turns the light off and gets into bed.

Cut to clock for time lapse of an hour.

Back to Stan and Babe fast asleep and Stan is snoring. The snoring causes the baby to wake up and it starts crying. Babe half wakes up and cuddles Stan up to him like a mother fondling a child. The baby continues to cry. Babe very sleepy reaches to the table, gets a bottle of milk and sticks it into Stan's mouth. Stan starts to enjoy it thoroughly in his sleep, sucking on it like a young calf. Babe still half asleep takes the bottle away and starts to put it down, but the baby starts crying again. Babe sticks the bottle back into Stan's mouth and starts singing "Rock-a-bye my baby."

Cuts to Stan enjoying the milk.

In the middle of this the baby starts crying again and Babe can't understand how the baby is crying with the milk bottle in its mouth. He gets a little suspicious, turns and pulls on the lamp, then looks back and sees the position he has Stan in. He gets very annoyed at this, pulls the milk bottle away from Stan, and not noticing that the nipple has come off in Stan's mouth, he places the bottle in back of him in bed. Stan takes the nipple out of his mouth before Babe turns again, and sits up in bed. Babe starts to bawl him out.

Suddenly Babe feels the warm milk pouring into bed and he does his usual takem, then discovers the empty bottle and jumps out of bed.

The baby starts to cry and Babe says, "You hold it while I get some more milk." Stan picks up the baby in bed and starts "Shushing" it. Babe puts on the light and exits to the kitchen. On his way out the light goes out again and he does another brodie with a big crash, and says "Will you stop playing with that light?" He then crosses to the switch and puts on the lights proper, and starts for the kitchen.

At this point the wife enters looking very beautiful. Babe turns and sees her and she says, "Oliver!" She crosses to him and they put their arms around each other. The wife says, "Will you forgive me, darling?" Babe says, "Certainly, honey, I knew you'd come back. You don't know how I've missed you."

Wife: "I know now what's been the matter with us. What we need is a baby in the family.

Babe: "That's just what I've been thinking."

Wife: "I knew you'd feel that way."

They embrace again, and we cut to a shot from Stan's angle, Babe embracing his wife and looking over her shoulder at Stan. Babe mentions for Stan to bring the baby. Stan starts to get out of bed.

Back to Babe and his wife. She says, "I'm so happy, darling." She turns and calls, "Oh Mama..." The mother enters through the door wheeling a perambulator with twins in it. At this point Stan comes down carrying the other baby. Babe takes it big when he sees the twins. The wife all enthused says, "Look what I've adopted, darling."

Babe: "Why two of them?"

Wife: "I wanted to make doubly sure of our happiness."

(Short finish to be added)

TOWED IN A HOLE

Production history: Production L-11. Script written late October 1932. Filmed Monday, October 31 through Wednesday, November 9. Released December 31. Copyrighted January 18, 1933 by MGM (LP 3577). Two reels.

Produced by Hal Roach. Directed by George Marshall. Photographed by Art Lloyd. Edited by Richard Currier. Sound by James Greene. *Uncredited Assistance:* Assistant Director, Lloyd French. Assistant Cameraman, Edward L. White. Story suggested by George Marshall. Additional material, Charles Rogers.

With Stan Laurel (Himself), Oliver Hardy (Himself), Billy Gilbert (Proprietor of Joe's Junk Yard).

At last Stan and Ollie are a success, driving their Model T through the Culver City streets and selling fish. Ollie sings "Fresh fish!" while Stan accompanies him by blowing a horn. Then Stan has a million-dollar idea: if they catch their own fish, their income will be clear profit. The boys buy a dilapidated old boat and try to repair and paint it themselves; Ollie is frequently soaked with water or paint, and Stan receives two black eyes for his blundering. Finally, their gleaming craft is ready to be towed to the pier; the boys' car is unable to pull it, so Stan suggests putting up the sail. A gust of wind sends the boat proudly pushing the car into a valley, destroying both vehicles. Stan runs to the wreckage; finding his horn undamaged, all is right in his world. Mr. Hardy does not share this view, and gives chase to his partner.

Stan Laurel loved all things aquatic. His birthplace, Ulverston, is very close to Morecambe Bay. His favorite recreation was fishing, and he caught many marlin and swordfish in frequent visits to Catalina Island, 26 miles from the California mainland. Stan recalled in a letter of February 24, 1960 to Peter Preece, "I was a Gold Button member of the Avalon Tuna Club at Catalina Island for several years - had a nice 45ft. boat fully equipped for fishing, twin Hall-Scott motors (275 H.P. each) with a speed of 22 knots. During World War II, the Navy took over Island (Catalina) for a training station, so no private craft was allowed in those waters, so I decided to get rid of it - no sense in letting it rot in Dry Dock." Stan's last two homes – apartments in Malibu and Santa Monica – had ocean views.

Boats and fishing figure in several Laurel and Hardy comedies. At one point in the early '30s, Stan and the writers were working on a story that had to do with fishing, but ultimately wasn't much of a catch. An undated and unfinished script survives with the title *Live Bait*, and it may well have been a preliminary idea that evolved into *Towed in a Hole*.

In it, Ollie's wife, Mrs. Phyllis Hardy, is a clubwoman, and it's her assignment to prepare a luncheon for the "Political Rights of the American Women" group. Stan and Ollie are attempting to peel potatoes and onions for the event, with Ollie getting an

Stan's not so melodious horn accompanies Ollie's singing "Fresh fish!"

unwelcome spritz in the eye from Stan's onion. Mrs. Hardy sends the boys to get fifty pounds of halibut. On the way, Stan sees two fishing poles in the window of a sporting goods store, and suggests to Ollie that if they catch the fish instead of buying it, then it will be really fresh.

The boys cast their lines from the deck of a live-bait boat, but an old sailor informs them that they'd have better luck if they actually used some bait. Ollie is annoyed at this, muttering to Stan, "And that man we bought these poles from said they were ready to use!" When Ollie asks the elderly gentleman what they should use to attract the fish, he replies, "Fish," which results in a misunderstanding:

> BABE: But how do we get them?
>
> MAN: Get what?
>
> STAN: Fish!
>
> MAN: Fish!

This confusion is interrupted by two fetching young ladies strolling by, who tell Stan and Ollie, "You need some live bait, and we'll show ya where to get it!" Stan is dismayed at the brashness of the two "freshies," but Ollie follows the girls over to the live-bait tank – and at this point, the script ends.

Laurel and the writers were having trouble developing a story in mid-October 1932. Henry Ginsberg had told a reporter for *The Hollywood Filmograph* that a new L&H

While repairing and painting their boat, little messes –

picture would be put into production on October 17th, but on the 22nd, the publication reported that the team's new film was still "Preparing," with director George Marshall as the only person assigned to the project.

Marshall caught a good story idea while driving to the Roach studio one morning. "I passed in Culver City one of these little fish wagons, it could've been on a Friday; and this fellow was touting his wares with a long horn, on the street. So I went on and I said, 'Well, maybe that could be the answer, with the boys selling the fish, but to make more money, catching their own fish.' That was the idea. I had about that much when I got to the studio and Stan was sitting there in his room. I told him about the idea and he said, 'Yeah, that just might work.'" Marshall, Stan and Charlie Rogers began making notes and developing the storyline of Stan and Ollie needing a boat to catch their own fish.

Their First Mistake had needed only a few inexpensive interior sets; this may have allowed more funding for this film, which was shot entirely outdoors. The opening scene was shot on Culver City's Madison Avenue (which had earlier been the location for *Hog Wild*), while the rest of the film was shot on the ten acre "Arnaz Ranch" property Roach owned a mile north of the studio. The supporting cast couldn't have been very costly, as it consisted solely of Billy Gilbert, who received prominent billing in the opening titles for a performance that lasts all of 13 seconds.

The movie's opening scene is very close to the scripted version. The most significant difference is when Stan is trying to repeat his brilliant idea to Ollie and concludes in the

-- soon turn into big ones.

film with, "then the profits would – they'd go to the fish." This is the first of four "Tell me that again" routines, the others being in *The Devil's Brother, Oliver the Eighth,* and *The Fixer Uppers.*

Billy Gilbert's part as the proprietor of the junk yard was cut in half; in the film, he has only the first line that we see in the script, which also clarifies that Stan and Ollie are fixing up the boat at the junk yard.

In the script, Stan has the idea to fill the boat with water in order to find its leaks; in the movie, this is Ollie's brainstorm.

The boys' battle of the water buckets almost has a second round in the film, when Stan says, "Well, you started it," and Ollie refutes this, prompting a new escalation of tensions.

In the script, Stan suggests that they take out "this big post" in the cabin so they could stock more fish. Neither he nor Babe realizes that this is the bottom part of the mast, which Babe is about to paint. This is reworked more plausibly in the film. Stan

In the film, Ollie falls into a puddle, but Stan does not join him.

Watching the culmination of their dreams.

All is not lost – Stan's horn remains intact.

has been exiled to the cabin, sporting a newly-acquired black eye as a result of some trespass against Babe. He amuses himself by playing a solitary game of tic-tac-toe, plays a discordant tune on a now-musical saw, and then – in one move that goes immediately from a pose of leisure to one of distress – gets his head caught behind the mast. In order to extricate himself, he starts sawing away at it, prompting some quizzical looks at us from Ollie, who is on a ladder and painting the top part of the very pillar that Stan is sawing. This of course results in a "brodie" from Mr. Hardy when the freshly sawn mast gives way.

Stan told his friend, actor Chuck McCann, that the unscripted tic-tac-toe scene was an idea he thought up while doing another scene. "He got the idea out there at the ranch while blocking out some other scene around the boat," McCann recalled. "Then they had to drive back to the studio, find a stage, and construct a cabin set with a porthole so they could shoot that interior."

Ollie's commanding "Come here!" to Stan after taking the fall, possibly portending another battle of water buckets, was replaced with the gag of Stan first revealing one black eye, and then both.

The script's suggestion that Stan is bound hand and foot to a tree in order to keep him from doing any more damage was replaced in the film by having Stan's hands bound to a barrel.

In an interview with Jordan R. Young in 1974, George Marshall fondly recalled the

A coffee break between takes.

Another laugh between takes.

final sequence that had originally been written. "The sales and releases depended on a certain length of footage, at that time about 1,800 feet. We had the two of them going through traffic, Babe out in front with the car, and Stan in the back with the sailboat, trying to throw out the anchor… We never shot it because we had enough." (Jordan has provided more about this in a Kindle book available from Amazon, *Directing Laurel and Hardy: An Interview with George Marshall.*)

Two days after Marshall finished directing *Towed in a Hole,* Henry Ginsberg fired him. The director had done very well by L&H with *Their First Mistake* and *Pack Up Your Troubles*, also providing a wonderful performance in that film as a malevolent Army cook. He continued to direct films and television episodes until 1972, and essayed a couple of acting roles just before his death at 83 in Los Angeles on February 17, 1975. He retained fond memories of his association with Laurel and Hardy to the end of his days. "Stan was wonderful," he said. "I learned a lot from him rather than he learning anything from me."

The original one-sheet poster.

L-12 - LAUREL & HARDY

Fade in on Stan and Babe coming down the street in a little Ford with a crude looking ice box tied onto the back. On the side of the ice box is printed, "Laurel & Hardy, Dealers in high grade fish. Crabs a specialty." Also hanging on the back is an old fashioned scoop scale. Stan is blowing a fish horn and Babe is singing out, "Fish, nice fresh fish."

Go to closeup of Stan and Babe; they are both seemingly very happy. Babe says, "Well, at last we are a success. Here we are in the fish business and for the first time in our lives making money." Stan agrees with him, then gets a little serious thought and says, "You know, Ollie, I've been thinking of something."

Babe: "What?"

Stan: "I know how we could make a lot more money."

Babe gets interested and asks him how.

Stan: "Well, if we caught our own fish, we wouldn't have to buy any, and whatever we sold would be clear profit."

Babe gives it deep thought and says, "Tell me that again." Stan starts to tell him and says, "Well, if we caught a fish, and whoever we sold it to, they wouldn't have to pay for it, then the profits would --- if you caught a fish ---" Babe stops him and says, "I understand what you mean. Eliminate the middle man." Stan nodes his head that that's what he was trying to get over, and Babe adds, "It's a pretty good idea. I can see it all. Here we are making pennies when we could be making thousands."

Stan: "All we need is a couple of fishing poles."

Babe: "Fishing poles! We're going to get ourselves a boat. Come on."

Stan goes into the big grin as we fade out.

Fade in on long shot of a general junk yard, with parts of old cars, etc., and on one side of the set there is an old boat in a cradle which has four wheels on it. The boat looks a little dilapidated and has evidently been there for several years. Chickens are walking around it, and probably a goat tied to the rudder. Stan and Babe are admiring it with the junk dealer.

The junk dealer is just folding the receipt, which he hands

to Babe and says, "Here's your receipt, Mr. Hardy. Outside of a couple of leaks I told you about, with a little fixing up you'll find she's the trimmest little craft that ever sailed the seven seas."

Babe: "We certainly got a bargain. By the way, if it's all the same to you, we'd like to fix her up here. We haven't any place to take her."

Man: "Sure, go ahead. Stay as long as you like. If you need any tools you'll find them down in the barn. Just help yourself. And if there's anything else you want, call on me."

The man exits. Babe says to Stan, "Well, so far so good. All we've got to do now is fix her up and everything will be plain sailing."

Stan: "What'll we do first?"

Babe: "Well, the first thing to do is to find the leaks."

Stan: "That's easy."

Stan looks over, sees a hose, takes it up on the boat and Babe says, "What are you going to do?" Stan says, "I'll squirt the water inside and if any comes out you will know where it leaks." Babe tells him that's a good idea and starts to take his coat off.

Cut to Stan in the cabin. He turns on the hose and starts spraying the side of the boat.

Cut to Babe on the outside. A stream of water comes out through a little hole and Babe gets it in the eye. He hollers to Stan, "Wait a minute, I found one." Stan comes out with the water still running, looks over the side of the boat with the hose in his hand and says, "Where?" The hose is pointing right at Babe. Babe gets mad, grabs the hose from Stan and puts it into the port hole, then says, "Now let the boat fill up with water and you stay out here. You just do the cleaning up while I do all the important work." Fade Out.

Fade in. Stan is scrubbing the deck and Babe is down on the ground painting the hull. He walks around to the rudder and starts to paint that. Babe calls up to Stan, "Ahoy there!" Stan takes it and Babe says, "See if the boat is full of water yet."

Stan looks down the hatch and we see the boat partly filled. He says to Babe, "Pretty near." Babe says "O. K., as soon as I finish this we'll start looking for leaks."

Stan goes back to his scrubbing. He moves the tiller over

to make more room.

Cut down below and the painted side of the rudder smears up against Babe. He gives a disgusted look and pushes the rudder back into position.

Cut to Stan and the tiller hits him on the fanny. He takes it and pushes the tiller back a little harder. This time it hits Babe and he sits in a paint pot. He gets up pretty mad and pushes the rudder again, and this time it knocks Stan's water bucket over. Stan is sitting on the deck scrubbing between his legs when the bucket behind him upsets, wetting his fanny. He gets up, gets another bucket of water and continues to scrub. This time he moves the tiller the other way, and the rudder smears Babe on the other side. Babe yells up, "What are you trying to do?" Stan stands up with the bucket of water.

Babe gives him a dirty look and slams the rudder over, which causes the tiller to hit Stan on the shins. He lets out a yell and the bucket of water goes overboard.

Cut down below and show the bucket hit Babe. He runs around and starts up on the deck. Stan sees him coming out and runs around the other side. As Babe reaches the deck, cut to Stan on the ground running by the rudder, which he pulls to give more room, which causes the tiller to hit Babe on the shins. Stan hears him holler, stops and looks up. Babe in his fury throws the bucket at Stan. It misses, hits against an old bed spring, bounces back and hits Babe, knocking him right down into the cabin. A terrific splash comes out of the cabin and water pours out of the port holes. Babe comes to a port hole and looks out with one of his helpless expressions. Stan looks at him dumbly and out of embarrassment says, "Let's look for the leaks." Babe does one of his wild exits.

Cut to the upper deck. Babe enters on the run, slips on a bar of soap with a big thud and just lies there.

Cut from Babe's angle to the other end of the deck and Stan looks over.

Back to Babe; he slowly gets up, very nonchalantly picks up the bucket, takes one step into the cabin, fills the bucket with water and walks calmly to the ground. Stan is watching all this, looking a little curious.

Babe starts walking around the boat toward Stan. Stan

notices him coming and starts slowly walking the other way. They both continue looking around corners at each other. Finally Babe catches Stan looking and says, "Come here." Stan pays no attention. Babe repeats, "Come here!" a little more firmly each time. Stan finally edges over to him. Babe takes Stan's hat off and hands it to him, and very daintily pours the water over Stan's head. Stan takes it all. The bucket is finally empty and Babe very daintily scrapes the inside of the bucket to get the last drop, flicking it in Stan's face, and finally gives him one of those "That-for-you" looks.

Babe then hands Stan the bucket. Stan takes it, fills it up with water from the cabin and deliberately throws it at Babe. Babe takes the bucket, fills it up and throws it at Stan. Stan takes it, fills the bucket again and throws it on Babe.

Babe: "Now wait a minute. Isn't this silly?"

Stan: "What?

Babe: "What! Here we are two grown up men acting like a couple of children – quarreling over little trivial matters when we should be thinking big. Just think of it, a big business future ahead of us and we stand here throwing water at each other. We ought to be ashamed of ourselves. Now let's put our brains together so that we can forge ahead. I'll go and get cleaned up while you fix up the cabin. Let's get this thing ship-shape. Remember, united we stand, divided we fall!"

They shake hands, Babe pats Stan on the shoulder and starts out. He slips on the cake of soap again and does another brodie. Fade Out.

Fade in. Babe enters to the boat, all cleaned up, carrying a bucket of paint. He gets up on the deck, looks down into the hold and says, "How you coming?"

Stan: "Say, Ollie, you see this big post in here?"

Babe: "Yes."

Stan: "Well, you know if we took that out we could put in a lot more fish."

Babe: "That's the way to think! Now we're going to get some place."

Babe walks over and starts painting the mast.

Cut to Stan sawing the lower part of the mast in the cabin.

Back to Babe; he has reached as high as he can go with the paint. He pulls up a ladder and leans it against the mast.

Back to Stan still sawing.

Back to Babe climbing the ladder. He reaches the top and starts to paint.

Back to Stan; he finally saws through the mast.

Cut to Babe and the mast starts leaning, finally falling over with ladder, Babe and all. Babe ends up in the duck pond.

Cut to Stan struggling to get the lower part of the mast out of the boat.

Babe gets out furious and starts toward the boat on the run.

Back to Stan inside. The mast suddenly comes out of the socket, which throws Stan against the side of the boat with a terrific thud.

Cut to the exterior. Babe reaches the boat just as the board springs away from the side of the boat, smacks him in the face and knocks him back into the duck pond.

Stan comes up on deck and does a double takem when he sees there is no mast. He looks over and sees Babe, throws down the piece of mast, reaches a life buoy out of the cabin and throws it over to Babe.

Babe gives him a dirty look and says, "Come here." Stan not knowing exactly what he has done doesn't make any move. Babe repeats "Come here!" Stan starts to exit off the boat, suddenly notices the empty bucket, picks it up and exits toward Babe.

Stan enters to Babe. Babe gets out of the water, takes the bucket from Stan and throws it away, shaking his head.
Fade Out.

Fade in on the boat all finished, looking pretty good. Babe has the car hitched to the boat to tow it. Fully satisfied that everything is in order, he exits.

Bring Babe into a setup at a tree where Stan is bound hand and foot. Babe cuts the ropes and releases Stan, and without a word they both get into the car. Babe starts the car and they pull the boat out of the scene.

They come out onto the boulevard, turn a corner and come to the bottom of a steep hill, and the car stops, with the motor still running. The boat is too heavy for the car to pull up the hill. Stan suggests that if they put the sail up the wind might help them get up the hill. Babe O.K.s the idea and Stan proceeds to put up the sail. Babe tells him to tie it off good and tight so that it won't slip. Stan does so and we show the sail suddenly bulge out with the force of the wind.

Back to medium shot and the boat starts moving, pushing the car up the hill. Babe jumps into the car to steer. Everything is fine until they reach the top of the hill and start down the other side. The force of the wind in the sail and the momentum the boat gains makes the car uncontrollable; in other words the car has to go wherever the boat pushes it.

Babe starts yelling to Stan to do something to help him and to let down the sail. Stan is struggling trying to untie the knots. Babe yells to throw out the anchor, which is on the back of the boat. Stan does so and the anchor is now being dragged along the boulevard. It swings over and catches onto a hydrant and pulls it off, and water starts squirting out. They finally go into some wild finish which demolishes both car and boat.

Lap dissolve to the street, similar to the opening location. Stan and Babe are now walking along the sidewalk minus their car, peddling fish. Babe is on crutches and Stan has his arm in a sling. Stan is blowing the horn as Babe is singing "Fresh fish."

Closeup of Babe as he looks at Stan with disgust and says, "Eliminate the middle man!" Fade Out.

TICKETS FOR TWO

The Roach studio closed for its 1933 annual one-month hiatus in mid-April, but after everyone reconvened in May, Stan and the writers were again struggling to come up with an acceptable story idea.

As June began, they had a script that seemed to be workable, and *The Hollywood Reporter* of June 10, 1933 noted:

Laurel-Hardy Starting
Laurel and Hardy will start their first comedy for the new season within the next week. It is titled "Tickets for Two," and deals with the trials and tribulations of a couple of prize fight enthusiasts. Lloyd French directs.

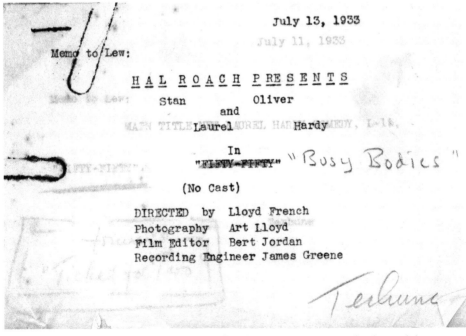

This note is from editor William Terhune to "Lew," or Louis McManus, who designed the main titles. The page visible underneath shows that *Busy Bodies*, formerly *Fifty-Fifty*, was even more formerly *Tickets for Two*.

Fade in on long shot of a lumber yard, a lot of activity going on.

Lap Dissolve to a large buzz saw. On each side of the travelling track which moves toward the saw is a runway wide enough for a person to walk along. There is a character feeding planks onto the runway to the buzz saw, showing the saw cutting the planks in two. This will have to be tricked through the medium of inserts showing the saw cutting the wood. Two or three men with planks on their shoulders walk up the runway, hand the planks to the man who is feeding the saw, and exit for more lumber.

After a couple of characters have gone through, Babe enters with a plank on his shoulder, followed by Stan. They start up the runway and Stan's plank accidentally catches Babe in back of the neck, causing Babe to lose his balance, and he steps onto the moving track. He has to run like hell to keep from being cut in two by the saw. He starts hollering for Stan to help him, but Stan just looks on in a dumb manner. He finally realizes the seriousness of it, throws down his plank and reaches out to grab Babe's hand to pull him off, but Babe being the stronger of the two pulls Stan onto the track in the same position. The man who is feeding the lumber takes it big, runs to the lever and throws it in reverse. The belt makes a sudden stop and starts going the other way, throwing Stan and Babe off the platform into a large pile of lumber with a terrific crash.

At this point we hear the whistle blow for lunch. Stan

This is the front page of the script which, aside from some mentions in trade papers, is about all that survives of *Tickets for Two*.

On June 17, however, the story was still waiting to be committed to film. *The Hollywood Reporter* again noted:

Three Comedies Ready to Start at Roach Lot

Hal Roach has three comedies ready to go into production as soon as work resumes at the studio on June 26. The three are "Tickets for Two" with Laurel and Hardy, a Charley Chase short, and an Our Gang short.

But it wasn't quite ready to go into production. Rather than make the *Tickets for Two* script, Stan and his crew decided to craft an entirely different story, even though they were running over schedule. A new L&H short was supposed to have been in release by June 17th, and this one didn't begin filming until the 19th. Its initial title was *Calling Car Thirteen*, which was replaced during the filming by *Calling All Cars*. It finally reached theaters early in August as *The Midnight Patrol*.

As for the *Tickets for Two* idea, part of it had some merit. The lengthy scene in a stadium parking lot would be expensive and difficult to film, but the idea of Stan and Ollie working in a planing mill presented some interesting possibilities that could be developed.

Virtually unknown since 1933, here is the complete script for the mostly unfilmed *Tickets for Two*. Mostly unfilmed because the framing device of the boys working in the mill obviously developed into *Busy Bodies*; you can make a comparison with that film's script, also in this book.

Some of the sequence detailing the boys' difficulty in parking outside a sports arena resembles a situation encountered by W.C. Fields in his 1935 Paramount feature *Man on the Flying Trapeze*. One would suspect that a writer who had worked on *Tickets for Two* also worked on the Fields picture, but that film's Laurel and Hardy connections were director Clyde Bruckman and editor Richard Currier.

L-14 - LAUREL & HARDY

Fade in on long shot of a lumber yard, a lot of activity going on.

Lap Dissolve to a large buzz saw. On each side of the travelling track which moves toward the saw is a runway wide enough for a person to walk along. There is a character feeding planks onto the runway to the buzz saw, showing the saw cutting the planks in two. This will have to be tricked through the medium of inserts showing the saw cutting the wood. Two or three men with planks on their shoulders walk up the runway, hand the planks to the man who is feeding the saw, and exit for more lumber.

After a couple of characters have gone through, Babe enters with a plank on his shoulder, followed by Stan. They start up the runway and Stan's plank accidentally catches Babe in back of the neck, causing Babe to lose his balance, and he steps onto the moving track. He has to run like hell to keep from being cut in two by the saw. He starts hollering for Stan to help him, but Stan just looks on in a dumb manner. He finally realizes the seriousness of it, throws down his plank and reaches out to grab Babe's hand to pull him off, but Babe being the stronger of the two pulls Stan onto the track in the same position. The man who is feeding the lumber takes it big, runs to the lever and throws it in reverse. The belt makes a sudden stop and starts going the other way, throwing Stan and Babe off the platform into a large pile of lumber with a terrific crash.

At this point we hear the whistle blow for lunch. Stan and Babe pick themselves up and the foreman walks in, just looking at them. Babe gets all coy to the foreman and says, "You are just the man I wanted to see." The foreman says, "What's on your mind?" and Babe explains, "Well, it's like this. Mr. Laurel and I had a couple of tickets given to us for the champion fight, and if you don't mind we'd like to take the afternoon off." The foreman says, "Why, certainly – it's perfectly all right with me. Go ahead and have a good time." Babe thanks him very profusely and the foreman adds, "And don't come back!" and walks out. Stan and Babe watch him out of the scene. Stan then looks at Babe and says, "What did he mean, don't come back?" Babe says, "Now you see what you've gone and done? You've made us lose our jobs. Come on!" They exit.

Cut to another setup. They enter to their Ford, which is a little dilapidated. They get in and start out.

Lap dissolve to them coming along the street. Babe turns to Stan and says, "Let's have some music." In the dash board of the Ford is a small hole with a piece of string hanging out, and on the end of the string is a nail. Stan pulls the string and the mjsic starts playing. They drive along a little ways and the music starts to die down with a grating sound. Babe stops the car. Stan gets out in a matter-of-fact way, opens up the hood of the car and we insert an old phonograph with a horn. We also see a home-made rack with a few records. Stan turns the record over, sets the needle again, adjusts the string and puts down the hood. He then gets back into the car and pulls the string again, and we hear more music as they drive out.

Lap dissolve to the exterior of a prize fight stadium, with the usual announcements hanging out in front, and people going in. Pan over and alongside the stadium show an entrance with big sign, "FREE PARKING." There are a few cars in there as Stan and Babe drive in and park right up against the wall of the stadium. As they are doing this, other cars are driving in and parking. Stan and Babe exit to the stadium.

As they start to go in, Stan feels for the tickets. He looks in all his pockets and Babe says, "What's the matter?" Stan says, "I can't find the tickets." Babe gives him a dirty look and starts to help him, feeling in his pockets and pulling out marbles, string, etc., giving dirty looks at each thing he produces. Babe then pulls out a postal card from Stan's pocket. Stan grabs it quickly before Babe gets a chance to look at it. Babe says, "What's that?" and Stan says, "It's a postal card from Paris." Babe takes the card from him and bawls him out for having such a thing on his person. He is just about to look at it when a cop passes and Babe quickly hides it in his pocket, getting over the thought that it is a dirty picture. Babe finally sneaks a look at it, and we see it is a picture of the Eiffel Tower. Having gone through all the pockets, Stan takes his coat off and shakes it.

Babe then tries to con the gate man to let them through, telling him they have the tickets and will mail them on to him. They can't get any place with this, and Babe finally decides they had better go home and get the tickets.

They exit and re-enter the parking station. By this time the parking space is pretty well filled, and their car is completely engulfed. They start looking for it and finally spot it away over in the back. Stan says, "How are we going to get out?" Babe says, "Leave it to me. All it requires is a little brains." With Stan in the lead, they start climbing over bumpers to get to their car. They come to the one alongside of theirs and Stan gets off the bumper. Babe steps on it and it breaks off, and he does a brodie. Stan helps him up, and in picking up the bumper accidentally one end of it goes through the window of a closed car. Babe says, "Why don't you be careful?" He grabs the bumper from Stan and it goes through the windshield of another car.

In front of their car is parked a small automatic dump-truck filled with sand. In front of that is a closed car, and in front of that are two other cars. Babe looks the situation over and tells Stan to drive the first car out and Babe will drive the second. They get into the cars and start them up. Stan says, "Where will I put it?" and Babe says, "Park it over on the left there." Stan starts out, followed by Babe. He starts to the right, then realizes it and backs up quickly, smacking Babe's car and knocking the headlights and bumper off. Babe gets out, looks at the damage and says, "Now see what you've done? You drive this car and I'll drive the other." Babe gets into the first car and Stan gets into the second. Babe drives across the parking space and wheels the car around to back it in against the fence. As he does so, Stan happens to have the same thing in mind. He wheels his car around and backs into the space Babe intended to take. Babe not knowing Stan is there backs into him and smashes the radiator.

They try to patch this up the best they can, then go back to take out the closed car which is in front of the dump truck. Stan opens the car to get in and there is a big bulldog in there. It jumps out ferociously and Stan starts running, with the dog after him. Babe yells, "Let him chase you till I get the car parked."

As Stan is running around, Babe pulls the car out. Stan in desperation seeing another car quickly opens the door and jumps in. There are two more dogs in there and Stan dashes out the other door, followed by the three dogs. Babe has just about parked the other car. Stan jumps into that car, followed by the dogs, then exits out the other side, leaving Babe with the three dogs in the car. Stan helps Babe out the window as the dog tears the seat out of his pants. They finally get out of that predicament and come back to the dump truck.

(We have another gag that follows this, where Babe, hearing the excitement of the crowd, gets onto the top of a car to look through a window and see what's going on. As he does this, Stan takes it on himself to move the car alongside of him. There is a cop inside the stadium. He turns and sees Babe, bawls him out and tells him to buy a ticket if he wants to see the fight. Babe, a little embarrassed and thinking the other car is still there, steps off and does a brodie. As he lands on the ground, Stan decides to back up again, and runs over Babe. Babe comes up in front of the radiator looking at Stan, very much disheveled and resigned to the situation.)

Babe now tells Stan to move the dump truck and to be careful. Stan starts the motor. Babe is in back cranking the Ford. Stan pulls a lever and the automatic truck tips up, the whole load of sand going over Babe and covering him entirely. Stan pulls the truck out, comes back, sees the pile of sand but can't figure where Babe is. He starts looking around for him, whistling, etc. He finally gets into the Ford, starts it, and realizes he can't move because of the sand. He gets out again. Lying by the sand is a shovel which was originally on the truck. Stan starts to shovel the sand away. He gets a couple of shovelfuls off and on the third he discovers a derby in the sand. He shakes that out and starts to dig again, finally disclosing Babe. Babe naturally is very pleased. He gets up and starts to chase Stan.

While they are chasing their way through the cars, a police car drives in with two cops. They park in front of the Ford, lock their car and exit into the stadium.

Stan and Babe return and discover there is another car in their way. Babe gives a helpless look and goes to open the door of the car to drive it out, but discovers it is locked. He tries frantically to open the door, getting exasperated. He then suggests to Stan to get under the car, push up the floor board, reach in and open the window. Stan crawls under the car but goes a bit too far and gets under the next car. He comes up and finds himself sitting in the car next to the one he should be in. He now has to open the door, get out and repeat the business on the proper car. This time he can't get into the car and is trying to reach the window with his hand. Accidentally his hand lights on the button of the siren, which causes it to give a long, loud shriek.

Cut to the front of the stadium. The cops come out wondering what it is. They go to the entrance of the parking station and watch Stan and Babe monkeying around with their car.

Stan finally comes up and says he can't make it. Babe says, "Can you imagine anybody dumb enough to lock their car in a public parking space? I'm going to teach them a lesson!" He picks up a big rock and starts smashing the window. The cops take this and start toward their car. Stan does a double takem as he sees them. He tries to get Babe's attention as Babe gets into the car and starts wearing out the motor trying to start it. Babe finally sees the cops, gets all fussed, and the cops ask him what he is doing. Babe starts to explain, "Well, it was like this. My friend, Mr. Laurel, and I were going to the fights and he left the tickets home." The cop says, "Don't worry, "I'll give you a ticket." Babe thanks him profusely and says, "If it wouldn't inconvenience you, I'd like to have one for my friend Mr. Laurel." The cop says he will be delighted, and takes out the pad and starts writing two tickets.

While he is writing the tickets, the other cop drives the police car out. He hands Stan and Babe the tickets and we hear wild cheers from the crowds. The cops get excited and run to look through the window to see the knockout. Stan and Babe take this opportunity, jump into their car and beat it. The cops realize they have started out and follow them, with the siren going, etc.

Cut to a couple of speeding shots along the street, crossing intersections, through stop signals, etc.

They finally come to the set of the lumber yard again. Stan and Babe drive in, looking back for the cops. They run up the runway and the car goes right into the buzz saw, which cuts it clean in two. Stan picks up his hat and discovers that the tickets were in the hat band. FADE OUT.

BUSY BODIES

Production history: Production L-15. Script written mid-July 1933. Shot circa July 15-25. Copyrighted September 16, 1933 by MGM (LP 4129). Released October 7. Two reels.

Produced by Hal Roach. Directed by Lloyd French. Photographed by Art Lloyd. Edited by Bert Jordan. *Uncredited Assistance:* Assistant Director, Jack Roach. Sound by James Greene.

With Stan Laurel (Himself), Oliver Hardy (Himself), Charlie Hall (Mill worker), Tiny Sandford (Foreman), Charley Young (Co-worker with coat), Dick Gilbert (Shoveler), Jack Hill (Co-worker kicking barrel of shellac).

Stan and Ollie spend a happy morning in their Model T, driving to their jobs at a planing mill. The boys spend most of their workday cleaning up their own messes. Stan accidentally locks Ollie into a window frame, then strips away the seat of his trousers with a plane, then (not so accidentally) glues a paintbrush to his chin. Shaving off the brush results in Ollie angrily pulling a hose and yanking an entire sink off a wall; the impact sends him flying into a pulley, through a floor, and into a sawdust flue. After a wild ride through its path, he is ejected outside onto a shed, which he smashes. Their foreman chases Stan and Ollie to their car; in haste, they drive into a bandsaw, which slices the Ford neatly in half.

After completing *The Midnight Patrol*, Stan and the writers returned to the unused script for *Tickets for Two* and decided to develop what had just been a framing device, the idea of the boys working in a planing mill. Carpentry had prompted a number of the gags in Stan's 1924 two-reeler for Roach, *Smithy*, as well as the 1928 L&H release *The Finishing Touch*. Babe had played the brutish, whip-brandishing foreman of *The Sawmill* in Larry Semon's 1921 short. (By comparison, foreman Tiny Sandford in *Busy Bodies* is the personification of affability.)

The working title for this picture was *Fifty-Fifty*, which was rejected because it had already been registered by the Pathé studio. (In fact, there had already been at least six movies with this title.) *Busy Bodies* doesn't describe the boys' occupation here with any more detail than *Fifty-Fifty*, but it was deemed to be usable, because nobody realized that Pathé had also used this title in 1928 for a *Sport Pictorials* short featuring writer Grantland Rice.

As with *Towed in a Hole*, this script is just as notable for what it doesn't contain. As George Marshall had noted, "Sometimes the props would lead into better things than we had written." There are props galore in this setting, and Laurel and Hardy make the most of them.

In the opening scene, the boys have more dialogue in the script than in the film, where it's pared to its bare essentials.

Stan doesn't change the needle on the boys' "radio," he swaps out records. However,

Ollie has been framed.

what's supposed to be a different record resumes with "Smile When the Raindrops Fall," which was the tune on the first record. Radios in automobiles were a new option in 1933, which made this a topical gag.

In the film, a rivalry between the boys and Charlie Hall is established when Stan and Ollie arrive in their Model T and loudly honk the horn just as Charlie has finished picking up a large bundle of wood. At the end of this scene in the movie, just as Stan is pulling his bag of tools out of the car's trunk, Ollie closes the lid too soon and it slams onto Stan's fingers. As Stan waves his hand in pain, Ollie reprimands him with, "Clumsy!" This is a subtle but telling illustration of Ollie's character. (Babe Hardy described him as "the guy who's dumber than the dumb guy, only he doesn't know it.")

The film has a perfectly-timed sequence as the boys enter the main workshop. Just as Ollie is about to walk in, another workman outside and behind him yells, "Got a match?" Ollie replies, "Sorry, I don't smoke!" As he's saying this, another workman is walking in front of him, carrying a large plank, so that when Ollie turns around, he walks smack into it and falls down. Stan and Ollie both run into another plank-bearing workman before they can finally run into the shop.

Having given co-worker Charlie Hall a cigar, Stan now alerts foreman Tiny Sandford to this gross violation of the shop's "No Smoking" policy.

In the script Ollie breaks a window frame over Stan's head, but in the film, Stan makes Ollie contort himself into all sorts of twisted positions while trying to extricate his hands from the window frame. Eventually, Ollie, Stan and the window frame all crash onto passing workman Charlie Hall, who complains, "That's the second time you've picked on me!" Also in the film but not in the script is the moment when Stan looks at some blueprints and Ollie asks what he's doing. Stan says, "I was looking at the blueprint, trying to open the window." Ollie replies, "Why, that's a blueprint of the Boulder Dam!"

The scenes in the script following the moment when Stan "planes off" the seat of Babe's trousers are a little more complex than they are in the film, and likely pay more attention to Mr. Hardy's derriere than he would have appreciated. Also more than many regional censor boards would have appreciated.

Those of us who are not mechanically inclined will appreciate learning what some of the implements in the carpentry shop are called. I had to look up "spokeshave," though. It's a small blade with handles for both hands; in the film, however, Stan uses a standard wood plane. It looks much more menacing as a device for shaving the face, hence the closeup of Ollie looking apprehensive when Stan sharpens it and tests the blade by snapping it with his thumb, resulting in a resonant "ping!"

In the film, when Ollie is stuck in the flue, Stan does not return to where Ollie fell and intentionally drop a barrel of shellac to prompt his expulsion; instead, Mr. Laurel

A lunch break – shown in several stills, but not in the film.

climbs up a long ladder to the suction outlet and hands Ollie his derby, since that's the most important item of business at the moment. Another workman, kicking the barrel of shellac, accidentally drops it down the hole in the floor; it travels through the flue and sends Stan and Ollie diving into a tool shed.

Tiny Sandford's wordless but impressive performance as the shop foreman is nowhere to be found in the script. The film has him as referee during one of Stan and Ollie's skirmishes with Charlie Hall, and both Sandford and Hall wind up on the receiving end of Stan and Ollie's dramatic fall from the highly elevated suction pipe.

Tiny runs into a tool shed, which is immediately flattened by Stan, Ollie and their ladder. Charlie, in trying to escape this fate, runs and trips into a trough which appears to be filled with whitewash. As the boys recover from their fall, sitting in the debris of the tool shed, Ollie says, "Will you let go of my ears?," since Stan has been hanging onto them all through their rapid descent. They hear a knocking from a door, then realize that one is lying flat in front of them. They open it to reveal Mr. Sandford, whose glowering countenance promises a quick dismissal from employment, and maybe from the planet.

The script's elaborate gag of having Ollie being carried on a moving belt toward a band saw (the old melodrama routine employed by top-hatted villains against comely young maidens) was scrapped in favor of just having the boys run back to the Model T we saw at the start of the film and – as per the script, "our last routine of cutting the Ford in two."

An altercation between the boys results in Ollie's new beard – a brush glued to his chin.

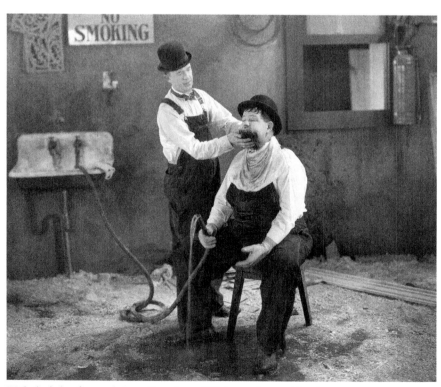

With the help of a wood plane, Stan shaves Ollie's unwelcome chin adornment.

Ollie has the flue – or it has him.

Mr. Hardy has toppled onto a shed, demolishing it; foreman Sandford, who was in it, is about to give chase.

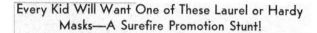

Every Kid Will Want One of These Laurel or Hardy Masks—A Surefire Promotion Stunt!

Here's an exploitation stunt that has 'em all stopped! A cardboard mask of Stan Laurel or Oliver Hardy. Every kid will want one. They're a sensation at parties, parades or any other festive occasion.

The mask consists of a life-size reproduction of Laurel or Hardy—full face—to be held in place on the face of the wearer by means of rubber bands attached to each side and on the back of each mask. The mask is reproduced in full color lithography (not less than four color printings).

Prices: 500—$11; 1-5000 at $20 per thousand; 5-10,000 at $18.75 per thousand; 10-25,000 at $18 per thousand; 25-50,000 at $16 per thousand; 50,000 and over at $15 per thousand. For complete details write Einson-Freeman Co., Long Island City, N. Y.

The press sheet offered these promotional masks. Many grown-up kids would want those today.

Those masks as modeled by the genuine articles.

L-15. Laurel & Hardy.

Fade in – Stan and Babe riding in their Ford on their way to work. They are both very happy. Babe says: "What a beautiful morning." Stan says: "It sure is. You know, we're havin' a lot of weather lately." Babe, without thinking, says: "We sure are. It's good to be alive." Stan says: "Yes, the air's full of it." Babe says: "What d'ya mean, the air's full of it? Let's have some music. Turn on the radio." Stan reaches to the dashboard and - -

We see a hole in it with a piece of string through it with a nail attached to the end.

Stan pulls the string and the music starts playing. Babe continues: "Yes, sir. We have everything to live for. A swell job; a nice car, nearly paid for; and the whole world seems bright. Even you look bright." Stan beams at this, then does a take 'em and tries to think over just what Babe said. At this point, the music starts slowing down. Babe stops the car.

Stan steps out of the car, lifts up the hood and we - -

Show an old phonograph sitting alongside the motor.

Stan lifts up the needle, turns over the record, replaces the needle, gets back into the car.

Stan pulls the string on the dashboard again, and as he does - -

We insert the lever of the phonograph being pulled by the piece of string and the record starts revolving. Music continues to play.

We now cut to a lumber yard and show a lot of activity going on.

Stan and Babe enter in their Ford and in a very businesslike manner, stop, get out of the car, take their lunch pails, etc. Both exit and - -

We take them into the carpenter shop. They greet everybody with a good morning. Both take off their coats and diligently start in to work. Stan gets all his tools set, finds his gum under the bench and starts planing. A little distance from him is Babe, who is fixing a window sash. It has two practical completed windows in it. Babe is having trouble trying to make the windows work. He calls over to Stan and says: "Come and help me with these windows. I can't get them up or down."

Stan goes over. Babe gives him a hammer and tells him to level it off on the top while he holds it. Stan gets up on the bench in order to reach the top. The lower half of the window is up. Babe is holding one side of the window frame and his hand is resting on the lower part. Stan hits the top of the frame with the hammer and both the upper and lower parts of the window drop onto Babe's hand with a terrific snap.

Babe lets out a holler and reaches to the top of the window to try and pull the windows off his hand. Stan, simultaneously, lifts the upper part of the window and shoves it up with terrific force, catching Babe's other hand in the top of the window. Stan then locks the catch, not noticing that Babe's hands are caught, and goes back to his hammering. Perfectly satisfied with his job, he throws the hammer down on the bench and says: "If there's anything else you need, call me." Stan goes back to his planning.

Babe says: "Come here." Stan goes back to Babe. Babe says: "Will you do me a favor?" Stan says: "What?" Babe says: "Would you mind opening the window?" Stan goes over to a window in the carpenter shop and opens it. Babe walks over to Stan with the whole window frame and breaks it over Stan's head. Stan takes it and goes back to his planing.

Babe then picks up a small piece of lumber, walks alongside of Stan and slams it down on the bench. Stan, at this point, turns away from Babe to clean the savings out of his plane. Simultaneously, Babe lays across the bench to reach a small plane, which is on the other side. Babe's fanny is now in line with the lumber that Stan is planing. Stan turns and making a big sweep with the plane, shaves the fanny out of Babe's pants and underwear. Babe remains laying across the bench with a very injured look. Stan takes it big and, realizing what he has done, becomes a little befuddled. He picks up the piece of material from Babe's pants and the seat of underwear, which is in two parts, the button being undone. Stan places them on the bench and very carefully buttons up the two halves of the underwear.

Babe watches all of this with a resigned look.

Stan then reaches over to the glue pot and, dipping a large brush into it, smears the glue onto the two pieces of material, carefully placing one on top of the other. He shakes them out and carefully places them on Babe's fanny.

Cut to Babe's rear and show insert that Stan has made a mistake and stuck the seat of the pants against his fanny and the underwear part is on the outside.

Babe looks back and views his fanny and again gives a helpless look. Stan, realizing that he has made another mistake, tries to pull it off of Babe's fanny. Babe lets out a holler, getting over that the glue has stuck good and fast. Stan, in utter bewilderment, now quickly sees the paint pot and paints Babe's fanny, covering the white underwear.

Babe now gets up off the bench, examines his fanny and gets an idea. He tells Stan to lay over the bench. Stan dumbly does so. Babe very calmly picks up the plane and, making a large sweeping gesture, takes the seat out of Stan's pants. Babe picks up the piece of cloth, examines it and looks back again. He then deliberately picks up the plane and gives another sweeping gesture, taking the underwear, which he had missed. He very carefully glues them together in a very fancy manner and, to make it a little worse, he pours the glue onto Stan's fanny and uses the brush to smear it around with, ending up with a violent dig with the brush into Stan's fanny. During this, you can see Stan is getting a little burned. Babe finally sticks on the seat of the pants and the underwear onto Stan's fanny and places the brush into the glue pot, slams it down on the bench and gives Stan a defiant nod.

Stan gets off the bench, examines his fanny, then losing his head entirely, he grabs the big glue brush and violently sticks it onto Babe's chin, pushing him out of the scene. We hear a terrific crash and - -

Cut to a setup against a wall. There are a lot of gallon cans around. Babe is laying on his back. Above him is a shelf, which has been knocked loose by the fall and we see a lot of cans still falling onto Babe from the shelf. Babe finally sits up and he has one of these cans on his head which looks something like a helmet and, as he sits up, he looks like a Roman soldier. Babe goes to take the brush off his chin and discovers the glue is stuck fast. He tries two or three times to pull it off, but to no avail. Stan walks into the set, squats down alongside of Babe and is very interested in seeing Babe trying to remove the brush. Babe gives up and looks at Stan. Stan takes hold of the handle of the brush with the good intention of trying to pull it off. He yanks it a little too hard, which pulls Babe's head down onto a square five gallon can, which is in front of him, giving him another terrific bump on the head. Babe is beyond speech. Stan motions for Babe to get up. Babe does so, wondering what Stan will do next. Stan takes him by the handle of the brush and leads him out of the set.

They enter to the bench where they originally started. On the end of it is a vise. Stan opens the vise and pushes Babe's head down toward it and puts the handle of the brush into the vise. Stan then tightens the vise, gets up onto the bench and, with both hands around Babe's neck, gives a terrific heave. Babe lets out a holler and comes up into the picture with all the bristles from the brush sticking to his chin. Stan takes it and looks down at the vise and - -

We insert the handle of the brush sticking firmly in the vise.

Stan looks a little sorry about this, his efforts having failed. He then tries to pull the bristles off of Babe's chin. Babe flinches each time Stan pulls. Stan decides that won't do. Babe is still passive. Stan takes Babe again by the hand and leads him out of the set.

Come in to another setup where there is a wash basin and towel hanging along the side. On one of the faucets is attached an old piece of hose. There is also a bottle of liquid soap in a bracket, nailed to the wall. Stan sits Babe down on a small four-legged stool, places the towel around his neck, takes the hose, turns the faucet on. Stan puts his thumb at the top of the hose and makes the effect of a spray. He then turns to Babe and sprays the bristles. Babe, with the water trickling down his face is looking very dejected. Stan finishes spraying the bristles, takes his thumb off the top of the hose and gives it to Babe to hold. Babe unconsciously is holding it, and the water is running into his lap. Stan then goes over to the basin and takes the liquid soap out of the bracket, comes back and sprinkles it on Babe's face in barberlike manner. He then returns to the basin and puts the soap back. He comes back to Babe and starts rubbing the bristles. He suddenly notices the hose running and, instead of taking it out of Babe's hand, he goes back to the basin and turns the faucet off. Babe, with a pitiful look as Stan returns, says: "Thank you." Stan now starts to rub Babe's beard and works up a good lather. This done, he exits out of the set.

He enters to his own bench and picks up a small spokeshave. Stan starts to return to Babe but, upon examining the blade, decides to sharpen it up.

Near the bench is a small electric emery wheel. Stan goes over to it and placing the blade against the wheel, it shoots out a lot of sparks. Stan examines the blade again and picks up a piece of wood and whittles it a couple of times. He nods affirmatively, exits back to Babe.

Stan commences to shave Babe. In several strokes, he gets Babe's face clean. He feels Babe's face all over to see if it is smooth. Satisfied that it is a clean shave, he goes to the basin, turns the hose on again. Babe is still holding the hose in his hand. Stan returns and takes the hose out of Babe's hand, fixes his thumb again at the top of it and sprays Babe's face again, washing it clean of the soap. He hands the hose, still running, back to Babe.

Babe has had just about as much as he can stand. He shoves Stan aside and, in a terrific heat of temper, gives one big pull on the hose to pull it away from the faucet but, instead of it doing that, the whole basin comes away from the wall and the hose, acting like a rubber band, snaps the wash basin right at Babe's head, knocking him backwards alongside a perpendicular belt, which is propelling some machinery, which we don't see. The belt is in motion and, as Babe falls against it, he grabs hold of it to save himself. The belt takes him up in the air and makes a complete revolution with him. As he lands on the floor on the other side, he crashes through the floor.

Cut and show the interior of a big sawdust and shavings suction pipe. Babe drops down into it and is sucked through various setups of this pipe, horizontally, perpendicularly, horizontally, then into a loop, then horizontally again and finally, perpendicularly.

Stan runs and looks down the hole where Babe fell through and realizes what has happened. He exits on the run.

Cut to exterior of the building and high up toward the roof is a pipe sticking out, which is evidently the outlet of the suction line. Get over the fact that Babe has travelled all over the building. We hear a long "Oh-h-h-h- -" coming. Stan runs out and stands watching.

Babe suddenly pops out of the suction outlet. He gets

stuck half way and is up there hollering: "Do something to help me! Etc."

Stan hollers back, "What can I do?"

Babe says: "Do anything. Just get me out of here."

Stan exits back on the run to the set where Babe fell through the floor, figures for a minute and then, seeing a small keg, which is marked 'Shellac' he rolls the keg over and drops it through the floor and - -

We see it drop into the suction pipe and it is blown through the same setups that Babe went through.

Stan exits on the run out of the set.

Cut to exterior and show Stan looking up at Babe and waiting for something to happen. Babe yells: "What did you do?" Stan says: "You'll be out in a minute," and holds his arms as if to catch Babe when he falls. Babe is suddenly shot out through the air, followed by the keg. Babe falls into a big pile of sawdust and shavings and, as he sits up, the barrel enters and breaks all over him. He picks himself up and all the shavings are sticking to him in every conceivable way. Stan says: "Did you hurt yourself?" Babe says: "Not a bit." Stan hands Babe his hat and says: "Here. You dropped this." Babe takes his hat and puts it on, gives a hopeless gesture, slapping his hands against his legs. He goes to exit and PAN OVER and he trips into the lime trough. Stan, very sorry for this, kneels down and sits on the edge of the trough as Babe looks at him. Stan says: "Can I help you?" Babe says: "Will you get away from me? You're getting in my hair!" Babe jumps up quickly and starts after Stan. Both exit.

Come in where the band saw is. Stan in the lead, jumps over the moving belt. Babe doesn't jump and lands in the middle of it and is carried toward the band saw. Babe realizes the danger and starts running, trying to get away from it. He now hollers to Stan to stop it or do something to help him.

Stan rushes over to the control lever and throws it into reverse.

The belt quickly reverses and Babe is carried off, on the run out of the set.

THERE IS ANOTHER GAG HERE, then go into our last routine of cutting the Ford in two.

THE END

OLIVER THE EIGHTH

Production history: Production L-17. Script written early December 1933. Filmed Friday, December 15 through Wednesday, December 20, then from Monday, January 8 through Tuesday, January 16, 1934. Copyrighted February 13, 1934 by MGM (LP 4494). Released circa February 13. Three reels.

Produced by Hal Roach. Directed by Lloyd French. Photographed by Art Lloyd. Edited by Bert Jordan. Sound by Warren B. Delaplain. *Uncredited Assistance:* Assistant Director, Chet Brandenburg.

With Stan Laurel (Himself), Oliver Hardy (Himself) Mae Busch (Wealthy widow at Box 204J), Jack Barty (Jitters, the butler).

Stan and Ollie own a barber shop. Stan reads a newspaper advertisement from a wealthy widow, "object matrimony." They both decide to answer it, but Ollie hides Stan's letter, hoping to win the lady's affections without competition. She accepts Ollie as a new husband, and he leaves Stan, preparing for a life of luxury. The lady and her butler behave very strangely – as Stan also finds out, after discovering his unmailed letter and following Ollie to the widow's home. The butler confides to Ollie that the widow was once jilted by a man named Oliver, and has exacted her vengeance by murdering seven other men with that name. The boys spend a sleepless night trying to evade her evil intent. Just before he's about to become her latest victim, Ollie wakes up – he's just had a very bad dream.

Hal Roach provided the idea for this film, after seeing a similar newspaper advertisement. *Oliver the Eighth* also may have been inspired to some degree by the recent Charles Laughton feature *The Private Life of Henry VIII*, which of course would include some references to beheadings. (The film was retitled in England as *The Private Life of Oliver the Eighth*, and other countries used a translation of this.)

Universal had proven that horror films were sure-fire box-office with *Dracula, Frankenstein, The Mummy,* and *The Old Dark House,* while *The Laurel-Hardy Murder Case* was one of the most popular of the team's comedies. *Oliver the Eighth* repeats that film's setting of a spooky old house (even using the earlier film's sets), along with the promise of a financial windfall, a restless and terrifying night, and the "just a dream" finale.

Jack Barty makes his only appearance with L&H as Jitters, the crazy butler. Stan and Babe had seen him onstage in a production of *Casanova* on July 27th, 1932, at the Coliseum Theatre in London. Comedians Douglas Wakefield and Billy Nelson were also in the cast of this show, and by the summer of 1933 all three were working at the Hal Roach Studio.

The script for *Oliver the Eighth* is very similar to the film. The first item not found in

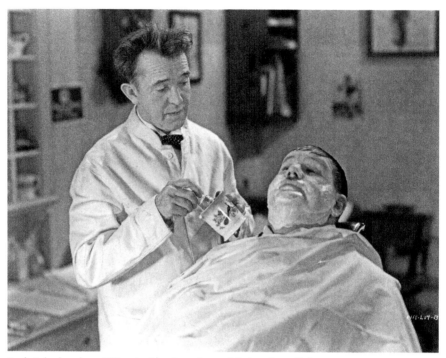

In their barber shop, Ollie asks Stan for a shave while he takes a little nap.

the film is the little bit of business where Jitters cuts off the toe of the widow's stocking to remove a hole in it. This would have established early on that they're both nuts, but of course that's already evident from the widow's declaration that she's killed seven other Olivers just because the first one left her at the altar.

The film offers some slightly more colorful dialogue in the scene where Ollie explains that he's getting married. He tells Stan, "She fell for me like a ton of bricks!" When Stan sees her picture, he whistles and remarks, "She's a pip!" The "Riviera" dialogue is not in the film.

The scene with the laundryman was evidently filmed but omitted in the final cut. The part was intended for Charlie Hall.

Mr. Hardy's middle name, originally his first name, is correctly spelled "Norvell," which he helpfully explained on the December 1, 1954 episode of *This Is Your Life*.

Ollie seems awfully unconcerned about leaving Stan and the barber shop. Stan has assumed that he's going to join the happy new couple, but Ollie tells him, "I'm sorry, but my social position won't permit it." After Stan finds his unmailed letter, he barges in to the widow's home (one wonders how he found the address, as the newspaper advertisement gave only "Box 204J") and demands of Ollie, "I want half of what you're going to get. I want my cut!" Stan doesn't realize the irony of this, as Ollie is really going to get his cut.

In the film, when Stan is displaying what he swapped for the barber shop, he mentions that the fellow who gave him that brick "told me to keep it 'til we got back on the gold

A scene not in the film – Ollie reads the wealthy widow's affirmative response.

standard." On April 5, 1933, President Roosevelt had ordered all Americans to turn in gold coins, bullion and certificates worth more than $100 to the Federal Reserve, for the set price of $20.67 per ounce. The value of gold rapidly depreciated, although it was almost certainly still worth more than the painted brick so prized by Mr. Laurel. The film adds that Stan received something else of value for the barber shop – some nuts.

In the film, when the widow first sees Stan, she points to him and asks Ollie, "What is that?," as if he's an inanimate object.

Invisibility provides two of the most memorable scenes. At one point, Jitters invites the boys to pick a card from an invisible deck. The best gag was created on the set, during the filming. It comes after Ollie has swatted away the invisible cards, and the butler pantomimes picking them up from the floor. He exits, but Stan whistles for him to come back and says, "You dropped one."

Later, the boys are served an invisible meal; Stan really gets into the spirit of things, having to unbutton his vest because he's so full. This gag had been used in the 1929 *Our Gang* comedy *Moan and Groan, Inc.*, with crazy Max Davidson serving up the invisible vittles to Farina. A similar routine would show up with the meal in capsule form in the 1944 20th Century-Fox L&H feature *The Big Noise*, which also had a lady of dubious sanity brandishing a blade late at night.

Stan brandishes a blade in this film, giving Ollie a shave while he falls asleep. Aside from providing a reason for the method of Mr. Hardy's demise in his dream, there

Stan – bearing the "solid gold" brick and the nuts he got in trade for the shop – meets Ollie's future bride.

Dinner is served – invisibly, by Jitters the butler (Jack Barty).

Jitters helpfully points out that "She's the one who's crazy, not me!" The jury's out on that last part.

With the help of a candle, a string, a brick and a shotgun, Stan tries to prevent Ollie's demise.

isn't much made of the boys as barbers. (One wonders if Stan wouldn't accidentally accomplish what Mae Busch intends to do.)

The unused gag of cutting the hole out of the stocking was reworked and replaced with a moment where the widow asks Stan for a pair of scissors. Being a barber, he naturally has one on his person, which the widow uses to cut off Ollie's necktie. This lets Stan and Ollie both know that the widow is crazy, too, which the earlier gag wouldn't have done. It also provides some foreshadowing of the widow's intended method of dispatching Ollie.

The imaginary meal is a little more elaborate in the film; Mae asks for salt, and after Ollie passes her a shaker, she says, "Oh, this is the pepper."

In the film, the butler reveals the widow's plan to both of the boys, not just Stan.

The script states Ollie's indelible catch-phrase as "Well, here's another nice mess you got me into." In the film, as in all others, while it is indeed a nice mess and not a fine one, it is one "you've gotten me into."

In the script, when Ollie is explaining that they'll take turns staying awake, Stan has a line that usually belongs to Ollie – which would have been a funny reference to the first scene in the movie.

We can all be glad that the butler's description of what he did to the cat is nowhere to be found in the film, which is grisly enough as it is. The hackneyed punchline isn't worth the gruesome setup.

Finally, we can be doubly glad that the final line proposed by the script is not the one used in the film, which is, "I just had a terrible dream."

Emulating a recent Charles Laughton feature, the film was retitled *The Private Life of Oliver the Eighth* in England, in Germany (left), and in Spain (right), among other countries.

L-17 – Laurel and Hardy.

Fade in on a small barber shop. Babe is standing in front of the mirror combing his hair. Stan is busy cutting up some newspapers into squares and sticking them on a hook to be used as lather papers. He notices on one of the pieces of paper that has cut out part of a personal column on which there is an ad. Stan reads it, turns to Babe and says, "Listen to this." Babe says "What?"

Stan reads the ad to Babe, which says, "Wealthy Widow with large fortune wishes to communicate with congenial young man. Object matrimony. Box 204-J."

Babe: "Oh, it's probably some old crab with a face that would stop a clock. Nobody would want to marry her no matter how much money she's got."

Stan: "Well I'd marry her. You know, beauty is only skin deep. I'd take some of that money and have her face lifted, then with the rest I'd be able to settle down and I wouldn't have to work any more."

Babe: "Tell me that again."

Stan: "Well, beauty's only knee deep – skin deep – and I'd take part of the money and have her skinned, then with the rest of the money she'd be able to look at a clock and I wouldn't have to work any more because we'd be congenial."

Babe: "That's a good idea."

Stan: "You bet it is. I'm going to answer this right away."

Babe: "What do you mean, you're going to answer it?"

Stan: "Well, I found it."

Babe takes the ad and says, "Well, it's my paper, and I'm going to answer it!"

Stan: "I've got just as much right as you have."

Babe: "All right, I'll tell you what we'll do. We'll both answer it, and may the best man win!"

Lap dissolve to insert of addressed envelope, Babe's hand sticking a stamp on it.

Pull back and show Stan in front of the mirror. He cuts off

a lock of his hair, puts it in his envelope and seals it. Babe gives him a dirty look and says, "Get this place cleaned up. I'll go and mail the letters."

Stan gets a broom and starts to sweep up a lot of hair off the floor.

Cut to Babe. He comes to the mail box and starts to mail the letters. He then has a thought, changes his mind and just mails one letter, which is his own. He sticks Stan's letter in his pocket and comes back to the shop.

Stan is busy sweeping up the hair, etc., onto a little dust pan. Babe comes in very unconcerned and when Stan isn't looking he ditches Stan's letter in the basket that contains the used towels.

Cut to Stan cleaning around the cuspidor. He lifts it from the floor and places it on top of one of those kitchen garbage cans, the kind that flies open when you step on the lever. He finishes cleaning up and is going to make an exit to empty the dust pan. He passes the garbage can and accidentally steps on the lever, causing the lid to fly open and throw the cuspidor into the air. It lands on Babe's head with a "bong" and knocks him for a loop.

Cut to Stan wondering what's happened. Go to two shot. Babe walks in and says, "Put those things away. I want you to give me a shave." Babe sits in the barber chair and Stan throws the sheet over him, tying it around his neck, then picks up the lather cup and brush and starts to lather Babe as we fade out.

Fade in on long shot of the Widow's boudoir. She is in a negligee seated at her dressing table. A butler enters the room carrying a tray with breakfast and places it on a little table near a chaise lounge, then speaks, "Your breakfast is ready, Madame."

The Widow crosses from the dressing table to the chaise lounge and drapes herself on it. On the tray there is also a large stack of mail. As the butler is pouring out the coffee, the Widow reaches for the mail and starts looking through it. One of the letters interests her and she picks it out of the stack, and as she looks at it we insert the envelope of Hardy's letter. She opens it and takes out the letter and a photograph of Hardy, which we insert. He is in some funny pose.

The Widow throws the picture on the table and starts to

read the letter. The butler looking at the picture says, "Another Oliver?" The Widow nods. The butler in a nutty attitude rubs his hands and says with a fiendish smile, "Oliver the eighth!" The Widow nods again. The Butler says, "Is he to share the same fate as the other seven Olivers?" The Widow says, "Why not? It was an Oliver who first came into my life and double crossed me – left me on the eve of my wedding – and I've sworn to take revenge on every Oliver that crosses my path." The butler says, "Strange that on the eve of every wedding you walk in your sleep – and the next morning they're found with their throats cut!"

The Widow discovers a small hole in the toe of her stocking and says, "Look, Jitters, how did that get there?" He says "You must have put on your stocking inside out. Just a minute, Madame, I'll cut the hole out for you." He pulls a pair of scissors out of his pocket, draws the stocking toe away from her foot and deliberately cuts off the toe of the stocking. Holding the end of the stocking with the hole in it, with a delighted smile he throws it away. She says, "Thank you, Jitters, that's much better." Fade out.

Fade in on the barber shop. Babe is on all dressed up, looking in the mirror and perfuming himself with an atomizer. He is singing, "I'm Sitting on Top of the World."

Stan enters, takes off his hat and coat, putting on his white coat. He keeps looking at Babe, wondering why he is so exuberant. He finally asks him, "Where are you going?"

Babe: "Oh, that's right. I forgot to tell you. I'm going away – I'm going to be married."

Stan: "Who to?"

Babe: "Remember that wealthy widow we wrote to? Well, I got a letter from her and she has accepted me, and we're going to be married as soon as I can get there. Look, here's her picture. Isn't she gorgeous?"

Stan: "She certainly is. I wonder what she could see in you?"

Babe: "Well, she probably thinks that I - - What do you mean, what could she see in me?"

Stan: "It's funny she didn't answer my letter."

Babe: "There's nothing funny about that. You just

weren't the type."

Stan: "What time do we have to go?"

Babe: "What do you mean, <u>we</u> have to go? You're not going."

Stan: "Aren't you going to take me with you?"

Babe: "Certainly not. Have I got to be your keeper all my life? You must learn to depend on yourself. Besides, the best of friends must part."

Stan: "Won't I see you any more?"

Babe: "I'm afraid not. I'll possibly be going to Europe – a honeymoon on the Riviera."

Stan: "What's a Riviera?"

Babe: "Don't waste my valuable time. You wouldn't know if I could think of it."

Babe by this time has his Inverness coat on. He picks up his suitcase and umbrella and says, "Well, I'll be seeing you."

Stan: "What about your laundry?"

Babe: "Oh, that's right. You can send it on to me. Here's the address."

He tears the address off the envelope and gives it to Stan. He picks up his suitcase and umbrella again and starts singing "I'm sitting on top of the world" as he exits out of the shop, leaving Stan there alone. Babe passes the shop window on the outside and waves to Stan as he exits.

Stan crosses to the door and looks up the street, getting sympathy.

The laundry man enters with a package of laundry. He starts to exit and Stan says, "Wait a minute – I'll give you some dirty towels." He crosses to the laundry basket, empties the towels on the floor and starts to count them. He comes across the letter that Babe was supposed to mail for him. He picks it up, looks at it and sighs, not realizing for a minute that it shouldn't have been there. He places it on the shelf and starts to count towels again, then does a double takem. He looks at the letter, opens it, takes out the lock of hair that he cut off, matches it with his own, then takes out the letter and the picture and looks at them.

Still very puzzled, Stan turns to the laundry man, holds the picture in front of him and says, "Who is that?" The laundry man looks at the picture and at Stan and says, "Why, it's you." Stan says, "Well, what was it doing in there?" The laundry man says, "I don't know!"

Stan then looks on the wall and sees an 8 x 10 still of Babe and himself standing in front of the barber shop shaking hands. We feel that this was taken at the opening of the shop. Stan takes the picture off the wall and tears it in half, intending to throw Babe's half in the garbage can, but by mistake throws his own half in and nails Babe's half back on the wall. He then suddenly realizes what he has done and gets all mixed up as we fade out.

Fade in on the hallway of the Widow's home. The butler is sitting in the hallway at a little card table playing an imaginary game of solitaire, using no cards. The door bell rings. He leaves the table, crosses over to the front door, opens it and Babe is discovered there all smiles.

Babe: "Good evening."

Butler: "What is the name, please?"

Babe: "Oliver Norval Hardy. I'd like to see the future Mrs. Hardy."

Butler: "Step this way."

Babe enters and the butler closes the door. He takes Babe's hat and coat, puts them on himself and looks in the mirror to see how they fit. He gets over he is very satisfied with them. He then feels the material in Babe's clothes. Babe takes this a little puzzled.

The butler gives Babe a fiendish smile, then crosses to the foot of the stairs, picks up a big bell and rings it. He places the bell back on the floor or table and says to Babe, "Madame will be down in a minute." He motions Babe to sit down, which he does. The butler then sits down at the card table and continues his imaginary game of solitaire, Babe taking it with wonderment. Babe says, "What are you doing?" and the butler answers, "I'm playing solitaire. It passes many hours away." Babe gives him another puzzled look.

The door bell rings again and the butler opens the front door, disclosing Stan, who brushes right past the butler and crosses over to Babe.

Babe: "What are you doing here?"

Stan pulls out the letter and shows it to Babe. Babe takes it with a shrug of his shoulders and says, "Well, what about it? All's fair in love and war."

Stan: "If you don't cut me in on this fortune, I'll tell her - - "

Babe: "What do you mean, cut you in?"

Stan: "Well, I want half of what you're going to get."

Babe: "What do you mean, you want half of what I'm going to get?"

Stan: "Well, I want my cut. And furthermore I'm going to stay here till I get it."

Babe: "All right, if you keep your mouth shut I'll see that you get it. What did you do with the barber shop?

Stan: "I sold it."

Babe: "How much did you get?"

Stan: "Well, I didn't exactly sell it – I swapped it."

Stan pulls out a brick wrapped in newspaper with a string around it. Babe looks very puzzled while Stan opens the package. As he opens it he discloses a brick painted gold, and printed on it are the words "Solid Gold." Babe gives one of his exasperated looks.

At this point the Widow enters at the top of the stairs and walks majestically down. Babe crosses to the foot of the stairs to greet her. She holds out her hand to Babe and says, "Oliver!" Babe kisses her hand, then introduces Stan, saying, "This is my friend, Mr. Laurel." The Widow acknowledges the introduction and says, "Is your name Oliver too?" Stan says, "No, my name's Stanley. I just came here to get my cut." Babe puts his hand over Stan's mouth to shut him up. He then takes the Widow by the arm and says, "Come, darling, let's make our plans for the wedding." They exit to the living-dining room, leaving Stan standing there.

Stan turns and looks at the butler playing solitaire. It is the first time he has noticed him, and he does a double takem. The butler throws down the imaginary deck, starts scraping them together and says, "That makes three hundred games I've played and it only came out once." He then shuffles the cards and says to Stan, "Take one." Stan looks puzzled and the butler repeats, "Take one." Stan takes one from the "deck" and the butler says, "Show it to me." Stan shows it to him and the butler says, "The seven of diamonds!" He takes it from Stan and starts shuffling the deck. He then hands the deck to Stan and says, "Show it to your friend."

Stan enters the living room, followed by the butler, and comes in to Babe who is seated on the settee with the widow, having quite a flirtation. She is stroking his neck and Babe is enjoying it immensely. Stan nudges Babe, who turns, and Stan pantomimes opening the deck of cards and says, "Take one." Babe looks at him puzzled and says, "Take one what?" Stan says, "Take a card out of this deck." Babe looks disgusted and slaps Stan's hands. Stan pantomimes the cards have fallen to the floor and the butler starts to pick up the imaginary cards. Babe does a double takem.

The Widow says, "What time is dinner, Jitters?" He says, "Right away, Madame," and exits. Babe looking very puzzled says to the Widow, "What's the matter with him?" She becomes very mysterious and says, "Don't pay any attention to him. He's crazy. He imagines things." Babe says, "Is he dangerous?" and she says, "Not if you humor him. You have to make believe too."

The butler re-enters, bows and says, "Dinner is served, Madame." Stan and Babe and the widow cross over to the dining room table and sit down. The butler says, "Would you care for soup, Madame?" She says, "Thank you, Jitters." He takes the lid off the soup tureen and with a big ladle serves imaginary soup onto her plate, then does the same to Babe and Stan. They do a routine eating an imaginary meal, passing the butter, bread, etc. While they are doing this the butler is filling up glasses of imaginary water.

The butler then says to Stan, "Would you care for some more soup?" Stan gets disgusted and says, "You're nuts!" Babe tries to quiet Stan, saying "Humor him." The butler motions for Stan to go into the hallway. Stan looks a little worried and Babe says, "Go ahead – see what he wants and humor him."

Stan enters the hall with the butler. The butler very confidentially says, "Who said I was nuts?" Stan pointing to the Widow says, "She did." The butler becomes a little enraged and says, "Oh, she double crossed me, did she? Well, I'm going to tell you something. It's not me, it's her that's crazy. I'll prove it to you." He points toward Babe and says, "When he's asleep tonight she's going to cut his throat, the same as she did to seven other Olivers." He walks away very mysteriously.

Stan then tries to whistle to Babe to get his attention. Babe is taking another helping of soup and says, "Don't annoy me. Can't you see I'm busy?" Stan finally induces Babe to come out to the hallway.

Stan: "Do you know what he said?"

Babe: "What?"

Stan: "He said it isn't him that's crazy, it's her (pointing to the widow). And when you go to sleep tonight she's going to cut your throat, the same as she's done to seven other Olivers."

Babe: "What do you mean, she's crazy? There's nothing wrong with her."

He looks over toward her and the butler is standing at her side with a tray full of sharp looking carving knives. She is feeling them and says, "That one will do."

Babe does a double takem, looks at Stan and says, "We better get out of here." Stan says, "I think so too." They get their hats and coats, getting all balled up. Babe calls to the widow, "Well, we've had a lovely time. We'll see you later." They try to make a hurried exit and discover the door is locked. The widow calmly walks into the hallway, followed by the butler. She turns to the butler and says, "Jitters, are all the doors and windows securely locked?" He bows and says, "Yes, Madame." She says, "Then show these gentlemen to the guest chamber." The butler picks up Babe's suitcase and says, "This way, please." Stan and Babe, realizing they are trapped, follow the butler up the stairs.

Cut to the guest bedroom. The door opens and the butler enters, followed by Stan and Babe. He says, "This is the guest chamber. I hope you'll have a nice long sleep." Stan and Babe take it. With a fiendish grin the butler takes the key from the inside of the door, places it in the key hole on the outside, then closes the door very mysteriously and we hear the key turn in the lock.

Babe looks at Stan and says, "Well, here's another nice mess you got me into."

Stan: "What are we going to do now?"

Babe: "There's nothing to do but to sit up all night and see that she doesn't cut my throat."

Stan: "I can't sit up all night."

Babe: "Why?"

Stan: "I can't afford to lose my rest."

Babe: "You don't have to lose your rest. We'll take turns. I'll sleep a while while you stay awake, then you sleep a while while I stay awake. It's simple."

Stan: "Tell me that again."

Babe: "Well, you sleep – What do you mean, tell me that again?"

Stan: "Well, I can't stay awake."

Babe: "Why not?"

Stan: "I don't want to see you get your throat cut."

Babe gives him a push and says, "Do as I tell you!"

Cut to the boudoir. The Widow is on dressed in negligee. There is a knock at the door and she says, "Who is it?" The butler opens the door and says, "It's me, Madame." He is carrying a tray with a large carving knife, sharpening steel and a pair of surgical gloves on it.

Widow: "Is everything in readiness?"

Butler: "Yes, Madame."

Widow: (Picking up the knife) "Is it good and sharp?"

Butler: "Yes, Madame. I tried it out on the cat."

He pantomimes holding the cat by the ears and cutting its head off.

Widow: "Success?"

Butler: "Big success. But a very strange thing happened. The head was laying over there, and the body laying over there. As I was leaving the room, the head of the cat started to sing."

Widow: "What was it singing, Jitters?"

The butler sings with a silly grin on his face, "I ain't got no body - - " He goes into a weird laugh and makes an exit, rubbing his hands.

Cut back to Stan and Babe. They have their pajamas on now and Stan goes to hang his clothes in the closet. As he hangs them on a hook he notices a pump gun standing in the corner of the closet. He picks it up and says to Babe, "Look." Babe is standing on the other side of the room. Stan, examining the gun, has the barrel of it pointed toward Babe. Babe says, "Is it loaded?" Stan deliberately pulls the trigger and the shell explodes.

At this point Babe was in the act of shaking his pants. We go to closeup of him and show that the seat of the pants is completely blown off and he holds up the two legs. Stan comes over and inspects the pants, looks at Babe and says, "It's a good thing you weren't in them." Babe grabs the gun from Stan and says, "Get to bed!"

Stan gets into bed and Babe puts the gun alongside of the bed, then gets into bed and discovers that Stan has made himself very comfortable and is going to sleep. Babe nudges him and says, "It's my turn to sleep first. You keep awake and if you see anybody coming, use that gun. But don't point it at me!"

Babe starts to go to sleep and Stan is left sitting up in bed. He scratches his head, then starts to whistle. Babe wakes up and very annoyed says, "Keep quiet!" He goes back to sleep again. Stan suddenly thinks of something, quietly gets out of bed, goes to his pants, feels in the pockets and brings out three or four nuts. He quietly gets back into bed and tries to crack the nuts with his teeth. He then gets the idea to break them with the heel of his shoe. He leans out of bed, puts the nut on the floor, picks up his shoe and starts to hit the nut with the heel, but realizes the noise might wake Babe up. He looks around, takes his pillow and placing it over the nut he hits the pillow with his shoe. He then looks under the pillow to see if it is cracked, but it has made no impression.

He then gets another idea. He quietly gets out of bed, crosses over to the closet and standing on the inside of the closet he places the nut in the hinge of the door. He pulls the door to crack the nut, and the door closes on him, locking him in. He starts knocking on the door from the inside.

Babe wakes up all scared, grabs the gun and says, "Who's in there?" Stan says, "It's me." Babe opens the door and with a disgusted look says, "I can't sleep when you're making all this noise!" Stan says, "Well, I can't keep awake unless I have something to occupy my mind." Babe says, "Just a minute – I'll get something to occupy your mind. Where's that gold brick?"

Stan hands him the brick and Babe unwraps the string from it, tying the string to a leg of the table that the candle is on. He wraps the string once around the candle about an inch down from the lighted wick. He then continues the string over a wall bracket which is above the back of the bed and extends out from the wall. Babe then ties the brick onto the end of the string and makes Stan get into bed. Stan gets into bed and the brick is dangling over his head. Babe gets into bed and Stan says, "That's liable to drop and hit me on the head." Babe says, "That's just the idea. As the flame gets near the string, you move the string down. If you don't, it will burn the string and the brick will hit you on the head. Now you've got something to occupy your mind and you'll have to stay awake." Babe settles down and Stan watches the candle and keeps looking up at the brick.

Babe stretches a little big and his foot comes out of the covers at the bottom of the bed, his toes accidentally resting on the rail of the bed. Stan notices the foot, becomes very scared and nudges Babe. Babe wakes up and says, "What?" Stan says, "Don't look now, but there's a hand on the foot of the bed."

Babe takes a little quick glance out of the corner of his eye and whispers to Stan, "Get that gun, and shoot to kill." Stan gets the gun very carefully and fires. It blows off the bottom of the bed. Babe jumps up holding his toe, jumping around the room hollering bloody murder.

He finally settles down and very disgustedly comes to Stan's side of the bed and tells him to move over. He says, "You go to sleep and I'll stay awake!" Stan moves over to Babe's side of the bed. Babe throws the covers over to get into bed.

Insert the candle burning the string.

Back to Babe. The brick is released and it drops on his head with a thud, which knocks him out. He staggers back to an arm chair which is near the bed and as he sits in the chair his head lies back, exposing his throat all ready to be cut.

Stan gets up and tries to wake Babe up.

Cut to the hallway. The Widow comes out with a glassy stare, sharpening the knife on the steel. She has on the surgical gloves, and walks with measured steps toward the room where Stan and Babe are.

Cut back to Stan trying to bring Babe to. He suddenly hears the key turn in the lock, gets all scared, grabs the gun and creeps over toward the closet door with the intention of hiding behind the closet door and shooting at the critical moment. The closet door is situated next to the hall door and the doors are swung so that as the Widow opens the hall door it pushes the closet door closed, locking Stan in the closet with the shot gun. The Widow starts toward Babe with the same measured steps, at each step sharpening the knife.

Stan in the closet is having a hell of a time trying to get the gun leveled, but the closet is too small.

Babe is still knocked out, with his neck bared. The Widow is now alongside of him. She finally throws the steel onto the bed and very slowly starts her hand with the knife toward Babe's throat. She has just got the blade on his neck when suddenly there is an explosion in the closet and a crash, which causes the Widow to pull back from Babe's neck.

We then go to a big head closeup of Babe as he comes to. He opens his eyes and lets out a terrific yell.

Cut and show that Babe is really sitting in the barber chair with Stan shaving him. Babe continues his yelling, jumps out of the chair, looks in the mirror to see if his throat is cut, looks at his pants and feels his head to see if he is all there.

He finally relaxes and Stan looks at him and says, "What's the matter?" Babe says, "It must have been something I et." FADE OUT.

GOING BYE-BYE!

Production history: Production L-18. Script written circa May 15-20, 1934. Filmed Monday, May 21 through Saturday, May 26. Copyrighted June 20, 1934 by MGM (LP 4785). Released June 23. Two reels.

Produced by Hal Roach. Directed by Charles Rogers. Photographed by Francis Corby. Edited by Bert Jordan. Sound by Harry Baker. *Uncredited Assistance*: Written by Charles Rogers, Frank Terry. Assistant Director, Chet Brandenburg.

With Stan Laurel (Himself), Oliver Hardy (Himself), Walter Long (Butch Long), Mae Busch (Mae), Harry Dunkinson (Judge), Murdock MacQuarrie (Jury foreman), Ellinor Vanderveer, Fay Holderness, Jack "Tiny" Lipson, William J. O'Brien (Jury members), Baldwin Cooke (Court officer), Lester Dorr (Guard), Charles Dorety, Fred Holmes (Courtroom spectators). Sam Lufkin (Man who gives warning).

Stan and Ollie are in a courtroom, having testified against notorious criminal Butch Long. When the judge pronounces that Long will be in prison "for the rest of your natural life," Stan blurts out, "Aren't you going to hang him?" This does not endear him to Long, who swears vengeance on them: "I'm gonna break off your legs and wrap 'em around your necks!" The boys decide to get out of town, and place an advertisement for someone to help drive and share expenses. A vivacious lady responds and asks if her boyfriend – who somehow has gotten locked in a trunk – might join them. Despite their best efforts to open the trunk with a brace-and-bit, blowtorch and hose, Long manages to break free – and gets his revenge precisely as described.

Four months passed between the production of *Oliver the Eighth* and the team's next short, much of that time taken up with a disagreement between Stan and Hal Roach over the story for an upcoming feature, *Babes in Toyland.* Stan was also maintaining that he was ill and unable to work, a ploy to modify the alimony agreement he'd made with first wife Lois, which gave her 50 percent of his earnings. (It didn't work.)

When Stan finally returned to the studio, he worked with the writers, including Charlie Rogers and Frank Terry, on a story called *Public Enemies* and then *On Their Way Out* before being christened as *Going Bye-Bye!* Gangsters were very much in the news. John Dillinger would be killed by three FBI agents one month after *Going Bye-Bye!* was released. He was leaving the Biograph Theater in Chicago after watching *Manhattan Melodrama*, which like *Going Bye-Bye!* was an MGM release. One wonders if the L&H short was on the supporting program. (Newspaper advertisements and surviving photographs don't provide any clues, alas.)

During the four-month layoff after *Oliver the Eighth*, director Lloyd French moved to New York to make short musicals and comedies for Warner Bros. Charlie Rogers, a writer and sometime actor who was Stan's closest co-worker at the Roach lot, was

Newly sentenced to prison for life thanks to Stan and Ollie's testimony, Butch Long vows revenge.

promoted to director. Given their personal and professional compatibility, Stan's method of subtly directing the director would certainly remain the standard operating procedure.

Walter Long, who had been so vital to Laurel and Hardy's *Pardon Us* and *Any Old Port*, was making his third (of five) appearances with the team. *Going Bye-Bye!* also marked Mae Busch's ninth film (of 14) with the comedians. She was enjoying a new prominence with Laurel and Hardy. Mae appeared in seven of the team's eight films from *Sons of the Desert* through *The Fixer Uppers*, the sole exception being *Babes in Toyland*.

The story for *Going Bye-Bye!* is similar to *Do Detectives Think?*, since both films are about a convict who seeks his revenge. This would also be an important element of the plot for the 20th Century-Fox L&H feature *The Bullfighters* (1945).

The courtroom sequence and the boys' conversation in the car outside is filmed virtually as written. Stan's remark about buttering your bread wasn't used, unfortunately. The boys' doubles (usually Ham Kinsey for Stan and Cy Slocum for Babe) earned their paycheck when everyone runs in panic out of the courthouse; instead of just exiting "scared stiff," Stan and Ollie (or Ham and Cy) stumble at the entrance and are practically trampled by the other spectators.

There's nothing in the film to indicate that Sam Lufkin – the man who compares Butch Long to an elephant – is his attorney, but it's nice that the script adds this detail.

"Everything would have been all right if you hadn't said, 'Aren't you going to hang him?'"

In the scene where Stan enters the boys' apartment bearing the newspaper, he manages to accidentally push Ollie into the framework of their bed, trapping his head between two posts. This is followed by some business where Stan needs his glasses to read the newspaper, can't see well through them and then manages to sit on them and break them. When Ollie responds with, "It serves you right," Stan says, "No wonder I couldn't see through them – they're yours!"

In the film, Ollie, not Stan, reads the classified ad as printed, which also includes a final note – "P.S. Those not interested, do not answer." Ollie seems to be pleased with the advertisement in the script, but not so in the film; since classified ads are paid by the word, Ollie is not happy about the superfluous verbiage.

The film's best-remembered line of dialogue is tremendously improved by editing in the film. No doubt Babe Hardy saw that "I'll be with you as soon as I get a towel" was unwieldy and spoiled the joke by explaining too much. He instead begs Mae's momentary patience with, "Excuse me, please, my ear is full of milk." That can of milk causes much more trouble in the script than it does in the film; similarly, in the movie, Ollie does not wipe his face with a rag covered with shoe polish.

Walter Long's promise to butter Stan and Ollie's bread was evidently thought to be a bit too poetic or fanciful; in the movie, he simply says, "I'm gonna search this town from end to end, 'til I find them."

Stan's reaction to Mae's story about Butch doing some packing and accidentally

Stan reads his brief and right-to-the-point advertisement. "Those not interested, do not answer."

Mr. Hardy introduces Mae to his friend, Mr. Laurel.

A posed still – in the film, Butch is firmly locked inside the trunk.

falling into the trunk and getting locked in is more pointed in the movie: "It *could* happen." Stan may be thinking of the many highly unlikely physical predicaments he and Ollie have gotten into – such as Ollie getting his head caught in their bed's framework earlier in the film.

The idea of Stan and Ollie yelling "Tuck!" repeatedly to warn Walter Long when to move inside the trunk must have proven unwieldy, because the only evidence of its existence in the film is one lone "Tuck!" from Stan on the soundtrack. The gag with Ollie's vest being caught on the drill and pulled through the trunk to Stan was probably too intricate to, ah, pull off.

The scenes with Mae talking to Jerry, and returning to the apartment, are not in the movie; as soon as she leaves to see Jerry, she finds that the police have indeed surrounded

Stan ventilates the trunk, as Ollie holds the flowers intended for Mae.

Ollie asks Butch if the fire is out yet.

Another posed still, as the boys are in an offscreen entanglement when the cops arrive.

the apartment, and they escort her off to the police station before she can get any help.

Long's unusual method of revenge is nowhere in the script. Nor is the gag – so subtle that it could be overlooked – of the boys constantly handing each other the flowers which they've brought for Mae, a cute and unforced gag which was evidently the product of on-the-set inspiration.

A suggested elaborate final sequence would have necessitated filming outside on the backlot at night, always an expensive proposition. Instead, the film concludes in Mae's apartment. After Stan and Ollie nearly barbecue Long to death inside the trunk with the blow torch, they then almost drown him by putting out the blaze with a nearby fire hose. The script proposes that the trunk walk all by itself down the street before it's recaptured. This does conjure up an amusing visual, but not quite as indelible as the movie's final scene, which shows that Long has carried out his threat (very efficiently and quickly, as he has only a few seconds alone with Stan and Ollie before the cops take him away), and that the boys now have their legs wrapped around their necks. There's the possibility that Stan had this idea in mind during the writing and didn't want to propose it to Hal Roach, who didn't like these "freak" finales. However, as Mr. Roach said to me in 1981, "I *always* saw the dailies," so there would have been no way to hide it from him. Similar gags would mark the endings of *The Live Ghost, Thicker Than Water,* and *The Bohemian Girl,* but Roach vetoed one intended for *Block-Heads.* Perhaps the ultimate freak finish is in *The Bullfighters* (1945), with Stan and Ollie's skeletons rattling back home to Peoria.

L-18 – Laurel & Hardy.

Fade in on court room, showing judge, jury, witnesses, attorneys, a few spectators, and the prisoner (Walter Long) in the dock. As the jury have filed in, cut to the Judge, who says, "Gentlemen, have you reached your verdict?" The foreman of the jury stands up and says, "Yes, your honor. We find the defendant guilty."

Cut to Stan and Babe seated at a table. They are very much pleased with the verdict and give each other a satisfied nod.

Cut to Walter Long, who is looking daggers at them.

Back to the judge. He looks toward Stan and Babe and says, "Gentlemen, I want to thank you on behalf of the state for the valuable evidence you have furnished this court in bringing this criminal to justice. It's men like you our country should be proud of."

Stan and Babe are very pleased, and Stan applauds. Babe stops him. The Judge turns to the prisoner and says, "The defendant will rise and receive sentence." Stan and Babe rise, then discover he doesn't mean them and sit down. Long stands up in a very surly manner. He is wearing a straight-jacket. The Judge continues, "I regret that the law allows me to give you only the maximum sentence – imprisonment for LIFE."

Stan speaks up in a disappointed tone, "Aren't you going to hang him?" Babe nudges him to shut up. Long looks at them menacingly and threatens to get them if it's the last thing he does, etc. Babe wiggles his tie a little sickly, and Stan says, "It's no use crying over spilt milk. You buttered your bread, now lay on it!"

This is too much for Long. With brute strength he tears off the straight jacket and makes a wild leap at Stan and Babe. The whole court room is thrown into a panic. The cops rush over and grab Long, tables are overturned, the Judge leaves in a hurry for parts unknown and Long is dragged out of the room. Stan and Babe exit, scared stiff.

Cut to the front of the court house. Stan and Babe come down the stairs, get into their car and Babe slams the door. Long's attorney steps up to the car and advises them to get out of town, because if Long ever escapes – "Well, he's like an elephant – he never forgets." He exits.

Babe looks at Stan and says, "Why don't you keep your mouth shut?"

Stan: "What did I do?"

Babe: "Here's what you did – you put us right on the spot! Everything would have been all right if you hadn't said 'Aren't you going to hang him.' Couldn't you see that he was annoyed? If he ever gets out of there, our lives won't be worth five cents!"

Stan: "Maybe we better get out of town."

Babe: "How are we going to get out of town?"

Stan: "Well, we've got a car."

Babe: "What are we going to run it on?"

Stan: "On the road."

Babe: "What are we going to use for gas?"

Stan: "Well, we've got enough money to buy some gas."

Babe: "Not enough to go as far as I want to go."

Stan: "That gives me an idea."

Babe: "What?"

Stan: "Why don't we advertise for someone to go with us, help drive and share expenses – like when we came out here."

Babe: "That was a great idea of mine. For once you've used my brains! We'll go to the newspaper office and put in an ad immediately."

Babe starts the motor and the car balks. A little puzzled, he takes it out of gear. Stan looks out over his side of the car and says, "Wait a minute." He then pulls up a strap which is attached to the door, and on the end of it we see a round weight which is used for "anchoring" horses. He throws it in the bottom of the car and they drive out. FADE OUT.

FADE IN on Stan and Babe's room. Babe is singing and busying himself with the packing. He brushes a pair of pants before putting them into the suitcase. He then looks at his shoes, gets a towel, puts his foot on a chair and starts shining his shoes. He hangs up the towel, not noticing that it is all black on one side.

Stan enters with a newspaper and Babe says, "Did you put the advertisement in?"

Stan: "Yes, and they printed it."

Babe: "What does it say?"

Stan: "Do you want me to read it?"

Babe: "Certainly – read it!"

Stan: (reading) "To whom it may concern. Two young men who are proud of their country are more than anxious to make a motor trip east – semi-colon – would like traveling companion to help drive and share expenses like when we came out here – stop – Please phone Main 489. Sincerely yours, Mr. Laurel and Mr. Hardy."

He looks up and says, "What do you think of it?"

Babe: "That's very nice. It's brief and to the point."

Stan: "I thought you'd like it."

Babe goes on with his packing and Stan says, "Can I help you with anything?" Babe looks around and says, "Yes – pack up the things out of that cabinet."

Stan goes to the cabinet, which is above the sink. As he opens it we discover among other things a little Sterno stove, folding pan and a can of condensed milk which has been opened. He starts to take them down and in doing so knocks over a razor blade, which falls into a clothes brush. The telephone rings and Babe says, "See who that is." Stan crosses to the phone, carrying in one hand the can of condensed milk.

As he answers the phone, we cut to the other end, which is in Mae Busch's apartment. She speaks into the phone, "Are you the party who advertised for a travelling companion to share expenses?"

Back to Stan and he says, "Yes – like when we came out here."

Mae: "I'm more than interested."

Stan: "And so am I."

Mae gives a little laugh and says, "If you're as nice as you sound, I'll bet you're cute."

Stan: "Do you think so?"

Mae: "I sure do. Where have you been all my life?"

Stan: "I've been with him." (pointing to Babe)

Babe turns and says, "Who is that?"

Stan: "A lady."

Babe: "Give me that phone!"

Stan: "Just a minute – my friend Mr. Hardy would like to speak to you."

Stan, a little befuddled, hands Babe the can of milk instead of the receiver. Babe puts it up to his ear and says very sweetly, "How do you do?" The milk trickles down his neck and he discovers what has happened. He hands Stan the can of milk and grabs up the receiver. Feeling the milk on the side of his face he says, "Get me a towel!" While stan is going for the towel Babe says into the phone, "Excuse me. I'll be with you as soon as I get a towel – my ear's full of milk."

Stan hands Babe the towel and Babe gives him the receiver while he wipes his face with the black side of the towel, making his face all black. He again takes the can of milk by mistake and puts it to the other ear. He discovers it, and becoming exasperated hands Stan the can of milk upside down. He puts the receiver to his ear and continues his conversation, during which Stan is standing alongside of hm, very interested and trying to listen, while the milk is pouring onto Babe's clean shoes.

Babe: "Pardon the delay. What was the nature of your business?"

Mae: "I understand that you are motoring East and I would like to accompany you."

Babe: "The pleasure is all mine."

Stan: (into phone) "And mine too."

Babe tells him to keep quiet.

Mae: "How soon do you expect to leave?"

Babe: "As soon as possible."

Mae: "That suits me fine."

Babe: "What was the address? . . Okay, we'll be right over. Goodbye."

Stan: "Goodbye."

Babe discovers the milk all over his shoes and says, "Give me that towel!" As Stan goes to get the towel, Babe takes off his coat. Stan returns with the towel and hands it to Babe, who gives him the coat and says, "Brush that off, and hurry." As Babe cleans his shoes, Stan starts to brush the coat. We insert the razor blade in the brush, which cuts the coat to shreds. FADE OUT.

FADE IN on bedroom of Mae's apartment, night. There is an open trunk in the center of the floor and she is taking clothes out of this and putting them into suitcases. She hears a mysterious tapping on the window. Very slowly she looks around.

Cut and show the window in the living room, which has a fire escape. There is a figure out there motioning to Mae to let him in. A little scared, she crosses to the window and looks through the glass. The character lowers his dark glasses and we see that it is Walter Long. She quickly opens the window and lets him in. He closes the window, glances down toward the street and pulls the shade.

Mae: "Butch! What are you doing here?"

Long: "I just took a little vacation."

Mae: "Why do you do that? You know they'll get you."

Long: "I've got a little account to settle."

Mae: "Did any of the gang double-cross you?"

Long: "No – a couple of mugs opened their traps too wide."

Mae: "So what?"

Long: "I know how to shut them up. Where's my gat?"

Mae: "You left it with your took kit. It's under the bed."

Long: "I'm gonna search this town from end to end, and when I catch up with them, I'll butter their bread!"

Mae: "You can't stay here! This is the first place the bulls will look for you."

The door bell rings and they both take it. They go into a whispered conversation. Mae says, "Here they are now. Quick, Butch – down the fire escape!" She crosses to open the window but he stops her and says, "Wait a minute – not a chance! They'll have the place surrounded." Mae says, "Hide in here, and if the worst comes to the worst, you can shoot your way out."

She rushes into the bedroom. He follows and gets into the trunk. She slams down the lid, takes a little cover from some place and places a lamp or bowl of flowers on top. During this the door bell has been ringing several times.

Finally cut to the hall and we discover Stan and Babe at the door. Stan is ringing the bell. Babe brushes him aside, saying, "I'll do it. Your ring lacks authority." Babe does a wind-up with his finger and jabs it forcibly into the push button, and his finger goes right in to the knuckle. The bell continues ringing and Babe is trying to pull his finger out. Stan pulls his arm to help him, and they pull the whole button off the wall with a spiral spring attached.

Mae opens the door and Babe quickly gets the bell off his finger, takes his hat off very gallantly and enters. Stan starts to follow but is still interested in the bell, which continues ringing. He looks into the hole where the spring was and inquisitively puts his finger in to feel. There is a little explosion and a puff of smoke as he causes a short circuit.

Cut quickly to the bell inside. There is a puff of smoke and it drops from the wall, hitting Babe on the head.

Stan takes it as Babe angrily motions for him to come in.

On the inside Babe introduces himself, saying "I'm Mr. Hardy. This is my friend, Mr. Laurel." She says, "How do you do?" and Stan says, "We came to answer the advertisement we put in." Babe shuts him up again and says to Mae, "Well, are we all ready to go?"

Mae: "Yes, but I'm in a bit of a dilemma. Maybe you can help me out."

Babe: "At your service."

Mae: "A friend of mine just dropped in, and he's most anxious to go east. Could you make room for him?"

Babe: "The more, the merrier."

Mae: "That's awfully nice of you. He'll be so delighted. If you'll excuse me a moment I'll have him come out and meet you."

They take seats and Mae exits.

In the bedroom Mae goes to the trunk and says, "It's Okay, Butch – you can come out." She takes the lamp off the trunk, placing it on another table. Long's voice inside the trunk says, "Who was it?"

Mae: "Oh, just friends of mine. I want you to meet them."

Long: "Okay – open the trunk."

She discovers it is locked and tells him so.

Long: "Well, get the key!"

Mae: "I haven't got it, Butch. You had it on you when you were arrested."

Long: "Well that's swell! You dumb cluck! Maybe you can get your friends to open it. And make it snappy – there's no air in here."

Mae goes back to the living room and says, "Have you guys got any keys?"

Babe: "Keys?"

Mae: "Yes – my friend got locked in the trunk and he can't get out."

Babe: "Locked in a trunk?"

Mae: (a little nervous) "Well, he was . . packing, and he . . accidentally fell in."

Stan: (to Babe) "Well, that could happen."

Babe: "Just show me the trunk and I'll have him out in a jiffy."

They exit with Mae to the bedroom. Long inside the trunk says, "Hurry up and get me out of here, will you? I can't breathe!"

Mae: "Take it easy. My friends are going to help you."

Stan takes out his Ford key and sticks it in the lock, but it breaks off. He examines the lock and says, "It's locked."

Babe: "Of course it's locked! That's why he can't get out. (to Mae:) If I had a hammer I could break it off."

Mae says "Wait a minute." She reaches under the bed and pulls out an elaborate burglar kit with drills, blow torch, hammers, etc. She lays it down and Babe opens it and looks at the tools. He takes out a hammer and starts hammering on the lock.

Long: "Wait a minute – wait a minute! Mae!!"

Mae: "What?"

Long: "Slip over and get Jerry. He'll open it."

Mae: "Okay. I'll be right back."

She rushes out. Long makes a noise in the trunk like he is choking.

Babe: "Is there anything we can do for you?"

Stan: "Can we get you a sandwich or something?"

Long: "Sandwich, NO! There's no air in this place! I'm choking to death!"

Stan walks over and opens the window and says, "How's that?" Babe says, "That's no good! The best thing to do is drill some holes." Stan picks up a drill and starts drilling. The drill suddenly breaks through the wall of the trunk and the whole length of it goes into the trunk. Long lets out one terrible yell. Stan very excitedly pulls the drill back out. Long is still groaning.

Babe: "Why don't you be careful?"

Stan: "Well I couldn't help it. I didn't know his . . . his head was at the other end."

Babe: "Now put some more in, and be careful."

Stan: "I've got an idea."

Babe: "What?"

Stan: "Well, when it's about to break through, we'll say Tuck, and that will be his signal to get out of the way."

Babe: (to Long) "Did you hear that?"

Long: "What?"

Babe: "When we say Tuck, you move up to the front end."

Long: "Okay."

Stan inserts the drill again and starts drilling. As it starts to go through the wall of the trunk we cut to the interior, showing Long. We see the end of the drill nearly breaking through. Finally as it breaks through we hear Stan and Babe say "Tuck!" Long draws his fanny in and the drill just misses it.

Cut to the outside of the trunk and Babe says, "How's that?" Long says "Okay." Babe then points to another section of the trunk and says to Stan, "Now put one over here."

Stan starts to drill. Babe is directly opposite him on the other side of the trunk, on his knees, pushing with his stomach toward the trunk. The drill breaks through and Stan says "Tuck!"

Cut to Babe's side and show that the drill has come through the other wall and has caught in his vest. Babe hasn't noticed it. He says, "Okay," and Stan starts to pull the drill out.

Babe looks down and sees his vest being taken from him and drawn through the hole. He turns to the camera with a disgusted look. Stan pulls the drill through the other side with Babe's vest on it. He takes it off, not knowing what it is, looks over to Babe, discovers his vest is missing and hands it to him.

Stan starts to drill again and Babe says, "That's enough. From now on I'll handle this. He comes around the trunk, takes the drill from Stan and throws it down into the kit.

Cut to the inside and Long looks through the hole, seeing Stan and Babe. His eyes open wide. His main thought now is to get at them, so he speaks: "Hey, you guys, just do as I tell you and you can get me out of here. See that blow torch?"

Babe: "Yes."

Long: "Light it and melt the lock off."

Babe: "How does it work?"

Long: "Just pump it up and light it."

Babe places the blow torch on the floor and starts pumping it up. Stan is feeling in his pockets for a match to light it with. He hasn't any so he speaks to Long in the trunk, "Have you got a match?" Babe says, "Don't bother him. Here's one." He hands Stan a match. Stan strikes it and lights the torch, which shoots out one long flame directly into one of the holes in the trunk. Long lets out a yell and the trunk does a "108."

Cut to a cigar stand. A couple of shady characters are on, playing "26." We hear the voices of newsboys shouting "Extra! Butch Long makes sensational escape," etc. Mae enters hurriedly with a newspaper and says to the man behind the counter, "Hello, Jerry." He is taking score for the dice game. He says, "Hi, Mae. What's eatin' you?" Mae shows him the newspaper and says, "Heard the news, didn't you?"

Jerry: "Yeah. I saw it an hour ago."

Mae: "Listen – I want you to come over to the apartment."

Jerry: "Is Butch over there?"

Mae: "Yes – he got locked in a trunk and I can't get him out."

Jerry: "Not me. I ain't comin' over there. One more jam

and I'm sunk."

Mae: "What am I going to do?"

Jerry: "Get the trunk over here. Bring it in the back way."

Mae: "I get you."

She exits.

Segue – Bedroom of the apartment. Stan and Babe are trying to saw the trunk open.

Cut to the living room. Mae enters and crosses to the bedroom. She stops Stan and Babe from sawing, and speaking to the trunk says, "Hey, Butch!"

Long: "Did you get Jerry?"

Mae: "No, he couldn't get over."

Long: "Well help get me out of here, will you?"

Mae: "We haven't got time to get you out here. We've got to take the trunk over to Jerry. We can't stay here a minute longer. The papers are full of your escape and your mug's smeared all over the front page!"

Stan and Babe see the newspaper, take it big and Stan motions to Babe that they'd better leave. Babe tries to calm himself and says to Mae, "I'm sorry, but we'll have to be going. We've had a very pleasant time, and . . a very pleasant time." Long shouts, "Don't let those mugs go! Make 'em take me over to Jerry's so's I can get out of here." Mae says, "That's a good idea," then to Stan and Babe: "Put this trunk in your car and drive us over."

Babe: "I'm sorry, but we can't start the car. They key is broken."

Long: "Make 'em carry me!"

(During this scene we hear the faint sounds of newsboys crying, "Extra – Butch Long escapes," and the sirens of police cars.)

Babe: "What do you think we are?"

Mae picks up her bag and puts her hand in it, pantomiming that she has a gun in there, and holding it toward Stan and Babe says, "Don't argue! Get this trunk out of here!" As they are picking up the trunk she continues, "And remember, I'm right behind you!" They start to exit with the trunk through the bedroom door, which is at the head of the stairs in the hallway. They start down the stairs struggling with the trunk, Babe in the lead. Mae is directly behind Stan. She slips on something, maybe the door mat, and lights on her fanny. The gun goes off in the bag and Stan takes the shot on the fanny, lets go of the trunk which causes Babe to fall down the stairs with the trunk after him. (Sound effect of "Oh's" and bumps.)

Cut to the front door at the street. The trunk and Babe come flying through the window of the door, followed by Stan and Mae. The trunk lands on the sidewalk and we see that Long's feet have gone through the bottom of it.

Babe picks himself up and Stan helps him to straighten up the trunk. They haven't seen the feet. Mae says, "Go ahead two blocks and turn to your right. And don't forget what I told you!" Stan and Babe pick up the trunk and start walking away with it, with Mae in the rear, and we see the picture of the pair of legs walking along under the trunk. As they are going along, Stan says to Babe, "You know, this trunk isn't as heavy as I thought it was."

They come to a corner where the boy is yelling, "Extra!" He waves the newspaper in Babe's face and says, "Read all about the sensational escape of Butch Long." Babe says, "I don't have to read about. I know about it."

Mae comes up alongside of Babe and says, "Down this way." They turn the corner onto a dark street. They walk along a little ways and suddenly a spotlight shines on their backs, lighting up Stan and Babe and the trunk with the feet beneath it. A police car drives into the scene and the cops make Stan and Babe stop.

Quick flash of Mae. She sees the situation, turns and runs.

The cops start to question Stan and Babe, and while they are trying to explain, the trunk starts walking away. They run and get it and bring it back. One of the cops says, "What have you got in the trunk?" Babe says, "It's a friend of ours. He got locked in here and we were just taking it to have it opened." The cop says "Oh, yeah? I'll open it for you." He takes out his revolver and places the muzzle against the lock of the trunk. Just as he is about to fire Stan yells "TUCK!" The gun goes off and the trunk falls to pieces. Long is discovered by the cops. We go for a wow finish and fade out.

- - - -

THEM THAR HILLS

Production history: Production L-19. Script written late May-early June 1934. Filmed Monday, June 11 through Wednesday, June 20. Copyrighted July 18, 1934 by MGM (LP 4849). Released July 21.

Produced by Hal Roach. Directed by Charles Rogers. Photographed by Art Lloyd. Edited by Bert Jordan. Sound by James Greene.

With Stan Laurel (Himself), Oliver Hardy (Himself), Mae Busch (Mrs. Hall), Charlie Hall (Mr. Hall), Billy Gilbert (Doctor), Bobby Dunn, Sam Lufkin, Richard Alexander (Moonshiners), Bobby Burns, Baldwin Cooke, Eddie Baker (Revenuers).

Ollie has "the worst case of gout I ever saw," according to his doctor, who prescribes a trip into the mountains, where he can "drink plenty of water — and lots of it!" Stan suggests renting a trailer; they drive into the hills, where they find a little cabin and a charming old well. They don't know that this has just been vacated by a gang of moonshiners who have dumped their highly alcoholic product into the well — and lots of it. The boys prepare lunch, drinking plenty of water and feeling no pain because of "the iron in it." Mr. Hall and his wife, motorists who have run out of gas, pay a visit and Ollie tells Mr. Hall to help himself to the boys' spare supply. Hall goes back to fill his car, then returns to find the boys and his wife happily hammered. Mr. Hall is not charmed by this, and a reciprocal fracas proceeds.

One of the best Laurel and Hardy shorts, *Them Thar Hills* was supposed to have been filmed from June 11th through the 16th of 1934, but California's "June gloom" caused the crew to vacate their location in Santa Ynez Canyon, about 15 miles northwest of the Roach studio. The moonshiners' cabin and well were duplicated on a Roach sound stage, where the film was completed from June 18th through the 20th.

Oddly, an article in *Hollywood Filmograph* of June 16th lists Francis Corby as the cameraman, with Elmer Raguse once again tending to the sound recording. The longtime Roach prop man Don Sandstrom is credited in this article as the Assistant Director. None of these gentlemen is credited in the film's titles, but it's possible that they worked on the film before the crew abandoned the Santa Ynez Canyon location.

Billy Gilbert had recently finished co-starring in a series for Hal Roach, as one of the German "Schmaltz Brothers" with Billy Bletcher. *Daily Variety* of June 9th noted, "Gilbert, formerly under contract to Hal Roach Studios, returns to that studio for a supporting part in the Laurel and Hardy two-reeler, which Charley Rogers directs." No doubt Billy was getting a higher fee as a freelancer than he'd gotten under contract to Roach. Soon after this, he appeared in several comedy shorts for Educational and Columbia, including a memorable turn as a crazy hospital patient tended to by Doctors Howard, Fine and Howard (the Three Stooges) in *Men in Black*.

In a scene not in the film, Stan attends to his friend's gouty foot.

The good doctor (Billy Gilbert) demands that Ollie travel to the mountains, drink water, "and lots of it!"

Stan attempts to carry Ollie to the car –

When the Doctor gives Ollie his advice, he hammers home that Mr. Hardy should "Drink plenty of water – and lots of it!" This, of course, is to plant the idea of the boys drinking copious amounts of that water that tickles which they get from the well.

In the film, when the boys are discussing the rental of a trailer, there's some byplay wherein Ollie is trying to pour some medicine, and when Stan tries to get his attention, Ollie accidentally pours it into his upturned hat. Stan finishes explaining his idea with, "We could get it for next to nothing. I bet if we paid cash, we could get it for less than that." However, he doesn't offer to carry Ollie downstairs; instead, Ollie says, "Help me down to the car," and Stan replies, "Isn't there any other way to carry you down? My back's broken carrying you up and down these stairs." Ollie is disgusted, and remarks,

-- but falls backward into the tub, fortunately filled.

"That would be like you – to desert a friend in his hour of need."

The dramatic scene showing the moonshiners being captured by the Federal agents also emphasizes a key plot point with a closeup of Bobby Dunn (later the genial shoplifter in *Tit for Tat*) yelling, "We'll dump the liquor in the well!" This line isn't in the script, but it's necessary to clarify the reasons for the boys' subsequent tipsiness.

Perhaps the most notable change from *Them Thar Hills'* script to its film counterpart comes when Ollie suggests what they'll have for dinner: "How about a plate of beans and a pot of steaming hot coffee?" Stan responds, "Swell. You sure know how to plan a meal!" This puts a much stronger "bow ribbon" on the scene.

Ollie accidentally "opens" and ruins a decorative coffee tin as the boys make lunch. Pom-pom!

Another key point of the story is emphasized more in the film, when Stan attempts to get water from the trailer's faucet, then tells Ollie there is none. "Draw some from the well," Ollie commands. "That's what wells are for!"

The very involved scripted sequence of Stan attempting to draw water from the well, which takes a half-page of a six-page script, is not in the film. It likely would have added another three or four minutes of running time, more than its modest humor content justifies.

Even though Ollie doesn't mention it in the film, they do have some "health bread," which Stan butters by cutting off a slice, buttering the edge of the remaining loaf, cutting off that slice, and continuing the process. (Ollie slices it in the script.)

While "The Old Spinning Wheel" is explicitly referenced in the script as the tune Ollie sings, the only hint of Stan's "pom-pom" countermelody at first is "They go into the singing routine with interruptions." At the later point in the script and film, when Mr. Hall returns to find his wife and her new companions drinking plenty of water and lots of it, the script notes, "they are singing 'Spinning Wheel' with the 'pom-pom' business." Evidently "the singing routine" and "pom-pom" had been discussed prior to this script being written.

The script writers seem to have forgotten about Ollie's bandaged foot, as several proposed scenes call for him to be more easily ambulatory than his case of gout would allow.

That good old mountain water is good for your nerves, and tickles in a variety of ways.

Stranded motorist Mrs. Hall enjoys a roisterous luncheon.

Mr. Hall, adorned with plunger, "beard," and baked beans, exacts his revenge.

The boys drink much more copiously in the script than they do in the film. The Production Code Administration of the Motion Picture Producers and Distributors of America, which greatly censored what could be depicted in American films, put the Code into effect on July 15, 1934. *Them Thar Hills* was released six days later, on July 21. If the drinking scenes were filmed (and there's no indication that they were), they almost certainly would have been eliminated by the "Hays Office," named for Will Hays, head of the MPPDA, supervised by Joseph I. Breen.

In the film, when Stan first draws a bucket of water from the well, he remarks to Ollie that it has a funny color. Ollie confidently tells him, "It's the iron in it!," an observation he also makes to Mae – who seems to take it as a clever euphemism, as surely these two gentlemen must know that they're drinking some very potent alcohol. The script describes her reaction as "a knowing wink."

The script and the main titles for *Them Thar Hills* spell Mr. Hall's first name as "Charley," but in his many surviving letters he consistently spelled it as "Charlie." So, for that matter, did Charlie Rogers, frequent L&H gag man and occasional director. Since supporting actors were rarely billed at all in the Hal Roach comedies, we can't imagine that Mr. Hall was terribly upset at the variant spelling.

In the film, after Mae says, "Why, I'm so hungry I could eat a horse's neck," there's a much better response: Stan gets a small hatchet and is about to exit the trailer when

Not in the film – the aftermath of Ollie's plunge into the well and subsequent landing.

Ollie asks, "Where are you going?" Stan replies, "I'm going to look for a horse." Ollie orders him to sit down, which Stan does, briefly, on the hot stove. Instead of the suggested montage of buckets of water being poured and more coffee going into cups, we just have a quick fade out; when we fade in again to see Charlie Hall arriving at the trailer, the raucous singing of Stan, Ollie and Mae tells us all we need to know about how much water they've consumed.

The film's final group of "retaliation gags" are not as violent as those suggested in the script. Instead of doing significant physical injury with a hornets' nest and a car fire, the gags focus more on personal embarrassment. Charlie gets a plunger stuck on his forehead; Ollie cuts his belt and this loosens his trousers, the insides of which are soon filled with baked beans.

Them Thar Hills was so well received that it prompted Laurel and Hardy's only deliberate sequel, *Tit for Tat*. The script for that film is included in *The Laurel & Hardy Movie Scripts*. (This book is a sequel to that one.)

L-19 – Laurel & Hardy.

Fade in on Babe's apartment. Stan, Babe and a doctor are discovered. Babe is seated inan arm chair with his foot resting on an ottoman and the doctor has just finished bandaging it up.

Doctor: "It's the worst case of gout I ever saw."

Babe: "What's the cause of it, doctor?"

The doctor with a warning tone says, "Too much high living."

Stan: "Maybe we better move in the basement."

Babe: "Shut up!"

Doctor: "You've got to lead a simpler life. Cut out the rich foods What you need is a rest in the country. Get away from this wild life. Remember, you can't burn the candle at both ends."

Stan looking puzzled says, "But we don't burn candles. We've got an electric light." Babe kicks Stan with his gouty foot, takes it and very annoyed says, "Would you mind standing on my good side?" Stan crosses to the other side of him.

Babe: "Do you know a good place to go, doctor?"

Doctor: "The best place for you would be up in the mountains – a high altitude. Get yourself a tent. Drink plenty of water – get to bed early and relax. When you come back you won't know yourself."

Stan: (to Babe) "See?"

Doctor: (to Stan) "And that goes for you too!"

Stan looks in the mirror, then at his feet. The doctor finishes packing his bag, goes to the door, turns and says, "Now do what I tell you. Get away and try to forget everything. Goodbye."

Stan and Babe say "Goodbye" in unison.

Stan: "You know what would be a good idea?"

Babe: "What?"

Stan: "Why don't we get one of those conveniences to hook on the back of our car?"

Babe: "Conveniences! You mean conveyance!"

Stan: "Well, we could live in it much better than a tent."

Babe: "Can you take those things up in the mountains?"

Stan: "Sure – right up in the high multitude."

Babe: "Not multitude – attitude!"

Stan: "I know where we can rent one for next to nothing. Maybe cheaper. Let's go take a look at it."

Babe: "How am I going to get downstairs with my bad foot?"

Stan: "I can carry you down."

Babe: "You can't carry me!"

Stan: "Sure I can. All you got to do is relax and lean forward."

Stan gives Babe his hat, helps him up out of the chair and helps him sit on the table. Stan then backs up to him and gets Babe's legs around his waist, Babe putting his arms around Stan's shoulders. Stan starts to struggle toward the door but gradually overbalances and starts going backwards. Babe starts hollering "Be careful! Careful! Careful!" They back into the bath room and right into the bath tub, which is full of water.

Go to close shot of Babe lying in the bath tub with his gouty foot sticking up in the air. Stan looks at him and sits on the little stool alongside the tub. For something to say, Stan says, "You didn't relax and lean forward." Babe suddenly takes a long-handled bath brush and clunks Stan on the head with it. Fade Out.

Fade in on a location up in the mountains. There is an old rough looking shack, and nearby it an old fashioned well. We hear several shots, windows are broken, and shots are exchanged from the shack.

During this we cut to the interior of the shack. Several moonshiners are firing through the windows. A few of them are carrying barrels of liquor out the back door and dumping it into the well. The Federal men finally break into the cabin, arresting the moonshiners as we fade out.

Fade in on Stan and Babe in their Ford pulling the trailer along the road.

Cut to a close shot. They are both seemingly very happy.

Babe points off and says, "There's a beautiful spot – let's park there." They swing out of the picture and we cut to a setup at the location of the moonshiners' hut. Stan and Babe drive in.

Go to close shot. Stan pulls on the brakes suddenly. The car stops with a jerk and Babe's bandaged foot, which has been resting on the windshield, goes between the upper and the lower halves of the windshield, locking his foot in there. He has great difficulty extricating himself, and for the first time in the picture says, "Why don't you be careful?" He looks the place over and says, "What a beautiful spot! The highest point of the mountains." Stan, looking, says, "Look at the well – we've got water and everything."

Babe: "Um-hum. Well, let's fix something to eat. I'm starving to death."

Stan: "What'll we have?"

Babe: "How about a nice plate of beans, health bread and a pot of coffee?"

Stan: "That's swell."

Babe: "You fix up the coffee and I'll take care of the rest."

Stan gets two buckets and exits toward the well.

Cut to the well setup. Stan enters, puts down the two buckets and starts to operate the well pole to draw a bucket of water. As he pushes the pole to the ground, the bucket comes out of the well. He is too far away to reach it. He lets go quickly and tries to grab the bucket before it goes down the well again, but misses it. He tries several ways to reach the bucket each time he draws it up.

Cut to Babe watching him. Finally in utter disgust Babe comes over to help and take charge. He explains to Stan how simple it is. He draws a bucket of water and maneuvers it to the edge of the well. Stan pours the water into one of his buckets, and in throwing the bucket into the well causes the end of the well pole to come up, hitting Babe under the chin. Babe takes it and says, "Wait a minute – I'll do the next one. You come over here."

Stan takes the end of the pole and draws a bucket of water, swinging it like Babe did to the edge of the well. He swings it a little too far and the bucket drops onto Babe's foot. Babe doesn't say a word, but comes over to Stan, takes the pole from him, swings the bucket into position, lowers it into the well and draws another bucket of water. Pushing the pole down to the ground he says, "Put your foot on that. That's all I ask you to do."

Stan puts his foot on the end of the pole. Babe goes over and pours the water into their bucket, placing the well bucket back on the rope, turns to Stan and says, "All right." Stan takes his foot off the pole and the other end drops down, clunking Babe on the head. Laying on the edge of the well is a dipper made of half a cocoanut shell with a stick through it. Babe picks this up and hits Stan on the head. (Try to get sound effect of horses' hooves.)

Babe then dips the dipper into the bucket of water and drinks it, smacking his lips, and says, "Even the water tastes different up here." He hands the dipper to Stan, who takes a good drink, smacks his lips and hands the dipper back to Babe. They pick up the buckets and exit toward the trailer.

Cut to the trailer setup. Stan and Babe enter. Stan takes one bucket of water into the trailer and Babe sets the other one down by the door.

Cut to interior of the trailer. Stan is getting out the coffee pot, coffee, etc. Babe enters, gets a card table and exits.

Cut to exterior; Babe comes out of the car, sets up the four legs of the table in a dainty manner, starts back into the trailer, looks at the bucket and calls to Stan, "Hand me one of those cups." Stan comes to the door and hands Babe a tin cup. He dips it into the bucket and as he finishes drinking he again smacks his lips, then exits back into the trailer.

Cut to interior, where Stan is just finishing drinking a cup of water out of his bucket. Babe enters, goes to a drawer, takes out a table cloth and some knives and forks and starts humming, "The Old Spinning Wheel." While he is doing this, Stan is putting the coffee into the pot and pouring the water from the bucket into the pot.

Cut to exterior; Babe comes out singing, puts the table cloth and knives onto the table, and just goes to spread the cloth when he notices the bucket and again takes a drink, smacking his lips. He continues singing with more vigor, laying out the knives and forks.

Back to Stan. He has filled up the coffee pot and has half a cup of water left. He goes to pour it back but decides to drink it. He then starts to put some kindling into the stove.

Back to Babe. He starts to go into the trailer, sees the bucket again and drinks another cupful. Singing all the louder, he enters the trailer.

Cut to interior; Stan is trying to get some kindling wood into the stove but the wood is too large. Babe gets out a loaf of bread, knife, can of beans and an opener, and again exits from the trailer, still singing. Stan, realizing he can't get the wood into the stove, opens the cupboard and takes out a hatchet. He exits from the trailer.

Exterior. Babe is now slicing the bread, still continuing his singing. Stan kneels down and starts chopping the kindling wood to make it smaller. They go into the singing routine with interruptions. Babe finally comes over to bawl Stan out for interrupting his song. Stan goes to chop a piece of wood and accidentally chops the toe off Babe's shoe.

Babe grabs the hatchet from Stan; the head of it comes off and flies out of the scene.

Cut to a wheel of the trailer. The hatchet enters and sticks into the tire and we hear a whistling noise as the air escapes and the tire flattens.

Babe takes it and kicks Stan in the fanny with his good foot. Stan resents this. He holds his fist in front of Babe's face, then quickly grabs Babe's tie and pulls his face into the fist. Babe loses his head and makes a wild kick at Stan with his bum foot. Stan ducks and the big bandage flies off of Babe's foot, sailing through the air and landing in something. Babe says "Now look what you've done! Get back in there and fix that coffee!" Stan picks up some of the wood and goes back into the trailer. Babe starts to follow, and seeing the bucket he takes another drink.

Interior. Stan is also taking another drink. Babe enters and Stan puts the kindling into the fire, puts the coffee pot on top, takes out a match, lights the fire and closes the door of the grate. He goes to blow the match out and the fumes of his breath cause a big flame to shoot out from the match, catching Babe on the fanny as he is bending over. They both look at each other puzzled. Fade out.

Fade in on Charley Hall and Mae Busch walking along the

road. Charley is carrying a gallon gasoline can. Mae is bawling him out somewhat to this effect:

Mae: "I told you when we passed the last station to get some gas! You never pay any attention to me!"

Charley: "Aw, shut up!"

Mae: "I won't shut up!"

Charley: "Then keep on talking!"

Mae: "I won't keep on talking! I haven't the strength! I haven't had a bite to eat since morning!"

She suddenly looks off and says, "Look – there's some people over there with a trailer. Maybe we can buy some gas from them." They exit.

Cut to the trailer setup. Mae and Charley enter and knock on the door of the trailer. As they are doing so Stan and Babe, a little unsteady, enter carrying a couple of buckets, water pitcher and stew pot full of water on a long stick, each holding an end.

Babe wants to know what their business is, and there is a general introduction all around. Charley asks what all the water is for, and Babe explains that they are out here under doctor's orders and that he told them to drink lots of water, adding, "We've only been drinking this for an hour, and you've no idea how much better we feel."

Stan: "Yes, and he told us when we get back we wouldn't know each other."

Babe: "Is there anything we can do for you?"

Charley: "Yes. We ran out of gas. If you have any to spare, would you be kind enough to sell us some?"

Babe: "Why, certainly."

Babe turns to Stan and says, "You'll find that spare gasoline under the sink. Give it to the gentleman." Stan takes the can from Charley and goes into the trailer.

Charley: "Thanks very much."

Mae: "We certainly appreciate it."

Babe: "Don't mention it. Won't you have a drink of water?"

Charley: "No, thanks."

Babe: (to Mae) "You?"

Mae: "Don't mind if I do."

Babe dips a cup of water and hands it to her. He dips another for himself and raising it in a toast says, "Here's to the simple life." They both drink and Mae has a reaction which Babe doesn't see. She kind of likes it.

Mae: "That sure is swell water." (Gives him a knowing wink) "Do you mind if I have another?"

Babe: "Help yourself."

Mae dips a cup, turns to Charley and says, "Why don't you try some?" Charley says, "I told you I didn't want any!" Mae says, "Okay, baby. You don't know what you're missing." She starts to drink.

At this point Stan comes out with the can of gas and hands it to Charley. He says, "Thanks very much," then turns to Mae and says, "You wait here while I get the car." He exits.

Mae sees the table all set and says to Babe, "Getting ready to eat?" Babe says, "Yes, would you like to join us?" Mae says, "I sure would. I could eat a horse's neck," and Stan speaks up, "We haven't any. All we've got is beans." Babe helps Mae to sit down at the table and says, "Stanley, get the coffee." Stan brings the coffee and there is general business of getting the beans onto the plates, etc.

For lapse of time, quick flashes of more buckets of water, coffee steaming, hand pouring coffee into cups, cans of beans being opened, etc.

Go to exterior of the trailer and we hear a lot of hilarity going on, the three inside singing "Spinning Wheel" and laughing; noises of tin cups and plates, etc. Charley drives in with the car, stops and gets out. He looks puzzled, hearing all this racket going on.

Cut inside the trailer and we show Stan and Babe and Mae well intoxicated. Mae has on Stan's hat; Babe has on Mae's beret; they are singing "Spinning Wheel" with the "pom-pom" business, and drinking coffee. On the table are beans, hot cakes, molasses, etc. Babe tells Stan, "Put on another pot of coffee. Make it two pots!" Stan says, "I did. They'll be ready in a minute." They all laugh again and continue their hilarity.

The door behind them opens and Charley looks in, looking not a bit pleased. Several things are done while he is watching, which makes him burn all the more. They finally turn and see him, and laugh all the louder. Mae puts her arm around Charley and says, "Hello, baby." He throws her arm and the laughter kind of stops as they realize Charley is a little bit sore.

Charley: "What's going on here?"

Stan: "Who are you?"

Charley: "If you've been doing what I think you've been doing, you'll find out who I am!"

He smells the coffee, then tastes it and says to Babe, "What do you mean, getting my wife drunk?" He hauls off and socks Babe on the nose, which starts a routine of retaliation gags, including:

Stan pouring a can of molasses over Charley, then throwing a lot of feathers at him.

Stan gets a pair of bellows, sticks the nozzle into the coffee pot, fills the bellows with coffee and squirts it into Hall's face. Babe laughs, thinking it is a great gag. Hall takes the bellows from Stan to repeat the business, fills it with coffee, levels it at Babe and as he presses the bellows together the coffee backfires and goes into Hall's face. Stan and Babe laugh again.

They throw hornets' nest into Hall's car.

Hall lifts the hood of Stan and Babe's car, lights a packet of matches, throws it on the engine, puts the hood down, setting it on fire. Stan and Babe go over to Charley's car, kick a hole in the radiator, water squirts out and extinguishes the fire in their car. They give Charley the nod and go back into their trailer.

Charley comes over, uncouples the trailer from the car and the trailer tips over with all the noise of dishes, etc. sliding to one end.

Finish with Hall pouring lamp oil over Babe's fanny. He feels for a match, then asks Stan, "Have you got a match?" Stan gives him one and he lights the oil on Babe's fanny, then gets in his car and drives away. Babe runs around yelling. Stan tells him to dive into the well. He does so and there is a terrific explosion, leaving Stan and Babe in some funny position for a fade out.

THE FIXER UPPERS

Production history: Script written early January 1935. Filmed Wednesday, January 9 through Saturday, January 19. Released February 9, 1935. Copyrighted February 26, 1935 by MGM (LP 5371). Two reels.

Produced by Hal Roach. Directed by Charles Rogers. Photographed by Art Lloyd, ASC. Edited by Bert Jordan. Sound by James Greene.

With Stan Laurel (Himself), Oliver Hardy (Himself), Arthur Housman (Friendly drunk who had a mother), Mae Busch (Madame Gustave), Charles Middleton (Pierre Gustave), Noah Young (Bartender), James C. Morton, Jack Hill, Dick Gilbert (Taxi drivers), Bobby Dunn (Apartment dweller with a cold), Bob O'Conor (Waiter).

Stan and Ollie are selling their home-made Christmas cards door-to-door. They encounter a lady who is distraught because her artist husband, Pierre Gustave, isn't showing her any attention. Stan recalls a case like this in which a third party was hired to make the husband jealous and realize his

The original 1935 title lobby card.

Two Christmas card salesmen attempt to cheer the neglected Mrs. Gustave.

thoughtlessness. Mrs. Gustave offers Ollie $50 if he will be the third party. The ruse works too well, and the enraged artist insists that Ollie return for a duel to the death. The boys are distraught, drowning their sorrows with beer, until they realize that Pierre doesn't know where they live. They celebrate with a tipsy customer and pass out. The customer makes sure they get home – three taxi drivers take them all to the address on Pierre's card, which was in Ollie's pocket. The duel isn't fatal, because Mrs. Gustave has put blank cartridges in the pistols – but when Pierre pledges to cut Ollie's body into pieces, Mr. Hardy suddenly springs back to life and the boys run away.

The idea of a frustrated wife hiring another man to make her husband jealous had formed the story of *Slipping Wives* filmed in October and early November 1926. In that picture, Stan as a paint delivery man was the gigolo, and Babe was a butler doing his best to get rid of him. The development of the Stan and Ollie characters over the following eight years makes the retelling of the plot much funnier.

Many Gallic references show up in *The Fixer Uppers*. The artist, Pierre Gustave, is "the best shot in all Paris." Stan and Ollie drown their sorrows at the "Café des Artistes." When Pierre asks Ollie if he's ready to begin the duel, he responds, "Oui, monsieur. Je suis pret. Vive la France!" However, Pierre's card gives his address as "14 Gramercy Place." This would indicate that the film's setting is in an artist's colony in the Gramercy area of Manhattan.

The script's opening scene with Mae Busch and Charles Middleton is not in the film, which begins instead with Stan and Ollie walking up the stairs to Arthur Housman's

Mrs. Gustave demonstrates how her husband used to show his affection.

Ollie's attempt to make Mr. Gustave jealous has succeeded spectacularly.

The boys drown their sorrows while Ollie awaits his fate.

apartment. Arthur's surname is misspelled as "Houseman" in the script – and frequently elsewhere.

The dialogue exchange with Mr. Housman is shorter in the film – and it's only one visit, not two. After Ollie reads his "Hot-cha-cha" card, Arthur says, "A beautiful thought; I'll take one." The scene ends there, so the boys do make a sale, since Arthur doesn't complain about the price as he does in the script. This keeps him on friendly terms with the boys, as required for his scenes later in the film.

Stan's recounting of the "hired man" story is the fourth and last of the "tell me that again" routines, the others being in *Towed in a Hole*, *The Devil's Brother*, and *Oliver the Eighth*. This is such a distinctive and endearing bit of business, one wishes it had been used in subsequent films.

When Mrs. Gustave demonstrates how she was once kissed by Pierre, her smooching of Stan lasts 43 seconds. The Production Code had stipulated that a kiss could not last longer than five seconds, which may well be why there are several cutaways to Ollie looking at us, checking his watch, assuring us that it's working, and registering astonishment.

The revelation in the script about the identity of "the other woman" is not in the film, probably because such a situation seems highly out of character for at least one of the participants. It also introduces an error because Stan had indicated that the couple "got married all over again," indicating that he would still have a wife.

Realizing that Pierre doesn't know where to find them, Stan and Ollie celebrate with their sozzled but friendly customer (Arthur Housman).

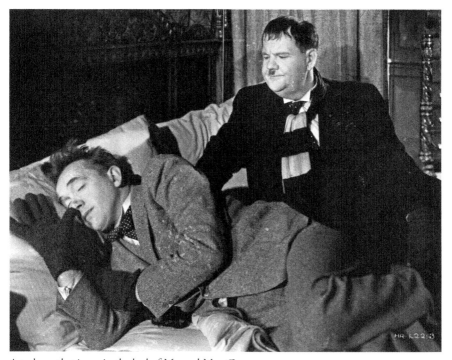

A rude awakening – in the bed of Mr. and Mrs. Gustave.

Pierre and Ollie have chosen their weapons. Note the slashed portrait of Mae in the background; a possible deleted scene may have shown Pierre destroying it in anger.

The scripted slapstick involving the four mugs of beer and changing of tables is not in the film; however, the movie does offer a nice moment where the pay phone rings in the saloon and Stan answers it. He says, "Hello? It sure is!" Ollie asks him who it was, and Stan replies, "Oh, just some fella having a joke." Ollie asks, "Well, what did he say?" Stan responds, "Well, I said hello, and the fella says, 'It's a long distance from Atlanta, Georgia.' And I said it sure is! Silliest thing I ever heard." Ollie agrees and says, "I wish there were some way to put a stop to those practical jokers!" This also plants the idea of the pay phone, which helps provide the last section of the story.

This script was originally formatted in two columns, reflecting the much greater emphasis on dialogue than usual. This story has a more complex plot than most L&H two-reelers, but since the emphasis is always on Stan and Ollie and not on secondary characters, as sometimes occurs in the feature films, it's still consistently entertaining.

Ollie's threat to return to the apartment was not retained in the film, and Stan's boast was replaced with a much funnier and more characteristic line: "If you had a face like mine, you'd punch me right in the nose. And I'm just the fella that can do it!"

In the background of some shots set in the artist's apartment, there's a portrait of Patsy Kelly, which had been made for the 1934 Todd-Kelly short *Done in Oil.* One can also see a portrait of Mrs. Gustave, which has been slashed to ribbons. How and why this happened is not mentioned in film or script. On January 15, 1935, during the filming of *The Fixer Uppers*, a fire broke out in a film editing room, causing its

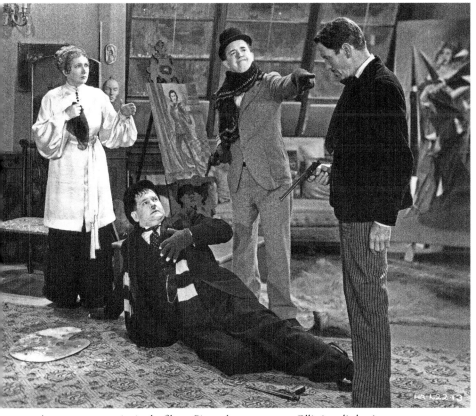

A moment not quite in the film – Pierre threatens to cut Ollie into little pieces.

complete destruction. *Daily Variety* reported, "Three cutters working in the room escaped, uninjured. A small amount of positive and negative went up into flames." One wonders if a scene explaining the defacing of the portrait might have been incinerated.

The scene in the saloon, the return of the boys to the artist's apartment, and the scene in the bedroom are all much more concise in the film. We do see three taxi drivers bringing the unconscious Stan and Ollie into the artist's apartment, but we never see three taxis. Also, Stan remains in bed and doesn't get up as he does in the script. Nor does the artist yank the mattress onto the floor with Stan and Babe still on it – no doubt this would have been very difficult to do with the dramatic flourish which was clearly intended.

The final gag proposed in the script was a favorite finale at the Roach lot; it had been used previously in *Wrong Again* and would show up later in *A Chump at Oxford*. The film instead ends with Mr. Laurel tapping on the lid of a garbage can in which Mr. Hardy has been hiding; he says, "You can come out now, he's gone." Stan hears a whistle and looks off to sees Ollie among the refuse that's piled on the platform of a garbage truck, which heads down the street and turns a corner as we fade out.

L-22 Laurel & Hardy.

FADE IN on an artist's studio, where we see Mae Busch posing for her husband, who is the artist. He is a type like Charlie Middleton, and is just putting the finishing touches on the canvas. He puts down his brush and turns to Mae:

ARTIST: Thank goodness that's finished.

MAE: Why, are you sorry you had to paint it?

ARTIST: Oh no, dear, but it has held me up on my other work. (Looks at his watch) By George, I almost missed my appointment! I'm having lunch with the President of Grafton Galleries.

He starts to remove his smock.

MAE: Aren't you going to take me with you?

ARTIST: I'm sorry, dear, but this is strictly business.

MAE: Do you realize you haven't taken me out in the last three months?

ARTIST: I know, my dear, but you know – business before pleasure.

MAE: Do you know what day this is?

ARTIST: Certainly – Tuesday.

MAE: It's our fourth anniversary.

ARTIST: Why, so it is! (Starts to laugh) Can you imagine – I completely forgot about it!

He goes toward her as though to give her a kiss, when the phone rings and he stops and picks it up. He listens a moment, then:

ARTIST: Oh yes – I'm ready to leave now. I'll be right over.

He hangs up and starts toward the door.

ARTIST: Goodbye, dear.

MAE: Haven't you forgotten something?

He looks a little puzzled, then suddenly:

ARTIST: Oh yes – my hat.

He picks up his hat and exits, closing the door. Mae sits down and starts to cry.

Cut to the hall. Stan and Babe enter up the stairs to an apartment which is situated at the head of the stairs. Babe is carrying a large scrap book filled with samples of Christmas cards. He daintily raps on the knocker.

The door opens and Arthur Houseman appears, dressed in pajamas, an ice bag on his head and an awful hangover.

BABE: (In his brightest manner) Good morning!

Houseman hiccups a "good morning."

BABE: We're taking orders for Christmas cards. I designed them myself and my friend Mr. Laurel has written the beautiful verses.

ARTHUR: Swell!

BABE: (Pulling out a card) Here's a beautiful number that might interest you. May I read it for you?

ARTHUR: Go ahead!

BABE: (Reading)

> 'Twas Christmas day in the poor house
>
> And the boys were feeling blue;
>
> The boys in gray were fighting –
>
> A Merry Christmas to you!

ARTHUR: And a Happy New Year to you! Could anything be fairer and squarer than that?

With this he closes the door in their face. Stan and Babe give each other a look and Babe knocks on the door again. Houseman opens it.

ARTHUR: What do you want?

BABE: We're taking orders for Christmas cards.

ARTHUR: That's funny – there was a couple of fellows here a minute ago.

STAN: What a small world!

ARTHUR: Well, what have you got to show me? State your business! State your business!

BABE: It's a pleasure! Now I have here a card that appeals to the ladies - -

(Pulls out a card and reads it:)

Jingle bells, Jingle bells

Coming thru' the rye –

I wish you a Merry Christmas,

Even as you and I.

At this point there is a character walking up the stairs. As Babe completes the verse, the character casually blows his nose, giving the effect of a "razzberry." Houseman looks over at him.

ARTHUR: You took the very words out of my mouth.

BABE: (a little hurt) What's the matter with it?

ARTHUR: Not enough sentiment.

This gives a lead to Stan, who whispers to Babe:

STAN: Ask him if he he has a mother. That generally gets 'em.

BABE: You ask him.

STAN: (To Houseman:) Pardon me, but have you ever had a mother?

ARTHUR: (With gestures) Now you've hit me!

BABE: I have a beautiful card here. May I read it to you?

ARTHUR: Go ahead!

BABE: (Reading)

Merry Christmas, Mother –

Merry Christmas, Ma –

Hi, Mommy Mommy,

And a Hot-cha-cha!

ARTHUR: A beautiful sentiment!

BABE: I thought you'd like it. May I take your order?

ARTHUR: Yes – give me one.

BABE: Only one?

ARTHUR: I've only got one mother!

BABE: It'll cost you just as much for one as it would for fifty.

ARTHUR: It's too much!

He closes the door again.

Stan and Babe cross over to the Artist's door and knock.

Cut to the inside; the wife is still seated, sobbing quietly. She hears the knock.

MAE: Come in.

Stan and Babe enter.

BABE: (Very breezy) Good morning, Madam. Pardon our intrusion.

MAE: What is your business?

BABE: We're taking orders for Christmas cards. I designed them and my friend Mr. Laurel wrote the beautiful verses. May I show you our display?

MAE: No, thank you, I wouldn't be interested.

STAN: (Whispers to Babe:) Read her the one about the husband. That'll get her!

BABE: Excuse my insistence. You don't have to buy this card, but I'd like to read it to you because it conveys such a beautiful thought. Doesn't it, Stanley?

STAN: It certainly does. That's one of my best efforts.

BABE: (Reading the card)

> Merry Christmas, Husband –
>
> Happy New Year's nigh;
>
> I wish you Easter Greetings;
>
> Hurray for the 4th of July.

That's what we call our four-in-one. You can use it all the year around.

MAE: No, thank you, I'm still not interested.

Stan and Babe start to exit. Mae goes back to her sobbing, which attracts their attention. They look over, look at each other a little puzzled and come back to her.

BABE: What's the matter? Did we do anything to upset you?

MAE: (Sniffling) No - -

BABE: What are you crying for?

MAE: I'm very unhappy.

BABE: I'm so sorry! Is there anything I can do to help you?

MAE: I'm afraid not. You wouldn't be interested in my troubles.

BABE: On the contrary, whatever it is, I want to help you.

MAE: Well, I'm afraid I've lost my husband's affections. I think he still loves me, but he doesn't give me the thoughtful attentions that he used to.

BABE: Tsk! Tsk! Tsk!

MAE: If there was only something I could do to make him realize he has been so neglectful!

STAN: You know what?

BABE: What?

STAN: (To Mae:) I knew of a woman once that had a case exactly like yours. But do you know what she did? She got a fellow to make violent love to her in front of her husband, but the husband got jealous and she knew that he loved her just because he was jealous. When the husband found out he was jealous he took her in his arms and they got married all over again. And then they had a little - -

BABE: Just a minute. What became of the fellow that made love to the wife?

STAN: The husband was so grateful that he gave him a lot of money, and they all lived happily ever after!

BABE: That's a splendid idea! (To Mae:) Why don't you do that?

MAE: It's a great thought. Will you help me out?

BABE: Well – a - -

MAE: If you help me I'll give you fifty dollars.

BABE: How long do you think it would take?

MAE: It wouldn't take more than a day.

STAN: He could do it much cheaper by the week.

MAE: (To Babe) Please do help me. It means so much to me.

Babe weakens a little, then turns to Stan:

BABE: Tell me again – what happened to the other fellow?

STAN: The husband was so pleased when he found out he was jealous, he gave him a lot of money and they all lived happy ever after. You see, her husband might give you a bonus.

Babe turns to Mae, completely sold:

BABE: Madam, I am at your service!

MAE: A thousand thanks! (To Stan:) And to you, too. You'll never regret it. Won't you sit down and help figure out a plan?

All three sit down on the settee.

BABE: Now, just what would you suggest? You know, this is a little out of my line.

MAE: I know what would make him jealous!

BABE: What?

MAE: If he saw you kissing me like he kissed me the first time we met, I'm sure that would do the trick!

BABE: How did he kiss you?

She turns to Stan to demonstrate for Babe.

MAE: He put his arms around me like this - -

She places Stan's arms around her, then continues:

MAE: And I had my arms around him like this - - (demonstrating) We were pressed tightly together - - and his lips met mine - -

She goes into a soul-kiss with Stan and they lean back on the pillow of the settee. It seems like the kiss will never end. Babe is getting a little concerned and refers to his wrist watch to see how long they have been at it.

Mae finally releases her hold, pulls away from Stan and turns to Babe. Stan is out cold, but Babe doesn't notice this.

MAE: Now, when you hear my husband coming, that's all you have to do.

Babe looks a little embarrassed.

MAE: Don't you think you could do that?

BABE: With a little practice, yes.

Babe suddenly turns and realizes that Stan is out cold. He gets up in a hurry and shakes Stan to wake him up. Stan comes out of it in a daze, looks at Mae and gets over he is sore at her for kissing him that way. He puts his arms around her and before she knows it he has her leaning back and is giving her a soul kiss.

Babe watches this with amazement, looks at his watch, thinks it is long enough and taps Stan on the shoulder. Stan pulls away, leaving Mae out cold as he gives her one of those hods getting over, "What do you think of that?"

BABE: What are you trying to do?

STAN: Well, she started it!

BABE: She was showing me - -

He turns, sees that Mae is out, gets all worried and starts fanning her.

BABE: Quick, get some water!

As Stan is looking for a glass of water, Babe picks Mae up in his arms, trying to revive her.

Mae comes to, and just as she opens her eyes she sees that her husband has entered the room. He is standing in back of Babe.

MAE: (Whispering to Babe) Kiss me! (Babe does so) Again – Again - -

Babe continues to kiss her. The husband is becoming infuriated, but is lost for words.

Stan enters the scene with a glass of water and stands alongside the husband watching Mae and Babe.

STAN: (to husband) Are you looking for somebody?

At this point Babe turns, sees the husband and quickly breaks away from Mae. The husband glares at Babe.

ARTIST: Yes, I'm looking for the viper who destroyed the sanctity of my home!

MAE: You're not jealous, Pierre?

ARTIST: Certainly I'm jealous!

Mae throws her arms around his:

MAE: Pierre, I'm so happy! Now I know you love me!

She kisses him but he pushes her aside:

ARTIST: Away, false one!

MAE: Pierre, let me explain!

ARTIST: There's nothing to explain. I know it all!

He walks over to Babe and glares at him.

MAE: Don't be foolish, dear. This man means nothing to me!

ARTIST: I'll find out! (To Babe) If I divorced her, would you marry her and take care of her for the rest of her life?

BABE: No, sir.

ARTIST: Just as I thought!

With that he slaps Babe across the face with his glove, then pulls out a card and hands it to Babe.

BABE: What's this for?

ARTIST: It means that at twelve o'clock tonight we will meet here in mortal combat – (Babe takes it) – a duel to the death!

MAE: Pierre! This is all a terrible mistake!

He pushes her aside.

ARTIST: Mistake, huh?

MAE: Pierre! Do you realize what you're doing? You, who were the best pistol shot in all of France! It's cold, premeditated murder! They'll hang you for this!

ARTIST: What do I care? I have nothing to live for.

MAE: Be reasonable, Pierre. This gentleman can explain everything - - (Indicating Stan)

STAN   Yes sir. I knew a fellow once, and his wife was - -

ARTIST: SCRAM!

Stan picks up the book of Christmas cards, gives Babe the signal and they start to leave.

ARTIST: Just a minute! I'll trouble you for your card!

BABE: Card?

ARTIST: Yes. It's the custom in my country to exchange cards after a challenge!

Stan opens the book and hands him a Christmas card as we FADE OUT.

FADE IN on Saloon set. This is a basement affair with steps leading down from the street and windows showing the feet of pedestrians walking by. A few characters are on – odd looking types a la Greenwich Village; also a couple of musicians playing soft music.

Stan and Babe enter, both looking very glum. They sit down at a table and a waiter enters to them.

BABE: Two beers. (To Stan) What'll you have?

STAN: I'll take two beers too.

Babe takes this as the waiter exits.

BABE: Well, you fixed me all up, didn't you? A nice little fixer upper!

Stan looks very brow-beaten.

BABE: If you hadn't said anything about that other woman getting somebody to make love to her, I wouldn't be in this mess! By the way, who was she?

STAN: Who?

BABE: The other woman you were referring to.

STAN: That was my wife.

Babe does a big takem at this.

BABE: Do you mean to tell me you gave another fellow money for making love to your wife?

STAN: Well, I didn't exactly give him money – I gave him an I.O.U.

BABE: I thought you said they lived happily ever after.

STAN: They did – after I left.

The waiter brings in four mugs of beer and exits.

STAN: Which is mine?

BABE: Never mind which is yours!

They each pick up a mug. Babe takes a sip. Stan starts to

do the same, then gets the idea to blow the froth off. As he does so, it goes into Babe's lap.

Babe gives that very helpless, disgusted look, reaches down and scoops up the foam and flips it over into Stan's lap. Stan rises to brush it off his lap, and in doing so accidentally tilts the table a little, which causes the four mugs of beer to slide off into Babe's lap. We hear the beer pouring onto the floor as Babe very nonchalantly picks one mug at a time out of his lap, placing them on the table. He gives a little sigh and calls the waiter, who enters.

BABE: One more beer.

STAN: Same for me.

WAITER: Yes, sir. How do you like our new beer?

BABE: Very lovely!

He gives Stan a dirty look as the waiter starts to exit.

BABE: Just a minute! Just bring him a bottle!

WAITER: Yes, sir.

The waiter exits. Babe then looks down in his lap, gets over there is something very uncomfortable, reaches down and brings his shoe up into the picture. He looks into it, sees it is full of beer, and pours it out, giving Stan another dirty look.

The waiter re-enters, places a mug of beer in front of Babe and the bottle of beer in front of Stan, throwing an opener onto the table, and exits. Babe starts to drink his beer and eat a pretzel.

Stan is having a lot of trouble opening the bottle. In trying to open it we see that he is shaking it up and down. He finally breaks the opener. Babe is just watching him to see how far it will go.

STAN: Have you got an opener?

Babe reaches in his vest pocket and brings out an opener which is attached to a chain, fastened in a buttonhole of his vest. He places the opener on the edge of the table and starts to unfasten the chain from his vest. Stan reaches over, not thinking, picks up the opener and pulls it toward him, and we hear a loud rip as half of Babe's vest comes off. Stan again looks all bewildered.

Babe finally burns up and grabs the bottle and opener from Stan:

BABE: Give me that!

Babe viciously opens the bottle and the beer, having been shaken up, pours out a steady stream of foam into his lap. (We will do this by pressure and let the scene run long.) Babe just continues to look down at it.

Stan gets a little inquisitive and stands up to look into Babe's lap, and in doing so again tips the table, which causes Babe's mug of beer to slide off into his lap.

Babe picks the mug out of his lap, places it back on the table, goes to push the bottle aside and as he does it gives a last gasp, shooting a little stream of froth into the air.

This last happening to Babe is the straw that broke the camel's back, but instead of getting violent he reaches back into his pocket, brings out a handkerchief, and his lips quiver with emotion as he puts the handkerchief to his eyes and starts sobbing as if his heart would break:

BABE: (In a plaintive voice – between sobs) Haven't you done enough to me?

This breaks Stan up and he also bursts into tears.

STAN: I couldn't help it.

BABE: Isn't it bad enough that I'm going to be shot at midnight, without you making my last few hours on earth miserable?

STAN: I wish we could figure out a way so you wouldn't have to be shot.

BABE: There's no way out of it. I've got to be there at twelve o'clock.

STAN: Suppose you didn't show up?

BABE: Then he'd come and get me!

STAN: How could he? He doesn't know where we live.

BABE: (Brightens up suddenly) That's right! If I don't show up, I can't get shot! (Calling off) Waiter, two more beers!

Babe is now back in his old character:

BABE: Now why didn't you think of that before? Here I

was worrying all that time! Selfish!

The waiter enters with two more beers. Babe thanks him, picks up his mug of beer and walks over to another table, giving Stan the nod.

STAN: You know what?

BABE: What?

Stan picks up his glass, goes over to Babe's table. Without a word Babe picks up his beer and comes back to the original table.

BABE: Now. What?

STAN: Why don't you phone up that fellow and tell him you won't be there tonight?

BABE: What for?

STAN: Well, he might have something else to do. Or he might want to go to bed.

BABE: A splendid idea!

He feels in his pocket, brings out the card that the artist gave him and looks at it.

BABE: I'll give him a piece of my mind!

He exits from the table.

Cut to the Artist's studio. The phone rings and he picks it up.

ARTIST: Hello.

Cut to Babe and Stan at a wall phone in the saloon.

BABE: Pardon me, but are you Mr. Pierre? Well, I'm the fellow you think you're going to kill tonight. Now listen to me, you cheap brush pusher, if you think I'm going to waste my time coming over to your place, you're crazy! In short, I won't be there!

Cut back to the artist as he says threateningly:

ARTIST: You better be here at twelve o'clock. If you're not, I'll search every corner of this town till I find you!

Back to Babe as he laughs heartily and wiggles his tie at the phone.

BABE: You better not leave your apartment, because

if you do I'll go back there and kiss your wife again. - - And very nice, too.

Stan nudges Babe.

BABE: Just a minute – my friend wants to speak to you.

STAN: (Into phone) That goes for me, too. And by the way, you ask your wife how I can kiss!

Stan puts the receiver up against the transmitter, causing a whistling noise.

Back to the artist. The whistle comes over the phone, blowing his beret off. He hangs up in a rage, grabs a gun out of a drawer, puts it in his back pocket, puts on his hat and starts to leave.

MAE: Pierre, what are you going to do?

ARTIST: I'm going to find your lover and kill him on the spot!

MAE: (Grabs him – pleading) Please, Pierre – think what you're doing!

He thrusts her aside and exits, slamming the door. Mae, who is now dressed in negligee, grabs her coat and hurriedly exits after him.

Cut back to the saloon. Stan and Babe are now seated at their original table. Babe is laughing and Stan is all smiles.

BABE: (Boasting) Lucky thing for him I decided not to go over!

Stan nods, all pleased.

Cut to the steps at the front of the saloon. Houseman enters, staggers down the steps to the bar and motions the bartender over.

ARTHUR: (Whispering) Gimme a small big one!

BARTENDER: Sorry, I can't serve you any more.

ARTHUR: Aw, come on!

BARTENDER: Do you want me to lose my license? Get out of here!

The bartender walks away. Houseman turns to look the place over, and brightens up as he sees Stan and Babe.

ARTHUR: (Waving to them) Hi, mommy mommy!

He goes over and sits down at their table.

ARTHUR: Listen, fellows, if you'll help me out, I'll help you out.

BABE: How do you mean?

ARTHUR: When you order a drink, order one for me on the side. Make out it's for you. If you'll do that for me I'll buy all the Christmas cards you've got.

BABE: Sold!

Babe shakes hands with Houseman, then calls the waiter over.

BABE: A beer for Mr. Laurel. A beer for myself and a straight whiskey on the side. (Pointing to Arthur) My friend doesn't want any.

He winks slyly at Houseman, who in turn gives hm a very exaggerated wink. The waiter exits.

ARTHUR: Have you got a card that says something about father?

BABE: (Reading a card)

Merry Christmas father,

How proud of you I am –

You're a better man than I am –

Three cheers for Uncle Sam!

Oh Joyous Day!

ARTHUR: Well, a bargain's a bargain. I'll have to take them.

The waiter enters with two mugs of beer, places one in front of Stan, the other in front of Babe, and the whiskey beside Babe's mug, then exits.

Babe glances around to sees that nobody is looking, then quickly pushes the whiskey over to Houseman, who holds his coat up beside his face so that nobody will see him taking the drink.

Cut to the bartender, back of Babe, looking through the mirror and seeing the action of Houseman.

Houseman drinks the whiskey and passes the glass back to Babe. Babe takes it, makes a motion as if having swallowed the liquor, then coughs a little, trying to convey to the bartender that he drank it.

ARTHUR: Let's have another!

BABE: (Turning to bartender) Another one on the side.

Stan, Babe and Houseman are all very pleased that they are getting by with their little scheme.

Cut to the bartender and a waiter.

BARTENDER: Did you get those mugs slipping that bum a drink? I'll fix them! Get me that bottle of - - (goes into a whisper).

DISSOLVE to a clock. We hear the chime through the dissolve, and as we are in clear we see that the hands read eleven o'clock.

DISSOLVE back to the saloon. Stan and Babe are fast asleep. The other customers are leaving, saying "Goodnight" etc.

The bartender comes over and shakes Stan and Babe, trying to wake them up, but they don't come to. He then shakes Houseman, who comes out of it.

BARTENDER: Come on, get out of here and take your pals home.

ARTHUR: I don't know where they live.

BARTENDER: Well, get 'em out of here anyway!

The bartender starts to exit –

ARTHUR: Make it three! We'll all have one. They're pals of mine!

The bartender goes up the stairs and whistles, motioning for the taxis to come and holding up three fingers.

We hear the noise of the taxis pulling up in front of the saloon, doors slamming, etc. The waiter starts back down the stairs, followed by the three taxi drivers.

DISSOLVE to the Artist's studio. The door opens and two of the drivers enter with Stan and Babe on their shoulders, followed by Houseman and the third driver.

ARTHUR: Are you sure this is where they live?

The driver has the card which was given to Babe by the Artist, and points to it:

DRIVER: It must be. This is the only card he had on him with an address.

ARTHUR: I guess it's all right then.

DRIVER: Where will we put 'em?

ARTHUR: The best place for them is in bed. That's where they always put me.

The drivers look around, then make for the bedroom.

Cut to the bedroom; they all enter and the driver who is with Houseman parts the curtains of the canopy, pulls back the covers, and the other two throw Stan and Babe into bed and cover them up.

ARTHUR: Wait till I tuck them in.

He tucks Stan and Babe in, at the same time singing "Go To Sleep My Baby" accompanied by hiccups. One of the drivers finally stops him.

DRIVER: Wait a minute. Where do you live?

ARTHUR: (pointing off) Right across the hall.

With this he collapses into their arms and they drag him out.

Cut to the hall. They drag Houseman across and into his apartment, and just as the door closes Mae enters up the stairs and goes toward her apartment.

Cut to interior of apartment. Mae enters, throws off her coat and goes toward the bedroom.

Cut to the bedroom. Mae sits at the dressing table, very worried, and starts to powder her nose.   Cut to the studio. The husband enters and slams the door. He plainly show that he has been defeated in his purpose.

Cut to the bedroom:

MAE: Is that you, Pierre?

Cut to Babe waking up and peeping out through the curtains as the husband enters:

ARTIST: Yes, it's Pierre! Who did you expect?

MAE: Don't be foolish, dear. You know you're the only man I love. If I didn't love you so much I wouldn't have tried to make you jealous. But you just neglected me.

ARTIST: (Weakening) Forgive me, darling. I'll never leave you alone again.

They embrace and go into a soul kiss.

Cut to the bed. Babe is looking out through the curtains as Stan, still fast asleep, breaks into a loud snore.

The artist and Mae take this big.

Babe, scared to death, puts his hand over Stan's mouth to stop the snore, but Stan breathes through his nose, causing the snore to become a whistle. This wakes Stan up. He looks around in a daze and suddenly decides to get out of bed, which he does. Babe is petrified.

Stan crosses the room and enters the bath room, paying no attention to the couple. They are dumbfounded.

Cut to the bathroom. Stan enters, goes to the wash stand, fills a glass of water and starts to gargle.

Back to the bedroom and we hear the sound of gargling coming over. This time as he gargles he runs the scale. We hold the scene and Stan enters from the bath room, gives them a "Hi," motion with his hand and starts back to bed. He suddenly stops, takes off his coat, drops it on the floor, then sees the alarm clock, winds it up and gets into bed, starting to make himself comfortable.

The husband can stand no more. He rushes over, takes a corner of the mattress and pulls the whole thing out onto the floor with Stan and Babe on it. He glares down at them:

ARTIST: What are you doing in my bed?

STAN: You told us to be here at twelve o'clock, and we got tired of waiting. Didn't we, Ollie?

Babe "shushes" him.

ARTIST: Very well. You'll wait no longer. Follow me.

Stan and Babe get up and follow him as he exits to the studio.

Cut to the studio and the husband enters, followed by Stan and Babe. The Artist locks the door to the hall and puts the key in his pocket.

ARTIST: (To Babe) You understand the conditions and rules of this duel? We stand back to back, take six paces and at a given signal we turn and fire. The truest shot will win. Understand?

BABE: Yes, sir.

ARTIST: Wait here till I get my guns.

He exits to the bedroom.

Mae is on, having followed Stan and Babe from the bedroom. She crosses over to Babe and hurriedly whispers:

MAE: Don't worry. I've taken out the real bullets and put in blanks, so when he fires, you pretend to die. I'll get him out of here and you can make your escape.

At this point the Artist re-enters with a regular case containing a brace of dueling pistols. He sets the case on the table, opens it, takes out the two pistols, and laying the handles over his arm he crosses to Babe.

ARTIST: Choose your weapon!

Babe takes one of the guns and Stan takes the other. The artist grabs the one from Stan:

ARTIST: That's not for you!

He reaches in his back pocket, pulls out the revolver and hands it to Stan:

ARTIST: This is for you to give the signal for us to fire.

Babe, knowing that the pistols contain blanks, is now very brave.

ARTIST: Are you ready, M'sieur?

BABE: Oui, M'sieur. Je suis pret. (To Mae:) Au revoir, Madame. Vive la France!

Babe and the artist stand back to back, take six paces and stop.

Stan, holding the revolver in the air, fires a shot, which knocks a globe off the chandelier. It drops onto Babe's head with a crash just as the husband turns and fires.

Babe sinks to the floor and pretends to die. The wife does a foney faint, while the husband puts his gun away.

Near Babe is the artist's palette with daubs of paint on it. Stan kneels down beside Babe, who gives him the wink. To make the scene more realistic, Stan smears his hand in the red paint on the palette and rubs it on Babe's shirt over his heart.

The husband comes over, throws Babe's coat open and sees what he thinks is a bloody wound.

ARTIST: Right through the heart!

He then exits quickly to the kitchen, and we hear the sound of him going through a lot of cutlery in a drawer.

Mae comes to as the husband rushes back into the room carrying a big knife.

MAE: (Screaming) Pierre! What are you going to do?

ARTIST: I have to dispose of the body, so I'm going to cut it up in little pieces!

Babe can't stand it any longer. He jumps up and runs around, followed by Stan.

BABE: OOoh-o-o-o- -

They chase around the apartment, with the artist brandishing the knife. Babe runs clean through the closed door, followed by Stan and the artist.

Cut to a corner setup on the street. It is snowing. Stan and Babe enter the scene and exit around the corner on the run. The Artist runs in, reaches the corner, stops and fires two shots out of the scene.

Hold the scene a moment and a cop enters, sore as hell, and takes the gun from the artist.

COP: What's the big idea?

ARTIST: I'm sorry, officer.

COP: What do you mean, sorry? You nearly blew my brains out! Come on!

He takes the artist by the arm, whirls him around, and as the two exit across the street we see that the cop's fanny has been shot and is smoldering.

FADE OUT.

THICKER THAN WATER

Production history: Production L-23. Script written mid-June 1935. Filmed circa Monday, July 1 through Monday, July 8. Copyrighted August 6, 1935 by MGM (LP 5709). Released circa August 6. Two reels.

Produced by Hal Roach. Directed by James W. Horne. Photographed by Art Lloyd. Edited by Ray Snyder. Sound by William Randall. *Uncredited Assistance:* Effects by Roy Seawright.

With Stan Laurel (Himself), Oliver Hardy (Himself), Daphne Pollard (Mrs. Daphne Hardy), James Finlayson (Mr. Finlayson), Harry Bowen (Auctioneer), Gladys Gale (Auction bidder on grandfather clock), Lester Dorr (Amused man sitting behind Ollie at auction), Charlie Hall (Mr. Sidney, bank teller), Ed Brandenburg (Bank teller), Allan Cavan (Dr. F. D. Allen), Grace Goodall (Nurse Goodall), Bess Flowers (Nurse), Baldwin Cooke (Hospital visitor).

Stan is a boarder with Ollie and his tempestuous wife. After a morning spent breaking more dishes than they wash, the boys are visited by Mr. Finlayson, who wants the $37 he's owed for a furniture payment. Stan convinces Ollie to withdraw their savings of $300 and buy the furniture to avoid future such embarrassments. En route home from the bank, the boys are enticed into an auction. A lady bidding on a grandfather clock discovers she's left her money at home and asks Ollie to keep bidding on her behalf. Ollie submits the winning bid – for $290 – but the lady never returns. Stan and Ollie try to carry their new purchase home, but unwisely set it down in an intersection, where a truck immediately runs over it. Mrs. Hardy is already well aware of the boys' misadventures, having met with Mr. Finlayson, whose store was the site of the auction. Returning home, she clobbers Ollie with a frying pan, which necessitates an emergency trip to the hospital. Mr. Hardy needs a transfusion, and Stan is recruited as a donor. The procedure goes awry; Stan acquires Ollie's look, voice and characteristics, and Ollie receives Stan's.

A press release for this film contained some bittersweet news: "For more than seven years Laurel and Hardy have romped through two-reel pictures, only occasionally appearing in films of greater length. Now, the demand is so great for comedies of greater length as vehicles for the famous fun duo, that Hal Roach has decided to grant the public's request and in the future there will be no more two-reelers with this stellar combination." In fact, a couple of weeks before *Thicker Than Water* began filming, the team had completed *Bonnie Scotland*, their first film under the new "features only" policy.

Thicker Than Water has a wonderfully cinematic gag that serves as a concise transition between scenes. Whenever the boys need to go to a new locale, one of them goes to the edge of the frame and pulls the next scene into view. Roy Seawright's optical effects work here is superb, providing some of the most memorable moments in the film.

Stan wrote a partial script which has an opening scene very similar to the one in the

The tiny terror Mrs. Hardy (Daphne Pollard) insists that the boys do the dishes and forget about the ball game.

film. (It's reprinted in full in John McCabe's book *The Comedy World of Stan Laurel.*) It opens with Ollie, his wife Molly-o, and boarder Stan finishing their lunch. Having finished a piece of pie, Stan attempts to also enjoy Mrs. Hardy's when she demands that he put it down. She tells Ollie, "I am full up – and fed up… You brought this tapeworm friend of yours to live with us as a boarder, six months ago. He's eating me out of house and home, and hasn't paid me a cent for his room and board yet." Stan protests that he gave his rent money to Ollie, who hands it over to the wife with, "I thought I'd save it for you, honey. And surprise you at Christmas!"

The boys are about to leave for the racetrack, but Molly-o demands that they instead stay and wash the dishes. As they wash a few dishes and break more, Stan wonders if a horse, conveniently also named Molly-o, will be running today. He's heard from a friend, "a feller who lives next door to a guy who doesn't have to work. He knows a relative of the jockey's grandfather – the same jockey that's riding Molly-o, and he gets his tips from him. Right on the nose!" Hearing that the odds are 100 to one, Ollie says, "If we get a tip on Molly-o, bang goes the whole works. Right on the nose." Stan calls his friend on the phone, gets a tip, and then tells Ollie, "It's all set. Put everything you can beg, borrow and steal."

The script ends there, but it's likely that the boys will lose all of their money at the track (something with which Babe Hardy was well acquainted in real life), and that the

Ollie will soon regret his command that Stan put the dishes in a "nice, dry place."

Mr. Finlayson wants his furniture payment "without any detour."

Ollie has withdrawn all $300 of the family savings. "Don't spend it all in one place" would apply here. However –

wife will deliver her own rendition of "right on the nose."

The final script has one major difference and several which are more subtle. Mr. Finlayson's reaction to the roundabout way in which he receives his payment is more colorful and concise in the film: "She gave it to you and you gave it to him and who give it to what – why, you're all NUTS!" Stan never seems to realize that he hasn't really paid his rent, he's just given back to Mrs. Hardy her own money, which she intended for the furniture payment.

When Stan gets a good idea about the furniture payment, one expects Ollie to say, "Tell me that again," prompting a garbled reiteration from Stan. That doesn't happen here nor in the film, nor does Stan's "no place like home" comment.

The female auction attendee bidding on the grandfather clock is a matronly lady in the film; in the script she is identified only as "Girl," indicating that the character was first thought of as being younger. It does seem more plausible that an older and very well-dressed lady would be more likely to have more than two hundred dollars to spend on a luxury such as this clock. (The entire auction scene, and its aftermath, was repeated almost verbatim in the 1943 20th Century-Fox feature *The Dancing Masters*.)

The idea of leaving a card for the lady who was first bidding on the clock doesn't seem to occur to Stan and Ollie in the film. Nor does the reprise of the "I gave it to him" business, which undoubtedly would have gotten a laugh. It's surprising that this was

-- Ollie's chivalry toward a lady bidding on a grandfather clock soon turns to grief.

not included in the film, as the whole sequence seems to be set up for such a dialogue exchange.

In the film, after Ollie reluctantly pays for the grandfather clock, he and Stan attempt to carry it, but stop to rest and put it on the ground for a moment; a truck immediately comes along and neatly demolishes their new acquisition. The script instead proposes that they actually carry the clock to the top of a double-decker bus, and engage in some highly interesting sightseeing.

In the movie, the exchange between Finlayson and Mrs. Hardy outside the auction house has a snappier finish. Finlayson says, "He bought himself a grandfather's clock." Mrs. Hardy: "A clock?! What for?" Finlayson: "For two hundred and ninety dollars, that's what for!"

The script does include the clever transition from one scene to the next – Stan or Ollie grabbing the edge of the frame and dragging it along as it "wipes" to the next location. However, the final scene of Ollie needing a transfusion and getting it from Stan, thus co-mingling their personalities so that Ollie behaves like Stan, while Mr. Laurel acquires the dainty gestures and voice of Mr. Hardy, is not in the script. The mention of Stan grabbing "the Hospital Wipe" indicates that the writers already planned to have the final scene set in a hospital. Likely they had the entire sequence in mind, but did not want it in print, lest someone in the cast or crew reveal the surprise. (The blood transfusion gag is almost revealed by the film's title.)

The lady bidder still absent, Ollie is forced to give Mr. Finlayson $290 for this unwanted purchase.

Laurel and Hardy's final starring two-reeler has echoes of *That's My Wife*, with Stan as a boarder who infuriates Mrs. Hardy, and *Hog Wild*, with the boys altering their plans because the wife insists they perform a chore. There's also another "freak ending," continuing the trend established in *Going Bye-Bye!* and *The Live Ghost*. Finally, having played their own sons in *Brats* and their sisters in *Twice Two*, Stan and Ollie now get to portray each other.

It's appropriate that the team's last starring short subject would have echoes of many previous releases, making this a fond farewell to their preferred format. Hal Roach would have continued with the two-reelers, but the changing economics of the movie industry made it clear that he had to go into feature film production, or go out of business, as had short subject producers Mack Sennett and Al Christie.

Roach said in January 1981, "The greatest comedies that were made by anybody were made in two reels, I don't care who it was. It's a simple damn thing. If you can stop after 20 minutes, you've only got to go up to this peak for your last laugh. But if you've got to go clear to 60 minutes, the last laugh is three times harder. It's that simple. And I don't care how funny a guy is, if you listen to him long enough, you're going to be bored to hell with him."

Buyer's remorse.

Armed with a skillet, Mrs. Hardy cooks her husband's goose.

L-39

FADE IN on Dining Room of Babe's home. Babe, his wife (Daphne Pollard) and Stan are seated at the table, just finishing their meal. Babe finishes his coffee and daintily wipes his lips on a napkin. Stan folds his napkin and unconsciously sticks it in his coat pocket, then finishes a glass of water.

Daphne reaches over, pulls the napkin out and slams it down on the table.

WIFE: That's where my napkins have been going! And incidentally, when are you going to pay for your room and board?

STAN: What do you mean, when am I going to pay? (Pointing to Babe:) I gave it to him.

Babe is probably drinking a glass of water at this moment. He splutters that out and gives Stan a dirty look for spilling the beans.

Daphne takes it big and looks at Stan:

WIFE: What did you give it to him for?

STAN: Well, he said he was the boss.

She gives Babe a dirty look and holds out her hand:

WIFE: Give me that money!

Babe sheepishly hands it over and pats her on the back in a jovial manner.

BABE: Don't get sore, honey – I was only kidding.

WIFE: (To Stan) Hereafter you pay your money to me.

Babe looks at his watch, jumps up from the table and grabs his hat.

BABE: Well, darling, I've got to be going.

At this point Stan is getting his hat.

WIFE: Going where?

BABE: Why – er – Stanley and I were going to the ball game. You know, we business men have got to relax once in a while.

WIFE: Oh no you don't! If you want to relax you can stay home and help me wash the dishes!

BABE: What do you mean – wash the dishes?

STAN: Yes – what would his friends think?

She turns on Stan and kicks him on the fanny.

WIFE: You keep out of this!

Babe in disgust throws his hat down on a chair or on the hat-rack, then goes to pick up the dirty dishes off the table. The Wife takes them out of his hands and puts them back on the table.

WIFE: I'll do that! You get in the kitchen and wash them!

BABE: (Pointing to Stan) Well if I've got to wash them, he'll have to dry them!

STAN: After we finish them can we go to the ball game?

WIFE: You can do as you like - -

STAN: (Tickled at this) Thank you, honey – Mrs. Hardy.

BABE: You heard what she said! We're not going to the ball game!

STAN: What do you mean we're not going? I can do what I want.

BABE: Don't argue! I'm master of this house!

Before he can say any more Daphne crowns him with a plate.

BABE: She's boss of this house, and we're not going to the ball game. Are we, Mrs. Hardy? I mean Honey. (To Stan) COME ON!

Stan and Babe exit to the kitchen and Daphne starts picking up the dishes.

Cut to the kitchen. Babe, very sore, puts on an apron, gets the dish pan from under the sink, places it in the sink and fills it with water.

BABE: Get the soap powder!

At this point Daphne comes in, puts some dirty dishes on the sink.

WIFE: Don't forget to rinse them off.

She exits.

While Babe is scraping the plates, Stan gets the package of soap powder and empties the entire contents into the dish pan, then swishes it around with his hand.

Babe shoves him aside:

BABE: Look out!

He places a pile of dishes in the pan, then does a takem.

Cut and show that Stan has put so much powder into it, it looks like whipped cream (Palmolive Shaving Cream).

Babe gives Stan a disgusted look:

BABE: Can't you do anything right?

He turns the faucet on with great violence and the water hits the top plate, throwing a spray of lather into Babe's face and all over the kitchen. Babe turns off the faucet and cleans himself up. He then takes the dishes out of the pan, empties the soap suds into the sink, fills up the pan with fresh water, puts the dishes back into it. He then turns to Stan and points to the cutting board under the drain board.

BABE: Pull that out!

He turns to reach for the dish pan with both hands as Stan pulls the cutting board completely out. Babe turns to place the pan on the board, which isn't there, and the dish pan drops to the floor. Stan, bewildered, hands Babe the cutting board. Babe, exasperated, throws up his hands.

Babe takes the board, puts it back in place, places the dish pan on it and starts to wash dishes. He finishes one plate, steps to the faucet, rinses it off and hands it to Stan, who starts to dry it.

Babe completes another plate and as he steps to the faucet to rinse it, Stan puts the dry plate back into the dish pan. Babe hands him the other plate and goes on washing.

Repeat this once or twice, then as Stan has finished drying a plate – Babe being a little ahead of him hands Stan a rinsed plate and Stan hands him the dry one. Babe puts it in the dish water and starts to wash it, then realizes what he is doing.

Stan then tries to dry two plates at once and gets all mixed up.

BABE: (Annoyed) Just dry one at a time! Haste makes waste!

Stan then places one of the plates back in the dish pan and starts to dry the other one. Babe sees this.

BABE: Don't keep putting them back in here! As soon as you dry them, stack them up where they'll be nice and dry!

Stan looks around and puts the plate on the stove.

Insert shows that the gas hasn't been turned off.

They complete the dishes, Stan placing each one on top of the other on the stove.

BABE: Now see? Isn't it simple?

He empties the dish pan, dries his hands very daintily, walks over and picks up the dishes, which are by this time nearly red-hot. He drops them with a crash and runs around the kitchen wringing his hands. Stan rushes over to Babe, puts his hands under the cold water, blows on them, etc.

At this point the door bell rings.

BABE: See who that is.

Stan exits to the front door, opens it and Finlayson is standing there.

FIN: Is Mr. Hardy home?

STAN: Yes sir, but he's not in just now.

Stan closes the door and exits.

Cut to Finlayson taking it big. He rings the bell again.

Back to Interior. Babe's wife comes to the door and opens it.

WIFE: Good afternoon, Mr. Finlayson.

FIN: (Curtly) Good afternoon!

He brushes her aside and walks right into the room.

WIFE: What's the idea?

FIN: I'm here to collect the payment on the furniture.

WIFE: It was paid yesterday.

FIN: Not to me, it wasn't!

She takes this and calls off:

WIFE: O-l-i-v-e-r! (As Babe enters:) Did I or did I not give you the money to make the payment on the furniture?

BABE: You certainly did.

WIFE: Then why wasn't it paid?

BABE: (Pointing to Stan) I gave it to him to pay it for me.

WIFE: (To Stan:) What did you do with it?

STAN: (Pointing to Babe:) I gave it to him.

BABE: You gave it to me?

STAN: Yes, for my rent. Don't you remember – you had to give it to her.

WIFE: (To Stan:) Do you mean to say that the money he gave to you that you gave to him and he gave to me, was the money I gave to him (Babe) to pay him (Fin)?

STAN: Well, if it's the money you gave to him (Babe) that he gave to me to pay him (Fin), it must be the money that I gave to him (Babe), and I saw him give it to you. So I'm all square.

Babe throws up both hands in despair.

FIN: Well, where do I get off?

WIFE: My, my! I owe you an apology. This money must belong to you.

She hands him the money.

FIN: Next time I want this payment without any detours! You gave to him to give to him to give to – BAH! If it ever happens again I'll back up a wagon and move you into the street!

He exits, slamming the door.

WIFE: (To Babe:) You big dumbbell! I can't trust you to do a thing!

STAN: That's right. Next time you pay it yourself.

WIFE: You shut up! I've a good mind to throw you out!

STAN: You can't do it!

WIFE: What do you mean, I can't do it?

STAN: Because I just paid my rent a month in advance.

BABE: What do you mean? That was the money she gave to me and I gave to you to give to him and you gave it to me and I had to give it back to her!

STAN: That's right! And if she wanted to give it to him, that's her business!

WIFE: Oh, cut it out! (To Babe:) From now on I'll not trust you with anything! I'm going to do everything myself!

She gives a grunt of disgust and exits.

BABE:　What humiliation! Creditors hounding me at my very fireside!

STAN:　You know what?

BABE:　What?

STAN:　I got a good idea.

BABE:　What?

STAN:　How much money have you and your wife got in the bank?

BABE:　Well, if it's any of your business, we've a joint account of around three hundred dollars. Why?

STAN:　Why don't you draw the money out of the bank, pay off the furniture and own it right out? You'd save the interest and all the humiliation, and you wouldn't have any hounds in your fireplace. You know, if you own the furniture – be it ever so humbug there's no place like home.

BABE:　That's a good idea.

At this point the wife comes on, wearing her hat and carrying a market basket.

BABE:　Oh, honey – Stanley has a very good idea.

WIFE:　What now?

BABE:　Well, Stanley was saying the thing to do would be draw the money out of the bank and pay the furniture off, then we wouldn't be humiliated any more.

WIFE:　We'll do nothing of the kind! That money stays right where it is! (To Stan:) And from now on, you mind your own business! (To Babe:) Huh! Draw the money out of the bank! The very idea! I've come to the conclusion that you haven't got an ounce of brains! Now I'm going out to do some shopping. You wait here till I come back. By that time I suppose you'll have some more screwy ideas.

She goes out and slams the door. Stan turns to Babe:

STAN:　Are you going to stand for that?

BABE:　I certainly am not!

STAN:　I never heard of such a thing – she talks to you like water off a duck's back! If she was my wife, I'd draw her out of the bank and go buy some furniture! Why don't you take a firm stand? Never put off till tomorrow what you can do today. And who knows, this may be tomorrow!

BABE: You're absolutely right! I'll learn her! Come on, Stanley, we'll draw the money out of the bank and pay for the furniture, and at the same time give that Finlayson a piece of our mind!

They put on their hats, go to the edge of the picture – Babe reaches over, takes hold of the Bank Wipe and they walk out of the scene with it.

Exterior of Bank. Stan and Babe come out, Babe counting the money.

BABE: Three hundred dollars!

STAN: That's a lot of money.

BABE: It certainly is.

STAN: I had no idea that three hundred dollars was so much. Maybe you better go put it back.

BABE: What for?

STAN: Well, maybe your wife is the boss, and she wouldn't like it.

BABE: A Hardy never retreats! Come on!

They exit.

Cut to Exterior Front of Auction Room. Over the scene we hear the voice of the auctioneer:

VOICE: One hundred and fifty dollars! My dear madam – this clock is worth twenty-five hundred of anybody's money, and I'm bid a hundred and fifty dollars!

MAN'S VOICE: One hundred and sixty-five!

GIRL'S VOICE: One hundred and seventy-five!

Stan and Babe enter and see a sign in the window which reads: "Step Inside. We are actually giving things away today."

BABE: Let's go in. Maybe we'll get something for nothing.

They enter the store.

Interior. The Auctioneer is standing behind the counter and a few people are listening to the sale. There is a big Grandfather clock in evidence in front of the counter, which is the object of the sale.

AUCT: One seventy-five! One seventy-five! Going at one seventy-five!

VOICE: Two hundred!

AUCT: Two hundred! I'm offered two hundred. Only two hundred?

He sees Stan and Babe in the doorway:

AUCT: Stop this way, gentlemen – Please don't block the doorway. I'm offered only two hundred dollars for this beautiful antique Grandfather's clock that's worth twenty-five hundred!

Stan and Babe move up to the foreground. Next to them is a girl:

GIRL: Two hundred and five!

AUCT: Thank you. Two hundred and five. Do I hear any more?

MAN: Two hundred and ten.

AUCT: Two ten!

GIRL: Two hundred and twenty!

She starts to reach in her purse as the auctioneer continues:

AUCT: Thank you. Two hundred and twenty.

MAN: Two hundred and twenty-five.

AUCT: Two twenty-five. Thank you.

The girl discovers that she has left her money home and takes it big. She turns to Babe:

GIRL: Please, sir, would you do me a favor? My heart is set on having that clock and I find I've left my money at home. Will you keep the bidding going till I go home and get it? Don't let anyone have it under any condition. I'll pay you well for your trouble.

BABE: We'll be glad to oblige – won't we, Stanley?

During this we hear the Auctioneer pleading for more money.

AUCT: Going at two hundred and twenty-five!

VOICE: Two hundred and thirty!

BABE: Two hundred and thirty-five.

GIRL: (To Babe) Thank you.

She hurries out.

MAN: Two hundred and forty.

BABE: Two hundred and forty-five.

STAN: Two hundred and fifty.

BABE: Two hundred and fifty-five!

STAN: Two hundred and sixty.

BABE: Two hundred and seventy! What are you bidding against me for?

STAN: Well, you're bidding against me.

AUCT: Going at two hundred and seventy.

BABE: Two hundred and seventy-five!

STAN: Two hundred and eighty!

BABE: (Holding his hand over Stan's mouth:) Two hundred and ninety!

AUCT: Two hundred and ninety! Going at two hundred and ninety dollars. Thank you, sir! Sold to the jolly gentleman on my right for two hundred and ninety dollars! Well, folks, that's all for today. I thank you one and all.

The people start to leave the store. The auctioneer looks at Babe, who is just standing there dumbfounded.

AUCT: Well, come on! Business is over! Get your clock and leave!

BABE: You'll pardon me, but I really wasn't bidding for myself! It was for a lady. She went home to get her money.

AUCT: You did the bidding and you'll do the paying, or I'll call the proprietor!

He beckons off and the proprietor, Finlayson, enters. He has a big takem as he sees Stan and Babe, as so do they.

FIN: What's the matter?

AUCT: These fellows tried to get out of paying for this clock!

FIN: (To Auctioneer) I'll take care of this! I've had trouble with these birds before.

STAN: (To Babe:) Why don't you pay him? Then you won't be humiliated.

Babe reluctantly pays the money to the Auctioneer.

BABE: Do you mind if I wait here till the lady returns?

AUCT: Sorry, but we've got to close up.

STAN: Why don't you leave your address with him so when the lady returns she will know where to come and get her clock?

BABE: I never thought of that.

He pulls out a card and hands it to the Auctioneer:

BABE: When the lady calls for the clock, will you kindly give her this address and tell her not to worry – her clock is in safe hands.

STAN: (To Auctioneer) And don't forget to collect the two hundred and ninety dollars from her. Then you can give the money back to him (Babe) that he gave to you.

AUCT: How do you mean?

STAN: Well, we don't want you to get mixed up like he was. You see, his wife gave him some money to pay him (Fin), and he gave it to me and I gave it back to him to give to his wife for my rent, but he (Fin) never got it till his (Babe's) wife gave it to him (Fin). Then because his wife got mad he drew the money out of the bank to pay him (Fin), but he gave it to you, so you'll have to get the money from the woman to give back the money he (Babe) gave to you so he can give it to him (Fin) – then everybody will be square again.

Finlayson has been listening to this and burning. He finally blows up:

FIN: GET OUT!!

BABE: (To Stan) Come on – he's not interested in our affairs. Give me a hand.

Stan holds out his hand. Babe slaps it down:

BABE: Come on – help me pick up this antique!

STAN: We can't carry that thing all the way home

BABE: Just help me to the corner – we'll take a bus.

WIPE to a street corner. Stan and Babe are struggling

onto a double-decker bus with the clock. The Conductor probably gets his hat knocked off or something.

CONDUCTOR: You'll have to take that thing on top.

The bus starts and Stan and Babe struggle with the clock to the upper deck, making their way through the seats, much to the discomfort of the other passengers, and finally arrive at the front seat. They stand the clock up against the rail.

A young fellow and his girl are seated in the next seat to Stan and Babe. It is evident from their conversation that it is the first time the girl has been in this neighborhood, and she is taking in all the sights. The young fellow points off.

FELLOW: There's Chaplin's home.

A little pause.

BABE: Charley?

FELLOW: No. Sid. (He points off again) There's Bennett's home.

BABE: Constance?

FELLOW: No. Joan.

Stan humors this with a smile – first to the young fellow and then to Babe, who by this time is somewhat embarrassed. Another pause, then:

FELLOW: There's the house of Barrymore.

BABE: (Hoping to guess one right) John?

FELLOW: Lionel!

Again the little smile of Stan's to the fellow, then to Babe.

FELLOW: That's Beery's home.

BABE: Wally?

FELLOW: Noah!

Stan seems to be enjoying this, but Babe is a little embarrassed. There is a little more pause. The girl points off:

GIRL: Whose statue is that?

BOY: That's the famous statue of Washington. The father of our country.

STAN: (Turns to Babe) Ask him if it's George. You can't be wrong all the time.

The young fellow presses the button to get off the bus, which comes to such a quick stop that the clock falls over the side. We hear a terrific crash and as Stan and Babe look over the rail they see a truck run over the clock, leaving a lot of dangling springs, works, etc.

Cut to exterior of the Bank. Babe's wife enters and goes into the bank.

Interior, at Teller's window.

TELLER: Good afternoon, Mrs. Hardy.

WIFE: Good afternoon. I'd like to put a stop order against anyone taking any money out of my account. You know – personal reasons.

TELLER: I'm sorry, Mrs. Hardy, but your husband was just here and drew your money out.

WIFE: (It doesn't sink in at first) Oh, I see. That's fine - - (A sudden big takem) WHAT DID YOU SAY?

TELLER: Mr. Hardy drew out the whole amount.

WIFE: (With murder in her eyes) Thank you! (She exits)

Cut to the front of the Auction Store. Finlayson is just locking up as Babe's wife enters and sees him.

WIFE: Oh Mr. Finlayson, have you seen my husband?

FIN: He was here a while ago.

WIFE: (Relieved) Did he pay you for the furniture?

FIN: He did not!

WIFE: Then what was he doing here?

FIN: He bought a beautiful clock.

WIFE: A clock? What did he buy a clock for?

FIN: (With relish) For two hundred and ninety bucks!

Cut to the living room of Babe's home. The door opens and Stan and Babe sneak in.

STAN: What are you going to tell her?

BABE: We'll tell her nothing – keep everything in the dark. And if you'll keep your mouth shut, nobody'll be any the wiser.

STAN: I think you're right. No news is good news.

At this point the wife enters. Babe takes it a little but regains his nonchalance.

BABE: Hello, honey.

WIFE: Don't honey me!

BABE: What's the matter?

WIFE: Where's that clock?

BABE: What clock?

WIFE: The one you bought for two hundred and ninety dollars!

BABE: Now don't be silly, honey – where would I get two hundred and ninety dollars?

WIFE: You know very well! (To Stan:) Where's the clock?

STAN: He's keeping it in the dark, and if I keep my mouth shut nobody'll be any the wiser.

The wife becomes exasperated. She looks like she wants to kill Babe but doesn't know how to do it. She gets a sudden thought and exits to the kitchen. Hold the set, and she immediately comes back with a big iron skillet.

WIFE: (To Stan) Bring me that chair.

Stan pulls a chair up alongside of Babe.

STAN: What are you going to do – cook something?

WIFE: Yes – I'm going to cook his goose!

With that she raises the skillet and brings it down on Babe's head with all her might.

SOUND: A terrific 'BONG'.

Babe does a high brodie and all the pictures fall off the wall. Stan takes it big, runs to the side of the set, grabs the Hospital Wipe and exits with it – the wife watching in wonderment.

EPILOGUE

Thicker Than Water was Laurel and Hardy's last starring short at the Hal Roach studio, but it wasn't the last time they ever appeared in a two-reeler made on the Lot of Fun. Charley Chase continued to make short subjects into the next season, and found a cute way to work Stan and Ollie into *On the Wrong Trek*. Charley, his young wife (Rosina Lawrence) and her mother (Bonita Weber) are on a motoring vacation from Salt Lake City to California. The script describes this cameo appearance:

> DISSOLVE TO: TRUCKING SHOT of the car going along and passing several hitch-hikers.
>
> ROSINA: I've never seen so many hitch-hikers before.
>
> CHARLEY: Maybe we should give one of them a lift. We have plenty of room.
>
> MOTHER: I wouldn't, if I were you.
>
> CHARLEY: Why not?
>
> MOTHER: Because most of the hitch-hikers are nothing but bums!
>
> Charley looks ahead and sees a couple of hitch-hikers dressed in sailor outfits.
>
> CLOSEUP of Laurel and Hardy trying to "thumb" a ride.
>
> Back to Charley driving. He starts to say something. Rosina places a hand on his shoulder.
>
> ROSINA: Now, Charley – mother knows best!

Evidently Charley Chase's scripts were revised during filming as much as Laurel and Hardy's were. In the film, it's the mother-in-law who suggests that they give the two hitch-hikers a ride. Stan and Ollie are dressed in their usual costumes, not in sailor outfits. This idea may have been proposed because the boys were filming their nautical adventure *Our Relations* at the time. They improvised a bit of business by having Stan thumb for a ride in the opposite direction from Ollie. Charley mutters, "They look like a couple of horse thieves to me!," and then imitates Stan's smile and head-scratching gesture.

Stan and Ollie ride away from the Hal Roach short subjects.

After this, the team appeared in only one more short, *The Tree in a Test Tube*, made in 16mm Kodachrome for the U.S. Department of Agriculture. Stan and Babe's improvised antics displaying various products made from wood are cute, but the film's main asset is in providing five minutes of them in color footage.

Laurel and Hardy made several excellent features, but Stan always regretted the end of the short subjects. He told biographer John McCabe, "You can't take a whole, long series of things we do and stick them all together in eight reels, and expect to get a well-balanced picture out of it. We didn't want to go into feature films in the first place, and even though I've got some favorites among them, I'm sorry we ever did go beyond the two- and three-reelers."

Happily, Laurel and Hardy made 72 silent and sound shorts (and another 14 foreign-language editions of them), providing a wonderful bounty of timeless comedy. These films have remained popular since their initial release, and ongoing restoration work is helping to ensure that they'll be preserved for future generations.